JUDY GARLAND
ON JUDY GARLAND

JUDY GARLAND
ON JUDY GARLAND
INTERVIEWS AND ENCOUNTERS

EDITED BY RANDY L. SCHMIDT

CHICAGO
REVIEW
PRESS

An A Cappella Book

Copyright © 2014 by Randy L. Schmidt
All rights reserved
First edition
Published by Chicago Review Press, Incorporated
814 North Franklin Street
Chicago, Illinois 60610

ISBN 978-1-61374-945-6

A list of credits and copyright notices for the individual pieces in this collection can
be found on pages 437–38.

Interior and cover design: Jon Hahn

Library of Congress Cataloging-in-Publication Data
Garland, Judy.
  Judy Garland on Judy Garland : interviews and encounters / edited by Randy L.
Schmidt. — First edition.
      pages cm
  Includes bibliographical references and index.
  ISBN 978-1-61374-945-6 (cloth)
  1. Garland, Judy. 2. Garland, Judy—Interviews. 3. Singers—United States—
Interviews. 4. Motion picture actors and actresses—United States—Interviews. I.
Schmidt, Randy (Randy L.) editor. II. Title.
  ML420.G253A5 2014
  772.42164092—dc23
                          2014010486

Printed in the United States of America
5 4 3 2 1

Would that my throat were blessed by the nightingale
That I could but sing of my heart's great love
In some lonely tree flooded with silver,
Sing till I burst my breast with such passion,
Sing, then fall dead to lay at your feet.

—FROM "THE WISH," A POEM BY JUDY GARLAND, 1939

CONTENTS

PART II · THE 1940s

ACKNOWLEDGMENTS

I am indebted to my exceptional and thorough editor Yuval Taylor, who felt this title warranted a place amongst the fine titles already in the Musicians in Their Own Words series. I also wish to express my thanks to Amelia Estrich, Mary Kravenas, and rest of the staff at Chicago Review Press for their encouragement and support throughout the production.

A number of individuals provided support at various stages throughout the project. Thanks to Rebekah Ankrom, Daniel Berghaus, Frank Bonito, Walter Briski Jr., Scott Brogan, Jeff Burger, Gerald Clarke, Steve Cox, Tom Early, Rick Ewigleben, Kyle Hall, Dean Hanvey, Sam Harris, Sam Irvin, Richard Tyler Jordan, Sara Jordan, Garry Kief and Stiletto Entertainment, Jeremy Kinser, Frank Labrador, Patrick Lillis (my Avedon angel), Steven Lippman, Chris May, Jeff Marquis, John Meyer, Jon Perdue, the Punchy Players, Michael Riedel, Tom Santopietro, Hillary Banks Self, Michael Siewert, Anthony Slide, Buzz Stephens, Chris Tassin, Donna Trammell, and Scott Zone. An extra special thanks to Laura Adam and Alex Williams for their assistance in transcribing several important radio and television interviews.

I am grateful to Gary Horrocks and the International Judy Garland Club (est. 1963, www.judygarlandclub.org) for images supplied and quotes shared from *Judy Garland—A Celebration* and *Rainbow Review*. I also wish to acknowledge the late Coyne Steven Sanders, author of *Rainbow's End: The Judy Garland Show*, whom I had the privilege of meeting in Chicago just weeks before his untimely death. Steve was genuinely interested in the concept of this book and was a source of encouragement to me during its inception.

My appreciation also goes out to the following libraries and organizations, and especially the librarians and representatives who offered such valuable assistance: the Academy of Motion Picture Arts and Sciences / Margaret Herrick Library, Los Angeles Public Library, West Hollywood Public Library, Butler Library at Columbia University, University of North Texas Library, Southern Methodist University Library, New York Public Library for the Performing Arts (specifically the Collections of Scott Schechter, Amanda Gee, and Charlotte Stevenson), the Richard Avedon Foundation, and the New-York Historical Society / Patricia D. Klingenstein Library. Additionally, I extend thanks to the various online communities of Judy fans, namely the Judy Garland Database, the Judy Garland Experience, the Judy Garland Message Board, and the Judy Room.

For their encouragement of my passion for exploration, research, and writing, I acknowledge my family. First, thanks to my parents and sister for putting up with me during those formative years filled with collecting and conventions. And to those I have the honor and privilege of coming home to at the end of each day: Jaime Rodriguez, my patient and reassuring partner, spent many late-night hours typing and reading aloud to me for this project, while daughters Camryn and Kaylee continually serve as an inspiring, captive audience. Because of them, there really is no place like home.

PREFACE

"A book for which publishers have been angling for years has been signed and sealed," proclaimed Random House in a press release dated January 4, 1960. "We expect that *The Judy Garland Story* will be our ACT ONE for 1960," added publisher Bennett Cerf.* What promised to be the book deal of the decade was personally negotiated by Cerf during a visit to Judy Garland's room at Manhattan's Doctors Hospital, where she spent seven weeks near the end of 1959.

"Those great, hypnotic brown eyes of hers were not there." recalled Judy's ghostwriter Freddie Finklehoffe, a longtime friend and Metro-Goldwyn-Mayer scenarist. "Just little dark spots, sunken in the fat and bloat of her face. Those famous legs, the ankles of a gazelle, were fat and heavy and she had trouble getting into her shoes. . . . [The doctors] announced the verdict. Sid [Luft] told me. 'Hepatitis and very bad.' That's what he told Judy. But he was lying to her as he lied to me. She had cirrhosis of the liver—and very bad." With physicians prescribing retirement and saying she'd forever be a "semi-invalid," the thirty-seven-year-old's career seemed at its end.

It has been said that husband Sid Luft pitched Judy's autobiography to Bennett Cerf as soon as he realized his wife would not be fit to return to performing and touring anytime soon, and maybe never. Upon signing the book deal with Random House, Judy was reportedly paid an advance in the amount of $35,000. Cerf later recalled an advance of $20,000 to be

---

*Cerf was referencing *ACT ONE: An Autobiography* by Moss Hart, the playwright's best seller published in 1959 by Random House. The book spent 22 weeks at number one and remained on the *New York Times* list for nearly a year.

split with Finklehoffe. Either way, Judy never saw a dime. Some say it was later that same day that Sid bet and lost the entire sum at the horse races.

"There have been a lot of stories written about me . . . some of them fantastically distorted," Judy announced in a press statement given from her hospital bed. "This book is going to set the record straight." Still terribly ill, she was discharged on January 5, 1960, and returned to Los Angeles to begin what promised to be a lengthy recuperation period. Recalling the incident a year later, Judy said: "You want to know something funny? I didn't care. All I cared about was that my children needed me. Suddenly the pressure was off. I just laid there, watched TV, read novels, and thought, no more pills ever, now I'm free. I'll find a way to be happy."*

Judy may have lost the ability to sing, but it was during this time that she found another voice. Working closely with Finklehoffe, she recorded a number of stories and reminiscences on audiotape. Random House execs expected a quick turnaround, but on September 26, 1960, Cerf stated in a letter published in the *Garland Gazette*, a fan club journal, that he'd "not yet seen one line of manuscript of the Judy Garland autobiography."

In an effort to appease the publisher, Finklehoffe delivered sixty-five pages of rough draft, but the project with Random House soon fizzled as Judy made a full recovery, abandoned the book, and returned to work. According to Cerf, Finklehoffe "vanished into thin air. I hoarded those pages, and every once in a while, Judy would say, 'I'm really going to finish that, you know.' She felt very guilty about it. She's a good girl. She doesn't mean to do unforgivable things, but she is absolutely discombobulated between liquor and pills." Random House eventually reclaimed its advance when it sold Judy's story to *McCall's* and Finklehoffe's pages came together to create a two-part feature for the magazine in 1964. "We got back our money and a little bit more," Cerf said. "But there's no book."

It was an angry, bitter, and obviously overmedicated Judy who revisited the idea of an autobiography during the spring of 1964, following the cancellation of her CBS television series. "I'm going to talk," she demanded. "And somebody's going to print this. Even if I have to put up the money myself, I'll print it in a little book . . . maybe somebody will

---

*From "Judy: She's Broken Through the Dark Clouds at Last. Ahead—the Rainbow," Jane Ardmore, *The American Weekly*, October 1, 1961.

read it . . . and maybe somebody will *learn* a little of the truth of this so-called legend! That's what I'm supposed to be, a legend. Judy Garland. Alright, then read about her. Read the *truth*, though!"

Again, during the summer of 1966, Judy took time to record more of her memories and thoughts to tape. "I think that I have every right to write a book," she said. "I think I'm interesting. I have perspective about me." The earliest recordings made during this period were thoughtful and honest, but quickly took on a more jaded and resentful tone. "I'd like to expose a lot of people who deserve it [. . .] and I'd also like a few questions answered . . . questions that I'm sure I'll find my own answers to by talk-ing about things that I've buried within myself too long. . . . *Why? Why* did the agents do this? *Why* did M-G-M behave the way they did? *Why* have the newspapers printed such idiotic and messy stories? *Why* was I not allowed to talk? *Why* was I overworked? *Why* was I . . . I think I know *why*. I just don't think anybody's ever taken the time to listen."

At times Judy was clearly in a narcotized state and even became enraged. She took to screaming and shouting into the recorder, saying, "I'm *not* something you wind up and put on the stage that sings Carnegie Hall album and you put her in the closet [. . .] I'm gonna write a book, and I'm gonna talk, because I can do something besides sing, you know. I don't always have to sing a song. There is something besides 'The Man That Got Away' or 'Over the Rainbow' or 'The Trolley Song.' There's a *woman*. There are three children. There's *me*! There's a lot of *life* going here. I wanted to believe and I tried my *damndest* to believe in the rain-bow that I tried to get over and I *couldn't. SO WHAT!*"

Judy phoned Cerf again in 1966, but her pleas for another book deal were not met with any sort of monetary advance from the publisher as she hoped. "I've always loved Judy Garland," Cerf said the following year. "She is an irresistible little woman—but one of the most tragic in the world. I'm sure that one day she's going to do herself in."*

That would be Judy's last effort to tell her own story. Discouraged, but easily distracted, she put the elusive book project back on the shelf. "When you have lived the life I've lived," she explained in 1967, "when you've loved and suffered, and been madly happy and desperately sad—

---

*From Bennett Cerf's 1967–68 interviews for the Oral History Research Office at Columbia University.

well, that's when you realize you'll never be able to set it all down. Maybe you'd rather die first."*

For all the chaotic tirades, there were moments of passion and tenderness, too, with Judy seeming genuinely determined and eager to tell her story. "I can guarantee you," she said in her final tapes, "even if I have to form a new publishing company and write this book, it's going to be one hell of a great—everlastingly great—book with humor, tears, fun, emotion, and love." She even toyed with ideas for a book title. She wittily told daughter Liza Minnelli her story would be titled *Ho-Hum: My Life*, and revealed to others that it might be called simply *Judy*, or *So Far So Good*, or *And Now, Ladies and Gentlemen, Miss Judy Garland*.

"How's your autobiography coming?" Judy was asked in 1968. "It's been quite a packed-in life," she answered. "It will take years."† Fueled by episodes of despair, stalled in moments of hope, Judy's efforts to compose an autobiography were inadequate and never resulted in much more than a few tapes of recorded rants and reminiscences. She abandoned her work repeatedly, and even Finklehoffe's sixty-five-page manuscript for Random House never amounted to much more than a disarranged transcription of the tapes the two made in 1960. With all such ventures incomplete, stalled, or suspended by the time of her death in 1969, it seemed as though Judy's telling of her life story would never come to fruition—until now.

Judy Garland on Judy Garland is the closest we will likely come to experiencing and exploring the legend's abandoned autobiography. Collecting and presenting many of Judy's most important interviews and encounters that took place between 1935 and 1969, this work opens with her first radio appearance under contract with Metro-Goldwyn-Mayer, and concludes with her last known interview, one taped for Radio Denmark just months before her death. Selections appear in chronological order and are arranged by decade. Most fall into one of two categories: The M-G-M Years (those published under the influence of the studio publicity machine in the 1930s and 1940s), and the Concert Years (from the 1950s and 1960s, with Judy on her own, telling *her* version of events, and

---

*From "When You've Lived the Life I've Lived . . . ," Ivor Davis, (London) *Daily Express*, March 11, 1967.
†From an interview with the Asbury Park Press, June 26, 1968.

attempting to set the record straight). Given that it was Judy's most vocal period, the 1960s section occupies nearly half of this book's pages.

What makes this collection unique and distinguishes it from the plethora of Garland biographies is that it places Judy in the role of story-teller. And what a great storyteller she was! True, a number of the stories herein have undertones of pathos, but many are decorated with witty bits of Judy's own brand of comedy. "You'll find that there's an awful lot of baggy-pants comedy in me," she declared in her 1966 tapes, later explain-ing, "I'm not the daughter of tragedy. [Judy Garland] wasn't her name. Her name was Ethel." Whether telling a story about her mother, Ethel ("the real life Wicked Witch of the West"), or being dismissed by M-G-M ("Leo the Lion bit me!"), Judy found ways to deal with even the most painful memories through the guise of humor. "I hope to *Christ* this comes out funny," she said of her planned book. "Otherwise it's really going to make Tchaikovsky sound like the Beatles!"

First Lady of Comedy Lucille Ball called Judy "the funniest lady in Hollywood," and Judy proved it again and again over the years through her spontaneous wisecracks and long, twisted tales. Speaking of tales, the task of separating fact from fiction is one of the challenges found in the process of untangling Judy's story. Such an undertaking requires fil-tering through many years of myths, half-truths, and some out-and-out lies. Stories tracing back to the studio should always be approached with some level of suspicion. Although a number of wonderful (and verifiable) truths are present, such tidbits may be hidden amongst other exaggerated anecdotes. It's important that readers navigate the information with care and an awareness of what is sometimes referred to as the "Hollywood hallucination."

M-G-M always boasted "more stars than there are in the heavens," and the biggest and best studio was, naturally, home to biggest and best marketing mouthpiece. Heading the studio's publicity department in its heyday was Howard Strickling, who—due to his reputation in the fine art of scandal dodging and cover-ups—held the title of Hollywood's leading "fixer." He was in close contact with all the major reporters, columnists, and fan magazine editors who, prior to publication, would often submit their features to Strickling's Culver City team for approval. When she arrived at M-G-M in 1935, young Judy had no real scandal to dodge or cover-up to make. Born Frances Ethel Gumm some 13 years earlier, she'd only been "Judy Garland" for a year or so.

With the success of *The Wizard of Oz* came public demand for more Judy, and Howard Strickling wasted no time fashioning a detailed biography for the popular youngster. As was customary in his department, the media magnate embellished Judy's story like an ornate and extravagant production number from a Metro musical. Her official studio biography, *The Life Story of Judy Garland* (dated 1940), was a 22-page mimeographed document with contents ranging from petty to preposterous:

- "The young star of today, idol of thousands, [once] faced the problem of conjuring a dinner for four out of two eggs and a moldy loaf of bread."

- "[At home,] Judy not only has her own room, but rooms—a suite of three. . . . Hidden somewhere in the recess of these three rooms are a secret closet and passage, known to Judy alone. These rooms are Judy's sanctuary."

- "She claims that when she is twenty-five, she will leave the screen, marry, settle down and have at least six children and do her own cooking."

- "Still says her prayers at the foot of her bed . . . never does she go to bed before she takes her setting-up exercises. Worries about being fat but consoles herself that it is only 'baby' fat and that she's bound to be thin the older she gets. So she keeps right on eating chocolate cake, ice cream with fudge sauce, spaghetti, and chili. She hates salads, but loves candy bars."

No M-G-M star could be average or ordinary. That is, unless that happened to be the slant the studio wanted to employ. "When a studio puts you under contract, its publicity department starts turning out news copy about you that you read with astonishment," Judy explained in a feature for *Cosmopolitan*. "You think, can this be me they're talking about? They don't really manufacture untruths, but they play up whatever makes interesting reading, and then a columnist adds his own little embellishments and another adds to that until there's a whole body of so-called 'facts' floating around—almost like another you—that simply isn't real. It isn't a lie, but it isn't real, either. . . . You can't very well go around denying the stories your studio releases when it is doing everything it can to make you a star, and sometimes you get to doubting your actual personality."*

It's important to note that Judy's arrival at M-G-M coincided with the untimely death of her father, and from that day she seemed to take on the persona and embrace the life prescribed for her by the studio. The death of Frank Gumm signaled the death of Frances Gumm. "I don't associate Frances Gumm with me—she's a girl I can read about the way other people do," Judy proclaimed in the aforementioned *Cosmo* piece. "I, Judy Garland, was born when I was twelve years old."

Biographer Christopher Finch, author of *Rainbow: The Stormy Life of Judy Garland*, described young Judy as an adolescent girl trying to cope with the loss of her father and in turn buying the stories sold to her by those in control:

Hollywood destroyed Judy Garland's childhood by trivializing it into oblivion, a process that started the day Metro-Goldwyn-Mayer's publicity department first turned its attention on her. She lacked the stability and security to resist the relentless erosion of fact and, eventually, she came to believe many of the myths invented for her. . . . She was just beginning her new life at M-G-M, and the aims of the studio and the aims of her subconscious coincided. M-G-M invented a surrogate childhood for her to escape to, thus destroying any hopes she might have had of finding roots and stability. The pills and the morphine and the rest of the junk would eventually finish the job—blurring whatever survived the fictionalizing process—but, to all intents and purposes, the truth was buried the day her father died. Eventually the happy times and all of the successes were obliterated, to be replaced by a catalogue of comic disasters.

---

*Judy Garland, as told to Michael Drury, "*My* Story," *Cosmopolitan*, January 1951 (this feature appears in its entirety later in this book).

Judy's split from M-G-M on September 29, 1950, proved in many ways to be her emancipation proclamation. She was finally free to speak her mind and formulate an identity apart from that created for her by the studio. In the succeeding years she made enormous efforts to triumph over the media's concentration on and exploitation of her personal struggles. It should be noted that, comparatively, the same media paid far less attention to her successes. But Judy had her say, as evidenced in this collection. She wrote a number of essays for various publications and sat for countless print, radio, and television interviews during the post-M-G-M era, particularly in the 1960s. These and the other autobiographical efforts made throughout what was to be the final chapter of her life are proof Judy wanted her story told, and wanted it told in her own words.

Aside from the occasional notating of blatant factual errors, I have elected to keep these interviews and encounters complete, intact, and uninterrupted, presenting them for the sake of presentation and preservation. I feel they all play an important role in Judy's telling of her story. Intentional stylized capitalization, creative wordplay, and other trendy literary devices used by various authors remain intact. Simple misspellings (especially names of well-known individuals, titles of films and songs, etc.) have been silently corrected. Editor's notes within a piece are indicated within brackets or as footnotes at the end of each page.

Interview transcriptions new to this volume were personally transcribed as accurately as possible, with only minor editing for readability. "You must get used to the fact—and I think that it should be written straight away—I don't talk well," Judy admitted in tapes recorded during the summer of 1966. "I don't finish any of my words lots of times because my mind goes faster and I stammer a lot." In an effort to smoothly adapt spoken word to print, I have omitted the excessive use of "um" and "uh," repeated words, and similarly unnecessary utterings by Judy and those who interviewed her. More substantial omissions are indicated with ellipses in brackets, while ellipses without brackets indicate hesitations or pauses. Most interviews are transcribed and presented in their entirety (or as much as survives on source recordings).

This book makes every attempt to present a thorough and detailed telling of Judy's story, but a collection such as this is not intended to cover the full breadth of such a complex life and illustrious career. Hers is a story that has been told many times and in many ways, in some cases by fine writers and Garland authorities. Those seeking additional reading and perspective are encouraged to review the Suggested Reading section of this book. Also, several pieces considered for inclusion but ultimately omitted for a variety of reasons include "The Real Me" by Judy, as told to Joe Hyams, which appeared in the April 1957 issue of *McCall's*. It was a virtual retelling of "My Story" from *Cosmopolitan* in 1951. Also, due to permission issues, 1964's "Judy Garland's Own Story: There'll Always Be an Encore" and 1967's "The Plot Against Judy Garland" (both features for *McCall's*) are absent from this volume, but recommended reads. Brief excerpts from these and other important pieces are included throughout the book and as "Judy Gems" between items.

My introduction to Judy Garland came in the spring of 1979. Just shy of my fourth birthday, I was indoctrinated into the Garland cult by way of the annual broadcast/event of *The Wizard of Oz*, like most fans of my generation. By the age of six I was aware of Judy Garland apart from Dorothy Gale, and I began exploring her other films, recordings, and fascinating career in entertainment. For years I collected feverishly, attended fan events, and even became curator of my own Over the Rainbow Museum and Sales Co. in a small building behind our house on my family's farm. Yes, I was *that* kid! As an adult, my interest ebbed and flowed (usually due to life events and various school/work obligations), but it never waned.

I have always found it difficult to put into words my gravitation toward the Garland phenomena. It's an inexplicable pull that only Judy has come close to identifying:

I have a machine in my throat that gets into many people's ears and affects them. . . . There's something about my voice that makes them see all the sadness and humor they've experienced. It makes them know they aren't too different; they aren't apart. That's the only reason I can give for people's liking to hear me sing, because I'm not that fine a singer. Sometimes my vibrato is too fast or too slow, although I've got good pitch. I have good diction, and I read a song much more than I sing it.

I try to bring the audience's own drama—tears and laughter they know about—to them. I try to match my lifelong experiences with theirs, and they match their own sadness and happiness to mine. I think that's it. Both men and women connect me with Dorothy in *The Wizard of Oz*, and they have a protective attitude toward me, which is rather sweet.*

Whether rooted in the protectiveness she referred to all those years ago, or perhaps some other characteristic yet to be determined, I am thrilled to have this opportunity to give Judy Garland the voice she always desired, and to present her story in her own words through this book full of the humor, the tears, the fun, the emotion, and the love she promised. "I'm going to talk in my own words," she assured us. "And tell the truth. So here goes."

---

*Judy Garland, "Judy Garland's Own Story: There'll Always Be an Encore," *McCall's*, February 1964.

PART I

THE 1930s

RADIO INTERVIEW

WALLACE BEERY | October 26, 1935, *Shell Chateau Hour*

Broadcast from the KFI Studios in Los Angeles, NBC's *Shell Chateau Hour* was a relatively new musical variety series in the fall of 1935 when Judy made her national radio debut on the program. With parents Frank and Ethel Gumm and sister Jimmie in the front row, host and M-G-M star Wallace Beery (subbing for usual host Al Jolson) declared Judy to be "only twelve years old," when in fact she had turned thirteen some four months prior. In what may have been an effort to magnify their daughter's already prodigious talents, Frank and Ethel listed Judy's birth date as January 10, 1923, on initial studio paperwork. It also seemed to be common practice for Metro's publicity department to intentionally misrepresent ages and birth dates in hopes of keeping their actresses seeming younger than they actually were.

Although the *Shell Chateau Hour* was Judy's first official appearance under the auspices of M-G-M, she was presented as a fresh discovery with no mention of the recent contract signed with the studio. Scripted chitchat with Beery gave way to the little girl with a big voice bursting forth with gusto in a tour de force execution of "Broadway Rhythm," the Arthur Freed–Nacio Herb Brown tune from Metro's *Broadway Melody of 1936*.

Wallace Beery: Now for the surprise of the evening, this is the opportunity spot of the show, one portion of the show we donate each week to someone whom we feel has exceptional ability and we want to help along. We have a girl here whom I think is going to be the sensation of pictures. She's only twelve years old, and I take great pleasure in presenting to you Judy Garland. Wait until you hear her. [*Audience applauds.*] Twelve years old. Come on, Judy. Come on. There you are. Here, Judy, if you're scared, you hang right on to me, honey. [*Judy laughs.*] I'm right with you. Now come on, we'll talk a minute. Now, where did you learn to sing?

Judy Garland: My mother taught me.

WB: Your ma, huh? Never had any regular music lessons at all, huh?

JG: Well, I did take some piano lessons.

WB: Well, can you play it pretty good?

JG: Oh, I don't know. Mom says I play pretty well.

WB: Well, of course. Mom would. All right, Judy, now tell me this. Now what do you want to do when you grow up to be a great big girl, huh?

JG: I want to be a singer, Mr. Beery. And I'd like to act, too.

WB: Well, you'll do it, Judy. Don't worry. Now, I'll tell you, you just stand here and sing that piece you sang for me the other day and show these folks what a singer you are. Now go right to it, and if you need me I'll be standing right there, you hear?

JG: [*Laughs.*] All right.

WB: Step right on it. Go ahead, Judy. I'll be right here.

[*Judy sings "Broadway Rhythm."*]

WB: That was marvelous. That was marvelous. Imagine . . . only twelve years old. We've got to get her back again.

RADIO INTERVIEW

WALLACE BEERY | November 16, 1935, *Shell Chateau Hour*

Judy returned to the KFI Studios three weeks later, this time accompanied only by Ethel. Frank Gumm had been hospitalized at Cedars of Lebanon Hospital earlier that day, diagnosed with virulent meningitis and given little chance of survival. Judy was not aware of the severity of her father's illness, but sensed the urgency in the voice of family doctor Marcus Rabwin when he phoned her at the studio prior to the broadcast. Rabwin told her that a radio had been placed at Frank's bedside and he would be listening.

Judy's performance of "Zing! Went the Strings of My Heart" outdid the rendition of "Broadway Rhythm" she'd sung several weeks earlier. Knowledge of her father's condition likely fueled the intensity with which she sang on this particular occasion, for it was one of the few early performances to foreshadow the force and potency of what was to come in the Judy Garland concert experiences of the 1960s. "I sang my heart out for him," she later recalled, "but by morning he was gone." By Sunday, November 17 (Ethel's birthday), Frank was in a coma. He died around 3:00 that afternoon. He was 49.

Wallace Beery: Now the little lady standing here beside me isn't exactly a celebrity *yet*. She's only twelve years old. She probably won't be famous, oh, maybe for a couple of years. Her name is Judy Garland, and I'm sure that you remember her singing here about four weeks ago. Well, since her last appearance here she signed a seven-year contract with the M-G-M Studio. Isn't that great? Gosh! And the minute she was signed, Sam Katz wrote her into his new picture *Yours and Mine*.* I knew that Judy would

---

* *Yours and Mine* was a project that never materialized.

make good. The last time she was here she was the cause that everybody said to me, "Wally, why, you've got to have that little Judy Garland back again." So here she is, and I'll tell you right now that we're very proud of her. Wait until you hear her sing. All right, Judy, whip along.

[*Judy sings "Zing! Went the Strings of My Heart."*]

WB: That was marvelous, Judy. Oh, how you can sing! Ladies and gentlemen, that was Judy Garland. That wasn't me singing. [*All laugh.*] I want to thank you for that, Judy. It was marvelous.

Judy Garland: Wait a minute, Mr. Beery. I wanna thank *you*!

WB: Oh, no, no, no.

JG: Yes, really, I do! I want to thank you for giving me two chances to come here and sing at *Shell Chateau* and for all the other things you've done for me.

WB: Oh, I'm so proud of you, Judy. I bet your mother's proud of you, too. Isn't that your ma sitting right down there in the front row?

JG: That's her!

WB: Mmm.

JG: Well, do you think my mother would care if I gave you a great big hug?

WB: Well, I don't know what she'd think, but maybe that little Carol Ann of mine might object. But go ahead! [*All laugh.*] Thanks, Judy! [*Audience applauds.*] That's awfully sweet of you. Now, come on. Just a little, little ditty . . . teeny weeny encore.

JG: All right.

WB: Go ahead!

[*Judy sings "Zing! Went the Strings of My Heart" reprise.*]

WB: Isn't that marvelous? A child twelve years old. Now that she's with M-G-M, I hope they give me the opportunity of being able to support her in a picture someday.

JUDY GARLAND FACES STARDOM

VICTORIA JOHNSON | August 1937, *Modern Movies*

In concurrence with the release of *Broadway Melody of 1938*, *Modern Movies* was one of two national fan magazines to feature Judy on its cover during August 1937 (the other was *Screen Juveniles*). Though it seems she was thirteen at the time of the interview, Judy was fifteen by the time of its publication.

Tradition turns topsy-turvy as this thirteen-year-old jostles her elders for first place

Judy Garland, child wonder of the screen, bursts upon an astonished world. She's the cutest little dancer and blues singer that's ever been seen or heard. She is only thirteen [*sic*], but already has years of professional life behind her.

Judy comes of a theatrical family and has been in almost every city in the United States with her parents "on the road." There were brief stays in Grand Rapids, Mich., Chicago and other cities. But she considers Los Angeles her home. Judy's stage work was as part of a trio, with her two sisters, Virginia and Suzanne.

She was born Frances Gumm in Murfreesboro, Tenn.,* but when George Jessel signed the trio for his act at the Oriental Theatre in Chicago,

---

* Judy was, of course, born in Grand Rapids, Minnesota. Upon signing with M-G-M, she supposedly listed her birthplace as "Murfreesboro, Tennessee," later explaining she thought it sounded more "glamorous."

he changed the last name—and Frances went him one better by switching over to her present "Judy."

"I had to fight for the name," she says. "But mother finally agreed to let me change."

Judy, for a child who has lived more or less in a world of make-believe, is striking in her lack of affectation. Her large, wide-set brown eyes are shy, yet they dance with interest, and smile. She is quite a movie fan, admiring particularly Jimmy Stewart, Clark Gable and Jeanette MacDonald. The world of pictures, which was opened to her two years ago, is exciting and full of promise. Yet she views it tentatively and gratefully—not as one who has come and conquered.

For nearly two years she was under contract before having a part. She had been seen while singing at Lake Tahoe, and an agent brought her to the attention of M-G-M.

"I didn't think I had much of a chance," she confesses, "I was just at the awkward age. It is funny, but even though there are lots of people my age in the world, few were interested in them. There's a big difference between Shirley Temple and Maureen O'Sullivan. But up until just a little while ago, there wasn't a place in between.

"That's why I'm grateful to Deanna Durbin. Her work proved to the public that people were interested in actresses or talent of the 'between age.' That was a break for all of us in our early 'teens.'

Judy is frankly thrilled with her role in *Broadway Melody of 1938*. In it she portrays Sophie Tucker's daughter. Sophie, in the film, is an ex-famous actress, whose vogue is passe. She tries to further the interests of her daughter, so the child can carry on where she herself left off.

In *Broadway Melody* Judy is given an opportunity to show her stuff. She sings, she dances—and acts. One of the big numbers in the picture features her coming onto the stage in a white streamlined car, lined in padded pink satin with a chauffeur and footman. Buddy Ebsen greets her in the middle of the stage, and off they dance.

The studio wisely made no attempt to push or retard her age. She is just a kid of thirteen with short dresses and bobby socks. And she has filled a place long vacant on the screen.

"I get so many letters from people my own age, saying how they enjoy seeing a person just like them on the screen. They get tired of seeing only small children or grown-ups, they write."

Judy admits she is at a confusing age. "You are all twisted up. Sometimes you'd like to make mud pies, or play with dolls, but think you're too old. At others, it would be fun to put on high heels and go dancing. Then you're ashamed, because you know you are not old enough. Oh, well, thirteen is a lot of fun, anyway. I've adopted it as my lucky number."

You cannot help admiring someone her age suddenly thrust into the glamorous world of films, who has remained balanced. Judy doesn't try to be "girly girly." And she is too smart to try to appear old, as do so many other girls her age.

"There are about fifteen years that you can be young," she philosophizes. "All the rest, you are grown-up. I think you appreciate being grown-up much better, if you don't try to be that way too soon.

"So I don't mind being teased now and then for my short skirts and flat heels. I tried some long hose and longer skirts once, but it wasn't any fun. Now I'll wait until I am ready for them instead of looking silly."

As for her career, the height of her ambition is to go into real dramatic parts someday. She'd like a picture in which she didn't sing even so much as one number—"just to show she didn't get by on her voice."

JUDY GARLAND LOOKS BACK OVER 10 YEARS IN THE SHOW BUSINESS

HELEN CHAMPION | August 1937, *Screen Juveniles*

At thirteen, Judy Garland is a veteran performer. They couldn't keep her off the stage!

At two, she determinedly held up proceedings for twenty minutes on amateur night in a little movie theater in Minnesota, while she lustily rendered "Jingle Bells" again and again.

She had climbed down from her grandmother's lap, and made her way behind the footlights to "put on her act."

First the crowd was amused, then restless, then annoyed.

It mattered not a bit to Judy.

She was singing, and she had an audience. Right then, the show business got her, and she's been at it ever since.

This, and a number of other things, I learned as bright-eyed, bubbling Miss Garland and her charmingly reticent little mother and I chatted over lunch in the huge Metro-Goldwyn-Mayer commissary recently.

She was particularly bright-eyed and bubbling that noon, what with the thrill of a smart new cream-colored makeup kit Norma Shearer had given her a few moments before, and Clark Gable sitting at the very next table to us.

What thirteen-year-old girl wouldn't be thrilled over a combination like that?

But before we go any further, you might as well know that while Judy has a great weakness for the Gable gentleman, Robert Donat is definitely "tops" in her screen affections.

"Sophie Tucker is a friend of his," she confided breathlessly, "and she's written to England asking him to send me an autographed picture. Isn't that grand?"

Miss Tucker, recently returned from English stage and screen engagements, is Judy's mother in *Broadway Melody of 1937* [retitled *Broadway Melody of 1938*], the Eleanor Powell picture currently before the camera at the studio.

"And wasn't it marvelous of Miss Shearer to give me this?" Judy wanted to know for the third time, as she lovingly patted the makeup kit beside her.

I could see plainly that I was starting out with a distinct handicap on that interview. Yet there is a certain honor in even competing with Norma Shearer and Clark Gable.

"You know, I didn't do a thing," Judy was saying. "I just went to a party Miss Shearer gave. That was all.

"But she's lovely, anyway. She's always doing nice things."

She smoothed a fold of her little dark blue sailor suit which the makeup kit had rumpled while she'd had it on her lap a few moments before, and with a happy sigh turned her attention to the toasted cheese sandwich the waitress set before her.

This Judy has acting and music in her blood from both sides of the family, I found. The movie theater in which she made that surprise debut at two was her father's. Her mother was pianist there, turning out by the hour that "atmospheric" music which always accompanied film showings in those days of the silents.

"Even now I think I could play 'Hearts and Flowers' with my eyes shut," she smiled, telling me about it.

The couple, Frank and Ethel Gumm, were veteran vaudeville troupers. As a boy soprano, Frank had worked his way through school by singing. As a man, he had a fine baritone voice. Ethel both played and sang well. At fourteen, she was ably holding down a job as pianist in a movie theater.

After their marriage, they toured the country in a singing act, as Jack and Virginia Lee. But the advent of Suzanne, Judy's eldest sister, stopped all that for a time.

Two years later, "Jimmie," (a girl in spite of her name) was born. Four years more, and Judy put in her appearance. She was known as Frances then.

They settled down in Grand Rapids, Minnesota, and Mr. Gumm bought a small moving picture theater.

The girls all showed talent. To their delight, their parents worked up a little singing and dancing act for them. They put on performances for their friends and at their father's theater.

When Judy was three, the family decided, with a suddenness characteristic of them, to take a trip to California. Partly as a lark, partly as a means of earning a little extra money, they "divided the family into two acts," as Judy puts it, and worked their way out here, staging performances in movie theaters along the route.

"That was my first professional work, and it was such fun," giggled Judy. "I can actually remember it. Daddy and mother were one act, and we three girls the other. We'd go on first, and then sit proudly out in front to watch our parents perform.

"As part of their act, mother used to sing 'I've Been Saving for a Rainy Day,' and it always made me cry. It was terribly sad!"

"It makes you cry even now when I sing it," teased Mrs. Gumm. Judy looked a little embarrassed.

They liked California so well that they decided to stay. Mr. Gumm bought a moving picture theater in Lancaster, about ninety miles inland from Hollywood, and the family settled down.

But don't think for a moment that anything could have kept those three girls in Lancaster. They slept there, but that was all. They'd had a taste of the stage, and their appetite was keen for more.

Agents liked their act, and they were booked steadily in small theaters in Los Angeles and Hollywood, and up and down the coast. Sometimes they made the long trip from Lancaster to Los Angeles twice in one day for a sudden engagement. They could always count on coming in at least four or five times a week.

Their mother came along, and played for their act. She was pianist for a number of dancing schools, in addition, and taught personality singing.

As we were discussing those days, Judy suddenly shouted with laughter.

"Do you remember the time we were putting on our act in Bishop, when I was five?" she asked her mother, "and just as I was to go on, I found I had my Oriental costume on wrong side out?"

"I'll never forget it," said Mrs. Gumm. "I was playing the piano, and looked up. There stood Judy in the wings, with not a stitch on, struggling to turn her dress right side out. Meanwhile, the other two girls were doggedly plowing through the chorus of 'Avalon Town' over and over again."

At that time, the youngsters' parents had considered pictures for them, but not seriously.

"We weren't sure there was a real place for them in films," said Mrs. Gumm. "When Judy was six, and her sisters ten and twelve, Gus Edwards arranged an audition for them here at Metro-Goldwyn-Mayer, but nothing ever came of it."

A little later, the owner of a dancing school, convinced of the talent of the three, particularly Judy, was knocking at studio doors in their interests. He was I. C. Overdorff, head of the Hollywood School of the Dance. The children's mother was playing for his students at the time.

Still nothing happened. So the girls continued merrily on with their act in the theaters.

"Why not take a trip to Chicago?" one of them suggested brightly, about three years ago. "We might do some good business."

Off they went, Mrs. Gumm and the girls. At the Oriental Theater there, they played on the same bill with George Jessel.

Through a mistake, they were billed as "The Glum Sisters."

Mr. Jessel, who had become quite interested in the trio, threw up his hands when he saw it.

"Let me give you a name to work under," said he. "Garland. Robert Garland, an old friend of mine, writes for the Sun and Telegraph in New York. I know he'll be glad to have you use his name. He's a grand fellow."

So the "Gumm" became "Garland."

The "Judy" made its appearance two years ago, when the family [was] on vacation at Lake Tahoe. It occurred to Frances that Judy was an interesting name, and she promptly adopted it.

It was the Lake Tahoe jaunt, too, that got her into pictures. By that time, Suzanne had married, and the act had broken up. The other two girls were each working on their own.

Their holiday at the Lake over, the family had started on the homeward journey in their car. Ten miles along the way, Judy remembered she'd left her music behind. They decided not to turn back.

Five miles more, and "Jimmie" discovered she'd left all her hats behind. That was different. You can't replace your favorite hats.

They returned to the Lake. When they arrived, they found that Lew Brown, the songwriter, had just arrived at the hotel. Someone insisted he hear Judy sing. All disheveled, and in her little rumpled sun shorts, she sang for him.

He worked fast.

Two days later, Judy was signed to a contract at Metro-Goldwyn-Mayer.

"Who has taught you to sing and dance, Judy?" I asked, curiously.

"Mostly my mother," replied the little girl, smiling at Mrs. Gumm across the table, "although of course I've picked up a lot of things here and there, being on the stage so much."

"She's worked hard, too," said Mrs. Gumm, "because she's been so interested in getting ahead. Roger Edens, who arranges all her songs and dances for her pictures here, has helped her a great deal."

The talk drifted to Judy's plans. Her brown eyes danced again as she told me about the new house that is to be built in Cheviot Hills, not far from the studio. It will be a red brick house, Colonial style, such as Judy has always longed for. Not a very large house, for the family is smaller now. Suzanne, of course, is married, and Mr. Gumm died a year and a half ago.

"But we're going to have it large enough to entertain when we want to," Judy assured me. "I love parties. And there'll be special accommodations for my pet duck, and my two dogs, two turtles and canary. We're going to have a swimming pool, too, and a tennis court.

"And besides that, I want to adopt a baby sister," she went on gravely. "Mother thinks it's a good idea, so we're going ahead with it right away.

"Why don't we go to that orphanage we were talking about, and see if we can't take a little girl over the weekend on trial?" she asked her mother.

"We ought to do it as soon as possible, don't you think? The more time the baby spends with us, the less time she'll have to be in an orphanage." Her brows wrinkled anxiously.

"We want her about a year and a half old," she explained to me, "and we're going to name her Penelope."

Besides all these activities, there will be ballet lessons. These are being arranged for now. Both Judy and her mother feel that this is one of the best ways to achieve grace and a properly poised body.

"And what's all this I hear about you and Jackie Cooper being such good friends?" I asked, when the time seemed to be right to bring up this important matter. "He says you're the grandest girl he knows."

Judy looked a bit upset.

"She and Jackie have had a little falling out," said her mother. "But it was really my fault. I didn't make myself clear to Jackie about a certain date. I'll fix it up," she smiled.

As we were saying good-bye outside the commissary door, and had stopped to show the new makeup kit to one of Judy's studio friends, we met Meredith Howard, the young woman publicity aide who had arranged our interview. Judy spied her charm bracelet and stopped to admire it.

"Oh, I'd so like to have one of those," she sighed.

"I've been planning to get you one for a long time," confessed her mother. "We'll see about it this afternoon."

"And you should have charms on it for your three pictures, *Every Sunday*, *Pigskin Parade*, and *Broadway Melody of 1937*," put in Miss Howard. "I'll get you the first."

"I'll get the second," I promised.

"And I'll get the third," added the gentleman to whom Judy had been exhibiting her new kit.

"What a day!" sighed Miss Garland blissfully.

JUDY GARLAND— GUEST EDITOR

JUDY GARLAND | **December 1937, *Movie Mirror***

Prepared during production for *Thoroughbreds Don't Cry*, the first of ten films Judy would make alongside Mickey Rooney, this piece for *Movie Mirror* is the earliest known example of her personal writing for publication.

Hello Juniors:

Freddie Bartholomew was telling me about the time he was guest editor for MOVIE MIRROR Junior and how much he enjoyed writing it, so when Miss Turner asked me if I would like to write the department this month, I jumped at the chance and I hope you like mine as much as you did Freddie's.

I've been on the stage ever since I was a few years old and I've been in pictures for the last two years. I'm fourteen now, and I hope to spend the rest of my life in pictures.

Mother and Dad were both vaudeville entertainers, but when my oldest sister, Suzanne, was born, they quit the stage and Dad bought a movie theater in Grand Rapids, Minnesota. I have two older sisters, and the three of us used to spend all the time we possibly could in Dad's theater watching the acts.

We were crazy about the stage, and my sisters got up a little act and the two of them used to put it on in the theater. They sang and danced, and I would cry because they wouldn't let me be in it, too, so when I was four years old I just determined to get up there anyhow. I got to the stage during their act and interrupted proceedings to give my version of a nursery song. It wasn't very good but, boy, it was plenty loud.

After that, they made a place for me and the three of us used to give regular performances in Dad's theater and for our friends. In fact, we'd put on that act for anyone who would stay still long enough to watch us dance and listen to us sing. We kept adding new songs and dances to it and spent all our spare time rehearsing.

My folks decided to take a trip to California and we thought it would be a lot of fun to act our way out there. So Mother and Dad got up an act of their own, and we three girls had ours. We put on performances in movie theaters all along the way from Minnesota to California, and I've never enjoyed a trip so much in my life. We'd give our act first, and then Mother and Dad would go on, and we three girls would sit out in front and watch them. We were tremendously proud of the whole thing.

We all liked California so much that my parents decided to stay out here, and Dad bought another movie theater in Lancaster, which is about eighty miles from Hollywood, and we all settled down there.

My sisters and I wanted to keep on acting, though, so we went to agents and managed to get bookings in theaters all up and down the coast. We were in a different theater almost every night. Lots of times we'd have to leave Lancaster on a moment's notice for a new engagement, and we'd scurry around like mad getting our things together and rushing off so we'd be in time for the theater. Mother always went along with us on these trips and played the piano for us.

Finally we thought it was about time for a vacation, so the whole family went up to Lake Tahoe for a few weeks. As we were driving back home, we discovered that we'd left all our hats at the hotel so we had to turn around and go back for them. When we got there, a friend of ours dashed out to the car and said, "Are you lucky, Judy! Lew Brown, the songwriter, just got here, and you're going to sing for him right away!" He started dragging me into the hotel, and before I knew what it was all about, there I was standing in front of Mr. Brown.

I was so excited that I hardly knew what I was doing, but I managed to open my mouth and start singing. He evidently liked it, because he said he thought I'd be good for pictures and he'd try to fix it up for me.

Well, I had been home for a couple of days and was just about recovering from all the excitement when the phone rang and it was Metro-Goldwyn-Mayer Studios telling me to come down and see them right away. My mother wasn't home to go with me, so Dad and I went right on down. I just had on a pair of slacks and a shirt, but we were so excited and in such a rush that I didn't have time to change them.

When we got to the studio I found that they had thought that I was older than twelve years, and weren't sure whether or not they could use a girl of that age. But they let me sing, and then called Mr. Mayer down to hear me. Finally they decided that they liked my songs and signed me to a contract. That was certainly one of life's big moments for me.

The first picture I did was a short with Deanna Durbin called *Every Sunday*. We sang together in that and she and I were great friends and still see a lot of each other. After that I was in *Pigskin Parade* at 20th Century Fox.

My next picture was *Broadway Melody of 1938*. Sophie Tucker played my mother in it, and we had a lot of fun on the set while we were working. I sing a song to Clark Gable called "Dear Mr. Gable" in the picture, and I sure put my heart and soul into it because he is such a grand person. After I finished the song, he gave me a lovely bracelet.

Robert Taylor became a candid camera fiend while we were making the picture, and in between scenes he would go around snapping pictures of everyone on the set. He got behind tables and up on chairs to get unusual angles, and it seemed that every time you turned around, you bumped into him taking pictures. He was having a swell time.

I kept my fingers crossed for days before the preview and during it I was so excited that I could hardly see the screen. That preview was another one of life's big moments for me.

I love going to movies and see as many as Mother will let me. I like parties, too, and we have a lot of them at home. Most of my friends used to be in vaudeville, too, and when we have parties they all get up and put on their acts and it's grand fun. I don't care for dances very much, though, because I think parties where you play games and do things are much more fun.

Ping-Pong is my idea of a swell game. I'm the champion Ping-Pong player at my house and pretty soon we're going to get up a Ping-Pong tournament, so I'm practicing all the time that I can.

Golf and riding and swimming are my favorite sports, and I'm crazy about baseball. I love going to baseball games and I generally cheer myself hoarse whenever anyone makes a home run.

I don't know if you have the same craze for roller coasters that I have. They scare me to death, but I love them. Whenever I can get someone to go down to the amusement pier with me, I spend most of the time on the roller coaster. Once my hat flew off, but fortunately the boy in back of me got hold of it as it soared over him. I hold on to the handrail so tightly that I wouldn't let go no matter what happened.

Well, I must go back on the set now, so I'll have to close this letter, but I want to tell you how much I enjoyed writing it and I do hope I hear from you in return.

Yours,
Judy Garland

If you will write to me and tell me whether you like musical pictures with singing and dancing best or if you would rather see just straight dramas or comedies without any music, I'll give ten autographed pictures of myself to the ten boys and girls who write the most interesting letters telling which type of movies they prefer and why. Miss Betty Turner and I will act as judges. Please write to me in care of MOVIE MIRROR, *Junior, 7751 Sunset Blvd., Hollywood, Cal., but be sure to mail your letter before December 5th, 1937.*

PUNCH AND JUDY

GLADYS HALL | **January 1938, *Motion Picture***

In 1937, Gladys Hall, known as the "Grand Old Dame of the Fannies," scored one of the first interviews with Judy Garland. The wife of noted Hollywood portrait photographer Russell E. Ball, Gladys was a founding member of the Hollywood Women's Press Club. The trusted friend and confidante of numerous Hollywood stars (including Judy), Hall was known to dine with at least three of her famous friends each week.

Here's the very first interview [for *Motion Picture* magazine] *with Judy Garland, the new child wonder of Hollywood. Called the next "Red Hot Mama" by Sophie Tucker, Judy can put punch into a song*

She still takes her Teddy Bear to bed with her. She puts her dolls to bed every night of her life.

Sophie Tucker (who ought to know) predicts that Judy Garland will be the next "red hot mama."

She is a sort of "nut brown maid," with dark hair and dark-brown eyes and rose-tan skin. She looks healthy and happy and wise without being sophisticated.

She adores the funny papers, with *Little Orphan Annie* nosing out the spinach-strong *Popeye* for her vote.

She reads "anything medical," her most recent favorites being *An American Doctor's Odyssey, I Was a Probationer, Hospital Nocturne* and *The Green Light*. She also read *Gone with the Wind* and Noël Coward's *Present Indicative.*

She reads all of the fan magazines. She is a Ping-Pong champion, beating the neighbor kids without much effort. She rides horseback, plays baseball, golf and tennis, the piano. She draws. She mimics other actors and actresses. She makes fudge.

Her hobby is collecting records and they include everything from swing music to the *Nutcracker Suite* and *the Afternoon of a Faun*. She adores Debussy.

She is a husky, hearty little girl with a huge appetite, an active body and an active mind. And she speaks her mind freely and frankly, without self-conscious fear of "what people will think." She doesn't want to grow up. She wears short skirts, no makeup off the set. Her mother says that she forgets she is a picture actress immediately she leaves the studio. She becomes, at once, "just a little girl," [when] roller-skating, making fudge, playing with dolls.

Judy is by no means one of those pathetic cases of all-work-and-no-play. If she were, her mother would see to it that No Work would be the verdict. She says: "If I study my script I get too stiff. I just sort of look at the lines. I never pose or make faces at myself in front of my mirror." She says, too: "I used to play house all the time. Well, that's acting, same thing."

She thinks that Hollywood is just the little old hometown where she has lived, between vaudeville tours, since she was three years old. It makes her "mad as a hornet" when people suggest that the little old hometown is mad and bad. She says: "That's crazy talk. I've been in lots of small towns and medium-sized towns and big towns when my sisters and I were a singing trio and Hollywood is just like any other small town, only better because it's more comfortable. You can go around wearing anything.

"People aren't stuck-up. People talk about other people but they do that everywhere. And they're not two-faced in Hollywood. One thing I can't stand is two-faced people—also onions and raisins and fruitcake. It also makes me sick about people with careers, even people in the movies, the way they say: 'I've sacrificed everything for my career.' That *does* make me sick. You don't sacrifice things, you *trade* things. Like me, I can't skate and play Ping-Pong and read as much as I'd like to but then I meet Clark Gable and Spencer Tracy and Jimmy Stewart and if that isn't a fair trade, what is?

"And Hollywood gives everybody a chance. Which is more than you can say for lots of other places. That's how I see Hollywood—as the place that gives everybody a chance. Hollywood gave me a chance. Which is really remarkable because, before Deanna Durbin made *Three Smart Girls*, fourteen-year-old girls didn't have a chance at all, in movies or on the stage. You might have thought, the way they acted, that there were no such things as fourteen-year-old girls. All fourteen-year-old girls were put away in mothballs and just not mentioned at all, except now and then by their families. Which is ridiculous as has been proven. Because fourteen-year-old girls are really very interesting people when you get to know them and they are also very interested people, which is a Point. They are the fans. They are the ones who fall in love with Clark Gable (like I did) and write most of the fan letters and fill up the theaters.

"It was very funny, the way I got my chance. As you may or may not have heard, Miss Hall, my sisters Suzanne (Suzanne is married now and Virginia, we call her 'Jimmie,' is at home), Virginia and I were a singing trio. Mummie always played for us. We sang and everything at the World's Fair in Chicago and lots of other places. I was born in Murfreesboro, Tennessee, if you think anyone is interested. Well, our real name is Gumm, our parents being Frank A. and Ethel Gumm, professional people, being vaudeville people and "legit" actors and also musicians. And my father was a theater-owner, which all makes it possible for me to say that 'the theater is in my blood.'

"Well, George Jessel changed my name. It was when we were touring and he named us the Garland Sisters. I guess the name of Gumm just didn't appeal to him, even though it was so well known. Now, Mummie has changed her name to Garland, too. Because people kept calling her 'Mrs. Garland' so she became Mrs. Garland to save explanations. Then Suzanne got married, and as I say, that broke up our act.

"Then we were in Hollywood and a Hollywood agent saw me and heard me sing and said, very kindly, that he wanted to manage me. He took me around to lots of the studios and no one would look at me. That is, they'd take one look and then say, more loudly than was necessary: 'I can't use her—get her away from here!'

"Then one day, after this had been going on for some time, my agent called me and said he wanted to take me to the M-G-M studio. For once, for the only time in my life, my mother wasn't home to go with me. My father went with us. Well, I just thought, oh, another old studio! I had on a pair of old slacks and an old polo shirt and I just went the way I was.

"Well, we got to M-G-M and I sang a song for Roger Edens, the musical director. I sang "Zing! Went the Strings of My Heart." My first surprise, not to say shock, was when he didn't sort of sink back like he felt sick and sort of groan: 'Get her away from here.' No, he called Mrs. Koverman who is a Very Important Person (put that in capitals, please) in this studio. I sang "Dinah" for her. And she didn't say 'get her away from here.' No, she called Mr. Mayer and asked him to come and hear me. Well then, Mr. Mayer, Mr. *Louis B.* Mayer, came in. He was in a Dark Mood and had a 'get her away from here' look on his face. So then I sang "Eli, Eli" for Mr. Mayer. He didn't seem to be looking at me. I couldn't tell whether he was listening or not. It was just like a big lull flew in. I thought, so what? Now I can go home and roller-skate some more. The next day I got my contract. *The very next day.**

"That's how I see Hollywood, too, as a place where Anything Can Happen, one big Surprise Package.

"So that was one of the Big Thrills (all the Thrills should be written capitals, I think, Miss Hall). But then, after that, nothing happened. They had Deanna Durbin under contract—at the time. Then after a while she wasn't there anymore. It looked like the fourteen-year-old girls were going back to the mothballs. I was doing radio broadcasts and things and I got so discouraged. I never get too discouraged, though, because I'm not the discouragable kind. I never mope or have Moods or interesting things like tantrums and all." Judy's mother says that the child has such a good disposition that she doesn't really remember her as a small child because she never Made Scenes. "Anyway," Judy added, "I did get kind of

---

*Judy's audition for Metro occurred on September 13, 1935. "Please prepare contract covering the services of JUDY GARLAND as an actress," read the inter-office communication memo dated three days later, September 16. It should be noted that this bit of misinformation appeared in numerous articles published throughout her career.

discouraged about my Career. I'd think, when I was on the stage I used to *accomplish* something.

"Then Mummie and I went to New York for a holiday and also because I'd never been to New York. There I had another Big Thrill. We went to Coney Island and it was wonderful. But while I was in New York M-G-M sent for me to come back. Which is one of Hollywood's peculiar characteristics, as I see it. When you are right here they don't seem to want you and the minute you go away, they do want you. I thought, At Last! But when I got back I found that they wanted me to make a *short*, a short with Deanna Durbin called *Every Sunday*.

"Deanna and I saw quite a lot of each other then but we haven't seen each other much lately. She is always busy. I guess she works harder than I do.

"Then I got loaned out to 20th Century Fox and played in *Pigskin Parade*. I hated myself in that. They wouldn't let me see the rushes which was too bad because if I had seen them I could have improved myself. I didn't wear any makeup and I sure looked it. I was afraid my freckles would show. Of course they didn't but I was conscious of them. But I have now got over my freckle-fear since I have observed that Myrna Loy and Katharine Hepburn and Joan Crawford also have freckles.

"Well, after a while Deanna made *Three Smart Girls* and then the motion picture industry rubbed its eyes and awoke to the fact that there are such things as fourteen-year-old girls and that they can be very smart girls, too, and what is known as Box Office. In the meantime, though, I went to Junior High School for a year, to public school which I had never been to before because I had always had tutors or gone to school on the M-G-M lot. But I wanted to go to public school so badly that Mummie asked the studio and they let me go. I graduated from Junior High and that was the Best Year of My Life. I loved it.

"So then I was taken right out of the movie mothballs and given a chance in *Broadway Melody of 1938*. And I like myself pretty well in that. The only thing I didn't like about me was the first line I had to speak. It was so precocious. I hate anything precocious. I am not precocious at all. I think like a grown-up and I like to be with older people and talk to older people but I am not a grown-up and I don't want to be. So, I didn't like the first line but after that it was all right and I think the song about Clark Gable (which I meant) sort of evened things up. Now I am playing in *Thoroughbreds Don't Cry* with Sophie Tucker and Mickey Rooney and after that I am to play in *The Ugly Duckling* with Allan Jones."

Judy doesn't want to be a singer. She doesn't want to place emphasis on the mezzo-soprano voice, which is a natural (she never studied voice). She says, "I want to act. I want to be a dramatic actress like Bette Davis and Margaret Sullavan and Norma Shearer, who are my favorites."

Judy, by the way, is one of the very, very few screen players ever to obtain a contract without having to undergo the formality of a screen test. The only others on record are Ramon Novarro and Janet Gaynor. And they were of the silent era. Since talkies came in Judy is the only "testless" player to be given a contract.*

"As I say," Judy was saying, "my favorite movie actresses are Bette Davis, Margaret Sullavan and Norma Shearer. When I grow up I want to be a little like all three of them. My favorite movie actors are Spencer Tracy, Clark Gable, Robert Donat and Charles Boyer. If I ever get married, which I do not intend to do until I am thirty because when I marry I intend to give up my career, I would like my husband to be a mixture of these four men.

"I love to go to the movies. I go almost every night of my life. I go with Mummie, with my sister Jimmie, who is twenty and my very best friend. Jimmie, by the way, takes a doll to bed with her every night, too. I hope you won't think we're all imbeciles. It's just being companionable, I guess. Anyway, I also go with Betty Jane Graham, my very best friend outside the family. Betty Jane and I play Ping-Pong, too, and ride and roller-skate and swim. Sometimes Mummie takes us to lunch at the Pig 'n Whistle. Then we go to a show afterwards and Betty Jane comes up with me and spends the night. Betty Jane has done things in pictures, too, and is a Very Fine Actress.

"Well, people have asked me about the Biggest Thrills I've had since I became a motion picture actress myself. Of course, as I've said, the first

---

*Although Judy was said to have been the only person ever signed to M-G-M without a screen test, similar claims have been made in reference to other Metro stars, too.

Big Thrill was when Mr. Mayer, whom I've come to love very much in Any Mood, sent me my contract the very day after I sang for him. Then there was the Coney Island thrill. Then the next one was meeting Benny Goodman. I got goose-flesh over that because I admire Benny Goodman beyond most men.

"The first picture star I ever met after I came to M-G-M was Jimmy Stewart. If anyone should ask me what I thought about him then I would answer: 'Just what I think about him now—he is wonderful.' He has a lot of fun with me, I guess. He keeps asking me when I'm going to marry him and I say that I am too young and he says that pretty soon he will be too old. Which is ridiculous because of course he's very young and is the type who will never be old.

"But speaking of the first movie star I ever met in my life—well, it was when I was three years old and we first came to Hollywood. My father being a theater-owner and all we visited most of the studios. One day we came to this studio, to M-G-M. After our visit during which we saw Frances Marion and her husband, Fred Thomson, who were awfully nice and jolly to us, we went to a little restaurant across the street to have lunch. As we went in I saw an earring lying on the sidewalk, quite an Oriental earring. I picked it up and took it to a waitress and she said: 'Oh, yes. I know who that belongs to. It belongs to that girl over at the counter having her lunch.' Well, I gave the earring back to the girl having lunch at the counter. And it was *Myrna Loy*!

"Then, another very Big Thrill was the night I was invited to Norma Shearer's for dinner. I got all dressed up for that. I met Carole Lombard there and also Charles Boyer and his wife and Basil Rathbone and his wife. The next day Miss Shearer sent me a beautiful makeup kit with my name on it. Which certainly goes to show you how big stars are in Hollywood.

"Another B. T. was when Clark Gable gave me a charm bracelet. One of the charms is a little sort of book with Clark's picture in it. I suppose he sent it to me on account of the song in *Broadway Melody* [*of 1938*]. I have also sung that song for him here in the commissary and on the sets and places. He always gets very red in the face when I sing it but I think he likes it.

"Then there was the time when I had my picture on the cover of a fan magazine. I let out a shriek when I saw that.

"The preview of *Broadway Melody* [*of 1938*] was a very Big Thrill. I got dressed about five hours before it was time to go. I always do that, get dressed five hours before it's time to go anywhere and then when it is time I'm all mussed up.

"I don't care very much for society, though. And I *hate* dances. I simply hate them. You dance and dance and no sooner do you stop dancing then someone grabs you and says: 'Come on, let's dance.' And you're off again. I went to a dance with Jackie Searl a few weeks ago. He and another boy took my friend Betty and me. They sent us corsages and everything. It was their School Dance. Mummie waited up for me at Mrs. Searl's house. They sat up for us together, Mummie and Mrs. Searl. Well, we got home about twelve thirty and I just kicked my shoes off then and there and thought, though I didn't say it on account of Jackie being so nice and polite and all, 'No More Dances For Me!'"

Judy had, I knew, "gone out" quite frequently with Jackie Cooper. They had been seen lunching at the Brown Derby, coming out of movie matinees, swimming and playing tennis together. I asked Judy about Jackie. She said affably, "Oh, I don't see him anymore. He's got another girl."

I said then: "Is there—I mean, are you interested in anyone else?"

Judy looked, for the first time, slightly embarrassed. She said to her mother, "Do you—do you think I ought to mention it? Do you think I ought to mention—*him?*"

And Judy's mother said, "Why not, dear? You like him and admire him and there's no harm in saying so."

"Well," laughed Judy, a little constrainedly, "for one thing, he's a—younger man, you see. That makes it rather awkward. But it is Freddie Bartholomew."

There was a slight pause during which I thought, sentimentally, that I could hear young Judy's warm heart beat a little faster. I felt, too, a little ashamed that I had asked her. You could tell that it was, with Judy, Kind of Sacred.

Then she said, changing the subject with great finesse: "Another Thrill will be the house we're going to build. It's being built from my plans, plans I drew up all by myself. And I have my room all planned out. The walls will be a sort of pale wood and there will be a beige rug and a big bed, the studio couch kind, done in brown corduroy and the hangings will be pale green.

She still plays dolls. Sophie Tucker calls her, "the next red hot mama." She is standing, though with eager, not reluctant feet, where the brook and river meet. She is a wise child, but a *child*. And she is bursting with "promise," all kinds and sorts of promises. She "sees" Hollywood as a Surprise Package. It is. And one of its most continuous "surprises" is going to be, I make bold to prophesy, this same Judy Garland.

JUDY GEM

On Growing Up

"I know lots of girls who think it's funny that I won't wear silk dresses and use makeup. Maybe it is—I don't happen to think so. When I am eighteen, I want to be able to enjoy the things that come with that age. And I won't be able to do the things that I do now. So I'm just living my age while I can. Then, when I'm eighteen, I'll have all the extra thrill of dressing in grown-up clothes and doing the things that grown-up people do. I am in no hurry."

—To Ted Magee, *Picture Play*, June 1938

JUDY GEM

On Dieting

"I don't believe in dieting . . . now. Maybe I will later . . . I don't know. But, gosh, when a girl has an appetite, she has to eat, doesn't she?"

—Unknown publication, July 29, 1938

JUDY GEM

On Beauty

"Of *course* I want to be beautiful! And Adrian—he's doing my costumes—says I *am* going to be beautiful in [*The Wizard of Oz*]! And I want to grow up to be very beautiful, too. Only I probably won't. But I do try. I take awfully good care of myself. I don't ever smoke or drink—I hate anything that has even the littlest fizz to it, even Coca-Cola. And I pay a lot of attention to my hands and even to my feet. Isn't that silly? I cold cream my feet every night, just like I do my hands and face!"

—*Hollywood*, October 1938

JUDY GEM

On Law School

"I've always thought it would be wonderful to be a lawyer. I know it takes a lot of work and study, but I wouldn't mind. I think everyone should have an extra profession on which to fall back, don't you?"

—*Picturegoer Summer Annual*, 1939

JUDY GEM

On Personal Appearances

"If I could have my own way, I'd like to do two pictures a year and spend the rest of the time on the road. I almost forgot that nice, warm feeling you get when the curtains part and you hear the orchestra and then the applause. You just want to give everything you have. Of course, I don't mean you haven't audiences in pictures, but you never see them until you go out in person. And audiences are so responsive and so spontaneous when they like you."

—*Picturegoer Summer Annual*, 1939

JUDY GEM

On *The Wizard of Oz*

"That was always my favorite story, only I never dared even dream that someday I'd be playing Princess Dorothy on the screen. And to make things even better, I'm willing to be a blonde. [Judy was referring to Dorothy as imagined by director Richard Thorpe, who lasted only two weeks on the *Oz* set. The long, curly blonde wig was quickly abandoned for a more natural look.] I'll bet every girl in the world with dark hair wishes she could have long, golden tresses. Well, I've tried mine on, and I can't even recognize myself in the mirror. I begged Mr. [Jack] Dawn, head of the makeup department, to let me wear my blonde hair to school but he thought it would be better to wait and spring it as a surprise when the picture starts. I suppose he's right."

—*Picturegoer Summer Annual*, 1939

SWEET SIXTEEN

ROBERT McILWAINE | August 1939, *Modern Screen*

The New York City appearance referenced in the first paragraph of this *Modern Screen* feature took place on February 10, 1938, exactly four months prior to Judy's sixteenth birthday. In support of the film *Everybody Sing*, which proclaimed the up-and-comer as "the nation's new singing star," this was Judy's debut at Loew's State Theatre on Broadway, where she performed four shows a day and reportedly grossed $10,000 more than the theater's average weekly gross at that time.

"Youngster is a resounding wallop in her first vaudeville appearance [as Judy Garland]," decreed *Variety*. "Comes to the house with a rep in films . . . Apparent from the outset that girl is no mere flash, but has both personality and the skill to develop into a box-office wow in any line of show business. Applause was solid, and she encored twice, finally begging off with an ingratiating and shrewd thank-you speech."

Judy Garland figures that now is the time for boyfriends and lots of fun

Remember how it felt to be sweet sixteen? Judy Garland *knows*, for she's just turned it, and is the first to tell you what goes on. In fact, it was on the eve of this eventful birthday that Judy journeyed to New York where she broke Jack Dempsey's all-time record for attendance at the theater where she appeared.

Now this in itself is somewhat of a major accomplishment, but not nearly so much, Judy feels, as the passing of those first fifteen years! When asked how it felt to be grown up, she grinned and said, "Oh, not much different. But gosh, everyone who knows me at all says I'm *not* grown up!"

Though appearances might dispute this opinion, Judy has arguments for each and every theory proffered. For instance, her high heels were the last word in smartness, but the kidding she takes to don them and show her face in public! As for her personal appearance these days, she's bordering dangerously near being glamorous. Her hair is a little lighter with just the right touch of gold to enhance those lovely eyes that feature dark curling lashes. Why the gal is even thinner and, what's more, with that engaging smile of hers, would make any guy's heart skip a beat or two just to pass her quickly on the street!

"Do I get razzed about these shoes!" Judy exclaimed, tossing a glance in their general direction. Then, looking up she laughed, "Why it's getting so I can only wear them in my dressing room and have any peace of mind. And just look at my hair! They had to change it for the color sequences in *The Wizard of Oz*. Now my friends kid me about that, too. You know we worked on that picture for six months and, even though it was the most pleasant time I've ever spent, I lost twelve pounds. So what do you think? All the gang thinks I'm reducing! Gosh, maybe I should at that! But really, it's only that I've grown taller and my weight is going to the right places!

Honestly, I'm in no hurry to grow up," Judy continued, her large eyes serious and a plaintive note of sincerity in her voice. "The way I figure it, you've only got about eighteen years in which to have fun—so why rush it? Heck, when you're grown, there're too many things to worry about, so while you're still young you should be able to enjoy yourself. All my friends, the gang I run around with, have the best time ever. Of course some of 'em, the boys especially, think they're pretty old. Why they even smoke cigarettes!"

After discussing Hollywood's promising youth we discovered our little friend had very definite ideas on the subject. Certain things were to be accepted. F'rinstance, several of her favorite pals even went so far as to smoke pipes! Of course, none are of the "veddy, viddy variety," as the handsome William Orr, who was the latest thorn in the side of one Andy Hardy! Judy can't believe any girl would prefer such a "fancy pants" as he portrayed to a real honest-to-goodness fellow. In fact, Judy has such sound reasoning and excellent ideas about companions that to date she can't decide just which boy she prefers. However, each has his points and plenty to offer, for Judy's far too intelligent to tolerate a dullard very long.

Concerning a few of the snapshots showing Judy steppin' out, she explained, "Oh I don't date very much. Mostly, we all go out together. Of course there's usually a fellow with a girl. Y'know we sorta pair up. Then we go dancing or just stay home and have fun.

"To give you an idea, I'll tell you what we do when Johnny Downs comes over." At the surprised look on our face, Judy hopped in and told us what a swell dancer and actor Mr. D. is. Having familiarized us with the gent, she continued, "Johnny will come over and bring a book along. We help Mother fix dinner and afterwards may spend the whole evening not saying a word, just sitting there reading. Then, when it's time for him to go home, we'll say good night and that's all there is to it. I think I like Johnny for this very reason. We don't have to put on at all to entertain each other. We can relax and not say a word and still have a simply grand time. He's very nice and very thoughtful, too, which is another reason I'm fond of him.

"Of course it's just the opposite with Mickey Rooney," Judy said and her eyes lighted up immediately, for all who know young Mr. R. have a very definite affection for him. "I think the thing I like about Mickey the most is that he's so much fun. When I go out with him I don't have to say a word. He keeps me laughing continuously. There's no one I know of that's so much fun to go dancing with, or just be around. And he's not a practical joker either. He's not at all like he seems on the screen. He may joke, but they're all on him and not at the expense of others, like a lot of wits. Y'know, he's not at all wild either, just the nicest person you could meet. I feel so sorry because his vacation wasn't as happy as it should have been.

"I guess everyone in New York expected him to be wild and crazy like the parts he plays, and when he wasn't, they weren't very nice to him. He only stayed a few days, then went to Florida. Of course he had more fun there cause he loves swimming and sports. He's really just like any other boy and a lot smarter than most. Of course, they're people who will try to make you think he's changed by sudden popularity and success, but he's been working so long and hard that it's not new. I don't think he'd ever change no matter how famous he became. That's why I like him—he's always the same Mickey.

"Another friend of mine," Judy continued, "is Jackie Cooper. He's awfully smart and loves music. We listen to lots of recordings together and sometimes go dancing with the gang. He smokes the biggest pipe. It's the only thing I can't seem to understand his liking. But then, I guess it's just another thing about men we women can't figure out," and, philosophically shaking her head, Judy pondered the profoundness of this astute observation. "You'd think he was awfully serious from the parts he plays, wouldn't you? Well, he's not a bit. He likes fun as much as anyone and is the first to get into the spirit of things and the last to sign off. I guess the main reason we have such a good time is because we enjoy the same things."

Then, Judy laughed and exclaimed, "Gee, if I'm not careful you'll think I'm bragging about beaux. But it's your fault because you wanted to know why I like certain people. I don't really get to go out often enough to be a gadabout. But, since you asked, here's the rest of my story.

"The birthday picture you asked about, the one lighting the candles, was with Billy Halop. Mostly everyone thinks the *Dead End* kids are tough, but they're not. Billy is just the opposite. Honestly, I don't see how he plays those characters so convincingly because he's not a bit that way. He's the most polite and thoughtful boy you can imagine. Why, if he takes you out he can't do enough to make you have a good time. He's pulling out your chair, or helping you up and down all the time. Billy has the most perfect manners of any boy I've met.

"Why, come to think of it, in real life Billy's just like the parts Jackie Moran plays on the screen. Jackie, of course, is the same on the screen and off. He's sweet, well mannered and always a gentleman. He's one of the nicest boys on the coast and everyone's crazy about him. I judge anyone a lot by their friends. I guess I just like nice people and when someone has lots of nice friends then I'm sure to get along with them. It's really an insight into their character to see what kind of people they go around with and like. That's why our gang very carefully looks over a new member before we pass judgment. We may seem overly friendly, but underneath we're a pretty cagey lot. Why, we have to be, or else we'd be dumb and completely taken in by everything. We may be young, but not quite that much—I hope.

"As soon as I get back home we're going to begin on *Babes in Arms*," said Judy, getting off the subject of gentlemen. "I didn't see the show last year, but I've read the play and I'm just crazy about it. I think Mickey will be wonderful in it, don't you?"

"A natural! You'll both be perfect," we admitted quickly and honestly. For Mickey's a lad that any of us could watch 'doing his stuff' till long past the curfew! And Judy—well, she's the tops in talkies, too!

"I can hardly wait to get started," she continued enthusiastically. And if you could have seen her eyes light up at the prospect of what was ahead, then you'd no doubt feel quite the same as Judy's many friends. Though in appearance Judy seemed quite a young lady, for all of her sixteen years, her face was that of a kid's before Christmas. However, the way Judy explains it is, "I guess maybe I look grown up, but honestly I don't feel it. The way I figure is that the first fifteen years are the hardest. Well, now I'm over that, the best part is right ahead of me, and I certainly plan to make the most of it.

"It's a lot like in *The Wizard of Oz*. When you're growing up you can hardly wait for the time to pass and things seem so dull and slow. Then one day you wake up and there you are just where you've always wanted to be, and it's wonderful. Well, it's like that in the picture. The cabin I live in is just plain and drab, y'know it's all in black and white. Then one day it's blown to the Land of Oz and when I open the door the lovely color of everything is like fairyland. You can't imagine what a contrast it is. That's about the way it feels to me now that I'm sixteen! Y'know, I always wondered just why they said, 'sweet sixteen.' Well, now I know, and gosh, but it's grand!"

JUDY'S CRUSHES

MAY MANN | August 1939, *Screenland*

Known for her syndicated "Going Hollywood" columns, May Mann visited with Judy for *Screenland* about her fascination with older men (Clark Gable, Victor Fleming) and the arranged publicity dates with boys closer to her age (Freddie Bartholomew, Mickey Rooney).

The little Garland girl is a famous movie star but that doesn't stop her from having the same cute romantic crushes as any sweet-sixteen schoolgirl

Judy Garland's got me remembering when I was just newly turned sixteen and fell in love with my piano teacher who was thirty-five-ish. I know just how Judy felt about [Clark] Gable, because one day my piano teacher (who was no Gable, but had a dimple on his chin) patted my hand in a grown-up way, and I suddenly discovered he was Prince Charming! I knew that if he'd wait a couple of years for me to grow up a little bit more, a great love would be ours. I pictured myself as the woman he adored, inspiring him to greater things—that is, until he introduced me to his real inspiration who was twenty-five-ish and proudly announced she was his new bride. You've no idea how tragic it was. Judy felt much the same way when Clark introduced her to Carole Lombard, and she suddenly realized how hopeless were her plans of their future together, Judy's and Clark's I mean.

"I meant every word of that song I sang to Clark Gable in my first picture," Judy seriously confided to me as she slipped off a little blue wool dress with the white lace petticoat trim showing two inches below the hem. And in the next breath, "Look at this note. It's from a boy who saw the afternoon show. He thinks that I should know that my petticoat is showing. Isn't that funny? He doesn't know that's the fashion."

Judy was in New York on personal appearance tour and I was on a holiday. We'd decided to see Times Square and Forty-Second Street and Broadway together—but the most we saw was the inside of taxicabs and crowds of people as we dashed about keeping Judy's numerous engagements. We'd just come from Judy's broadcast and were in her dressing-room, banked with baskets of flowers, when Judy and I began to wax confidential in true feminine fashion. The telephone was ringing when we entered. It was Los Angeles calling, with Judy's next-door-neighbor-boy-friend on the wire. Ten minutes later a new boy acquired on the New York holiday called for a date, and before a half hour had passed a couple more had called—one, being as Judy described him, "just perfectly wonderful—he's going to Yale and he's so distinguished and everything!" That's how we got onto the subject of boyfriends and then romance in general.

"Clark Gable was really the first man I ever thought seriously of," said Judy, brushing her gold-brown hair prior to getting ready for the evening show. "The first time I met him, I thought I'd faint, he was so wonderful! He was just exactly the way I'd always imagined he would be. He smiled and took my hand and held it just like he really meant it. He was so clean-looking and had such cute dimples. And the shaving lotion he used smelled so masculine and nice!

"After I sang that little song that I wrote to him in my first picture I was invited to his birthday party. I sang the song for him again. But Carole Lombard was there—and I soon realized that I didn't have much chance when he already had such a glamorous woman in love with him. She's so beautiful and so witty and keeps everyone laughing at the clever things she says. While me, I felt awkward and self-conscious, and I sat and twiddled my thumbs, which didn't get me very far. I didn't know what to say. All I could do was look at Clark and think how much I liked him and wish that there were two of him, one for Carole and one for me. I couldn't help noticing all of the time the way he looked at her—like she was something awfully precious. He just grinned when he looked at me.

"Soon after that Clark sent me a charm bracelet and I wore it right up to the day he married. It was awfully cute with a little gold book in which was inscribed, 'To My Best Girl, Judy—from Clark Gable.' And then when I was in that automobile accident he sent me a pair of lovebirds. But after meeting Miss Lombard I knew that Clark would never really be serious with me." And Judy began brushing the curls around her finger. She's very pretty and sweet sixteen-ish. Her large brown eyes are girlishly innocent and have a way of widening when she's serious. There's none of the coquette about Judy—not even when she's talking about her boy friends.

"Isn't that the Gable charm bracelet you are wearing now?" I asked, noting a clever one on her wrist.

"This is the one the boy who lives next door gave me," Judy explained. "He's a very nice boy who takes me to movies and occasionally to parties, and we go bicycling together. But he's very young—just sixteen. Well, I mean sixteen's young for a boy. Of course we're not a bit romantic—we're just friends," she added.

"How about Freddie Bartholomew?" I asked.

"Oh, that was one of those studio publicity romances," Judy said. "They were in vogue at the time. Sonja Henie and Tyrone Power, and Wayne Morris and Priscilla Lane. It really didn't mean a thing. We just posed for pictures and he took me to a premiere or two."

"Well," I asked, undaunted, "how about Mickey Rooney—is he your big moment like the papers say?"

"Oh, that's just *another* publicity story," Judy smiled. "We've really never been a bit serious about each other. In fact, he pesters me with his practical jokes all of the time. Every time I have a serious scene he stands off somewhere and tries to make me laugh at something and spoil it. Really, at times Mickey can be a terrible pest—but he's so sweet at others. In our next picture together, *Babes in Arms*, I win him for a change. In our last picture I lost him to Ann Rutherford."

Judy put on a little pink dress and seemed to be debating with herself before she spoke again. "If you really want to know a perfectly wonderful man, you should meet Victor Fleming," she said with a dreamy-eyed smile. "He directed my last picture, *The Wizard of Oz*,—and he's perfectly marvelous! He has the nicest low voice, and the kindest eyes. Besides, he realizes that a girl who is sixteen is practically grown up. He shows me all of the courtesies he would to Hedy Lamarr. That's very important to me. He rises when I enter the room and places a chair for me. He notices my clothes and the way I do my hair and remarks about them. After our first picture had been in production a week, I felt that I wanted to do something nice for him. I baked him a cake—and he was so appreciative. I asked mother if she thought it would be all right for me to give him a white carnation for his lapel. She couldn't see any harm in it—so I picked out the loveliest one in my shop (Judy owns a little florist shop in Hollywood) each morning and sent it to him. A man appreciates little things like that. Besides, it keeps him thinking of a person."

I readily agreed and pursued the subject. "Were you romantic about Mr. Fleming—momentarily?" I asked, remembering my piano teacher and all.

"Well, I might have been if I'd been older," Judy sighed. "He's such a wonderful man!" And the way Judy said that I knew distinctly how she'd felt—for I could detect a bit of "It might have been" in her voice, in the way that only a girl in her very early teens can express. Then the telephone rang.

Judy spoke in very low guarded tones. It was a local call from a New York swain. "He's the one who sent me those flowers," Judy smiled after the call, pointing to an enormous basket—such as prima donnas receive on first nights at the opera. "It really takes a more mature man to do things for a girl. Why, back in Hollywood, no one would ever think of sending me such a large basket of flowers. The boys back home usually send me a corsage of baby pink roses or lily of the valley. Now that I'm sixteen I'd like gardenias at least. And I've always wanted an orchid. But if they ever bring me gifts it's usually candy—which *they* sit and eat!

"You've no idea how perfectly miserable I've been waiting to grow up," Judy said wistfully. "And now I don't know *how* long it'll be before people will recognize the fact that I'm a young woman, and not an adolescent. Everyone calls me 'Baby' and 'Monkey' and no one takes me very seriously," she lamented. "While I'm really as serious as can be. I'm practically sixteen, which means that in a couple of years I should be playing romantic leads in grown-up parts.

"I'd like to tell you my ambition in life—that is, if you'll promise not to laugh—because it isn't a bit funny," Judy warned. I promised and she continued. "I want to play my first grown-up leading role opposite Clark Gable. I personally think this is a wonderful idea. Ever since I sang my song to Gable in my first picture our names have been linked together. I think the public would really like to see us together on the screen, don't you?"

I assured Judy that it seemed like a good idea—and in tune with my sympathetic understanding—because after all we're sisters under the skin with my memory of my piano teacher and Judy's crush on Gable, so Judy revealed to me her truly one *great* ambition in life. She wants to become another Bette Davis!

"I wouldn't care if I never sang again—if I could just become a great dramatic actress like Bette Davis. I don't care whether I'm beautiful or not. I want to sway the emotions of millions of people, make them weep and laugh and feel the things I'm feeling on the screen."

I interrupted Judy to tell her that really she was doing something like this on the screen in her current pictures—but Judy said that she wanted to be *very* dramatic as a grown-up actress. I'm very serious. I want to study drama. I've mentioned this to the studio and they just smile—the powers that be—and chuck me under the chin and say 'Run along, Judy, you're just a kid yet. You've got plenty of time for serious things.' They don't realize that I'm sixteen. They insist that I must wait for years and that you can't portray experiences you've never known. But they don't know the emotions I've already experienced."

I could feel with Judy—remembering that piano teacher. But luckily schoolgirl yearnings have a way of vanishing and are soon forgotten—though I'm sure Judy doesn't think so at present. But she will in just a few more years.

A bell rang and a call boy said, "First curtain, Miss Garland." Judy patted a bit of powder on her nose and hurried to the stage. I caught her mother, who accompanied Judy on the tour, coming up the stairs and we dashed down into the audience and stood in the aisle to catch Judy's numbers.

"Judy's been telling me that she wants to be a great actress," I whispered as we waited for Judy to appear.

"Yes, and she's very serious about it," her mother smiled. "Did she tell you she's got her heart set on being Clark Gable's leading lady when she's eighteen?" I nodded.

"Judy's just at that age where she's thrilled with everything," her mother whispered. "She had a crush on Clark Gable for a long time—but that finally wore off. Then she became very much interested in her accompanist. He's more like a father to her since her own Daddy passed on. Then her dancing master caught her fancy but that only lasted for a week. She discovered that he was married and had daughters older than herself.

"Judy's such an impressionable child—she goes about singing and laughing all day, but when she starts sitting around waiting for the telephone to ring we know she's in the midst of another romantic crush. Probably the person she has a crush on never knows it—but mothers can always tell. I never worry about her, for these schoolgirl crushes never last long. Judy's very proud that she's a young lady now. The other day she went shopping by herself and came home with her first pair of high-heeled slippers. They really look so much better than the flat-heeled slippers that I let her wear them and buy some more. Judy's still girlishly plump—and she wants to be pencil-slim like her two sisters, but I tell her she'll slim down in another year. My other girls did.

"You should have seen Judy when she picked up this morning's paper. There was an article saying that Judy Garland, the youngster, would now step into Deanna Durbin's shoes—for Deanna was now definitely a young woman. Judy felt terrible at being classified as a youngster. 'You'd think I was Jane Withers' age,' she said."

Judy came on stage then, and the applause was terrific. She looked sweet-sixteen and appealing; she sang several songs and then told the audience how she'd broken into the movies. A talent scout heard her sing on a lodge program at Lake Tahoe and sent for her. Louis B. Mayer of M-G-M heard her audition and promptly signed her on the dotted line.

On the way back to the dressing room her mother continued, "Judy's an unselfish child. She wants to do so much for her family. Though both of her sisters are married, she insists that they stay home and live with us. She wants us all to be together always. We have a new eleven-room house and there's plenty of room. Judy adores her two older sisters."

Judy was going through a handful of fan letters and mash notes sent back to her from out front. She was smiling over some and suggested to her mother that she really ought to see the writers and greet them since they were so nice to write back and ask to see her. At the stage door there were hundreds of them milling about—all waiting to get a glimpse of her. A high-school youth was carrying a florist's box and another had a box of candy—Judy's suitors!

Judy returned home the other day and so I dashed right over to her house in Beverly Hills to check up on her, as it were. And darned if the telephone didn't ring, right while I was there—and it was New York calling. Judy talked sweetly for five full minutes and then with sudden concern, "Oh, we've talked for five minutes—just think how much that will cost! I guess we'd better hang up!" And after she'd placed the receiver on the hook, I asked her point-blank, "Well, which one was that?" And Judy replied, "He's a boy I met in New York. He took mother and me out to dinner and to see Katharine Hepburn in *The Philadelphia Story* [the play]. Really he's a wonderful boy. So thoughtful." Meaning probably that he's another one of Judy Garland's romantic crushes!

"I'VE BEEN TO THE LAND OF OZ!"

JUDY GARLAND AS TOLD TO GLADYS HALL | **September 1939, *Child Life***

This is the first in a series of Judy's "as told to" stories by prolific Hollywood fan magazine writer Gladys Hall. Based on Hall's personal interviews and meetings with Judy (and in all probability some of M-G-M's press material, too), this *Child Life* feature gives a charming look at *The Wizard of Oz* through the eyes of its "Dorothy."

It is, of course, impossible to determine how much of these stories were made up of direct Judy quotes versus amalgamated passages shaped by Hall and other writers. Regardless, the idea of a sixteen-year-old Judy communicating the joys of her experiences on the *Oz* set—even if by proxy—makes for a rare and delightful reading experience.

I'll try to be calm and tell you about *Oz*—the movie, I mean—as sensibly and sanely as I can. Although it's a little bit too much to expect a girl who has really been in the Land of Oz to talk sensibly! Anyway, the picture tells the story of *The Wizard of Oz*, which was the first of the Oz books by L. Frank Baum. Now there are thirty of them.* We follow the book very faithfully. There are a few little differences at the beginning and at the end. And there are songs which have been written in for some of us to sing.

I'm not going to tell you the whole story, because you've probably read the book. And if you haven't read it, I don't want to give away too

---

Ozoplaning with the Wizard of Oz, published in 1939, was actually the thirty-third Oz book. Baum completed fourteen titles before his death in 1919, and the series continued under the pen of Ruth Plumly Thompson, who published a new Oz book each year between 1921 and 1939.

many of the surprises in store for you when you see the picture. I'll just tell you about some of the characters and about some of the things that happened while we were making the picture. I'll begin with Toto because Toto is certainly important. He's not only an important person and, as our director, Mr. Victor Fleming, said, "a very *great actor*," but also he is in just about every scene of the picture. Toto is played by a little cairn terrier whose real name is Terry. And you can't imagine a more clever little dog! We all wanted to buy him from his owner. Two weeks before we went to Oz—before we began the picture, I mean—they let me take Toto home with me so he'd get used to me. He slept in a little box in my bedroom. I fed him every day. After a few days he followed me everywhere, just as if I were his mistress.

It took him quite a time to get used to the Cowardly Lion, who is played by Mr. Bert Lahr. And no wonder! For Mr. Lahr just *is* the Cowardly Lion. He wears real honest-to-goodness lion skins which weigh fifty pounds. And though it seems a funny thing to say, Mr. Lahr really has a *liony* face so that he hardly needed any makeup on his face. It was the funniest sight in the world to see that great, big cowardly lion eating salads for lunch!

Near the beginning of the picture, I land in the Munchkin Country, the *loveliest* little country you ever saw, with ninety-two tiny, real houses, a bridge over a tiny river, a fountain, streets, and giant flowers to make the Munchkins look even littler. And the Munchkins themselves are real midgets. I think there are about 250 of them. Some of them are [Leo] Singer's midgets.

The Tin Woodman is Jack Haley, though I certainly got to believing that Jack Haley is really the Tin Woodman. He was *so* grateful to me when I oiled his joints! He kept offering to buy me ice cream cones every minute. He really had a hard life because his entire costume, from his jointed shoes to his funnel hat, was made of metal so that he couldn't sit down without the greatest difficulty, and when he did manage to sit down he couldn't get up again without help. One day it took thirty Munchkins to get him out of a chair. Every day his face was painted with ten dollars' worth of real silver. Every now and then it had to be polished with a soft cloth, the same as shoes are shined. He had to drink soup for lunch every day because he couldn't open his mouth for solids.

Ray Bolger is the Scarecrow. He was stuffed with dry straw and he said he was a fire hazard. Everywhere he went he was followed by men with fire extinguishers. He went around begging people not to light a match near him because of what might happen. When we did the scene where the Wicked Witch sets fire to him, three men with extinguishers stood by in case the fire spread past his arms, which were protected by asbestos under the coat and straw. Mr. Bolger didn't bat an eye, but Miss Hamilton, who did the black deed, was so unnerved that she had to lie down for half an hour. She took off her long, green metallic nose and just stretched out. One night, by the way, Miss Hamilton went to the theater and lost her purse, and her nose was in it. She was noseless and desperate, but the next day the nose came back in a package, and there was a note with it which said, "I found this. So this is Hollywood! I'm going back East—*today!*"

Billie Burke is Glinda, the Good, so beautiful you'll gasp! She comes into all the scenes in a big, glittery pink bubble, and it's just breathless! Don't ask me how it's done. I still don't know. I really half believe in magic after Oz! All of the scenes in Oz are in Technicolor, you know—such colors as even rainbows never dreamed of! The only scenes in black and white are the scenes on the Kansas farm. I can only say that Dorothy herself never felt so amazed when she walked through the streets of the wonderful Emerald City as I did. Honestly, it is an Emerald City, all shining green, every inch of it—houses, streets, everything, all studded with emeralds as big as boulders. And all the people are dressed in shining green, too, with white, white faces and real patent leather for hair.

Then there is the deadly Poppy Field—the most beautiful thing I've ever imagined. It covers a whole acre and a half, and there are forty thousand pastel poppies in it. Twenty men worked for a week, night and day, sticking the stems of the flowers into the ground.

When I met the Winged Monkeys—well, there was nothing make-believe about that, believe me! There I was in the Enchanted Forest with smoke that looked like real fog clinging to the ground and big black rocks, and the Winged Monkeys, eight of them, swooped down and carried me off. Of course, they were really midgets with condor wings, and we were really on wires, but it seemed very real. And just wait until you see the Talking, or Fighting, Trees, and then tell me how *you'd* like to take an apple off one of them, or try to, only to have the thing slap you! And then there are

PART II

THE 1940s

"I'M NOT BOY CRAZY!" ASSERTS JUDY GARLAND, DEBUNKING THE HOLLYWOOD MATCH-MAKERS' GOSSIP

JAMES CARSON | January 1940, *Modern Screen*

She had the top-selling hit song of 1939 with "Over the Rainbow," was invited to place her hand and footprints in the cement at Grauman's Chinese Theatre, and was presented with a special Oscar for Outstanding Performance by a Juvenile Actress in *The Wizard of Oz*. She called it her "Munchkin Award," but Judy entered the 1940s a mammoth star. In fact, she was a top-ten box office name in 1940, and would maintain such status for most of the decade.

Demand for all things Judy made her a favorite of the "fannies." The movie fan magazines couldn't get enough of her, and hardly a month went by without Judy being featured, interviewed, or appearing in a gossip column. Up until this point, her supposed teen crushes (most were mere publicity dates) had included Freddie Bartholomew, Jackie Cooper, and, of course, Mickey Rooney. But with this new decade came Judy's inevitable evolution from girlhood to young womanhood. She became interested in older, more sophisticated men, and the teenage puppy loves detailed in this piece for *Modern Screen* gave way to more serious romances.

Interviewed around the time of her romance with 29-year-old bandleader Artie Shaw, Judy details her perfect mate and dreams of marriage. Their love affair was short-lived, though, and turned out to be terribly one-sided. Judy was dazed and devastated to read in the newspapers of Shaw's elopement with Lana Turner in February 1940.

Judy Garland plucked the knife from its place beside her salad and waved it dangerously. Her pert nose quivered. Her dark eyes sparked.

"Honestly, I don't know why, but all the gossip writers keep painting me as if I'm boy crazy! Maybe it's because of the songs I sing. Yes, it must be. Those songs give the wrong impression. But gee, I'm not that way at all!"

"Take the stories about Mickey Rooney and myself. I'll give it to you straight. The columnists keep saying I'm in love with Mickey. It upsets me so; really it does. Because I'm not at all in love with him. Not a single bit. Oh sure, we're swell friends, very good friends. Mickey is so full of fun and I enjoy working with him. I'm looking forward to our next picture, *Strike Up the Band*. But outside of pictures, why, I rarely even see him! Neither one of us cares for the other—except as pals. And that's the truth!"

Judy Garland puts the knife down, and absently contemplated her salad. When she looked up, she gulped, glanced around to see if anyone at the crowded tables in the M-G-M commissary had overheard her outburst, and then looked at me with her shy smile.

"Gee, you understand, don't you? The papers have it wrong. I don't go mooning over some new fellow every other day. It's all so unfair. Why, right now I haven't got a special boyfriend. And I don't even go out much.

"Last night, for example, I was home reading that marvelous book, [*A Treasury of Art Masterpieces*] by [Thomas] Craven. Then, this morning— why—did you see this morning's paper? Someone reported that last night I was at Victor Hugo's holding hands under the table with some person I don't even know! It's very confusing, and I hope everyone doesn't believe all those things.

"The last time I went on a date was over a week ago. A concert violinist named Jimmy took me to see Katharine Cornell in *No Time for Comedy*. I won't be going out again until the Ballet Russe comes to town. I have a date for that. I'm dying to see the Ballet Russe. Have you seen it? I can't wait!"

Judy unclasped her light fur jacket and allowed it to fall back over her chair. She went at the cottage cheese in her salad. It was her favorite and it seemed to mellow her.

"I'm really not very enthused about going out places," she exclaimed. "Why should I be, when I live in such a marvelous home? Sometimes I see different boys, maybe twice a week, but they come over to the house. We sit in my music room and listen to symphony records. Now that's real fun!

"Most of my friends are nonprofessionals. That is, they're not movie people. After all, I spent nine years in vaudeville, and I met the finest people that ever lived. They're still my best friends."

Judy's red hair crept out from under her turban. She violently put her hair in its place.

"Do you really want to know how silly those rumors about me are?" she inquired, dead earnest. "I'll tell you. First the rumors said I was in love with Leonard Seuss, a musician. Now feature that. I've known Leonard for ten years! He's a sort of brother to me, a friend of the family. He's only seventeen, and supports his mother. Sometimes he works in my pictures.

"Then the rumors said I was in love with Peter Hayes, whose mother manages the Grace Hayes Lodge. Well, he's really a nice person. But I only went out with him three times in my life, and we were only pals.

"That's the way it is with everyone. When I make a new acquaintance or send someone I admire a note or flowers, I am madly in love. Imagine what people, reading about those different men and myself, must think. Boy-crazy Judy, they must say. And I'm not at all like that!"

Judy's intensity left her breathless. She sat back against her fur jacket and took a deep breath. She was a young girl being very and delightfully sincere.

Suddenly Judy Garland's eyes widened, and she leaned forward with a secret. "But one day I *am* going to fall in love—and it won't be a rumor."

Her voice quickened. "The man I'm going to marry is going to be honest. Yes he is. He's going to be a colorful and exciting man. I want him to have strong, sincere opinions, even if they're wrong. And as for looks, gosh, how a man looks doesn't matter at all with me!

"I've always vaguely dreamed of getting married at twenty-four. That age sounds just right, doesn't it? If I'm still good enough to be in the movies, I wouldn't want to retire when I'm married. But I wouldn't want a burdensome contract, either. My big dream is to have a husband, a big family, and do maybe one picture a year. That sounds ideal. Too ideal, I'm afraid. Maybe it's only a fairytale dream. I suppose things never happen like that, do they? But I pray this does."

And this certainly will. For, while Judy is only [seventeen], and much will happen to her as it does in all young lives, she will always and eternally be the same Judy—quick of enthusiasm, but sound of judgment and desire. She possesses an amazing sense of true values for one so young, and her seriousness and honesty are tempered by the most precious gift of all—laughter.

But Judy, at no one's expense, will always have her way and her desires, because she will always be Judy.

She hasn't changed a bit since she was Frances Ethel Gumm of Grand Rapids. Not even when, some seven years ago, she played on a vaudeville bill with George Jessel, and he said, "You can't get any place with a name like that—Gumm. Why, it sounds too much like crumb, bum, or dumb. I'll christen you with a new name. I'll name you after my best friend, the drama critic, Robert Garland." Even when she came to Hollywood five long years ago, her feet were on the ground. Even when she tried to sing, and they said she was too young, and she sang anyway—and so well that Mr. Louis B. Mayer himself was dragged in to hear her and to sign her.

Today, with applause loud in her ears after *Babes in Arms* and *The Wizard of Oz*, with critics and polls falling all over themselves to vote her among the best ten of the past year, Judy still manages to retain the old values. My contention is that, if the past five years haven't changed her, nothing ever will. She may be the great Judy Garland to the world but, in her heart, she's still plain Frances Gumm, who loves dill pickles, Debussy, Bette Davis, Italian operas and new, silly charms for her bracelets.

It is a sign of sophistication among the young to consider mother love naïve and blasé. Well, Judy Garland isn't sophisticated. There's only one way to put it—she's nuts about her mother.

"I just want everyone to know this," she insisted. "I've the most marvelous mother that ever lived. She's got such a regular sense of humor. She's so different from other movie mothers. She's not at all bossy. She never comes on the sets and tells me what to do. When I ask her advice, she gladly gives it, though she prefers that I do things on my own. And do you know, on certain matters, she even asks my opinion. Isn't that swell?

"She never used to lug me around to casting offices, either, like some stage mothers did. The first casting office I ever saw was when I came to

Hollywood at the age of eleven. And she's considerate. I'll never forget my last birthday. I woke up early in the morning, and there was a string tied to the bed. Beneath it was a note from Mother reading, 'Follow this string, Judy, to your present.' I followed it through all the rooms in the house, to all sorts of little gifts, then down through the living-room and through the door and into the street, where the string was tied to the bumper of a brand new wine-colored coupe. It was something I'd always wanted. I almost fainted!"

Next to mother, and waiving other members of her family like sister Suzanne "who I talk to for hours and hours," Judy's favorite is chubby Oscar Levant, whom you all know as the music expert on the radio program *Information, Please!* He's always been a sort of long-distance godfather to Judy.

"Oscar Levant is one of my truly best friends," Judy confided to me. "In fact, he's now married to another friend of mine, June Gale. Oscar's so intelligent. He's brilliant, absolutely. In the days when I was struggling, and when I was often blue, each week he would write me two and three letters, with good common sense in them. They would inspire me. I still have all his letters, tied with a ribbon." To this day, they still correspond.

Sprinkled through Judy's conversation are loads of names—big names and small names, friends and idols. People are her hobby.

"There's Alfred Vanderbilt. He's so nice. And his wife's baby is one of the cutest I've ever seen. And I adore Lana Turner. She's so outspoken. We make the funniest couple, Lana and I—she's so glamorous and I'm so unglamorous!"

Suddenly, in her conversation, Judy stopped cold. Her eyes were shining. They were staring over my shoulder. "Look!" she squealed. "It's Rhett Butler!"

I turned and saw Clark Gable, sleek in a dark gray afternoon suit, coming into the commissary. He waved to Judy. She waved back enthusiastically.

"Clark Gable is grand, isn't he?" she said to me. "I saw him in *Gone with the Wind* and I'll never forget his performance. He's another friend of mine. I mean, not as close as magazine stories make out, but a friend anyway. I'll never forget that song I sang to him on his birthday. I gave it all I had, because I admire him so. The next morning, a package arrived for me. In it was the most gorgeous charm bracelet in the world, with a miniature gold book attached. The book snapped open, and inside was Clark Gable's picture and the inscription. 'To Judy, my best girl, from her most ardent fan, Clark Gable.' What a thrill! And I love his wife. Carole Lombard is so intelligent and frank. Aren't they the grandest couple?"

The lunch was almost over. Judy's salad was reduced to ruins. She licked her lips and murmured, "Dessert time." She wanted a chocolate sundae. After the sundae materialized, and the blue-aproned waitress, humming a tune, left our table, Judy took up the humming and started in on her favorite conversational topic, music.

"My favorite popular song, the prettiest and most beautiful in the world, is 'Over the Rainbow,'" she said. "I think it's a relief from some of the other numbers you hear. Aren't the tunes orchestras play on the air awful? They're all so loud and sound exactly alike.

"When it comes to good orchestras, though, I'll settle for Duke Ellington. He's my choice, by a mile. I also enjoy Glenn Miller. But I'll let you in on something private. My brother-in-law, Bob Sherwood—he's married to my sister Virginia—now has a band of his own. He plays the guitar. It's a string band. Strings that swing. He'll be great yet, watch and see.

"My personal preferences go to the classics. I love to listen to classical music, but I have no desire to sing it. I'm satisfied with the popular stuff I do now. It gives me a kick. When I'm on the listening end, I prefer Ravel, Debussy and Tchaikovsky. I suppose Wagner was the greatest, but he's too heavy for me."

In the past year, she composed three songs of her own. At first she was hesitant about speaking of them. Then, finally, she did. "[Jerome] Robbins, the publisher, wanted to bring out the three songs I composed, but I wouldn't let him. I don't know, I think they're just not good enough, though my mother thinks they are wonderful. My best song is called "I'm Not Supposed to Know." The idea of the song is that, while I go to school and learn everything, I'm not supposed to know about love. It's a cute idea, I think. I do wish I had more time for composing."

On the subject of her own warbling, Judy made a confession. "Yes, I'll confess, I never took a singing lesson in my entire life. I bet some of my critics think I should have! But, anyway, two years ago Nelson Eddy's voice teacher took me aside and said, 'Don't ever get it into your head to take singing lessons, Judy. You're an intuitive singer. You have good memory and a good ear. Lessons will only mix you up.' I followed his advice. I can't read a single note of music! Can you imagine that? I just have a band play a tune over a couple of times and I get it that way."

Then, excitedly, Judy told me about her new home and about the special and spacious room she has for herself. With broad gestures, she described the white rug on the floor, the fireplace and the bed that resembled a chaise lounge.

She told me that she sleeps in a silk nightgown, that she must have eight hours of sleep or she's a wreck and that she often gathers her friends in her room and holds a back-scratching party. Everyone sits in a circle and scratches everyone else's back. "If you haven't had your back scratched, you haven't lived!" Judy said. "It's entirely inane, but so comfortable! Of course, everyone thinks we're crazy. We are. At dinner, our house is a madhouse."

Discussing home life led, of course, to a discussion of the root of all evil. I asked Judy if she received an allowance.

"About a year and a half ago I was put on an allowance of $5 a week. But at the end of the first week I had $4.78 left. I never spent money. I don't know why. But now I've discovered clothes—and bracelets. I have a passion for bracelets and shoes. And stockings—why, I wear out two pairs of stockings a day. Isn't that terrible?"

Like most humans, Judy is filled with a thousand different and sometimes contradicting likes and dislikes. She hates mayonnaise. She loves tea and hot chocolate. She is crazy about perfumes. She dislikes jitterbugging, despite publicity photos to the contrary. She spends hours having her red hair fixed in different styles. She doesn't ever want to be a typical glamour girl. She believes in having an outside income "in case of hard times" and owns a flower shop on Wilshire Boulevard. She gets a kick out of riding a bike, but prefers her car. *Love Finds Andy Hardy* is still one of her favorite pictures. She hopes to wear her grandmother's wedding gown at her own wedding.

And as for her Number One amusement, "I'll tell you, if you promise not to laugh. Movies!" Judy grinned. "Busman's holiday, I suppose, but when I have time, I would rather go to the movies than do anything else. I never get tired of them. And Bette Davis is my very favorite. I saw her in *Dark Victory* five times—and I cried myself sick!"

She glanced up at the wall clock and gasped. "Oh, dear, I'm twenty minutes late for school. I'll get killed for this!"

She pulled on her jacket and explained, "I have a private instructor in my dressing room. It's loads of fun. I graduated from high school courses last year, but the state law says you have to attend school until you're eighteen, so I'm taking a postgrad course of my favorite subjects, music appreciation, art appreciation and French. I'm learning oil painting, too. I've been at it five days. And I'm learning the history of art. When I visited the [Metropolitan] Museum in New York, I could tell who painted what without even looking at the names underneath. School really isn't bad this term. But last year! Ouch! I had geometry! And that was terrible!"

In a moment she had a mirror in front of her face, for a hurried checkup. If her fans, that moment, could have peeked over her shoulder, they would have seen an even more attractive Judy Garland. They would have noticed her light makeup and carefully rouged lips, her glistening eyes, tilted nose and determined chin.

As she gathered her belongings, her fans would have marveled at five feet two* of animation. When she rose, they would have guessed her to be 110 pounds in weight and they would have been right. They would have thought her off-screen figure amazingly slender, and one of the fans—a male, no doubt—would have emitted a whistle at her beautiful legs.

She left me with a wink and a lilting, "Be seeing you soon."

I wish I could pay her a compliment. Not only for her talent, but for her genuine lovableness. I wish I were smart enough to think of something startling and different.

However, I have heard it said that when a fellow sees a girl and immediately thinks, "There she is, the kind of girl I would one day want to marry," he is then paying her the greatest of human compliments.

---

*M-G-M's height for Judy was 5'2", but she was actually 4'11".

I have heard those who know Judy pay that compliment to her. Judy need not blush. Those who know her realize she is everything a fellow could want. They realize she's not boy crazy, not Hollywood, not anything more than little Miss Gumm from Grand Rapids.

And you see, Judy, I wrote this for those who don't know you, just to let them in on it and to reassure them that—well, that in the robust language of sportdom—you're the real McCoy!

WHO SAID "THE TERRIBLE TEENS"?

JAMES REID | May 1940, *Motion Picture*

The delayed publication of submissions by Hollywood writers was common-place in the 1930s and 1940s, as evidenced by this interview. Clearly conducted when Judy was sixteen, this piece was not published until just before her eighteenth birthday.

Judy Garland, 16, is no longer a child and not yet a grown-up. And the teens aren't so terrible with Judy representing them. You'll like the way she speaks up

"I don't think the teens are so terrible," said Judy Garland—as if she meant it. She even added a smile. It wasn't a pained smile. She didn't act as if she intended to be pleasant-even-if-it-hurt about being reminded that she wasn't grown up yet. Certainly she didn't give the impression that she was in a hurry to *look* grown up. In a commissary full of Pretty Young Things, some of them playing schoolgirls in a new picture, Judy was the only one who looked more like a schoolgirl than a movie actress. Her hair wasn't carefully coiffured; it was merely combed. Her eyelashes weren't long and artificial. Her lips weren't rouged. Her clothes weren't Fashion's latest gasp; she was wearing a jacket and skirt—both inconspicuously plain.

As it happened, the only reason why she was at the studio today was that, even between pictures, she had to go to school. You might think that a girl who had just been elected Feminine Star No. 3 in a nationwide newspaper poll would be embarrassed about letting anyone know that, till next June, she still had to go to school. But Judy wasn't embarrassed. Not on that score.

"Not after what has been happening to me ever since *The Wizard of Oz*," she said, darkly. "I've been accused of being twelve years old.

"You should see some of the disappointed looks I get, when people lay eyes on me in person. They expect someone in gingham, with braids, to come out singing 'Over the Rainbow.' And out I come, instead. I think some of them are pretty angry with me, too, for not wearing braids, and not dressing like *Dorothy*, and not being eleven or twelve. They've written in about it.

"I don't get any sympathy from anybody. People I've trusted all my life tell me, with perfectly straight faces, that I ought to feel flattered. 'It isn't every actress that people are willing to believe younger than she is.'"

She tossed up both hands in a you-can-see-what-I'm-up-against gesture.

"It's terrible to be halfway through the teens and not get credit for even being in them. But the teens themselves aren't terrible. Just inconvenient sometimes.

"Some people who know how old I am don't give me credit for having any sense—because I'm 'only 16.' That attitude is the only thing that really bothers me. I'd like to break it down. But apparently there's no way except to grow up. And I don't know if I want to grow up. I'm having a wonderful time."

Now, most adolescents don't enjoy being just that. They can't wait to be adults. They harbor the youthful delusion that adults lead more desirable lives. The movies encourage them in the delusion. The movies make adolescence something to laugh about or pity, and the grown-up state something romantic and poised and exciting. And Judy not only sees movies; she's in them.

Another thing: A girl six thousand miles from Hollywood can get ideas about trying to be more sophisticated, just from watching glamour girls on the screen. And here Judy is, right on the same lot with Hedy Lamarr, Norma Shearer, Joan Crawford; she sees them in person; and she isn't inspired to try to acquire that adult allure even off the screen.

She actually likes being an in-betweener: No longer a child, not yet a grown-up.

"I've thought a lot about it," she said earnestly. "I don't envy grown-ups. They take life sort of for granted. They don't get excited about it. Practically everything they do, they've done before. It's all old stuff. And having cares and worries cramps their fun.

"That's why I don't want to get ahead of myself; I don't want to grow up in a hurry. I want this to last a while. I mean— this being able to look forward constantly to something new, being able to get excited about things. I'm doing so many things for the first time. And there's no time like the first time.

"If I were 25 or so, and could go to the Victor Hugo [café in Hollywood] every night in the week, how much would it mean to me? But I get to go dinner-dancing about once a month—with my mother's permission—and it's an event. When I walk in the door, I may look casual about being there. But I'm really palpitatin' inside."

That made her sound like a normal 16-year-old. But how could she be a normal 16-year-old? She was a moom pitcher star. She had a career to think about. She disposed of that with: "Everybody my age likes to do some one thing more than anything else. What I like to do is sing good and loud. Or not so good maybe; but loud . . . I'm luckier than a lot of people, getting paid for doing what I like to do most; but that doesn't make me any less normal than anybody else.

"Of course, what's normal for one person might not be normal for somebody else. But it's normal for me to be mixed up in show business. I've been mixed up in it as long as I can remember. It isn't a career; it's a habit. I don't feel natural *not* working. This vacation right now is the longest I've had, and it's killing me. I wish they'd hurry up and start *Strike up the Band*. It's going to be a follow-up to *Babes in Arms*. Mickey and I are going to play a couple of kids on Broadway." She added pointedly, "A couple of normal kids—in show business."

Was she going to sit there, spooning up a large bowl of chicken broth (practically all that she was having for lunch), and try to insist, between spoonfuls, that anybody who had grown into the teens in show business could be normal? She certainly was going to try.

She said: "It gives me an awful pain when an actress hauls out her hanky and has a good cry about how she missed out on fun when she was a child, being on the stage. It's all in the mind. If you don't have fun as a kid, it's only because you think you don't.

"*I* had fun. I had a wonderful childhood. I did a lot of traveling, saw all kinds of interesting places. I met interesting people—people with stimulating minds. I learned countless things I'd never have learned just from books, and I liked that. What kid wouldn't?

"I've heard actresses wail that as children they were always with older people; they 'never knew what it was like' to have friends their own age. It's true that when you're a child on the stage, you're with older people more than most kids are. But I never had trouble finding friends my own age.

"I've heard actresses say, too, that they missed out on the fun of growing up gradually, being in show business. They had to grow up practically overnight. One day, they were doing child roles; the next, they had to play young grown-ups. Maybe that was true once upon a time, but it isn't true now. Pictures like the *Hardy Family* have made people expect adolescents to act their age.

"Nowadays, there's nothing to keep an in-betweener in show business from being as normal as any in-betweener anywhere. Not a thing."

Nothing except fame. How about the difficulty of doing things other people do, what with autograph-hunters swooping down in droves?

Judy grimaced. "Stars complain about not being able to go shopping, because they're recognized, and stampeded, and stuff. If they don't wear jewels and furs, they won't be bothered. I did all my Christmas shopping last year, myself. I just wore something simple, and I wasn't recognized once. Other shoppers weren't looking for a movie star. They had their own shopping to do."

She smiled mischievously. "Funny thing about movie stars. Put them in plain clothes and they look like plain people. Without the trimmings of glamour, they don't stand out in a crowd."

That took care of that. But was it normal for a growing girl to content herself with a chicken-broth lunch?

"Oh, I'm not contented," Judy said. "I love to eat. But I was eating too much. I used to put away steak and potatoes, *and* pie, at lunch—and then want to go somewhere and lie down the rest of the afternoon. . . . You should see the breakfasts I eat. No glamour girl ever eats such breakfasts. Truck drivers, maybe—but not glamour girls. Orange juice, scrambled eggs, sausage, toast, coffee. A real meal. It takes something like that to get me out of bed in the morning. Something worthwhile in the line of food."

She seemed to have a rebuttal for every supposition that she couldn't have a normal life, being a star at 16.

"I have a home. It so happened that I was lucky enough to be able to buy it, myself—and I'm going to get my money's worth out of it. It isn't a showplace. It's a place where I can be myself, and do things with my family. And, with my particular family, I don't get a chance to be a movie star around home. I don't get away with anything. I don't even get picked up after; I have to pick up after myself.

"Some of the things we have in the house are a little nicer than the things we used to have, but our life is just the same as it always was. We do the same sort of things. We have just as many laughs. Our friends are still the same ones we used to have. Mom still doesn't mind how much noise my crowd kicks up, if everybody's happy. She still bakes chocolate cake, and we still like it. My two sisters and I still trade clothes. And I still ask Mom first, if I want to do something."

Ah, that's a gruesome thing about being in the teens—still having to "ask Mom first."

"The way I look at it," said Judy, "it's a good thing—having somebody who has your best interests at heart and won't let you do anything unless it's safe and sane. You get a lot of crazy ideas."

Judy gave a short laugh.

"The only time Mom really slipped up was when she let me talk her into letting me have a motorbike. My idea of a place to try it out—with my girl-friend, Patty McCarthy, in the sidecar—was the middle of Hollywood Boulevard. The studio heard about it and told me to keep out of traffic. So

I tried the bridle path in the middle of Sunset Boulevard, out Beverly Hills way, where there wasn't even horse traffic. Somebody phoned the studio: 'Your Judy Garland is going up and down that bridle path at what looks like eighty miles an hour.' That was the last straw. A few executives had nervous breakdowns, what with *The Wizard of Oz* not yet finished, and I had to give up motorbiking."

Something that makes 16 terrible for most people is the self-consciousness that goes with it. Was she ever afflicted, even if she was an actress?

"Yes—when I can feel people getting the wrong impression. Like the time I went to the opera with [Peter] Lind Hayes, Grace Hayes' son, and on the way home he wanted to stop 'for five minutes' at Grace Hayes' Lodge. She asked me, in front of the crowd, to sing a song. I was embarrassed into doing it, not wanting to offend Lind's mother. But I could see what some people were thinking: That I was there just to show off. It was agonizing. And the next day five people phoned the Board of Education to see 'if something couldn't be done about keeping Judy Garland home nights, not chasing out to nightclubs.' And *that* got in the papers. And everybody was unhappy. Especially me. . . . Life doesn't get complicated like that very often, thank goodness."

A popular misimpression of Judy is that she is probably the hottest of Hollywood's jitterbugs. "I was a jitterbug for three weeks—but I couldn't stand the pace."

The columnists kept insisting that she was smitten first with this boy, then that. The impression was out that she was boy crazy. "Nobody thinks less about boys than I do," said Judy airily. "I don't go out much with boys, and the only reason I go out at all is, a girl has to have an escort. When I do go out, it's usually with Jimmy Cathcart. He isn't in the movies. We've known each other a long time.

"In one breath, people accuse me of being 12 years old. And in the next breath, they suspect me of having ideas about eloping. It's a great life.

"I don't want to get married till I'm 24. Why 24? Well, that sounds like a good long while away."

School isn't one of the terrible things about the teens, to Judy. "It was, while I was taking geometry. But now that that's behind me, life is worth living again. I really finished school last June. What I'm taking this year is a sort of postgraduate course—appreciation of arts, music appreciation, Shakespeare and French. All of which ought to do me some good."

You might not suspect it, but Judy, the jazz singer, collects the records of Tchaikovsky and Debussy, not the composers of Tin Pan Alley. She's serious about her music. She's considering voice lessons. (Something she has never had, up to now.) On her last trip East, of her own accord, she went to a famous teacher at the Metropolitan to have an audition—to see if the woman could do anything for her.

"She thought maybe she could help me sing soft. I don't know. I'm sort of sentimental about those loud notes. I've screamed this far."

Something else she did for the first time while East was to go skiing at Lake Placid. "I knew I was going, so I went shopping for a ski suit in Chicago. They talked me into buying a regular Swiss one, complete even to goggles. I got to Lake Placid, put on my suit, and strolled down into the lobby, looking like probably the most professional skier this side of the Alps. Everybody trooped out to watch me—and they thought I was only kidding when I went out to the beginners' slope. I started down, and I saw a couple of trees looming up a hundred feet ahead. I didn't know what to do to avoid them. I had visions of bashing my nose into my head. So—I just sat down. Ignominiously.

"I try *so* hard to be an outdoor girl, but I'm just not it. I'm awful at tennis. I can't hit a golf ball. I splash when I swim. The only sport I'm good at is skeet-shooting—and I don't know how that happens. I get most of my exercise with my eyes, reading."

One thing that makes the teens terrible for some people is the conflict of ambitions within them.

"Up to the time I was fifteen," said Judy, "I had all kinds of ambitions. Every time I passed UCLA, I wanted to go to college. Every time I read a fashion magazine, I wanted to be a designer. When I read *An American Doctor's Odyssey*, I could see myself in my lab with my test tubes.

"But now that I'm 16, I realize that if a person is having a good time doing something, that's what he or she ought to continue doing—instead of getting impossible ideas. If I'm lucky, I'd like to go on like this for five more years, and then quit.

"That's what everybody says, isn't it? Everybody likes to believe he or she will be able to quit 'five years from now.' But I'm not kidding myself one bit. I know I'll be keeping on till rigor mortis stops me."

The teens aren't so terrible—with Judy Garland representing them.

A LETTER FROM JUDY GARLAND

JUDY GARLAND | May 25, 1940, *Picture Show and Film Pictorial*

Judy updated her fans in the spring of 1940 with news of another installment in the Andy Hardy series. She also detailed some favorite hobbies, including painting and golf.

Dear *Picture Show and Film Pictorial* Readers,

I am now hard at work in *Andy Hardy Meets Debutante*. I'm Betsy Booth—if you remember *Love Finds Andy Hardy*, you'll know it—and I once again join forces with the Hardys. As I have to confess, clothes seem mighty important to me nowadays, and in this new picture Dolly Tree has made me some darling things. But, best of all, today I bought myself my first fur coat. It is a ruby fox and I couldn't resist wearing it to the studio today, even if it wasn't exactly appropriate. But then, Sue, my sister, won a part in *The Mortal Storm*, with Margaret Sullavan, Jimmy Stewart, Robert Young, and Frank Morgan, so I took her to lunch and told her I was wearing my new coat in celebration of her career. Not a bad excuse, eh?

With the start of the new Metro-Goldwyn-Mayer picture, I went back to my three-hour schedule. Before that I had been in school more than the required three hours just because I was so fascinated with it. Not with school, exactly, but with my artwork. Mrs. Carter, my teacher, says that I am not half bad at it, and after I finish my French and music lessons, she lets me spend the rest of the time painting. Yesterday I copied a picture of a girl by the artist Petty, and today I sketched my new coat on her.

Speaking of Sue working in pictures, the laugh is on her. For the last few years I've been the only one in the family who had to get up before six every morning in order to be at the studio made up and ready for work by nine. This morning Sue set her alarm for five-thirty, and when she woke up, she started to wail because it was still dark. Did I giggle! Now you should see how much more respectful she is to me. "To think you have been doing this for four years," she says—and looks astounded.

But I was glad she was working, for it gave me a chance to visit *The Mortal Storm* set this morning. There I met Robert Stack. You know, he is the young man who played with Deanna Durbin in *First Love*. I had met him before, but this was our first real talk. And we are going out together Saturday night. Isn't that grand?

I have started something new. It's golf, and I'm in love with it. Every morning at seven-thirty I go to the Bel-Air golf course and take a lesson. Now that I'm working I'll have to wait until Sundays to play, but I'm not going to let up on it. Do you know that I can drive one hundred and twenty yards already? My instructor tells me that is quite good. I hope so, because my one ambition is to be able to beat Mickey Rooney at golf. I wonder if I'll ever be able to do it?

Best wishes to you all, from
Judy Garland

THE UGLY DUCKLING WHO BECAME A SWAN

MARY JANE MANNERS | June 1940, *Silver Screen*

Judy added to the legend of a feud with Deanna Durbin and responded to the elopement of Artie Shaw with Lana Turner in this fan magazine feature.

It seems only yesterday when Judy Garland left a party in tears because friends of Deanna Durbin poked fun and laughed at her and said "Imagine her being a movie star!"

It was moonlight and the air was filled with the fragrance of flowers as a lone little figure, in a white party dress with a gardenia in her thick brown curls, trudged down a winding road in Brentwood, California. Unobserved, she had slipped out a side door of the big white house on the hill, where lights and music told plainly that a party was in progress.

At the fork of the road, the child, for she was discernibly a plump adolescent of teen-age, stopped and waited.

Suddenly, a sedan drove up. The car door opened and she flung herself in, heedless of the fragile ruffles on the dainty frock. Simultaneously, she broke into sobs.

"Why Judy Garland," said her mother, turning off the ignition switch, "whatever has happened? Why did you telephone me to come and get you? Why didn't you stay at the party?"

"I couldn't bear it, mother, they laughed at me! Some of the girls stood in a corner and whispered and poked fun at me," Judy sobbed in her mother's arms. "I heard one of Deanna Durbin's friends say, 'She'll never be an actress. She just thinks she can sing. She's too fat. Imagine her being a movie star!' Then they all laughed."

And then came afresh the release of pent up emotions and disappointment and child heartbreak.

A few seconds later the tears suddenly stopped. "I should have slapped their faces," exploded Judy, her quivering chin now rigid with indignation and determination. "But, I'll show them. I WILL be somebody in pictures. I WILL."

And she is.

"I was pretty mad," Judy remembers. "But I really owe some of my spunk to those 'catty' girls!

"When I was making a personal appearance in New York, a boy sent a note backstage to me. It said that I was a hypocrite singing that I loved New York and was happy. "You just live a glamorous life in Hollywood and don't know what real honest clean fun is! And you don't look so hot up there with your petticoat showing a couple of inches—and you on the stage! Yah!" he wrote.

"My temper didn't rise a bit at the note. I felt sorry that anyone should be so bitter about anyone else. I had the usher bring him backstage and we talked. I told him that I wasn't a hypocrite—and he said well he thought all people who had lots of money were two-faced!

"He'd just been released from a reform school—and didn't seem to like anyone or anything. I told him I had lots of fun. That I lived with my mother and sister and went with boys and girls my own age, and swam and played badminton, went to movies and did most anything any boy or girl does.

"Too, I explained that my petticoat was not showing, that my dress was made with a bottom ruffle. Well, he seemed really sorry for being so unkind. Said if he'd thought more, he wouldn't have sent such a note. The next day he sent a letter of apology. I believe he always will feel friendly towards me. Probably, if I had stopped and spoken to those girls at Deanna's party they might have become friends, too. I've thought about it a lot.

I know now that the way to deal with people who want to be unkind to you is to be so nice, they'll like you in spite of themselves."

Strangely, Judy lives in a new white house on a winding road near the very hilltop where jealousy first reared its ugly head and two thoughtless girls squelched her adolescent pride, but fired her determination.

"This is my very own house," Judy said, proudly showing me through the spacious rooms and out onto the patio where we glimpsed the badminton court and the new swimming pool. A huge St. Bernard dog rounded the corner and all but knocked Judy over in his attempt to bestow affection on his mistress.

"Mother was married shortly before last Christmas," Judy continued as we settled ourselves comfortably in beach chairs on the sun-drenched patio. "She spends part of the week here and the other part at Santa Paula—where she is Mrs. Gilmore. I really have two homes. Sue, my older sister (*she's* 24), is here with me. Mother put it straight to us girls whether she should marry or not. We told her to go right ahead. Now someday, when I get to be twenty-one or -two and find the right boy, and want to get married, I won't have to worry about mother being left alone. She's very happy."

Judy's mother will tell you that her youngest daughter might make a good press agent. Mrs. Garland had decided to keep her new marriage quiet. But Judy was so thrilled, she called up every columnist and radio broadcaster in town, even wiring Walter Winchell, to give him an "exclusive scoop" that her mother was slipping off secretly to Yuma to be married that night.

Since there's been so much to-do about a romance between Judy and Mickey Rooney, I asked her if it were true.

"Mickey's about the nicest and, at the same time, the funniest boy," she replied. "He's terribly restless and full of energy, you know. He never can sit still for more than a minute—then he must be up and doing. He'll call up suddenly and ask for a date. If I tell him I already have one, he'll name every day in the week until he gets one. We'll even argue about it. He'll come bursting in breathless and we'll rush somewhere—to a movie or bowling alley or something. Then he'll bring me home and I won't hear from him for weeks.

"It never occurs to Mickey to bring a girl flowers or candy, but he'll sit down and eat candy from the box the boy the night before brought. That's the way he is," she sighed. "But I like working with him better than anyone else in pictures and I think he likes working with me. Even so, sometimes we tell each other off, but we always make up. I sort of suspect that Mickey reads about us supposed to be going around together in the movie magazines and wants to feel that he has sort of first call on me for dates.

"Right now we're making *Andy Hardy Meets Debutante*, in which I again play Betsy Booth like I did in *Love Finds Andy Hardy*. Then we're to make *Strike Up the Band*. We get a lot of fun out of working together."

I asked Judy to tell me one of the most important of the many things that are happening to her in her rapid ascent to stardom.

"Going to the premiere of *Babes in Arms*, my first costarring picture, and having my hand and footprints taken in the forecourt of the Chinese Theatre," she replied without hesitation. "You should have seen my mother that night," she continued with a roll of her brown eyes. "This was really my first big starring role. I asked mother if I could have a very special dress to wear. She said that I might look around and find something and then I could let her know about it.

"My stand-in and I went shopping. Just for fun, and because it looked so impressive, we stopped in at Bernie Newman's. He had the most gorgeous white dress I've ever seen. It was terribly expensive, the kind Norma Shearer and the really big movie stars wear to premieres. He said it was so fragile, I really shouldn't even sit down in it. It was just made to stand and be seen in.

"I telephoned mother and coaxed her until she said I could have it. She spoils me terribly when I really want something very much. Well, when she saw me on my knees, in that dress, putting my hands in the cement at the theater, I thought she was going to faint. And that wasn't all! After the premiere, we went to the Cocoanut Grove and rode hobby horses—and, well, there wasn't much of my dress left but shreds by the time I got home. But somehow mother seemed to understand that it wasn't all my fault and she was a darling. She didn't scold."

The telephone interrupted. It was Cleveland calling Judy.

"That was a friend of mine. I met him on my personal appearance tour," Judy said on returning. "He's the nicest boy, calls up almost every day. His telephone bill will be as big as the national debt, I'm afraid. His family has invited Sue and me to spend a week with them in Ohio. We're going to soon, I think."

Since Judy's name has been closely linked, and romantically, with Artie Shaw's I commented on his marriage to Lana Turner. "It was a surprise to everyone," I ventured.

"Not at all," said Judy. "Artie's like that. Does whatever he feels like doing when he feels like doing it. He disbanded his orchestra and quit because he really didn't like leading a swing orchestra and playing for jitterbugs." The truth is that Artie long-distanced Judy and asked her advice before he quit, but he didn't mention his intention of eloping with Lana when he took Judy out to dinner at the Victor Hugo the week before he flew to Yuma to ring the wedding bells. Despite the difference in their ages, there was a strong bond of friendship between the former Swing-King and the little Swing-Singer.

At present, Judy and her sister are going with brothers, Jimmy and Jack Cathcart, age 21 and 24, respectively. "And made to order," laughs Judy. "We make a fine brother and sister act."

The younger of the brothers, who squires Judy, is a member of Ray Noble's orchestra. The other night Judy's mother arrived home at midnight to find Judy in the kitchen busily engaged in pouring cake materials into the electric mixer. "I'm baking a cake so's Jimmy and I can have cake and coffee when he stops by," Judy explained. Jimmy has to play with his orchestra practically every night, so much of his courting is being done over sandwiches and cold snacks in the Garland kitchen on the way home, or they play badminton in the mornings.

Judy makes three times her movie salary on the radio. Her present M-G-M contract has three years to go, and although she is one of the studio's best box office attractions, her weekly stipend remains around $750 a week. Even so, Judy has practically everything that a girl her age could desire. There's her home in Bel Air with its lovely bedroom and sitting room upstairs designed for her. Then comes her sports roadster and her dog and cat. In her closet is a sports skunk coat and a winter one trimmed with mink, for her mother believes that Judy is still too young for an entire mink one. There're rows of simple girlish dresses and the once elegant but now bedraggled Bernie Newman model. Judy still loves to look at it and its price tag and visualize it as it once was. Some day she hopes to be able to afford another like it. She dreamed of a star ruby, but later reasoned that she hadn't better buy her own jewelry, for after all she wants something left for a fiancé to buy her, if and when she decides on the boy.

When Judy was born almost [eighteen] years ago, her parents retired from vaudeville and bought a theater in Grand Rapids, [Minnesota,] and settled down to make a home for their three daughters.

"One Christmas Eve, when I was two," Judy says, "Daddy let me go out on the stage and sing, 'Jingle Bells.' Mother says they couldn't get me off. Finally, daddy had to walk out and carry me off.

"When my parents moved to California and bought a theater, they enrolled us in a school for training children for the stage. I was four and a half when I played Cupid in a prologue at a downtown Los Angeles theater. I sang 'I Can't Give You Anything but Love, Baby,' with a big sty on my eye. It came the morning of the show, but since I was supposed to be a trouper, I went on in spite of it.

"Gus Edwards saw us and said we sisters should be a trio. So, we became the Gumm Sisters and sang at benefits and wherever we could.

"A friend of mother's booked us into Chicago. By a mistake on the marquee, the sign read the Glum Sisters. That was perfectly tragic to us. George Jessel, who was on the same bill, suggested that to avert such a mistake, we should call ourselves the Garland Sisters. That's how I adopted my name.

"After an engagement at the Chicago World's Fair, we returned to California to settle down to school. Suzanne married and Virginia and I continued on singing together.

"A talent scout heard me sing at Lake Tahoe during a summer vacation and arranged my audition with Louis B. Mayer. Then I was signed to an M-G-M contract.

"My family and friends thought of course I would be a movie star right away. But I wasn't. It appeared as though they weren't going to do

JUDY GARLAND'S GUIDE BOOK TO DATING

KAY PROCTOR | August 1940, *Movie Mirror*

Judy shared her "grown-up" dating advice in this *Movie Mirror* feature, one of her many fan magazine cover stories during the 1940s.

A young modern gives her formula for whom to date and how often . . . where to go and what to wear . . . what to do and how late to stay out

Do you remember your first *grown-up* date? So does Judy Garland—at the ripe old age of seventeen. It happened about six months ago and if you were in a dither about yours, wait until you hear what happened to hers. It almost turned into a three-ring circus!

Judy told us about it the other day when we were talking about dates and what to do about them. Just because she is a movie star with all the trimmings doesn't mean the date question hasn't been a problem to her quite as much as it is to other seventeen-year-olds in the country. In her case, in fact, it has been an extra problem because of the spotlight of publicity's being focused on everything she did as she slipped from girlhood into charming and gracious young womanhood.

It was twenty-one-year-old Robert Stack who beaued Judy on her first honest-to-goodness grown-up date. The occasion was an invitation to Pickfair, which is a glamorous name to conjure within Hollywood. The world's most famous names, even royalty, have entered its portals and invitations don't grow on trees. Naturally, therefore, Miss Judy Garland was in a lather of excitement with a slick new evening dress to make everything perfect.

"I was so excited," Judy confessed, "that I started getting ready about four o'clock in the afternoon and was practically *rumpled* by the time we were ready to go.

Bob was supposed to call for her at eight; but nine o'clock came and went with still no sign of him. Judy was fit to be tied when the telephone finally rang. It was Bob, saying he couldn't find her house in the winding streets of Stone Canyon. To make matters worse, he didn't have her telephone number with him, so had to call all over town before he got it.

"The number is right out in front of the house," Judy started to say and then remembered that it wasn't! The house had been newly painted and the number had not been replaced. Whereupon she gave him explicit directions for reaching the home.

"The more I thought about it, the more I decided I hadn't better take any chances," she told us. "We had a loudspeaker system in the house with a microphone I use while practicing for my radio show, so I turned that on and hung it out the window broadcasting 'Judy Garland lives here! This is the house where Judy Garland lives!'"

Just in case that didn't do the trick, she sent her two older sisters, Sue and Jimmie, out to the curb with fresh white bedsheets to flag him down!

"He found the house all right," she said comfortably, "and we had a wonderful time. Gee, it was wonderful!"

A long sigh was choked off by enthusiasm for the chicken pot pie and chocolate sundae (with whipped cream, nuts and cherry) which lay on the table before her. For once she had time to relish every mouthful; her scenes in *Strike Up the Band* with Mickey Rooney were finished for the day and she had two full hours before rehearsal for her weekly radio show.

Technically speaking, the Pickfair date with Bob Stack wasn't her first grown-up date, if you mean being out unchaperoned with a man. When she was a sprout of fifteen, the venerable (all of twenty, at least!) Johnny Downs had taken her to an evening movie and a chocolate malt at the drugstore afterwards. On that memorable occasion, she remembers, she wore a navy blue gingham dress with blue bobby sox and flat-heeled shoes. It didn't really count, however, because she was sure Johnny looked on her as a baby and was just being nice.

There were no more dates in the Downs-Stack hiatus. "Nobody asked me," she explained with disarming honesty.

She isn't troubled with that nowadays. She has all the dates she wants and invitations for a lot she doesn't want. With those dates came the problem of how to handle them graciously and in good taste, the same as it does for thousands upon thousands of young girls like her. Whom to date with and how often. Where to go and what to wear. What to do and how late to stay out.

She has solved the problems with the right answers, apparently, for she has the admiration of her elders and the respect of the young people her own age. That's a triumph in itself. But if you expect she's going to mount a platform and start giving out advice to others, you are greatly mistaken.

"I think it's pretty silly for a seventeen-year-old to try to preach about *anything*," she said. "All I know is what *I* like and what has worked for *me*."

Judy catalogues her dates as "special" and "average." A "special" takes place maybe once in six weeks or so. An "average" happens once or twice a week when she's not working on a picture. Most of the time, however, she says the "bunch" get together and do something. The "bunch" includes Mickey Rooney, Bob Stack, Jackie Cooper, Jimmy Cathcart, Forrest Tucker, Bob Shaw, Jack Hopkins, Bonita Granville, Linda Darnell, Helen Parrish, Betty Jane Graham and Patty McCarty.

"What's a 'special' like?" we asked.

"Well, let's take an example," she said. "Bob took me to dinner and to see Katharine Cornell in the play *No Time for Comedy*. I'd call that a 'special.' It was on a Saturday night and we had dinner a little earlier than usual because we were going to the theater and I hate to be late. So he called for me about 6:30 or so. As usual, I started getting ready early, because it seems to make things last longer, don't you think? I had a new evening dress, which made it an 'extra special,' and Bob sent me a lovely corsage to wear. He wore his tuxedo and looked very handsome.

"He called for me in his own car and came in and talked to mother for a few minutes. Then we went to the Tail o' the Cock restaurant for dinner and had a tomato juice cocktail. That was to make it extra festive, sort of. I told him what I liked on the menu and he ordered the dinner. We talked about our hobbies and pictures we had seen and so on. Then it was time to go to the theater. We had wonderful seats down front and during intermission we went to the lobby to talk to friends.

"The play was out by eleven o'clock, and we were hungry again (seems like we're *always* hungry!) so we drove to a hamburger stand. I've been to swank, sophisticated places like Ciro's, just to see what they are like, but we have more fun at a hamburger drive-in. It was about midnight when we got home. Mother was still up, so Bob came in to say good night to her. Otherwise he would have left me at the door. So that's what a 'special's' like."

Judy said she realized it was a more expensive evening than many young people could afford. Bob, working in pictures, naturally has more money to spend. But the same sort of a date could be carried out on less expensive lines and with just as much fun.

"You might skip the dinner, for instance," she explained. "Or you could have dinner at some place like the Cocoanut Grove where there is dancing for the evening."

An "average" date would be like the one she had last Wednesday with Mickey Rooney, she said. Mickey called up about quarter to seven.

"What are you doing?" he opened the conversation.

"Nothing in particular," said Judy.

"Okay, let's go for a show. I'll pick you up in fifteen minutes. And say, got anything to eat at your house?"

At seven he breezed in, greeted Mrs. Garland, and made a beeline for the kitchen where Judy had rustled him a fried egg sandwich. While he was wolfing that sandwich they checked the theater ads and found a movie they wanted to see. Then out they dashed, climbed into his station wagon, and off for the show. On the way they stopped to buy a bag of jawbreakers, licorice drops and bubble gum. At the theater they found seats in their favorite spot, the front row center, and stayed for both features of a double bill. After that came a milkshake in a sweet shop across the street where they dropped a few nickels in the "jukebox" (phonograph record machine). Then home.

"Where," Judy said, "Mickey opens the door, shoves me in, yells good night and is half way to his car again before I have time to catch my breath."

Mrs. Ethel Garland, Judy's mother, never attempts to dictate about Judy's dates. As result, Judy talks them over with her freely and often asks advice. Mrs. Garland, however, does insist on one thing; that she meet the young man before Judy goes out with him. That's fine with Judy because, she says, she's always so proud to have her friends see what a wonderful mother she has.

"I think the most important thing about a date is to know the boy and what he's really like," Judy said. "That's just common sense, because otherwise you might get yourself in a jam. It hasn't happened to me, but I know girls who went out with some boys they did not really know and they took them to some sort of a cocktail place and started drinking. The girls were frightened and didn't know what to do. They wanted to go home and the boys wouldn't take them."

We asked Judy what she would do in a spot like that. She gave a direct and very wise answer.

"I'd telephone Mother to come get me," she said.

She thought it was a bad idea to date too much, to go out every night, Judy said. It gives a girl a reputation of "go-er" and makes her seem a little cheap and shallow.

"There are so many things that are fun to do at home if you only wake up to it," she said. "Play the piano, sing and dance, make candy, play games of all kinds. And I think it's silly to think it has to be boys, boys, boys all the time! Two girls can have grand fun together. You can play night tennis on the public courts, go bowling, practice driving on a golf driving range and all sorts of things. It seems to me it is important that other girls like you as well as boys. I know I wouldn't be proud of the fact other girls didn't like me, and that's what happens a lot of times to go-ers."

Judy said she didn't have any "rules" for behavior on dates, but there were a few things she tried to do and tried to avoid.

"I try to have poise," she told us, and then started to laugh because, as she said, you certainly couldn't call it poise the way she broadcast out the window and waved sheets in front of her house that night of the Pickfair date. But anyway, poise was important. Or maybe it was better to call it behaving in a ladylike manner. No loud talking, or giggling, or boisterous actions that would call attention to herself. She said she thought it embarrassed boys and made them uncomfortable.

"Of course, that doesn't mean I don't laugh at their jokes," she added seriously. "That's just smart, even if they're not very funny. The dumbest girl can seem smart if she keeps the conversation focused on the boy's interests, or at least keeps it steered on the one subject she knows most about."

It's just common decency to show regard for the condition of a date's pocketbook, she went on. In other words, she doesn't suggest doing things or going places she knows is more than the boy can afford, even though it is what she wants to do.

"Sometimes when I'm having dinner with a boy, though, I wish he would order first," she said plaintively. "That would give me an idea of how far I am supposed to go on prices."

She thought it was important to be "regular," which means not too feminine and not too independent. Boys have now outgrown a girl who is afraid of "ruining" her hair while she's in swimming, for instance, and they still won't stand for being bossed. She said she made it a point to express her appreciation for invitations and try to reciprocate whenever possible by having the date come to her house for an evening, or asking him to share free tickets when she got them. She tries to be a good dancer and always underdresses rather than overdresses for an occasion.

"If I know a boy doesn't have much money, I don't ask him if we are going to 'dress,'" she said. "I just take it for granted that we are not, and say nothing about it."

This modern freedom stuff is all right, Judy said, but she still lets her dates know she expects the old-fashioned courtesies like opening doors and things. If they neglect them at first, a half kidding remark like "After you, Alphonse" usually gets the idea over. When the courtesies are extended, however, she doesn't neglect to say "Thank you."

"What about necking?" we asked. "We've heard it's quite a problem to seventeen-year-old girls these days, and the girl who won't permit little liberties stays home alone."

"I don't believe in it," Judy answered. "Maybe that used to be so, but I think most boys and girls have so many other interests today, they just don't think about that other stuff."

Naturally, she admitted, she has had a good-night kiss stolen at the front door once in a while as has any girl. But it doesn't happen if she can help it. Either she kids the boy out of the idea or says a flat no. If it happens once, she forgets about it because it gives too much importance to the incident to make a fuss about it. If it happens the second time she crosses the date off her list and forgets about him as well as the kiss.

Now you know Judy Garland's guide book to dating. But here's something maybe you don't know: she may be famous and have a lot of money and fine clothes and scads of boys crazy about her, but it hasn't made her blasé. She gets just as excited about Saturday night as all the rest of us.

BEGINNING JUDY GARLAND'S GAY LIFE STORY

JUDY GARLAND AS TOLD TO GLADYS HALL | December 1940, *Screenland*

One of the more thorough and lengthy looks at Judy's early life story came in the form of this two-part "as told to" piece by Gladys Hall. It should be noted that the stylized (and often random) use of capitalization is not an error. It appears exactly as in the original manuscript.

PART I—MY PAST

I think First Things are Best Things! Wasn't it Robert Louis Stevenson who said that first sunsets, first loves, all the things we see for the first time, all the first experiences we have, are *always* best? Anyway, *I* think so. I know I'll always remember, most clearly and deeply and forever, the first things that have happened to me in my first eighteen years. The things that have happened to me in my first (and only) "Past," you might say, since now that I am eighteen, I think I can be said to have a Past. So, I got to thinking that maybe I'd write my first Life Story my own self in my own way. My "own way" probably won't be the Proper Way, at all. The Proper Way to write an Autobiography, I mean. Because I'm just going to sort of talk out loud, or write out loud, to my mother, to my friends, to my fans. I'm just going to go on and on, sort of Revealing to them all the Important, First Things (important to *me,* that is) that have made up my Past.

Like, for instance, my first day on this earth, which is certainly the *first*, First Thing! Well, Mom, as *you* may remember, my first day on this earth was the day of June 10, 1922—(I seem to remember that movie girls don't give the year of their birth—oh, well!)—and you may also recollect, Mom, that I first opened my eyes in Grand Rapids, Minnesota. You've got it down in my baby book that I weighed eight pounds when I was born and that my eyes were blue at birth and started to turn to brown when I was about five months old. You've also confessed to me that your first feeling about me was one of—terrible Disappointment! Because, having had two small daughters already, Suzanne and Virginia, naturally you and Daddy wanted some *novelty* in your children and just hoped and *prayed* that I would be a boy! You terribly wanted me to be a boy, you've said, you planned for me to be a boy, you even named me Francis Gumm, Jr., after Daddy. And not only did I turn out to be, NOT the answer to your prayers, but just another little girl, for Pete's sake. Also I was as red as an Indian, you said, and the reddest, *homeliest* baby anyone ever saw! You just made the best of it by changing the "i" to "e" and naming me Frances, anyway!

I was three months old (how often you've told me this, Mom!) when you first noticed what you called "the first signs talent" in me—you always sang to me when you rocked me to sleep, you've told me, and you noticed that when you sang just sort of usual songs, like "Baby's Shoes" or "[Rock-a-Bye], Baby," I'd go smack off to sleep. When you sang sort of rollicking, spirited, "Yo, Ho" songs, I'd gurgle and bat my eyes and flip my hands around as though I was telling the Sand Man to scat! And when you sang sad songs, especially "In the Gloaming" or "The End of a Perfect Day," I'd cry. I'd cry real wet, sobby tears!

That's how you first knew, you say, that I was "sensitive to music." Well, be that as it may, certainly my first sort of large, blurry memory is of music, music all the time, music all over the house. "We shall have music wherever we go" should have been the Gumm motto! I can remember how you and Daddy and Suzanne and Jimmie sang—in the bathtub, at meals, at your housework, as well as in the theater, of course. Daddy had a *beautiful* voice. Anyway, you've always insisted that my response to music "showed" abnormally early and was abnormally acute. And as it makes me feel rather "special" I like to think you were right—you always are, Mom, and that's not gross flattery!

The "First Tooth" is also one of your favorite "baby" stories about me. I was four months old to the day, it seems, and you had invited guests for dinner. And I made the dinner hour hideous by yowling my lungs out, *not* musically, and continued throughout the evening! When you couldn't stand it any longer, you gave me a thorough "searching" and discovered that I had cut, not my first tooth, but my first *teeth!* The two uppers had come through. Mom always tells people, "She was doing things double, even then!"

My First Word, I believe, was uttered at the ripe, old age of nine months. And the family was unimpressed because it seemed to be the very banal, baby word, "Goo." Then, Daddy noticed that whenever I said "Goo" or whatever it was, I always proceeded to *do* something, like throwing my rattle at the cat or putting a glass ornament in my mouth, and then they all realized that I was not saying "Goo" but "Do." (I still think that's a debatable point, Mom, but have it your own way!)

I took my First Step at the age of eleven months, Baby-Book History records. Previous to that first step, I've been told, I managed to get around by hitching myself across the floor, delicately balanced on one hip bone! Even my doting parents couldn't make anything precocious out of *that!*

My First Interest, it seems, was in picture books. Well, I can believe that. I've always been crazy about books. And I can remember for myself that my first real favorite was the story of *Aladdin and the Wonderful Lamp*. Right now, I'm reading *Mein Kampf* and finding it pretty tough going, too. But I honestly think that if we want to understand what's going on in Europe and how it got like this, we should read the book!

I never played with dolls, *never*. I'm told that when I was a mere infant, I'd make horrible faces if anyone just handed me a doll. And I remember myself that my first really nice doll was given me by Mary Pickford when I won the *Herald-Express*' "Better Babies" Contest. I think I was two and a half or something like that.* I don't remember the contest but I do remember that the Great, Big Beautiful Doll sat in my playroom along with other, not-so-elegant dolls and that I thought it was just a piece of bric-a-brac, not something to *play* with. I think I know why I hated dolls,

---

*The event Judy referenced here was the "Eighth Annual Los Angeles Evening Express 'Better Babies' Exposition" held at Paramount Studios on March 4, 1930. Judy was seven years old at the time and reportedly won second place in her age division.

they reminded me of little *dead* people! All cold and still. I liked live, warm, cuddly things. I still do. The first toys I ever really played with, I remember, really *used*, were a toy piano and a toy xylophone. I never had a piano lesson in my life but I liked to bang on that toy piano.

I'm not sure whether I really remember my first Public Appearance or whether I've just heard Mom and Daddy talk about it so often that I think I remember. I do remember that I sang "Jingle Bells" and that I chose that song my own self. I do remember it was Christmas week and I was about three years old, and that I wore a white dress which Mom made for me and that Suzanne and Jimmie (I always called Virginia, Jimmie) pinned sprigs of holly all over it, even where I sat down! And of course I remember, Mom, how you taught us three kids lots of songs. And you've told me that I amazed you by my persistence in making trios out of duets (so that I could be included in with my sisters!) and by my quickness in catching onto tricks and phrases. Anyway, so the Family Saga goes, when the curtains parted on this First Appearance on Any Stage of Baby Frances Gumm, there I stood, and when the orchestra gave me my cue, I started to sing, without a moment's hesitation or the slightest sign of shyness. You insist that I kept perfect pitch, perfect time, and didn't miss a word!

Well, when the chorus ended, so far as the orchestra was concerned, and it was time for me to bow off gracefully, I did nothing of the kind. I started the song all over again! Again it ended. Again I had other ideas. And after five verses and four choruses, Daddy had to march out on the stage, pick up his infant daughter and carry her into the wings amid quote tumultuous applause end quote! "I wanna sing some *more*," I kept protesting. I remember Daddy telling me this—"I wanna sing some more," and he said he was sure my voice could be heard out front long after I'd vanished, on his shoulder, into the fringe of canvas Christmas trees.*

---

*The official debut of the Gumm Sisters occurred on December 26, 1924, with the girls performing "When My Sugar Walks Down the Street" on the stage of their father's New Grand Theatre. Frances was scheduled to sing one verse and a chorus of "Jingle Bells," but the solo quickly became an event when she refused to leave the stage, fueled by the approving roar of the audience. Incidentally, the number of choruses of "Jingle Bells" seemed to grow with every retelling by Judy of this momentous occasion! Her first review was published several days later in the Grand Rapids *Herald-Review*: "The work of Frances, the two-year-old baby, was a genuine surprise. The little girl spoke and sang so as to be heard by everyone in the house and she joined in the dancing both alone and with her older sisters. The audience expressed their appreciation of the work of all three girls by vigorous applause."

That was amateur night, too, by the way. And *I won the first prize.* And Daddy wouldn't let me accept the prize because it was his theater and he said it was like a hostess not accepting the prize at her own party! That always sort of stuck in my mind and I thought to myself, "Huh, I'll win prizes someday, prizes I can accept!"

Anyway, that was my first heady draught of applause. I loved it then, apparently, and I've always loved it. Between you and me, folks, I think it's the *most* beautiful music in the whole world! And it can come in different ways, too, not only the sound of hands clapping, but in fan letters, good reviews, the shine in your director's eyes when you've done a good scene, lots of ways.

My first memory of my Mom and Dad is watching them doing their singing and dancing act as I sat in an orchestra seat between Suzanne and Jimmie. Especially, I remember hearing my mother sing "I'm Saving for a Rainy Day." That has always been my favorite song. I used to cry when she sang it. I still do.

I remember how Daddy always arranged the bill in his theater so that our acts followed one another. I mean, Mom and Dad would do their act first and we girls would sit in the audience and applaud. Then we would go on and do our trio singing and Mom and Daddy would sit out front and applaud *us.* That was my first practical lesson of the theater—that it *takes only one good friend to start the ball rolling.*

I have other First Memories of my Mom and Dad, too—especially how hard they worked for us—how my mother not only accompanied us on the piano but also made all our costumes, sometimes sewing all night long, and also arranged our music for us and also took care of our theatrical bookings. And Daddy did all the business end of things, took charge of the box office and our traveling arrangements and so on. And then, after all their back-of-the-scenes work was done, they'd get out there on the stage and do their act, fresh and peppy as kids! I don't think there's anything in the world so folksy as a Family Act. It really is "all for one and one for all."

And most of all, I remember how Dad introduced Mother to the audiences. He was so proud of her tiny hands. Like little, quick birds, they were, I always thought. Anyway, Dad would always do his short dance routine first and then he'd step forward to the footlights and hold up his hand for silence and say, "I want to introduce a tiny, pretty lady with tiny, pretty hands!"

Maybe it sounds kind of corny now, but it always brought a lump into my throat and tears into my eyes when I was a kid. And it still does, when I think about it, now that I'm eighteen.

I guess you *always* remember your First Best Friend. Margaret Shook was my First Friend. I didn't know until long after we'd left Grand Rapids that Mardie, I always called her Mardie, was the daughter of a maid who had worked for us before I was born. I remember how Daddy taught Mardie and me to sing "My Country 'Tis of Thee" and how he'd play it and we'd stand on the front steps and sing it and we'd make our kitten and puppy and lop-eared rabbit and trained duck stand at attention, too! Once Mardie threw red pepper in my eyes—remember, Mardie?—it was by mistake, of course—and I thought I was blind. Long after the sting had gone out of my eyes I went around making believe I was blind. I guess I liked the attention it got me. I always liked the spotlight, I'm afraid. I've always felt at home in it, like sitting by the fireside, cozy. And I remember that my First Punishment was being stood in a corner. I may as well admit to you now, Mom, that it was no *punishment!* In fact, I got a Kick out of it. It got so that I'd do something naughty deliberately-on-purpose and then I'd go and stand in a corner under my own steam! Because I *liked* standing in a corner. Because it was, in a manner of speaking, also standing in the spotlight! Suzanne and Jimmie would be so impressed when they saw me standing there, they'd sort of tiptoe around.

Well, I certainly remember my First Tour! We left Grand Rapids soon after I was three. I can remember hearing Mother and Dad talking about how California would be the best and healthiest place to bring up three small girls. I remember all the talk about Dad selling his theater in Grand Rapids and his plans for buying a new one in California. Being practical people, *and* vaudevillians, we decided to make one-night stands along the road on the way out. That's when I began to be The Pest of the Act. Being the smallest of the three, I always stood on the stage between the girls, with an arm around each sister. And I'd tickle first one and then the other! I broke up the act entirely. They'd just go to pieces but I'd go right on singing! Jimmie thought it was rather funny but Suzanne would chase me all over and around backstage, trying to catch me and spank me.

Sometimes we played jokes on the orchestra, too—and then one night, the orchestra turned the tables on us. We had to stand very near to the footlights, you see, being so little—and this bunch of boys got a very bright idea and *they all ate garlic* and the fumes nearly *asphyxiated us*! But that was nothing to what our First Audience did to us when we first played in California—it was in a small theater in a small northern town, I remember, and before we'd half-finished our first song, the entire house *walked out on us*! That was the night Dad decided that the theater was not for us. And that walkout was my First Introduction to California audiences!

Well, then we settled in Lancaster, California, and Daddy got his theater nearby. I think the first special thing I remember about Lancaster is when I did my first school play there. I must have been about four and a half, I think. Anyway, I was a *dwarf* and I had pillows stuffed all over me. At the end of our act, I was surprised to see the curtain go down before we, The Players, had taken any bows. What kind of a thing was *this*, I thought?—so I just went right out in front of the curtain and started to bow like mad and I just stayed out there, bowing and bowing, and then I had to crawl in under the curtain to get back again! I should have been mortified but I'm told that I wasn't.

My first "starring" role was also in a school play in Lancaster. I forget whether it was given by the dramatic school I attended for a while or the public school, but anyway, I was "Mrs. Goldilocks" and I wore a huge monument of a blonde wig. I had to swing back and forth in a rope swing under some canvas trees and in my zeal of enthusiasm, I swung so hard that I hit one of the backdrops and *knocked my wig off*! And there sat "Mrs. Goldilocks" with little, brown wisps for hair. They never gave me a starring role again! Oh, and as if I can *ever* forget the time I appeared in a school recital in the auditorium of the public school where Suzanne and Jimmie were going! The place was packed. Behind the scenes, my mother held my dress for me. I can see it to this day, a white dress, all ruffles, with panties attached so it would be easy for me to slip into with one motion—

well, just as Mom was holding it ready for me to step into, I heard the opening bars of my number and I rushed out onto the stage, *stark naked!*

I must say that I began my professional career as an ill-starred star. Like when I was five I became one of The Meglin Kiddies. And the next Public Appearance I made was in one of their revues in a Los Angeles theater. To us, a Los Angeles theater meant what the Palace did to Broadway. It was the Big Time! And not only was I in several of the ensembles but also, dressed as a Cupid, with bow and arrow and quivers in a silver case, I was to deliver myself of a solo, "I Can't Give You Anything but Love." And then, again, Disaster! For I awoke on the eventful morning with a cold sore, a sty on my right eye and the horrible results of my First Permanent almost totally disabling me. I couldn't see, my eye was practically shut, my mouth was swollen with the cold sore, and my hair looked like *Topsy's* after a pillow fight. We spent the day frantically trying first aid remedies and I kept my fingers crossed wishing—but you can't wish sties and cold sores away, nor permanents, either, they run their appointed courses. Anyway, Mom says that I showed then, for the first time, that the old "the Show must go on" slogan was in my bones because—a very sorry-looking Cupid did the blind staggers onto the stage. I couldn't even get the quivers out of my case on account of how I couldn't *see* to get them out!

But I've always said that I was born under a Lucky Star, somewhere Over the Rainbow—because that night Gus Edwards was in the audience and he came backstage and told my mother that my sisters and I should resume our trio singing—"With her ear," he said, "nothing musical is beyond her." I remember his exact words on account of how I thought he mentioned my ear because my ears were the only parts of me that were not disfigured!

It was soon after that that The Gumm Sisters got their first Professional Engagement at the Biltmore Theatre in L.A. Boy, did we celebrate! We always celebrated every Big, First Occasion at our house. That night we had ice cream and store cake and lemon pop and candy. We were Big Time! Well, sir, we even had a private dressing room *with maid service.* I kept asking the maid to go and get me ice cream sodas and chewing gum. I didn't know what else to ask her for. I still send people out to get me ice cream sodas and chewing gum when I'm working. Well, we were all so happy and elated we didn't even think to ask what our salaries would be. Mom had bought all three of us new dresses. I remember them so well because they were our first *bought* dresses. And all our friends came to the theater. Mom and Dad sat in the front row of the orchestra to get the applause going. And we got a lot of it, too. Lovely waves of it!

I guess that was the first time I ever had a conscious, sort of *formed* ambition to Be Someone I never thought of going in movies, never once in my life. But I did think, I'm going to be a Singer! I did think, I'm going to have lots of pretty clothes someday and a lovely house and a red automobile! They always say "As a man thinks" . . . well, *I* say that "As a *little girl thinks*" because I have them, now, the pretty clothes, my own house, even the red automobile!

But Pride certainly goeth, at times, before an awful belly-whopper—for that night, when we opened our pay envelopes after the show, we found *fifty cents apiece, in each*! So that was my First Paycheck—FIFTY CENTS! And Mom had paid ten dollars each for our dresses. I said "Are we bankrupt?" And Daddy laughed and said, "No, but I guess Woman's Place is In The Home—and in school, for you three!"

Buddy West—well, Mister West, I certainly remember *you*! *You* certainly belong among my Important Firsts on account of how you were the first boy I ever noticed, and *I hated you*! Maybe Dr. Freud and the psychologists would say that I was having an "overreaction" but I called it just plain hating you—in fact, I hated all boys after you, for ages, well, for *months—I* remember how, when Daddy would reminisce, saying "when I was a boy—" I'd say, passionately, "you weren't a boy, you weren't ever a nasty little boy!" You gave me my First Black Eye, Mister West, sir, if you care. You threw a stone at me and gave me the pip of a shiner! Mom laughed at me when I came home with the black beacon. She was very wise with me, my Mom, she always laughed off the little, hurtful things that happened to me. So that I wouldn't take misfortune, or myself, too seriously.

But the girls certainly knew how to make my life miserable. Whenever they wanted to tease me, they'd go around yodeling a little ditty they reworded. I can still remember every horrid word of it. It went like this:

"Frances is mad and I am glad,
And I know how to tease her,
A bottle of wine to make her shine,
And Buddy West to squeeze her!"

Ugh, I can get a cactus spine even now, when I think of it! But I got back at you, Mister West, *if* you recall. One day we were having a fire drill in school. I had an all-day sucker in my hand. We got in line and you tried to kiss me and I hit you in the face with the all-day sucker and it *stuck* there! Gosh, did *you* look funny!

I really had my First Heartbreak in Lancaster, too. I had quite a Hard Time there, really, in many ways. The kind of ways that hurt kids something fierce. When the neighborhood mothers heard that I'd been on the stage, that I was a "Theatrical Child," none of the children would play with me. Gee, they were mean to me, awful mean. Like I had a lot of costumes up in the attic, of course, real stage costumes and lots of times, especially Halloween, they'd all come to my house, so sweet, sugar wouldn't melt in their mouths, and they'd borrow costumes from me. And then, when they'd got what they wanted, they'd ditch me, leave me sitting alone in my costume. It almost broke my heart.

I never learned—hopefully I'd take the kids to Dad's theater night after night, for free. I'd buy them all candy and gum, Vera Shrimp, her little sister, Ardis Shrimp, Muggsy Ming, Laurana Blankenship (did you ever hear such names!) and the others—and they'd grab the candy and the tickets and then they'd scuttle in and leave me standing there, alone! Those little SHRIMPS! I'd think, fiercely, and never know how funny it was.

And of course I remember my First Fashion Show. Daddy was putting on a Fashion Show at his theater and Mom made me a frilly costume and fixed up an enormous frilly hat box which was to be carried out on the stage with me in it. I was to come out, all bowing and smiling, but—my "friends" had turned up and they gave me the Bronx Cheer and what I mean is, they put their hearts in it! I started to cry, right then and there. You and the girls were out front, Mom, making signs to me not to mind. But I did mind. And Daddy was *furious*. No one could make me cry when *he* was around. I was such a "Daddy's Girl"—so he just walked down the aisle of the theater and announced that "the rude, young people would please get out of the theater, get their money refunded at the box office from the cashier, and stay out!"

Then there was the time when I was going to the Professional School—Jimmie and I. Frankie Darro was in my class and that mortal boy spent every mortal minute whispering to me. One day the teacher grabbed Frankie by the back of his neck, while holding a croquet mallet in her hand. I piped up, "Atta girl!" and she hit me over the head with the mallet! I don't know what she was doing with a croquet mallet and I don't know why she hit *me* when I was taking up for her! But she did. And Jimmie was furious. She took me home right then and there and I never did go back!

Of course, I had *some* fun in Lancaster—now and then the two Shrimps would come over, or some of the others, and we'd play my favorite game of Kick The Can, in our backyard. I was a tomboy sort of a little girl, I guess. I never much cared how I looked. I was too busy kicking the can and ringing doorbells to care about clothes—we rang doorbells *every* night, whether it was Halloween or not. But just the same, I *do* remember my first Party Dress. Blue chiffon it was, accordion pleated, with little rosebuds just growing all over it!

I believe that when I changed my name, or rather when Mr. George Jessel changed it for me, that was the first real turn of the Wheel of Fortune for me! I believe in numerology. And I believe that the name Judy Garland is right for me—so I date my Beginning As An Actress from my Second Christening. Of course, there were to be a few Grim Detours, but nevertheless, I was On My Way.

Well, it was not so very long after our "financial crisis" at the Biltmore Theater that a theater manager in Chicago offered "The Gumm Sisters" an engagement at the Oriental Theatre in Chicago, with, he said, our names in electric lights! That's what got us, especially me! Applause and electric lights—yummy! Daddy didn't want us to go but after lots of coaxing and teasing he finally consented; the family exchequer yielded new dresses again, and The Gumm Sisters accompanied by their mother set forth to conquer the world!

I remember how I could hardly *wait* to get to Chicago to see our names in electric lights. That's all we talked about, all the way across the country. On opening night we got to the theater an hour and a half before opening time just so we could stand there and GLOAT! What's more, we took a *taxicab,* feeling that no extravagance was too great for this Great Moment. But when we got there, it wasn't "The Gumm Sisters" we saw, winking at us over the marquee, but—"The GLUM SISTERS!" The adjective "glum" was certainly appropriate to our mood for the rest of that evening.

But, once again, my Lucky Star did its stuff—this time it brought me a new, good friend and a new name. George Jessel was playing on the bill with us. George Knew How It Was. He tried to comfort the forlorn, sort of damp little trio that we were. He took me on his knee and told me I was "as pretty as a garland of flowers"—and then I remember how he stopped dead in his verbal tracks, so to speak, and exclaimed "Garland! Garland is a lovely name for you, little one, and they can't kick it around—how about changing your name to Garland?"

I said, "Yes. And Judy, I want Judy for a first name—let's name me Judy Garland!" So that very night, then and there, backstage, "Baby Frances Gumm" became Judy Garland.

We wired Daddy that night. I signed the wire "Judy Garland" and he wired back, "Have you lost your mind?" and I said to Mom, "Wire him back and say 'No, but I've found a name!'"

But the Fates are pretty funny old girls, I guess, and not very quick at doing a right-about-face. It took them quite some time to realize that they shouldn't treat Judy Garland quite so disrespectfully as they had been treating Baby Frances Gumm. The new name on the marquee didn't save us. For when our engagement at the Oriental was over, Chicago just didn't seem to know that we were there. We didn't want to write Daddy for money, having come against his wishes. Just in time we got an offer to appear at the Chicago World's Fair. But when our concession closed, our salary checks were held and, for the first time in our lives, we were penniless! And that was, also, the first time I ever bearded a manager in his den. I guess I wasn't a very good bearder, though, because although I demanded our money in loud, ferocious tones, he just turned on me and said, "Put up and git!"—and he looked so much like a gangster that we "got!"

So then I had my first and, I am happy to say, my only experience of Facing Starvation With A Smile! Mother and the girls were out canvassing the agencies and it was up to me to perform a miracle with the two eggs and the one aged piece of bread, which was all that remained to us of this world's goods. Well, sir, I just scrambled those eggs, to make them go farther, and I dried that bread in the oven, dryer than it *was*, I mean, and when Mom and the girls got back we had a celebration out of *that* little snack on account of how they'd landed us a job and it would mean enough money to get us home!

We got home. Dad didn't say anything. But he had that "Woman's Place Is In The Home" look in his eyes again, and back to school we went. We did do our act occasional weekends. But when audiences in the Valley Theater in Lancaster and the Strand Theatre in Long Beach tittered at our imitations of the Brox Sisters and when a smart-aleck boy in the balcony threw an orange at us one night—well, our weekends were spent at home, too!

I had my First Crush on a boy at about this time. I was getting over being allergic to boys by now. His name was Galen Reid and I think he must have "conditioned" me for my crush on Mr. Gable because he looked sort of like him, in a small way. Anyway, he sent me a Valentine on Valentine's Day. And that was not only my First Attention from A Boy but also it was the *fanciest* valentine of any girl in the school! He later confided to me that he had paid *twenty-five cents* for it and I was simply Overcome. I think it was then that I first began exercise my Feminine Wiles, like washing my hands now and then, you know, and combing my hair, and even putting some very white powder on my nose when Mom wasn't looking. Also, I would let Galen ride me home from school every afternoon on the handlebars of his bike. And as our house was directly across the street from the school, it took a little maneuvering. I always pretended I had turned my ankle or that the street was muddy or something so it wouldn't seem *too* silly.

Well, the next Momentous Occasion in my life was my First Meeting with Mickey! It took place in the corridor of Lawlor's Professional School where, after Suzanne was married and Jimmie was Keeping Company, I was enrolled. Mickey had been sent out into the hall for punishment. So had I. I sort of stuck around, eyeing him—and I saw that he was combing his hair and that he had got the comb stuck in his mop. Always the helpful type, I offered to help him get the comb out, and I nearly scalped him!

Oh, and my First Love Note was from Mickey! He sent it to me in the classroom. It said, "I love you. Do you love me?" I was almost fainting with excitement, with the Drama of It All! And I wanted to make the most dramatic answer possible. Just the night before, it so happened, I had seen the picture, *Silver Dollar*, and I remembered, word for word, the lines the heroine spoke when the hero told her he loved her. So I wrote them down on a piece of paper, made a spitball of it and threw it to Mickey. Then I waited, my pulse in an uproar. Then I saw him look at me, but—*with icy contempt in his eyes!* At the noon hour, he just brushed past me in the hall. "Oh," he sneered, simply *sneered*, "so *you* saw *Silver Dollar*, too, did you!" Well, you may *imagine* what came next!

Judy Garland's new contract, recently filed in Superior Court, shows that Judy will receive $2,000 per week for the next three years, $2500 for the following two years, and $3,000 for the last two years. That gives her a total salary of $680,000 for seven years. —(EDITOR'S NOTE.)

JUDY GARLAND'S GAY LIFE STORY

JUDY GARLAND AS TOLD TO GLADYS HALL | January 1941, *Screenland*

PART 2

Well, as I said in Part 1 of MY LIFE, you may imagine my embarrassment, me answering Mickey's love note, my first love note, too, with words copied right out of a movie heroine's mouth! I guess that was the first time in my life, speaking of firsts, I was ever acutely embarrassed, so embarrassed I wanted to die. And, of course, being young, I thought I would, most any moment. But Mickey is a very understanding boy, as boys go. After about two days, he didn't hold it against me anymore.

As a matter of fact, Mickey was the first boy I ever let kiss me without slapping him down. It was a birthday party kiss, only a kind of a kid kiss, but still—gosh, though, when I remember how we used to talk at Lawlor's Professional School, about how we'd be big stars on the stage someday and about how rich and famous and glamorous we would be—well, that's what's so amazing that we wound up together like this! Anyway, Mickey is my best pal. He always was, even when he teased me, he always will be, even if I do have to listen to him rave about other girls.

Right about now, along comes my first big break! Both my sisters got married, as girls will, and although I worked hard at school, was on the baseball, volleyball and basketball teams, had a lot of friends now, who didn't snoot me, still and all, I was lonely. I missed the girls. I missed the days when we were all in the theater together, so warm and cozy. Daddy sensed the way I felt. So he sent Mother and me to Lake Tahoe for a little vacation. I really do owe my break to Daddy. Because if he hadn't been thoughtful, if he hadn't sent us on that vacation—when I think—!

Well, so one night we were sitting around the campfire and I sang for the bunch. As Fate would have it, a talent scout was among the guests. He told Mother he wanted to take me to the M-G-M studios. He said I should be in the movies. Well, it was just like his words were dynamite. They blasted Mother and me right out of that hotel and onto the train and home. I kept saying, "Oh, he'll forget it—oh, he didn't mean it—oh, they won't want to see *me*!" but between us, in my bones I felt this is IT! It was what you call a premonition. I believe in premonitions.

And why not? For the call came. My first studio call! It just so happened that Mother wasn't home, so Daddy took me to the studio. It was the first time he'd ever done anything in a business way with us girls. He'd always left the bookings and interviews and such to Mother. I'm glad, now, that he did go with me. I like to feel he brought me luck.

Well, we got to the studio and went into the casting office and there they stopped me, dead in my tracks! They said "No Babies Today!" I told them I was Judy Garland (they looked blank). I told them I had been sent for (they let me in).

I sang for half a dozen people. And finally I was sent to Mr. Mayer's office. I sang everything I knew for him, every song I'd ever heard in my life. Like always, you couldn't stop me! When I had exhausted my repertoire, and myself, *and* Mr. Mayer, he asked me if I could sing "Eli, Eli." I said yes, and proceeded to wail my head off. When I got all through, Mr. Mayer didn't say one word, good or bad. He didn't smile or he didn't frown or *anything*. He just said, "Thank you very much," and I walked out. And I thought, another false alarm!

When I got home and told Mom where I had been, she gave one loud, piercing scream, and said, "You *didn't* go to Metro-Goldwyn-Mayer looking like THAT?" I said I did and I think she would have fainted, had she been the fainting kind. But three days later, the phone rang. I was told to come to Metro and sign my contract. I was just thirteen then. And it was the biggest day in our lives. I remember how, that evening, Mom and Daddy and I just stayed at home. We didn't even have one of our usual celebrations. We didn't need ice cream and store cake to make *that* evening a party! We were too happy to celebrate. I'm glad we were like that, that night, just the three of us, alone. For it wasn't to be the three of us, much longer.

Of course I went around in a daze, thinking, What will my first day be like? Will I play love scenes with Clark Gable? Who will I meet? Will everyone realize I'm a movie star? Where will I go first?

Guess where I *did* go first, for Pete's sake? Right *to school*! Much to my rage and disgust *and* amazement (I've always just detested school) that's where I went! It helped a lot to have Mickey there. "Hi, *you* again!" that's the way we greeted each other. And Deanna Durbin was there, Gene Reynolds, Terry Kilburn, quite a few of the kids. But especially, of course, it was fun to be with Mickey again. I remember how, that first day, he took me on a tour of the studio lot.

On our tour we saw Myrna Loy, Joan Crawford, Bob Young—and *Clark Gable*! Mickey practically had to support my tottering footsteps after I saw Mr. Gable. I remember him saying, "Gosh, dames are awful silly!" just because I acted up over Mr. Gable, and who wouldn't?

But to jump ahead a little (I told you I wouldn't be able to write a proper autobiography) my first real beau was Jackie Cooper. My first real crush. The first time I ever counted daisy petals and read poetry and sang sad songs with a "meaningful" look in my eyes was over Jackie Cooper. I had to maneuver ways to get to see him. And I did. Just the way I maneuvered with Galen Rice, when I was *very* young. Like I found out that Jackie was going to a party at Edith Fellows' house. Now, I hadn't seen or talked to Edith for *ages*. But I soon fixed that! I called her on the phone and was just too chummy for words. And I talked and I talked. Every time it looked as though we'd just have to hang up, I'd think of something else I just had to tell her. I talked until I am sure she invited me to her party just to shut me up.

Well, Jackie took me home from the party! It took me all evening to work that, lots of songs and sad eyes and such acting as I have *never* done on the screen! And boy, when he took me out to his car and I saw it was a chauffeur-driven car, did I ever feel like Lady Vere de Vere! Whoops, I thought, this is the life, a boy with a car and a chauffeur. We got home and,

Jackie being a perfect gentleman, he escorted me in. What was my horror to walk into the living room and find my Mother and Dad *down on the floor*, counting the nickels and dimes which were Dad's box-office "take" for the evening! Jackie said, in a whisper, "What do your folks do, run a slot machine?" I was SO mortified.

My first grief came soon after I'd signed my movie contract. It was my Dad's leaving us. Something I never thought could happen, something I know would never have happened, for any lesser reason than Death. He had meningitis. He went away in three days. One of the things that hurts now is knowing that if it had happened to him a little later, he might have been saved. Because now sulfanilamide is a cure for meningitis. But then, there was nothing they could do for him, they didn't know what to do. I had thought I was heartbroken many times before that. Now I knew what heartbreak *really* feels like. It makes you grow up, a thing like that, a loss that's deep and forever.

I did my first broadcast the night Daddy went to the hospital. We didn't know, of course, that he was anything like as ill as he was. It was on KHJ, Big Brother Ken's Program, and I recited "Boots" and sang "Zing! Went the Strings of My Heart."* I didn't have any mic fright at all. I never have any fright, mic or camera or stage. Anything that's entertaining, anything that's *theater* makes me feel right at home.

Well, my first screen appearance, as I am *afraid* some people will recall, was a short called *Every Sunday*, which Deanna and I made together. Deanna sang opera. I sang swing. We both would like to forget that sorry little shortie—but I am putting down all of the first things in my life, I can't skip that, much as I should like to. Then I made my first full-length picture, *Pigskin Parade*. I should also like to have amnesia when I recall *that*! I was loaned to 20th Century Fox for that picture and it was in that I saw myself, for the first time, on the screen. I can't TELL you! I was so disappointed I nearly blubbered out loud. I'd imagined the screen would sort of "magic" me. Well, I never got over it, I hated it so badly! I'd expected to see a Glamour Girl, as I say, and there I was, freckled, fat, with a snub nose, just little old kick-the-can *Baby Gumm!* And I tried so hard, I

---

*This seems to be inaccurate. As previosuly established, Judy performed on the Shell Chateau Hour the night of her father's hospitalization.

acted so forced—ohhh, it was revolting! It didn't help a bit that Mom and the director and lots of people said I was good.

But I get over things pretty quickly. Someone once told me I have a "volatile element" in me, whatever that means. Anyway, I started to work very hard. The studio began "grooming" me, I learned how to walk, how to carry myself better, I got to know the other players on the lot. And I began to work with Mrs. Rose Carter, who was engaged by the studio as my private tutor.

For the first time in my life, schoolwork became a pleasure. For instance, I had never been able to do geometry; it was plain nightmare to me. Well, Mrs. Carter found out how I love art, drawing and all, and she explained that geometry is nothing but a series of drawings worked out in figures instead of colors. I soon discovered I could solve angles, no matter how intricate. Then, thanks to Mrs. Carter, I learned to appreciate Bach, Beethoven, Brahms, Verdi. Now I have a collection of 2,500 records, including the classics and swing. It was Mrs. Carter who put me wise to the fact that modern fiction is pale compared with history. She encouraged me not only to love art but to *do* something about it, to sketch and a print and draw. That first year, on Mother's Day, my gift to Mom was a portrait of Dad that I made from an old tintype.

It's skipping way ahead to tell you about my graduation—anyway, last June, right after I was eighteen, I went into my dressing room (which was also my schoolroom) one day and there was Mrs. Carter, packing away books and portfolios and things, like mad.

"What are you doing, Rose?" I asked.

"Doing!" said Rose. "Why, I'm getting rid of these pesky schoolbooks! Isn't this a sight your eyes have been sore to see? Don't you realize you are through with them forever?"

And then, of all things, I began to cry! If anyone had ever told me I'd cry at the sight of some vanishing schoolbooks I'd have committed them to the loony bin. But I just blubbered, "I'm sorry I'm through and—but— well, if I *have* to be through, I want to graduate with a—with a *class*. I want to be like other girls my age, at my graduation, anyway!"

So, I did graduate with other girls, like other girls. On June 26th, 1940, I was a member of the graduating class of University High School. And I wasn't one speck different from any of the other 249 girls! I wore a plain blue organdy dress, like they all did, and carried a bouquet of sweetheart roses, just like the others. The flowers were provided by the school and I've got one of them pressed in my scrapbook. I almost missed my place in line, too, because Mother sent me a lovely corsage of mystery gardenias and Mickey sent me a cluster of *orchids* and I had to dash into the audience and explain to Mom that I *loved* the corsages but I just *couldn't* wear them. "I can't be different from the other girls, Mom," I said, "Please don't be hurt, but that's the way it is." Mom understood, like always. I wouldn't even let Mickey come to my graduation. I certainly *would* be "different," for Pete's sake, if I'd had Mickey Rooney at my graduation! And I wouldn't have any cameramen there, or anything—and it was all wonderful.

But now I have to go back three years, just a little hop, to the lots of first things that began to happen then. The first time I met Mr. Gable, in particular! Well, the way it happened, I was in Roger Edens's office on day (Roger is a musical coach at the studio, and my instructor) and I begged him to let me sing "Drums in My Heart" which he had arranged for Ethel Merman. He told me I was too young and unsophisticated to sing a song like that. Now, I have a quick, fiery temper and you know how a girl *hates* to be told she is "unsophisticated," not to mention "young," migosh! So I just stormed out of his office and then cooled off, *right* off, like always and came meekly back again. And Roger suggested that we compose a song just for me. He said, "Now, what or whom, would you like to sing about?" And I said, quick like, "Mr. Gable!" And Roger looked as if he was trying not to laugh and so then we made up the song, "Dear Mr. Gable."

Well, it was Mr. Gable's birthday, the first day I met him. Roger took me onto the set of *Parnell*, which Mr. Gable would like to forget but I have to just mention it, and I sang "Dear Mr. Gable" to him—and he cried! Imagine making Clark Gable cry! Imagine being *able* to! And then he came up to me and put his arms around me and he said, "You are the sweetest little girl I ever saw in my life!" And then *I* cried and it was simply heavenly!

Just a few days after this, came my first pieces of real jewelry—my charm bracelet from Mr. Gable. It's all tiny, gold musical instruments, a tiny piano, harp, drums, violin and so on—and the only other charm is a teensy golden book which opens and there is Mr. Gable's picture in it and an inscription which says: "To Judy, from her fan, Clark Gable." As long as I live and no matter how many jewels life may bring me I will always keep that bracelet, along with the little diamond cross my Dad gave me on my last birthday before he died, and my first wristwatch which was from Mother.

My first premiere came along about this time, too. It was *Captains Courageous* and it was at Grauman's Chinese Theatre and I went with Mickey! I wore my first long dress and my first fur coat, a gray squirrel, which I wore for daytimes and evenings, too. When I was seventeen, Mom gave me a ruby fox which I was only allowed to wear on special occasions and when I was eighteen she gave me my wonderful, white fox cape, full length! I got my first car on my seventeenth birthday, too, a *red* job, like I'd dreamed.

But I was talking about my first premiere—Mickey sent me a pikake lei instead of just a commonplace corsage. Pikakes are like small, white orchids, only with a heavenly fragrance, and they grow only in the tropics and Mickey'd had them flown by Clipper from Hawaii!

I suppose I'd call that first premiere my first date, too. And if there is anything more important than a first date in a girl's life, I don't know what it is.

Here's what I think about a first date: first of all, a girl should *act her age*. I mean, if you are fifteen or sixteen, you shouldn't go out looking as though you had just graduated from kindergarten, of course, but neither should you try to look like a Senior at a Glamour Girl School. If you are wearing your first long dress, or even any new dress, I think it's a swell idea to try it on several evenings before your date, just to sort of get acquainted with it. So that you can practice being nonchalant. So you won't fall on your face when you go into a theater or restaurant. And I don't think First-Daters should overdo the makeup stuff, either. I know I just used a little thin powder, just a touch of rouge because the excitement made me look like the ghost of my grandmother. And a very light dash of lipstick. And NO MASCARA! 'Cause if you forget and rub your eyes or laugh until the tears come, your face gets all smudged up. Most of all, on a date, I think a girl should *be herself*. It's a temptation not to be, I know. I've had my moments when I thought I'd try to act like Marlene Dietrich or even Garbo. And then I'd figure that it was my natural self, such as I am, that attracted my date in the beginning, so why take a chance on changing into something *he* might not like as well?

Well, anyway, lots of first things were happening, three years ago, like I said—I played in *Broadway Melody of 1938* and that was the first *real* step forward in my Career. Not to mention that it was then that I first met Robert Taylor!

Then I made *Love Finds Andy Hardy* and I really believe that's my favorite of my pictures. Mickey and I had lots of fun together while we were making that, same as we had fun making *Strike up the Band*—we'd tear down to the beach weekends and "do" the amusement piers, and we'd come home loaded to the gills with Kewpie dolls and Popeyes. Mickey is an expert shot with the rifle and I'm a dead-eye aim with baseballs, so we'd be pretty even-Stephen on prizes.

We had our "crowd" by this time, too—Mickey of course, Jackie Cooper, Bonita Granville, Bob Stack, Rita Quigley, Helen Parrish, Ann Rutherford, Leonard Seuss, most of them were in our gang then and are now—and in the evenings we'd get together at my house or one of the other kid's houses and we'd play records, dance, "feed" on hot chocolate, chili and beans, wienies, brownies, popcorn, Cokes, our favorite items of "light" refreshment!

We had jolly times, we still do—it was mostly all fun and nothing very serious. We'd all sort of date each other, I'd go out with Mickey, with Jackie, later with Bob Stack; the other girls would go out with them, too; there were very few jealousies—we were pretty deadly in earnest about our work—of course, I often thought I was in love—but I used to worship people from afar more than those who were dunking their doughnuts in my hot chocolate. I'd have crushes on people who thought I was a little girl—my doctor, for instance, I was *insane* about him—he's fifty, I think! And every time I'd have a crush, I'd think, this is real love! But in saner moments I know I have never *really* been in love, I always recover too quickly. Columnists and gossip are always trying to make out that I'm serious, about Bob Stack, for instance, or Dan Dailey, or this one or that. But *I'm not, I never have been* and *I don't intend to be,* for quite some time to come!

Now, let's see—dear me, I *hope* I'm getting what serious biographers call "Chronology" into this manuscript! Well, after I was fifteen, first things happened to me so sort of fast and furious, I get *addled*. Anyway, two very important first things come or [sic] in here, I know—I played Dorothy in *The Wizard of Oz* and *that* was a dream I'd dreamed ever since Daddy read the *Oz* stories to me, backstage, when I was just a kid. And just before I stopped being Judy and became Dorothy, I built—my own home! It's sprawling and it's white and it's surrounded by trees and flowers and a tennis court and, this year, we put in a swimming pool which is the rendezvous, every Sunday afternoon, for the crowd. My bedroom is all done in chartreuse and brown and the walls are lined with my favorite books. I have my own dressing room and bath, too.

Well, when I made *The Wizard of Oz* not only did I actually live in the Emerald City, not only did I pinch myself black and blue every day to make sure I was awake, not dreaming, but also Dorothy won me my first Academy Award for a performance by a Juvenile Actress! And Mickey presented me with the golden statue. Mickey and the statue looked like they were swimming, because of the tears in my eyes.

Next I think of *Babes in Arms* and, especially, of the preview which was at Grauman's Chinese and which was the first premiere of one of my pictures that I ever attended. Again with Mickey, naturally. And that was the night I was invited to put my footprints and handprints in the forecourt of the theater. Mickey's were already there and, of course, Clark Gable's, Harold Lloyd's, Shirley Temple's, oh, all the *big* stars'!

I wanted to look glamorous that night, as I had never wanted to before, or since. Well, I bite my fingernails and I felt sick because I couldn't have long, glittering ones like Joan Crawford's. So the manicurist fixed me up with artificial ones. After I placed my hands in the wet cement I went into the theater and after a while I thought a creeping paralysis had set in, beginning with my fingers! They felt all numb and heavy. I was in cold sweat until we left the theater and then I realized some of the cement had got under my nails and *hardened on the false ones!* I went to a party afterwards feeling like Dracula's daughter, with talons! The next day I had to have them *chopped off!* That was my first and last attempt at being glamorous.

After *Babes in Arms* the studio sent Mickey and me to New York on a personal appearance tour. We did six shows a day so, of course, we didn't have much time to sightsee. Mom said 10:30 was curfew and Mickey kept to that schedule, too. But we did manage to spend one evening at the Rainbow Room. We wanted to know how it felt to dance "on top of the world." That trip was the first time I really shopped in New York, too. Boy, did I sweep in and out of Fifth Avenue's finest! It was the first time I bought semi-grown-up clothes.

And that was the time Fred Waring asked me to appear as a guest on his radio program. Of course I accepted, thinking he just wanted me to say "hello." Do you know what he did? He had his entire program dedicated to *me!* And his theme song for the evening was "Over the Rainbow," which happens to be my favorite song. So I sang all the songs from *The Wizard of Oz* for him and a good time was had by all, most especially by me!

Oh, and I must tell about my sixteenth birthday. We had a party at my house and my brother-in-law, Robert Sherwood, brought along his La Maze orchestra. Mickey was the master of ceremonies and we staged an entertainment program of our own. I sang two numbers, and Jackie, Bonita, Ann, Helen, Buddy Pepper, all of them did turns. We had a Ping-Pong tournament, too, and Mr. Rooney walked off with the honors! At midnight we served a buffet supper. I wore a new, white, sharkskin sports dress with flowers appliqued on the pockets. And in my hair I wore the gardenias, which Mickey sent me—oh, and in the midst of the festivities, two blue lovebirds in a blue and white cage were delivered to me. And the card attached read, "Happy Birthday to My Best Girl, Judy—Clark Gable."

But I guess the *most* important first thing that happened in 1938 was that, for the first time, I became an aunt! Jimmie says it's really a little more important that *she* became A Mother than that I became an aunt. I wouldn't know about that. I only know that I always wanted to be an aunt. And that the circumstances of my aunthood befell me under circumstances which were pretty extraordinary! 'Cause *I* was in the hospital, too! It was right after my automobile accident. One bright morning, a few days later, my nurse told me she was going to take me "visiting." She bundled me into a wheelchair and we headed for the "baby floor." There, for the first time, seen under glass, so to speak, I first beheld my first niece, Judy Gayle [*sic*] Sherwood, my namesake as well as my niece! Born in the Cedars of Lebanon Hospital while I'd been recovering from my accident—both of us under the same roof!*

So now, I guess, I'm pretty much up to the Present. I made *Andy Hardy Meets Debutante* and then *Strike Up the Band*. And did we have ourselves a time, Mickey and I, while we were making that. After doing our "Conga" number, talk about being in a lather! Between scenes, Mickey'd mostly play the songs he was writing to me, and I'd make recordings for him and all. I was *just* like the character in the picture, where Mickey was concerned.

And now I'm playing my first grown-up, dramatic character part in *Little Nellie Kelly*. I even *die* in *Nellie*. And—and this is a VERY important first in my life, *I play my first grown-up love scene* in this picture, too! I'm really blushing even as I write about it. I, who have said I was never embarrassed on the stage, in front of a mic or a camera, take it all back now. George Murphy plays my sweetheart (*and* my husband, *I* play a dual role, too!) in the picture. And he was certainly the most perfect choice, for he is so kind and tender and understanding—and humorous, too. But just the same, after we made that love scene, I didn't know what to *do* or where to *look*. I'd just kind of go away between scenes because I *couldn't* look at him. He kept kidding me, too, saying he felt like he was "in Tennessee with my child bride!"

And—well, my goodness, I guess that's about all! I guess a girl hasn't *much* of a Life Story when she's just eighteen because, of course, she hasn't had much life! Although I do think I've had quite a Past and I know I'm old enough so that it's been fun to Remember. And I also know that, at the end of my first eighteen years, as I write "Finis, The End" to my first Life Story, I'd like to say some Thank Yous, quite a lot of Thank Yous—first of all to Mom and Daddy, of course, for all the things they did for me, for everything they were and are to me; and to my sisters for their patience

---

*The story surrounding the birth of niece Judy "Judaline" Gail Sherwood is quite deceiving. Although it is true that little Judaline, daughter of sister Jimmie and first husband, Bobby Sherwood, was born May 28, 1938, just four days after Judy's auto accident, birth records confirm Judaline's arrival occurred in La Porte, Indiana, some two thousand miles from Hollywood.

with me, and the fun we had; and to Mr. Mayer for believing in me; and to Mrs. Carter and Roger Edens and all the directors who have helped me and all the people who have worked with me—and to Mickey, naturally— I don't know what *for*, just for being Mickey, I guess—and to all the magazine and newspaper people who have been so kind to me—and to my fans, who are my friends, and who have made me what I am today— to—well, to just about everyone and everything—yes, to everything and everyone who have made my first eighteen years of being alive so swell, and such fun!

OLD ENOUGH TO KNOW
WHAT SHE WANTS

CAROL CRAIG | June 1941, *Motion Picture*

Though she claims there were no marriage plans in the near future, by the cover date on this issue of *Motion Picture*, Judy was preparing to marry musician David Rose. The two had dated since February 1940, and announced their engagement on May 28, 1941.

Don't class Judy Garland among the kiddies any longer. A big girl—going on 19—she's the same age as Deanna, and old enough to know what she wants. Like getting married.

We know people who are horrified to read in the gossip column that Judy Garland may be a bride before the year's over. The trouble is, they still think of Judy as a little girl in a pinafore and pigtails, singing "Over the Rainbow." They can't realize that she's a big girl now. Though there's a chance that they can after they see her *latest* picture.

She doesn't play a glorified schoolgirl. She plays a glorified showgirl. The title of the picture is *Ziegfeld Girl*—a title that refers to Judy just as much as it refers to Hedy Lamarr and Lana Turner, who are also present. In other words, she's old enough to be convincing as someone who would have caught the eye of the late great Florenz Ziegfeld, a connoisseur in alluring young womanhood. So she must be old enough to get married.

According to her birth certificate, Judy is 18. (An age which many girls become brides. As Anne Shirley, for example, did.) On June 10th,

Judy will be 19. (The age of Deanna Durbin, who, by the time you read this, will be a bride.)

If it seems like only yesterday that Judy was a child, that's because it was less than two years ago that she made *The Wizard of Oz*, in which she sang "Over the Rainbow." But she was 16 even then. She looked 12 only because the M-G-M makeup, hairdressing and wardrobe departments made her over for the role of *Dorothy*.

The makeup, hairdressing and wardrobe departments all contributed to Judy's appearance in *Ziegfeld Girl*. But they didn't have to make her over. We found that out, first thing, when we went out to her house the other day—to check up on those rumored marriage plans and/or whatever else was new in her life.

A year ago, Judy would have rushed into a room, betraying nervous excitement at the prospect of an interview. She would have been wearing a sweater-and-skirt outfit and sports shoes. Her hair would have looked windblown. She would have given the general impression that she was fresh from a high school hockey match.

Now there was a vast difference. She walked into the room. Calmly, gracefully. She was wearing a smartly simple one-piece dress—all black except for some gold embroidery near the neckline. Toeless pumps adorned her feet. Her reddish-blond hair, loosely waved in a long bob, had a freshly-combed look. The general effect suggested a well-groomed college girl. Someone interested in being considered adult, though young.

The effect wasn't that of a child in grown-up garb. She didn't wobble on her high heels. And her dress fitted snugly enough to reveal that she had trim curves —which un-grown-ups don't have.

Yet the effect wasn't that of A Glamour Girl At Home, either. She didn't glitter.

That has always been one of the refreshing things about Judy—she has never looked so much like a movie star as like a normal young girl. Even on the screen. (That's probably one of the secrets of her success.)

The last time we talked with her, a year or so ago, we had asked her how it felt to be halfway through the terrible teens—and she had been eloquent on the subject. So now, hopefully, we asked her how it felt to be grown-up. She gestured vaguely. "I don't feel grown-up," she said, "and I don't feel *not* grown-up. I don't know how to express it. I don't feel so much as if I've changed. It's more a sensation that things around me have changed.

"A year ago, for example, my contract specified certain types of roles for me—and I didn't even dream of having it revised. It seemed like a pretty good contract to me. But one day the Front Office called me in and said they were tearing it up and giving me a new one, because they had 'a little older' roles in mind for me, beginning with *Little Nellie Kelly*. 'You're eighteen now,' they said. So suddenly, my roles started being different— even though *I* didn't feel any different from how I had felt at seventeen or even sixteen.

"And Mother is letting me take over more and more business details. Like keeping my appointments straight, myself, and talking to agents and people myself. I used to depend on her to do everything. Now I feel as if I'm taking a little of the responsibility. Which is a good thing.

"She still takes care of the financial things," Judy continued, "but she's teaching me how, by degrees. Only sometimes I think she must get pretty discouraged. As a business manager, I'm as bad as she is good. I'm not extravagant. I don't throw money away. But I have an awful habit of not writing the amount on the check stub when I write a check. I can't be trusted to know how much I have in the bank." She smiled a self-chiding smile. "Though I can be trusted to drive a car by myself now," she added in self-defense.

Perhaps you have visions of Judy blithely tearing around the country-side in a sporty red roadster with the top down. Kindly disillusion your-self. She drives a sedan, if you please. And not because she can transport more of "the gang" at one time in a sedan, but because she feels safer, driving a heavy car. Which is good proof of Judy's sanity.

She denied having any ideas about taking up flying—which has become the great Hollywood urge. (It has supplanted ranching.) "I don't like flying," she said. "The *thought* of flying frightens me. Any form of trans-portation frightens me. The thought of trusting your life to machinery. It's almost a phobia. Maybe it is a phobia. I can't bear to go in an engine room. All that pounding machinery seems like a bunch of ominous monsters.

"When I'm on a train, I get to thinking about that one man up front, making everything go. What if he went crazy, all of a sudden, and decided to wreck the train —because things were so monotonous? And I've always been afraid of boats. I keep having a recurring dream about a boat.

"Did you ever have the same dream, time after time? This one is *awful*. I'm on the deck of a boat that's being launched, and everybody's standing at attention, and people are cheering and waving flags. A woman breaks a bottle of champagne on the bow of the boat, christening it, and it starts sliding down the ways. Only when it hits the water, it keeps on sliding down. I look around to see what everybody else is doing—and everybody else is still standing at attention, as if nothing is happening. I want to scream and I can't. The water comes over our ankles, then it's up to our waists—finally it's up to our necks. That's when I wake up. At least, so far, I have." She shuddered. "Let's change the subject."

She was willing to confess that she had become clothes-conscious, and that that was another proof that she was beginning to grow up. "Adrian has come into my life," she quipped. (He designed her wardrobe for *Ziegfeld Girl*.) "But I was clothes-conscious before that happened," she said, more seriously. "Though not long before. A year or so ago, I didn't give much thought to what I wore. One thing seemed as good as another, so long as it was decent. I'd wear a sweater and skirt with a fur coat. Then one day I went shopping and I saw a couple of smart things and—I just became conscious of the right ensemble. I guess that happens to every girl, when she reaches a certain age. Usually about the time she finishes school."

Judy finished school last June. "That's a big change in my life," she said, "—not having to combine schoolwork and screen work. Though after about a year's rest from textbooks, I'd like to start taking some college courses in the arts. There are some things I want to know that I can't learn any other way."

Singing lessons, however, still aren't anywhere on the schedule. "I've never had any, and now I'm afraid to take any. They might change my luck. And speaking of being afraid, maybe you think I wasn't scared this last year when I had to have my tonsils out. I was never so frightened in my life. The doctors couldn't guarantee that my voice would be the same afterward. It was more or less a gamble. But I had to have those tonsils out—they were poisoning my whole system. And the operation did change my voice. Only it helped. I can hit lower notes now, and higher notes."

But that hasn't changed her vocal ambitions. She's still swearing allegiance to songs with a hot beat—because they've done all right by her so far. Not because life is simpler, singing hot songs. If anything, it's more complicated.

Judy told us about that "Minnie from Trinidad" number in *Ziegfeld Girl*, by way of illustration. "Busby Berkeley shot two choruses of that number in one long take. I started singing at the top of some steps, and had to walk down them, singing—without looking at the steps—and then, at the bottom, count thirteen, take two steps forward, then turn and weave in and out of lines of people, and reach a certain spot on a certain note, without being able to look down and see if I had hit the mark, then count eight, turn, take a certain number of steps and count five more. And singing all the time. You get galloping hysterics after about eight hours of that."

On days like that, or on any other days, did she ever think she'd like to give it all up? "No, it's in my blood," she said. "I don't want to quit for a long time yet. I mean, I hope it's going to be a long time before I start slipping—because I want to quit just before that happens. And even then I'll probably keep on working on the radio and the stage."

But not nightclubs. It may be news to you, if you've been following the gossip columns, but Judy doesn't like nightclubs. "It's a funny thing," she said. "When I wasn't old enough to go to them, I thought that when I *was* old enough, I'd go every other night. But now that I am old enough, I go about once every three or four weeks. People think I go oftener because, every time I do go to one, it's printed about twenty different times. In most nightclubs, there's nothing to do but sit and talk and drink—and I don't drink and it's hard to talk, because of the noise. Even in the places where there's room to dance, there isn't *enough* room.

"So going to nightclubs seems like an awful waste of time. Unless it's to see some special entertainer or hear some special orchestra. I don't have to leave home to talk with my friends; they're all welcome here. And we have a radio, not to mention a phonograph. If we want to dance, we can dance right here."

Every Sunday, the Garland house is still the meeting place for "the gang"—which has few screen members. Most of them are family friends, friends of her two sisters as well as Judy. And what do they do when they gather? "We relax. If somebody feels like working a jigsaw puzzle, or playing cards, or reading a book, or sitting out in the patio getting a suntan, that's what he's free to do. We play a lot of quiz games and word games. We make up a lot of our own, on the spur of the moment. Like the newest one. I point at you, for example, and fire a question at you, only you aren't supposed to answer; somebody else has to answer, but fast. Then I fire a question at that person, and you have to answer. Another gag is seeing who can make up the saddest story. The last time we had one of those sessions, I made 'em all choke up."

She has taken to writing stories, also, this past year. She recently did a one-act play on the radio that she wrote, herself. And, for Christmas she gave her mother a specially printed volume of poems that she had written over a period of several months. All of which would indicate that Judy has unsuspected depths. A serious mind and an urge for serious self-expression—which she hasn't admitted even to herself, yet.

A year ago, she wasn't so serious minded. A fact made apparent by her being interested in no one boy. Whereas now she admitted, when asked, that she had only one male interest. For the benefit of latecomers, his name is David Rose, and he is a handsome and talented young music arranger.

"We met at a party, and started talking about music," said Judy, "and discovered that we liked the same things. And—well," she added, as if that explained everything, "we just sort of started going together. We have a lot of fun and a lot of mutual interests. And my family likes him, too."

And what about those rumored marriage plans?

"There's nothing definite yet," said Judy, seriously, "—nothing in the near future."

But whether she marries in 1941 or not, it's important to realize that she isn't a child any longer. She's a big girl now. An inch and a half taller than she was a year ago, and immeasurably more grown-up.

"MISTAKES I'LL NEVER MAKE AGAIN!"

JUDY GARLAND AS TOLD TO GLADYS HALL | November 1942, *Silver Screen*

Judy's plan to wed David Rose in September 1941 was quickly abandoned when, over dinner on the evening of July 27, they decided to elope. Accompanied by Judy's mother and stepfather, Will Gilmore, the lovebirds flew to Las Vegas that night and were married by 1:20 AM the next day.

Judy was due on the set of *Babes on Broadway* in a matter of hours when, at 2:00 AM, she wired Arthur Freed via Western Union: "Dear Mr. Freed, I am so very happy. Dave and I were married this AM. Please give me a little time and I will be back and finish the picture with one take on each scene. Love, Judy."

Although filming came to a halt for a day (production notes cite "layoff due to Judy Garland"), Metro would not allow Judy any time whatsoever for a honeymoon. Executives demanded she return to the set immediately. "Even if we don't get a honeymoon right now," the new Mrs. David Rose told reporters, "we're the happiest couple in the world."

Judy Garland, now a top-flight star and happily married young woman, may not have been either, she confesses to Gladys Hall, had she continued making silly, teen-age blunders

I'll pretend I have a grab bag in my hands. I'll fish around in it and bring up, one by one, the mistakes I once made, and try not to make any more. Some of them are the very usual mistakes we all make when we are, er, VERY young. Some of them are kind of pathetic, little boners. One of them was a mistake so serious that it might have meant the end of my career. Another, a mistake so grave that it might have ruined my personal happiness. Others are as funny as the things we read in the comics. Like my first formal dinner party. Hold on, I'll take that one out first!

It was at Jackie Cooper's house, the first formal dinner to which I was invited. There were six of us there. We were all about fourteen. From the elegant conversation going on around the festive board, you would have given us a neat forty. Suddenly I found myself in a predicament. At home, we always had meals served, country style. That is, everything right on the table and the longest arm got the extra ear of corn. So I had never been served, in formal style, from a platter. Being faced with a custom new to me, plus the fact that I am left-handed, really undid me. And as I couldn't make the transfer from the platter to my plate without going into contortions, I only tried once. I managed to make a four-point landing with one tiny drumstick and that is ALL I ate. I tried to look as spiritual as possible, and must have succeeded. For after dinner Jackie said to me, 'You certainly eat like a bird." "Yes," I said, with a wan smile, "I never eat very much."

When I got home, I ate the icebox, plus contents.

Now, I think, I never make the mistake of pretending. About anything, great or small. Now, if I were not sure of how to behave about something, I'd come out with it. "What gives here?" I'd say. Or I would tell a maid, "I'm left-handed. Will you please serve me from the other side?" The mistake of putting on airs causes so much real suffering not only to others, but to one's own self.

One of the mistakes I made at the beginning of my picture work (*I hate the word "career," sounds so pompous*), the serious one I mentioned, was that of wanting to be a star right away. I hadn't the patience of a midge. I wanted success so badly that, after a few months of marking time, as I thought, I asked Mr. Mayer to let me go. I didn't want to stay, I said, if I couldn't be Big right away. Mr. Mayer just looked at me. Then, "I didn't think you had a glass chin, Judy," he said.

I was ashamed, and properly so. I think it was what happened to Deanna Durbin that upset me. I know it was. For when she left M-G-M, she became a star, immediately. She shot right up. And she has stayed up. But it is a mistake to think we can all take the same path to success.

I know, now, that it is a mistake, for most of us, to get success too quickly. I *know* it is better to go slowly and surely, I know it is good for us to get a few knocks on the chin. Which can't be glass, if we are to survive. Now instead of envying the overnight successes, I think of stars like Joan Crawford, Bette Davis, Barbara Stanwyck, who have come up slowly, the hard way, and are still up. They are the ones, not to envy exactly, but to admire and to copy.

I also made the mistake, when 1 was about sixteen, of being antagonistic because everyone treated me like a child. It used to make me very angry. I tried to brush it off with all sorts of ridiculous gestures. Like the time I bought my first fur coat, without my mother to guide me. A ruby fox, it was. Not only did I get a ruby fox coat, but a hat *and* a muff, as well. *And* swept into the studio commissary, *rolling* in fur, and on a very hot day, too. Underneath, I had on a gingham dress. The titters burned me to a crisp. Short, fat people should never wear anything but flat furs. And I was both, short and fat. Youngsters should not wear fur at all, let alone ruby fox. Well, now that I'm married, they still treat me as a little girl. But now I like it. Now it's nice. For when people treat you as a child, they are gentle with you.

Along about the same age, sixteenish, I wanted to outgrow working with Mickey. I thought I could grow faster on my own. Also, I wanted to stop making musicals and go dramatic. I was too young, then, to realize that people like Youth on the screen. I know it now. Especially now, when everything is so terrible, it's kind of fun to see kids on the screen. They're noisy and exciting. They make you kind of forget, for a few minutes, what adults have done to the world—and to the kids.

Anyway, I have no yearning to do Great Dramatic Things now. Just singing gay things are okay by me.

A mistake of which I am very much ashamed comes up now. I am going to tell about it because it may serve to make other youngsters realize more keenly what mothers are, what swell people, what pals—if we give them half a chance.

When I wanted to get married, I thought that my mother would object. I had a regular complex about it. I was positive that she would put her foot down and that would be that, I couldn't get married. I thought everyone would oppose me but, of course, what your mother thinks matters most.

I didn't even dare tell her I was in love. When, at last, on a train coming back from New York, I mustered up courage and blurted out, "I'm in love!" she said, continuing her game of solitaire without missing a card, "I know. Why didn't you tell me sooner?" Then she added, pleasantly, "When do you want to announce your engagement?" "On my birthday," I bleated. "All right, who'll we have?" she said. "Let's make a list. And I think a garden party would be nice."

Even after that, when we made up our minds, while having dinner at Romanoff's one night, that we wanted to be married, then and there, that night, I was afraid to tell her. I wouldn't have run away without mother. Of course I wouldn't have done that. So, scared to death, we went home to break the news. Mother took one look at me and, before I had time to open my mouth, said, "Oh, my gosh, all right—let's go. I only wish you could have thought of this yesterday. I've just come back from Las Vegas. And it's a long drive."

I never again made the mistake of keeping anything from my mother, and never will. Not that I could, even if I wanted to. I learned *that.*

One mistake I never have made, by the way, is that of underestimating the good sense and intelligence of the fans. When I was warned that the fans would resent my marriage, that it might hurt me on the screen, I didn't believe it. And I was right. I didn't have one single letter that wasn't congratulatory and sweet and swell. After all, we're all *human.*

Of course, at fifteen, I made the common mistake of wanting to be sooo beautiful and exotic. I cried myself to sleep after I first saw myself on the screen, in *Pigskin Parade.* I thought so much depended on being beautiful. I used to sit for hours trying to make my nose go down and stay down. Every time I pressed it down, it flew up, higher than ever. I'd soak my face in buttermilk, nearly drowned in it, trying to get rid of my freckles. I dieted like crazy. Which *is* a mistake for girls in their early teens, as I found out. For when I was about seventeen or eighteen all my fat came off, just like that. It was baby fat and would have evaporated in the natural course of my growth, without all that fasting on my part.*

---

*By this time, Judy was well established in several serious habits that would haunt her for the rest of her life. She was only four feet eleven inches inches tall, and M-G-M expected her to maintain a camera-slim ninety-five pounds. Studio doctors prescribed their "miracle drug" of choice, Benzedrine, to assist Judy in keeping her energy up and weight down. She was then given barbiturates to counteract the "pep" and induce sleep.

Now I don't think that looks mean so much. I just try to look as well as I can and let it go at that. It's what's behind the face that puts you where you want to be, and keeps you there.

I used to overact an awful lot, of course. I thought that in order to get across on the screen you had to punch all the time. I gave out with all the overworked expressions. My voice was pitched too high and too loud, I screamed and gestured and mugged. Then I'd see the results and feel so discouraged I just didn't want to make pictures anymore. That's how I learned. For when I'd see rushes that were plain revolting I'd go into my next scene sort of limp and relaxed and so—what and lo, they'd turn out pretty good!

I know it's a mistake to try too hard about anything. A mistake to feel that what you are doing is THE most important thing in the world. I think very few of us make this mistake nowadays, though. For none of us can read the newspapers and really believe that what WE are doing belongs in the headlines.

I don't mean that we should be lax about what we do, or lazy. Heavens, no. But I do say that if we think, "Well, if it's good, it's good and if it's bad, it's bad—but there is always something else ahead," it will *be* good.

The next little prize package to come out of the grab bag is—our house. For the house we bought, though beautiful, was certainly a mistake. It was MY mistake, too, not Dave's. He knew that it was too big for just two people. But I took one look at it and felt that I could really be the Lady of the House. Now we are trying to sell it or rent it and when we do, we'll rent a small place in Westwood.

I really have an aversion to anything false. I believe I can honestly say that I never did make the mistake called "Going Hollywood"—unless it was that great big *house*.

As the Lady of which, by the way, I have made a couple of social errors that were dillies. For one horrible example: One night, not long ago, I got home from the studio, very tired. I removed my makeup. I slipped into a robe. Dave and I had dinner in the living room, in front of the fire. Just as we had finished, the doorbell rang and I heard voices in the hall. The voices of two very famous stars here in Hollywood. *Voices belonging to guests I had invited to dinner that night!* Colder than Juliet in her shroud,

I greeted them as they were ushered into the living room. I had *just* got home from the studio, I said, I hadn't had time to change, but would do so at once if they would please excuse me for ten minutes meanwhile, if they'd just make themselves at home . . . dinner would be a little late, so sorry . . . still chattering, I dove up the front stairs, then down the back stairs and told the cook she would HAVE to get a dinner on the table, yes, another dinner, any kind of a dinner, the best dinner she could whip together, but a *dinner*.

Half an hour later, we were all at table. And Dave and I had to eat all over again. Thanks to a slight social error on my part: that of not keeping track of my engagements.

Lack of responsibility about small things, but not so small when they rise up and bite you, has always been a fault of mine; has been responsible for many of my mistakes. I never carry any money with me, for example. With the result that, when I have the need for some, I just write off checks and then forget about them. When I was first married, I thought I could take care of everything, my work, my household, all of it. Before I knew it, there were piles of bills on my desk, mounting to the ceiling, with the little inscription, "Please Remit," on most of them. Mother came in one day, took one look at the tower of Please Remits and took over for me, as she had done before I married. And so the mistake of thinking I could do everything was corrected.

Most of my mistakes, by the way, seem to hover around dinner tables. They really are my undoing. I just thought of another horrible occasion, which occurred around the same time as Jackie Cooper's party. I was dining out in the home of people I didn't know very well. Just before dessert was served, I moved my finger bowl from its plate, but left the doily *on* the plate. When the chocolate soufflé was passed to me, I deposited my helping on the doily and proceeded to eat it, doily and all. When I realized what I was doing (*and that was with the first mouthful!*) there was no going back. I *couldn't* leave a half-eaten doily on the plate for servants to see. So I finished it. So help me.

Oh, and there were the little slips o' the tongue I made when I went on a tour of the camps. I was the first of the picture people to make such a tour and I didn't know what the insignia meant. So I called a colonel a corporal, a brigadier-general, a lieutenant, and so on. At Camp [Wolters] in [Texas], I pulled several of these boners, which certainly got me the laughs when I least expected them. After I got home, the boys sent me a whole chart with all the insignia and what they mean. I have it hanging in our dining room at home. I'm living and learning, General!

I'm afraid I've always made the mistake of being rather a skimmer. When I could get by, on the surface, I never bothered much about building the foundation. I never took singing or piano lessons, you know. I've seldom had occasion to play the piano and I got by with the voice on the stage, on the air, in pictures. That was good enough. Now, Dave is teaching me piano. He has showed me my mistake in not being familiar with the fundamentals of what I do. It's like the difference between walking on quicksand or on solid earth.

At one time, when I was a mere sixteen or so, I think I wanted to be rich more than anything in the world. And for the obvious reasons. So I could buy lots of swish clothes and jewelry and streamlined cars and things. Well, I've never had time to buy lots of clothes. My engagement ring and wedding ring comprise my "collection" of jewels. I have a good car, but people don't stop and stare as I drive by. And it *really* doesn't matter anymore. Not that I'm the "spiritual" type now, any more than I was when I starved myself at Jackie's dinner party. But I do know, now, that being happily married, being *happy*, is what I want more than anything in the world. Having money makes it all nicer, yes, but it's not necessary. For if you can't be happy without money, you haven't got the Bluebird by the tail, anyway.

I think, summing it all up, that my worst mistake, when young, was in being too tense about everything, too emotional, too "Oh-This-Is-The-End!"

I laugh, now, when I remember how I went on about some of my adolescent romances: Each was the Great Love, of course, desperate and dark. One boy in particular. I'll call him James because that was not his name. Well, I just thought that James and I, oh, my! One evening we had a date. James did not appear. The next morning, at breakfast, I said to my mother, "Strange, James didn't show up last night. Guess he was busy."

"I'll say he was," said mother—and handed me the morning paper—James had eloped with another girl!*

Well, of course I just dramatized myself all over the place about that. I had a broadcast to do that night and I drooped over the microphone like a wilting lily. Dave called for me after the show. We were Just Friends, Dave and I, or so I thought. I'd always tell him all my troubles and problems with my various crushes. I'd call him at any time of day or night to ask his advice about the most personal matters. He smiled when, on this occasion, he beheld my woebegone expression, took me out and bought me the most sensational piece of apple pie á la mode. Almost at once, I recuperated. I was rather disgusted with myself when I realized that nothing had ever happened to me that a good piece of apple pie couldn't cure!

And right then and there, I learned to correct another mistake, or mistaken idea of mine—that love, in order to be love; must be feverish and fatal and uncomfortable and wildly emotional. If I had not corrected that mistake—well, I might have mistaken the face of love, real love; when I saw it.

---

*An early draft (dated 8/20/42) of this "as told to" Gladys Hall piece for *Silver Screen* confirms that James was, of course, none other than Artie Shaw.

LONELY GIRL: A STORY BY JUDY GARLAND

JUDY GARLAND | November 1943, *Photoplay*

On December 7, 1941, Judy Garland and husband, David Rose, were at Fort Ord, near Monterey, California, for a live broadcast of the *Chase and Sanborn Hour* when news arrived of the Japanese attack on Pearl Harbor. The broadcast went on as scheduled, but with frequent interruptions for special news bulletins.

Answering the War Department's call to help boost morale in army camps around the country, Judy took her place as one of the first entertainers to sing for troops during World War II. Just weeks after Pearl Harbor, she and Rose left on a USO tour of the Midwest. Rose served as her accompanist during the demanding month of singing a program of twelve songs for three or four shows a day. By the time the travelers reached Camp Wolters in Mineral Wells, Texas, their fifth and final stop, Judy collapsed with a severe case of strep throat.

Back home in Los Angeles, Judy remained patriotic and continued to assist in the war effort by entertaining on numerous radio shows and at the Hollywood Canteen. She went back out on her own army camp circuit during the summer of 1943 and was soon invited by the Hollywood Victory Committee to join its Hollywood Bond Cavalcade, a sixteen-city tour that left Washington, DC, on September 8. The all-star troupe included Fred Astaire, Lucille Ball, James Cagney, Kathryn Grayson, Betty Hutton, Harpo Marx, and Mickey Rooney. In three weeks they traveled more than ten thousand miles, sang for more than seven million people, and raised $1,709,586,819 in war bonds as part of the Third War Loan drive.

It is likely that this hypothetical diary of sorts, published in *Photoplay,* dates to Judy's second USO camp tour in July and early August of 1943. Here she told the story of an all-too-familiar singer-actress she called "Joan." The referenced "Earl" was composer/lyricist Earl Brent, her accompanist that summer.

You may very likely guess who the girl in this story is—and you may be right. But more important than her identity is the understanding that came to her heart.

This is a true story about a real girl, whom I choose not to identify. So I shall just put down her story for you. Perhaps, though, you will recognize her . . .

"Try it again, Joan," Earl said, "and this time don't look gloomier than the song itself. Do you want the soldiers to commit mass suicide after hearing it?"

He played the introduction again to "Don't Get Around Much Anymore." Joan, who'd been stalking the hotel room rug as if it were a jungle trail, stopped beside the piano and began singing again. It was the twelfth popular song she had memorized in two days, closeted here in this strange New York hotel room—because, as Earl had pointed out, maybe the soldiers would ask for songs that she hadn't sung in her pictures.

Across the room she could see her mother sitting, knitting busily, but with a worried expression on her face—as worried as that of her pianist as he bent frowning over the keyboard.

She knew it was ridiculous to them that she felt so hopelessly depressed—but she'd been in this mood for weeks now. It had continued all the way across the continent from Hollywood, and it had lasted right through these packed two days of song rehearsing.

While she sang, she argued with herself about it. Why should she feel lost and hopelessly sad? At twenty-one, she was a famous movie star who thoroughly enjoyed making musical pictures. She was young, successful, surrounded by friends . . . and yet she felt as if life had no aim for her, that there was no one person who needed her and whom she needed. She was deeply lonely . . . and, though she knew loneliness was a disease, striking millions of other women in America right now, company didn't ease her misery. She certainly had—what would you call it?—the wartime blues.

The worst of it was, she couldn't shake them. They were still with her the next morning at eleven, when she mounted the rough wooden steps to a platform—in front of a murmuring, whistling, rustling mob of ten thousand uniformed men.

Earl sat at the piano, waiting for her. The heat was so oppressive that her powder had melted off her face on the way from her impromptu board dressing room, and now as she climbed the steps she shook out again the damp wrinkles of her gray jersey dress—a sixty-mile automobile ride in a temperature of 100 hadn't improved its lines.

Then she was standing there looking down at the suddenly quiet sea of faces above the half-mile mass of khaki—and she pushed her depression away by sheer force. Smiling, she stepped up to the microphone.

"I didn't come here to tell you how to fight the war," she said, and her light voice went out clearly into the great silence of the men. "All I know is that you *will* fight the war, and you will win it—and I and a hundred and thirty million other people will be forever indebted to you. So I came to give you a down payment on our indebtedness, with a piano and some songs. What would you like to hear?" A few hardy souls yelled song titles toward her, and then with a roar like the ocean surf, they were all shouting together.

Out of the turbulence she picked the five songs they called the most loudly for—and she was to sing those same five songs for thousands of other boys in a dozen other camps in the next crowded three weeks, for they were the favorite songs of Uncle Sam's Army. Three of them were from her pictures, and she sang them easily: "You Made Me Love You," "For Me and My Gal" and "Over the Rainbow." The other two she had learned only yesterday, in that hotel room—"Don't Get Around Much Anymore" and "Let's Get Lost."

After she had sung those five, she sang seven more—twelve altogether. She'd borrowed Earl's handkerchief after the second song and frankly mopped off her face with it, and she continued to mop while she sang in the suffocating heat.

When she finally came down the stairs again, hundreds of soldiers surged around her, waving pencils and autograph books, grabbing at the pink bows in her hair—snatching them off, shredding them, clutching at the tiny pieces for souvenirs. She stood there, dripping perspiration, signing and signing again for a good half hour . . . and then she was back in the car with Earl and her mother, driving miles across the enormous encampment to another platform, with another ten thousand soldiers already waiting to hear her songs.

She was to sing five times that day, to five gigantic, eager impatient audiences . . . singing good-bye to them, really, for this was an embarkation point, this camp, and so were all of the others scheduled for her tour.

But even though she shoved back that feeling of lost sadness while she sang—it was still there, waiting to take possession of her again the minute she was alone. The world seemed *so* overpoweringly sad—10,000 sadnesses after 10,000 sadnesses. And what could you do about it really. Don't kid yourself, Joan. You just aren't in this thing and you know it.

Technically for Joan, the tour went on. Five times a day she sang to enormous sprawling soldier audiences traveling in blisteringly hot trains from one camp to another. She learned that paratroopers always yell from emotional pressure as they leap from a plane—hoarse shouts of "Geronimo!" as they drop into space. She learned that soldiers always sing with unnatural loudness as they march down to their overseas boats—mainly the songs of the last war, like "Over There," and "I Want a Girl (Just Like the Girl That Married Dear Old Dad)," and "K-K-K-Katy!"

And she kept traveling. Once she was in three different states in one day, singing. Sometimes she lived right on the embarkation post with the soldiers—in old-fashioned little board houses, with ancient wind-it-yourself phonographs stocked with aged records. Night and day sentries marched in circles around her twenty-four-hour home, gun on shoulder . . . "Protecting me from either the Jap soldiers—or the American soldiers!" Joan laughed to her mother. "I'm sure I don't know which!"

She was touched by some of the things that happened to her—like the special love song written to her by one soldier and sung to her on an officers' club balcony like a G. I. Romeo and Juliet scene. And the time she went into an enlisted men's club and found a sign saying, "Welcome, Joan!" written in delicate paper flowers that a tough battalion had spent two weeks making by hand. And the time she ran into Clarence Stroud, now an Army pilot—whom she'd last seen eight years before in vaudeville.

There was another part of her camp activities—a part which was soon to play a vital role in Joan's life. At every camp she sang to an audience of patients in the recreation hall of the hospital provided by the Red Cross and with gentle "Gray Ladies," as the boys call the Red Cross nurses, visited six or seven wards, going to each bedside and talking to each man.

It was Joe who provided the vital link. Joe was just a sheeted bundle on the nineteenth bed from the door when she first saw him from the threshold of the ward. She worked her way down to him, going from bed to bed, holding each patient's hand, looking at each boy's ever-present snapshot of his sweetheart or his wife, speaking to each one of his hometown. And then she was holding Joe's hand—a calloused young hand with short, work-stained nails. Joe's young face went with that hand; and it was topped by a wide white bandage that matched the white wrapping around one leg hoisted in the air on a pulley.

It was Joe's simplicity that got her. Mostly the boys were too engrossed with the aura of being visited by a movie star to talk much about themselves in these short visits. But Joe was different.

Searching for a way of opening the conversation, Joan commented on the snapshot of a pretty, dark girl in a sweater and skirt on his bedstand. "Is that your girl, Joe? Does she know you're in the hospital?"

"Naw," he said in his Brooklyn voice. "But she won't care when she does know, 'cause she'll know I'll be well again—and I'm on'y in this war for her."

"For her?" said Joan, surprised.

"To protec' her," Joe explained, equally surprised that she didn't know that. "And my mother, too. We guys gotta fight so our women can be safe—but, gosh, you know that without me tellin' you."

"Oh," said Joan, and she sat down. Soon Joe was telling her all his plans—how he'd saved two thousand dollars while he worked as a riveter in a factory before the war and he'd signed over all his savings jointly to his girl and his mother —in case anything happened to him. How he'd reluctantly sold his adored car—"A real zooty car, with three searchlights and white skirts on the back fenders—printed with Ella's name," he finished, sighing. And how he was sending home everything he made except six dollars a month, which was for beers and occasional movies.

"Ella's savin' it all, for our marriage when I git back from overseas," he said then. "She's a swell girl, a good cook and thrifty. We'll have a house then, and lotsa kids." He blushed then, and said, "I hope."

Then suddenly he said reverently, "I gotta thank the Army for alla this, really. You see, I was kinda wild, just a wild kid until it come along. I joined the Army—and it got me to thinkin'. Fella's gotta have something to hook onto times like these. So first chance I got I asked Ella to marry me and I put those savin's in her name and my mother's, which I'd really been savin' for a bumming trip around the world. Now I'm goin' around the world with Uncle Sam, looks like; and I got an aim in life—Ella, and a home. And I—well, I'm a different guy now and I got the Army to thank for it. I'm thinkin' of staying right in it when we've beat those Germans and Japs, long's I live. It's give me everything." Then he added, "Believe me, I'm grateful."

And that was about it. Maybe it doesn't sound like much to you— just another soldier's ideas on living. But as Joan walked away from his bedside, she was thinking of Joe and his gratitude—and his clear-cut version of why they were fighting, and planning, and living for freedom and the right to a home and wife and children. In some strange way it seemed to include her. And Joe was the voice of ten million soldiers—Joe *was* ten million soldiers. Out of his loneliness and need in the Army he had become a man, with a man's philosophy and aim—and somehow he seemed to have given it to her. Why could not she too keep on plugging until she found the basic things she needed?

Thoughtfully she left the hospital and headed across the parade grounds for her rough boxlike dressing room. A milling crowd of khaki had already gathered outside. "We want Joan!" they were howling. "Where's your auto-graph, Joanie?" "Kiss the boys good-bye, Joan, like a good girl!" They were all kidding, boisterous, noisy—until suddenly the thin sound of music came over their shouts. It was faint and distant, but the boys instantly fell into deathly stillness. Lifting her head, Joan could hear plainly the strains of a Negro spiritual, high and sweet in the throbbing dusk. The backs of the soldiers were turned to her now as they silently watched a nearby road. She looked, too, with something prickling along her spine.

For there, swinging along in march time with full packs and ammunition were two thousand Negro soldiers—marching to the docks to board a boat for overseas. And as they marched they sang. The sergeants sang the verses, and two thousand rich, strong voices came in on the choruses—"Swing low, sweet chariot," they sang, "comin' for to carry me home!" Sweet and full came the song to Joan—and long after the two thousand marching black men had passed, with their song growing fainter and fainter in the distance—long after that came the rattle and clank of armored cars, tanks, guns, following them to the docks.

Her first sight of men actually going forth to battle lines. . . . This was it, she thought; this swelling, unbearable lump in her heart that must come forth or she would burst. Now at last she knew what she would do if they would let her. She would sing as those men had sung—not to soldiers in a distant, safe camp where she, too, was safe and distant, but to men riding to battle; shoulder to shoulder with them on the boats carrying them through the enemy-infested seas.

This was Joan, truly come to life!

And that's the story I've written for you. I hope you'll understand the things I've tried to explain, and I hope most of all you'll understand Joan, who is really happy now, I know. And she owes it all to a million men in uniform—and to one private in particular, named Joe!

THIS IS MYSELF

JUDY GARLAND | December 1943, *Movieland*

A cover story for *Movieland*, the following is a "fill-in-the-blank" style interest inventory that allowed Judy to touch on some of her likes and dislikes not often addressed in other features.

I USED TO:

. . . Work in small-time vaudeville theaters.

. . . Be called the leather-lunged blues singer, I'm ashamed to say; the little girl with the big voice.

. . . Dream that I was singing with a symphony orchestra—I felt as if I were still dreaming when at last it came true and I stood up to sing with Andre Kostelanetz.

I REMEMBER:

. . . Getting in the way of a forward-passed cheese sandwich one night when I was singing in a small-time vaudeville house and how furious I was; all I could say, over and over, was "Someday!"

. . . My Christmas dinner when I was ten. I was singing at Warner's Hollywood theater and couldn't have dinner at home. Mother promised she'd let me choose where I would eat and what I'd have. I went to a drugstore and ordered hot tamales.

. . . The white party dress I wore to the Academy dinner when I won my Oscar.

. . . Wearing that dress again when I was footprinted at Grauman's Chinese Theatre, and how Mickey Rooney held it up out of the cement for me.

MY FIRST:

. . . Appearances were made in our backyard shows where my sisters and I charged ten straight pins a show.

. . . Poem was composed when I was four and heard my sisters making up verse. I went in for rhythm not rhyme and the result was: *Bookie, Bookie, I saw a star. Money, money, salt, salt, salt.*

. . . Car was a Lincoln Zephyr convertible, a present on my sixteenth birthday, and I loved it, but I wasn't big enough to see what was behind me when I backed up, so after four months I was persuaded to give it up.

. . . Friend was Betty Jane Graham, who is still my closest girlfriend. We were four years old and met when we tried out for a part at Universal Studios. Betty Jane thought I would get the part, and I thought she would, so we brushed each other off. But when Cora Sue Collins got it, we fell into each other's arms.*

I LIKE:

. . . Bonfires on the beach. . . Baby chicks . . . Walking in the rain . . . Anything chocolate . . . Men who know how to handle head waiters . . . Christmas Eve.

I DISLIKE:

. . . Dull pencils . . . That put-on Southern accent . . . Salted peanuts . . . Getting telephone connections . . . Attending to details . . . Mayonnaise . . . Popcorn.

I'M GUILTY OF:

. . . Losing my keys . . . Eating too many chocolates . . . Forgetting appointments or being late.

. . . I've never worn a watch because I'd rather not know what time it is.

. . . And I'm the worst backseat driver in the world.

---

*The Universal film was *The Unexpected Father* (1932), and Judy was certainly older than four years old. It's likely that she was nine or ten at the time of the audition, and Betty Jane Graham was a year her junior.

I HATE TO:

... Have my nails filed ... Go home when the party's getting good ... Wait for people who said they'd positively be on time ... Hear a baby cry and nobody do anything about it ... Grow lovely long fingernails and then have one break off ... Get up early.

I LOVE TO:

... Cook, but I hate to clean up afterwards ... Make over hats and remodel clothes ... Play tennis, Guggenheim, Ghost ... Keep the radio going or records playing whenever I'm in the house ... Spoil my sister's baby—but I never do!

I'VE LEARNED:

... From my mother—practically all I know, including singing, playing the piano, cooking, and managing a house.

... From my sisters—How to get along with other girls, not to acquire a star complex.

... From Mickey Rooney—Anything I know about screen technique. The first day we worked together on a picture he said, "Let's promise each other never to work at each other but always with each other!" and we always have. He's given me plenty of good advice, including, "Don't worry!" But I'm still the world's champion worrier.*

... From Roger Edens (Who does all my musical arrangements) the songs that are best for me. When I was a child in vaudeville, my favorite numbers were tunes like "Stormy Weather," which I sang wrapped in a black shawl, sitting on a piano on a dark stage, only my face spotlighted. At the song's conclusion, I threw off the shawl and the lights came on. I then did my six-year-old curtsy. I wanted to do "Drums of My Heart" for my first screen song, but Roger said no. Simple songs were best for children. He wrote "Dear Mr. Gable" for me; he was right. The people liked it, and it started me on my real screen career.

---

*The picture was 1938's *Love Finds Andy Hardy*, their second film together. "Watching the rushes," Judy later recalled, "I saw that my scenes were more sincere and believable. I've kept that thought in mind ever since. But not until I played in that picture did I commence to enjoy myself and feel that I was beginning to find myself. . . . I learned from Mickey Rooney to be a natural, to be myself before the camera."

I'M LEFT-HANDED:

. . . When I write, my hand smudges the ink as I cross the page. I've discovered that putting talcum powder on my hand will permit it to ride along without smudging. Southpaws, attention!

I'M FOND OF:

. . . Penny candy . . . John Frederics cologne . . . Novelty jewelry . . . Good Humor ice cream . . . Biographies . . . Surprises . . . A Tuesday special (a hug and a kiss from my little niece).

I WONDER:

. . . Where all my best answers go when I wish I could think of them . . . Who invents those frightful lipsticks some girls wear . . . Why weeds grow so much larger than anything else in a victory garden . . . If hair that's flat on the top of the head will really come back soon . . . And when the war will end.

WHEN I WENT TO SCHOOL:

. . . At Lawlor's Professional School for children, twelve years ago, my schoolmates were Mickey Rooney, Anne Shirley (then Dawn O'Day), Jackie Cooper, Frankie Darro, Diana Lewis; they all made good, and we're all still friends. . . . I was always so busy trying to get out of studying that I never really learned anything.

I THINK IT'S FUN:

. . . To wash my own hair . . . Dust furniture that gleams after you dust it . . . Go into a shop and buy what I want without tiresome delays . . . To cry at movies and eat candy while I cry.

MY NICKNAME:

. . . "Judaline" was given me by Director Victor Fleming in *The Wizard of Oz*, but only my family uses it. My sister, Jimmie's baby, Judy Gail Sherwood, is also nicknamed "Judaline."

MY BIGGEST THRILL:

. . . Was my twenty-first birthday party last June. My sister, Jimmie, Danny Kaye, Keenan Wynn, Dore Schary, and Betty Asher surprised me by making records of a script they'd written called *The Life of Judy Garland*. It began with my first cry, which Danny Kaye gave to the tune of "Over the Rainbow" and continued in a kidding vein to tell what had happened to me in twenty-one years. It was terribly funny, but it ended with a serious little speech given by Keenan so beautiful that I cried—I was so touched and so happy.

MY SPECIAL HEROINE:

. . . Is [First Lady of the Republic of China] Madame Chiang Kai-shek.

MY FAVORITE FICTION CHAR.:

. . . Is [Rose Franken's] Claudia. And I want a little farm in Connecticut like the one she had, and a little house exactly like hers.

MY SECRET AMBITION:

. . . Is to write fiction. I've written a book of verse, and I love to write stories. I don't believe I'd care for literature as a living because I can't write unless I'm in the mood. But when I am in the mood, I can write for hours.

I'D LOVE TO:

. . . Do a big musical show on the New York stage.

I ADORE:

. . . Richard Tauber's recording of "Vienna, City of Dreams." I wish I could have seen Vienna as it was in his time. I'd like to have been part of that life where all women were glamorous, all men romantic, everything was exciting, and no one was ever dull or lonely or sad.

JUDY GEM

On Growing Up

"I wanted to stay like Dorothy in *The Wizard of Oz*. Life wasn't as complicated then. But I can't help growing up. No one can. Time won't stop and life won't stand still. But I have a feeling that if I just look backward once in a while at Dorothy, if I am off beat in any way, I'll get back on the sound track again. . . . Dorothy and I thought a lot alike when I made *The Wizard of Oz*. I like to think we still do."

—Unknown publication, April 1944

JUDY GEM

On Breakup with David Rose

"Marriage is important. If people break up, there should be solid reasons why they can't go on. Ours were personality reasons. Our personalities were so conflicting that we could hardly agree on one point. And yet we wanted to please the other so badly that these differences never came out into the open. . . . We really had too much respect for each other, too MUCH consideration for the feelings of the other. I would seem to agree with him because I didn't want to hurt him. He did the same thing. We tried hard to change, not the other person, but OURSELVES. We tried to make ourselves over from inside out, but you can't do that. You can't change the *real you*. You can only pretend to. So—there was a constant heaviness in the air."

—Unknown publication, April 1944

A VISIT WITH JUDY . . .

LILA STUART | **March 1945, *Screen Stars***

This interview was conducted on the set of *The Clock*, Judy's first straight dramatic role. She and costar Robert Walker began work on production during the summer of 1944 and continued through the fall.

A delightful chat with your favorite—Miss Judy Garland . . .

It was time to interview that veteran of ten years in pictures and twenty years in show business. Here was a trouper who should definitely have a story to tell. And she did!

Twenty-two-year-old Judy Garland was sitting in her pretty portable dressing room on the set. The decor is aqua and rose. Choo-Choo, Judy's pet miniature poodle, was happily settled in her lap when we arrived. She was between scenes of *The Clock*, her new picture at Metro.

Judy was very much the picture of "all's right with the world." And it very definitely is—with Judy's world. She is playing her first straight dramatic role. She's in love with the script written by the poet and novelist, Robert Nathan. She's going to move back home with her family and that's the best part of it all.

It started, Judy's return to the home hearth, when she had the flu. It was shortly before the start of *The Clock*. Judy's flu made her downright miserable. Mrs. Garland took her straight home. Sister Jimmie was home with an impacted wisdom tooth. Judy and Jimmie were tucked into twin beds, and Mrs. Garland babied them and nursed them back to health, just as she used to do when all of her girls were at home. Judy loved it.

"I really haven't been happy living alone," Judy confessed, her brown eyes wide, earnest, thoughtful. "The last few months I've felt restless—kind of lost. Then the flu came along and the answer to all my problems. I wanted to be home again. Mother recently found a house large enough for us all. You see, there's Mother, my grandmother, my sister Jimmie and my little niece, Judy. I guess I'm used to family life. It isn't much fun coming home after a long working day, to an empty house. Now it isn't going to be that way anymore. I'm going to be part of the family again.

"When I moved from my big home in Bel Air" (Judy's and Dave Rose's), Judy continued, "I took a tiny apartment. I didn't like to stay alone at night, and there was no room for a maid. Mother's place then was too small, so I was house hunting again. I moved into Mary Martin's house in Westwood. Mary was in New York for *One Touch of Venus* and she decided to sell her house. There was another moving day to experience.

"A doctor acquaintance went into the Navy, and I leased his house for six months. Then Mother found her perfectly wonderful house, and I have been wanting to move in with her—longer than I had realized. It was the most wonderful thing to go home—and be home again."

That talk about Judy being ill and thin and unhappy seemed grossly exaggerated. True, Judy is slim, happily so!

"I feel wonderful. I never felt better. I just lost my baby fat," she smiled. "Everyone began saying, 'Judy, how are you?' with anxious voices. I'd say, 'I am feeling wonderful.' Then aware of their concern, I found myself actually wondering, 'How am I?' I would like everyone to know that I am healthy and happy.

"Happy and quite concerned," Judy added. "This is my first straight dramatic role. No singing. And while I am terribly thrilled, I am also a little nervous about it. What if the audiences keep waiting for me to sing? I told Bob Walker perhaps the picture should be retitled "Without a Song." Then people will know what they are getting.

"This isn't a stark dramatic role, but it is a wonderful story. The story of a boy and a girl who meet under 'The Clock' at the Pennsylvania station in New York. He has a forty-eight-hour furlough, and they live a lifetime while the clock ticks off the forty-eight hours.

"It is a story of a twenty-year-old girl. I rather smile when I think of some of the parts I've wanted to play. I realize now that they wouldn't have been right for me. It was the same when I was fourteen and Roger Edens, my arranger, arranged a song 'Drums in My Heart' for Ethel Merman. I was wild to sing it.

"'You're too young, Judy,' he said. 'That song is for a woman, not a girl.'

"I was so enthused about it. I wanted to sing it so much. Roger said, 'Look, I'll write you a special song all of your own. If you don't like it better than the Merman number, you can sing "Drums in My Heart."' I came back from lunch and Mr. Edens had 'Dear Mr. Gable.' Of course, that song gave me my great opportunity on the screen. I have learned the advisability of waiting for the right thing to come along."

Judy paused. The quietness of the huge soundstage permeated the chintz walls of the dressing room. "Isn't it quiet?" Judy remarked. "No yelling, no screaming. I have always made musicals. You could always hear the noise all over the lot from my sets. The stages would be jumping with a playback going, Mickey pounding a piano, people dancing—rehearsing numbers in corners, a big boom overhead picking up the sound. Now [it is] just Bob and I alone in so many scenes. I couldn't get used to it at first. It didn't seem like we were working without the buzz of activity. Now I rather like it. It gives me a chance to write and work on my poetry."

Judy has already sold an article to a national magazine. And she has a book of poetry in print. No, she will not release it for publication. Judy is afraid it isn't good enough. Her theory being that it might be printed because Judy Garland wrote it, even if it was not good. If it was good no one would believe that she actually wrote it.

"I don't want to only play dramatic roles," Judy remarked—giving Choo-Choo a playful roll over and an affectionate pat. "I love musicals and I am thrilled beyond words at the prospect of my next picture, *The Belle of New York* opposite Fred Astaire. Imagine dancing with Fred Astaire!" Judy's eyes reflected admiring anticipation.*

---

*With a score by Richard Rodgers and Oscar Hammerstein II, *The Belle of New York* was first set for production in 1943. Script revisions and rewrites continued over the next four years, and composers Harry Warren and Johnny Mercer did their own take on the score, but the film never materialized during Judy's tenure at M-G-M. *Belle* was finally produced in 1951 with Astaire alongside Vera-Ellen.

"It will be good to get into costumes again." Judy ruefully observed the trim little navy blue suit and the soft white blouse that she wore. "It is pretty, I admit," she said, "and in the picture the girl wears it from the time she meets the boy—until dinnertime. That is perhaps six hours in her life—but in mine, two months. I've been wearing it for weeks!"

Clothes? Judy loves clothes and she wears smart clothes off the screen. "Now that I am so much thinner, I love clothes." She smiled. Judy was referring back to her adolescence—when she first became a star. "Everyone was so certain that I would be pudgy and fat." Judy laughed. "I have always loved chocolate and chocolate cake and peanut butter fudge. And I was always being warned that I must not eat the things I liked. I was the ugly duckling," Judy laughed.

But today, the slender pretty Judy at twenty-two has no diet worries. The baby fat has disappeared. Judy eats as she pleases. Which means chocolate.

"For my birthday I had a chocolate roll birthday cake. It happens to be my favorite. Today I received an entire carton of chocolate bars. Some soldiers on the studio lot on a visit discovered how much I like chocolate. They took turns daily going to the camp P.X. and finally collected this entire carton. Wasn't that wonderful of them?" Judy's nose wrinkled the way it does when she smiles and she's so very, very pleased.

"Radio is for me," Judy remarked. "I am given chances on the air— that I am never given on the screen. I played opposite Walter Pidgeon in *A Star is Born* and there was *Morning Glory* opposite Adolphe Menjou. People actually called up at home asking, 'Is that really Judy?'"

Judy's hair is now its natural shade of dark brown. "I lightened it to red when I made *The Wizard of Oz* . . . It seems years back," Judy remarked. "I hope to keep it its natural shade now. I like things natural, as they are, not merely what they seem to be. I admit I am a little on the old-fashioned side. The home type I suspect."

That's what Judy is to the boys in the service. "You're just like the girl next door at home," they write. "Thank God, you haven't gone glamorous."

Judy is hoping that the boys will like her latest pinup picture. It is a snapshot taken with a tiny brownie camera on her vacation at Del Monte.

Judy in a pair of shorts is standing by some rocks. Typically a picture the girl next door would take on her summer vacation.

Betty Jane Graham snapped the picture. And therein lies a story. Betty Jane is one of Judy's closest friends. They met when they were both small children and were auditioning for a picture at Universal. Judy thought Betty Jane would get the coveted part. Betty Jane resented Judy's certain assurance in winning the role. Alas, neither won. It was given to Cora Sue Collins. Instead of remaining bitter rivals, Judy and Betty Jane consoled each other's disappointment and became the fastest of friends.

A year ago Betty Jane married, and for months she followed her young soldier-husband from camp to camp. Recently she received word that he was killed in action on his second mission over Burma. Judy took Betty Jane with her to Del Monte. Now she is sponsoring Betty Jane's career at Metro.

"Yes, it is wonderful to be home and with the whole family again," Judy said. "Wonderful until the day when I can have a home and children of my own."

Then—she went on the set for her next scene in *The Clock*.

Thank you, Judy, for such a heart-to-heart chat. You've answered everything that all of your thousands of fans have wanted to hear for a very long time!

LOVE SONG FOR JUDY

ADELA ROGERS ST. JOHNS | **April 1945,** *Photoplay*

Judy's budding love affair with Vincente Minnelli began when the two worked together on *Meet Me in St. Louis*, and blossomed once Minnelli replaced director Fred Zinnemann on *The Clock*, which wrapped on November 21, 1944. Three days later, the new couple boarded a train bound for the New York premiere of *St. Louis* and announced their engagement soon after.

This two-part feature for *Photoplay* comes from the pen of the publication's best-known female writer. In her time, Adela Rogers St. Johns was something of a Barbara Walters figure in the media because of her aggressive approach to journalism. Her own alleged intimate affairs with several in the industry led to her becoming known as the "Mother Confessor of Hollywood."

The first time I ever saw Judy Garland and Vincente Minnelli together was in the cold gray dawn on a station platform in Pasadena.

I had gone out to meet a dear friend who was coming three thousand miles, but even the glow of welcome couldn't warm the wind that blew down from California's snow-capped peaks. Since misery loves company, I was glad to find a lot of other people waiting for the train and to discover that they were all there because Judy Garland was coming back from a trip to New York, and that Vincente Minnelli was on the same train.

There had been vague rumors that a romance was brewing between Judy and the young director who had piloted her *Meet Me in St. Louis* to such a triumphant success. But nobody seemed to be very sure about it because Judy had taken her separation and divorce from David Rose pretty seriously.

Personally, I was hopeful about it. I had never met Mr. Minnelli, but I felt that I knew him very well. Last summer when my youngest son worked as a messenger boy at the Metro-Goldwyn-Mayer studios, I learned Vincente was the idol of the messenger boys. If a messenger couldn't be found, he was out on the [*Ziegfeld*] *Follies* set watching Mr. Minnelli's picturesque methods of getting all the girls into their bubbles at the same time, or listening to his vivid and humorous vocabulary and admiring his directorial genius.

I am inclined to take the clear-eyed verdict of youth seriously myself, so I already felt a keen interest in and admiration for Mr. Minnelli.

Presently the Super Chief steamed proudly in and Judy and Vincente Minnelli got off the train and, all of a sudden, I was quite warm and happy. My friend touched me on the shoulder and I greeted her with the slightly inane remark, "But they're in love, I'm sure they are. Isn't that splendid?"

The reason I thought it was splendid was because, like everybody else, I adore Judy and to date her romances hadn't been lucky. So I decided, in spite of its being just before Christmas, to go and see Judy and ask her about it. Actually it was the day before Christmas when I waited for her in her dressing rooms, a suite with a charming little drawing room and a big room which, upon this occasion, was completely filled with packages and when Judy came in she was completely loaded with packages, too.

She dumped the packages and collapsed and I thought, she's such a very little girl, and she looks exhausted the way everybody does who has been banging around on those last-minute errands, and she isn't exactly beautiful nor exactly pretty, she's—she's just Judy Garland, not like anybody else in the world and isn't it nice to just sit and look at a girl who isn't like anybody else? For Judy is always Judy, with the biggest, brownest eyes and where in the world does that voice come from? Lily Pons is little but then she's a coloratura [soprano], but Judy's voice is big and rich and warm and dynamic.

I asked her, right away, about her rumored engagement to Minnelli.

Judy looked at me rather solemnly, and she said, "I don't know yet myself. We—we've been talking about it. But this time I want to be sure; this time I want to take everything into consideration, all the things that have to do with my work and his. There isn't any use saying—for me at least—that I'd give up my work and my singing. Vincente doesn't want me to do that. But—we want to be very sure. When you are a movie star," said Miss Garland very seriously, "you find that there are a lot of things to be taken into consideration that other people don't have." She paused a moment and then she smiled and added, "I like being a movie star. But maybe that's because I've been one so long it's become a habit."

"How long have you been here at M-G-M?" I asked.

"Ten years," said Judy, "but before that I was in vaudeville for ten years."

"And how old are you?" I inquired.

"I'm twenty-two," Judy Garland said.

Twenty-two. Ten years at M-G-M, ten years in vaudeville. Judy made her first appearance when she was two; she came to M-G-M when she was twelve.

But somehow there was a great deal more to it than that. Twenty-two is not so very old. You aren't supposed to be adult enough to vote until you are twenty-one. A great many girls are just graduating from college at twenty-two. Yet into those short years little Judy Garland has already crowded so much of living, so much of success and applause and hard work and problems.

I thought of something Lana Turner once said: "It's very difficult, growing up in public."

Judy has grown up in public. And now a new air of womanliness sits upon her, without in any way disturbing the little girl she still is.

"You've put on a little weight," I said. "It bothered me a little when you were so thin."

"It bothered *you*," said Judy, with a little shout of laughter. "You should know how it bothered me."

"I thought maybe you did it on purpose."

"I," said Judy, gravely, "have been trying to gain ten pounds for four years. I mean literally. First, I was too fat; I was sort of chunky—remember when I was with Mickey—so everybody was trying to get me thinner. Then I got thinner and thinner and thinner —and then everybody was trying to get me fatter. Now I've gained ten pounds—isn't it wonderful?"

But it set me to thinking, while Judy wrapped Christmas presents, of the crowded, incredibly hardworking life Judy Garland leads. The phone rang half a dozen times. Somebody was consulting Miss Garland about dance routines. Wardrobe wanted Miss Garland the day after Christmas for fittings. Songs had to be tried and recorded and rerecorded. The portrait gallery wanted a sitting. The publicity department wanted to arrange some interviews. All this, of course, in addition to making the picture.

Judy handled it all with ease and great good humor.

"You know, the way I feel about Christmas," Judy said suddenly, "I think the men overseas want to think of Christmas at home the way they always had it and loved it. Maybe it's funny to say, but I think we're really having Christmas for them so that if over there somewhere they're thinking about Christmas at home, they aren't kidding themselves. I like to think of it this year as sort of keeping in practice for them. That makes it easier. You know what I mean?"

Since one of my sons was somewhere with Patton's Third Army, I said I knew very well what she meant.

"Do you think people are more religious this Christmas than they've been in a long time?" Judy said, sitting down beside me on the big couch.

"Of course," I said, thinking how mature she was for one so young.

"You know, Judy, you didn't just grow up in public. You grew up as the baby of the entire Metro-Goldwyn-Mayer lot."

"Well," said Judy, with an enchanting grin, "they were all wonderful about it, at that. The only thing that ever bothered me was how hard it was to make anybody realize I wasn't still twelve years old. They still kind of think I am."

That, I knew, was true. When Judy married Dave Rose the whole lot took it as a personal matter, watched the progress of the love affair, talked about it and advised Judy about it. She had met Dave Rose somewhere at a party with her sister Virginia, who is her greatest chum. She was eighteen then and still to everybody who knew her a "baby." The thing that drew them together was music. Young Dave Rose was playing the piano when Judy walked in and that did it. From then on they were inseparable, they had musical evenings at Judy's house with her mother and sisters, they did songs together and soon they were in love and then they married, [shortly after] Judy's nineteenth birthday.

But it turned out that music was about all they had in common. There is a simple, direct quality about Judy Garland; she has the courage to look life right in the face and when it didn't work she met that, too. Not happily. With a good many tears and a good deal of regret that it hadn't worked.

Part of her growing up, that marriage was.

When I saw a preview of *The Clock*, her newest picture, it came over me that Judy Garland is a big star, a very important star in the movie heavens. For a long time I'd taken her for granted, just with a sort of affection for her, always going to see her pictures and enjoying them because she was Judy. But in *Meet Me in St. Louis* and most particularly in *The Clock*, as you will see, she is more than that. There are moments in *The Clock*, a divine story written by Paul Gallico, adapted for the screen by Robert Nathan and directed by Vincente Minnelli, in which Judy Garland does some magnificent and delicate acting worthy of Helen Hayes—acting so sincere and so encompassing that I found myself putting her in a much higher bracket.

Judy has come of age as a star as well as in her private life.

And she has brought with her the things that have made her. The heartbreak of an unhappy love affair might have been good for her, because every girl has to fall in love sometime with an older man who seems to represent life and glamour and the older phases of life she's read about. The marriage that was founded on music but got out of tune. The friendships, the big family, the years of hard work and the simple philosophy of doing your job well and trying not to jostle the other fellow and expecting the best from life. All these things are in Judy's eyes and voice and the simplicity of everything she does.

"Did you intend to become a movie star?" I asked her. "Did you have a direct ambition about it and set out to achieve it?"

Judy considered, curled up with her feet under her. "No," she said, "it just happened. All I wanted to do, I guess, was sing. I'm sure I never thought about acting. My father and mother were both on the stage. My father was a wonderful guy. He died just after I got my first M-G-M contract—and I was always glad he saw me sort of get started. When I was little, they just kept taking me around with them and letting me sing. My mother didn't always want to, and after we moved to California she always insisted I had to go to school. But—I had such a good time singing and it's no fun singing unless you sing to somebody, is it? So—I don't believe I ever thought of pictures, but little by little I sort of drifted into them because we were out here and it was a good place to sing. Then I learned to dance—my mother taught me. And that was part of it. I think it all just came about sort of naturally, you know. The way things do."

Of course. The way flowers grow, the way birds sing and fly, the way a garden comes into being.

Fat little Judy, leading the band and singing in *Pigskin Parade*. Little Judy with Mickey Rooney—and in *The Wizard of Oz*—and finally a star in her own right in *For Me and My Gal* and now a real artist in *The Clock*.

All in twenty-two years.

We went about our Christmas preparations in our own separate ways but I kept thinking that I would like very much to know more about Vincente Minnelli. I knew a good deal about the only two men who had been in Judy Garland's life up to this time. Both of them had served a purpose, both of them had helped her grow up. She spoke of them with a rather touching friendliness, a little wry humor, not blaming them that things hadn't worked out, not even blaming herself.

Now, it would be different.

A week or so later the phone rang and Judy said, "I'm starting my next picture much sooner than I thought, but I wanted you to meet Vincente. We're going to announce our engagement next week. Would you like to come and have lunch with us?"

I said I would like it almost better than anything and we set a date for two days from then.

It isn't every movie star that I wish those who see her on the screen could know personally. Some idols have feet of silver or gold. They do not always have feet of clay. That's why I want to take you with me to lunch with Judy Garland and the man she is going to marry.

Judy and Vincente tell this famed writer their marriage plans—at luncheon and thereafter. Join them next month—in May Photoplay.

LOVE SONG FOR JUDY

ADELA ROGERS ST. JOHNS | **May 1945**, *Photoplay*

It will be a wedding march—the scene will be the altar—the girl, Judy Garland, will meet the man, Vincente Minnelli—and both will say "I do!"

There is one thing about Judy Garland—maybe because she has music all the way through her: she is literally like a haunting melody. After you've been with her for any length of time, you remember her for days. You find yourself smiling and thinking of some little thing she did, of her enormous youthful gravity when she is serious about anything, of her rich chuckle when she is amused, of the impression of littleness and fragility she gives.

"I've put on ten pounds," Judy told me. "Isn't it wonderful?"

"I thought maybe you had that modern idea of being so terribly thin," I said.

"Me?" said Judy, and chuckled. "Of course when I was a kid I was chunky as anything. So then I was always trying to take off weight. It was awful! I had an appetite and I guess I was growing and I was always hungry—so I just couldn't diet. So I used to exercise. But it never did any good—I stayed chunky. Then all of a sudden I got thin. And I was too thin. So then I had to start trying to get fat. Now I've put on ten pounds—and I think that's about right."

The day Judy invited me over to have lunch with her and Vincente Minnelli, she was late. She's nearly always a few minutes late for everything; she's even late on the set.

"Where's the baby?" somebody will say. (She is still M-G-M's "baby.")
"She'll be along," somebody else says.

"The point is," says Miss Garland in explanation, "there's only one of
me. I have to be in so many different places at the same time."

The truth is that she is interested in so many things—music first and
foremost, the young American composers, the great conductors, the
political significance of Wagner's unquestioned genius. She is interested
in every detail in the war, in sports and the nickel World Series in St. Louis,
in collecting china, in the writers who have been produced by the war and
the books they've written. She's interested in everything that takes place in
Washington. I don't mean just surface patter—I don't mean that she's an
intellectual. She's just vitally *interested* in everything that's going on in the
world, which, of course, makes for richness of personality.

The first time we had talked about the possibility of her marrying
Vincente Minnelli was just before Christmas and her engagement to him
had not yet been announced.

"I made one mistake," Judy said then. When she looks at you seriously like that her eyes get darker and darker, shadowed by the intensity
of her inner thoughts, by her all-out integrity about herself. "I don't want
to make another.

"I love my work. I know there are girls who can give up their work and
get married and just live at home. I don't believe I could. I don't believe I'd
be happy. You see—"

Somebody came in with some papers for her to sign, the wardrobe wanted
to know if she'd be ready for a fitting at three, her secretary handed her
a list and Judy said, "These are the nobody-can-do-them-but-me things.
You know about those."

After a while she went on, "You see—my father and I were very close.
He loved music and the theater and everything about it. He sort of planted
it in me and when I was little and they found out I could sing—he began
to train me. I wasn't more than a foot high, I guess. My mother thought
I could do something long before anybody else did—she thought I could
maybe even act someday. We always belonged in the theater. I know that
lots of stars say they'd like to retire and I know some girls who really can

occupy their lives other ways—but—I've been singing and dancing and acting since I was two—ten years in vaudeville and ten in pictures. That's all my life. I don't believe I could ever be really happy and fulfilled without it now. But I do want babies awfully."

She took time out then to tell me about her young niece, her sister's little girl, who is five. It must be great fun to have Judy Garland for an aunt. Like every other aunt, Judy told a dozen stories about little Judy, her namesake and godchild, and they were just like all the other cute stories about five-year-old children but you could tell that Judy thought they were something very special indeed—and I liked that.

"So—it has to be somebody that understands about me and my work and thinks it's important and—we have to work together," Judy said. "Vincente is wonderful. He's the most interesting man I've ever known. He knows everything in the world, honestly, it just amazes me—he's read everything and heard every piece of music and been everywhere but you'd never think it just to meet him, he's so quiet and rather shy and always making you laugh. But he puts work first. I don't know yet—maybe it will be right for us. We both know that a marriage can either be the most wonderful thing on earth or it can gum up your whole life and spoil everything, including your work. We—we're thinking it over.

I remember I went away that day wondering how long two people in love can think about anything and then I realized that perhaps Judy didn't know how much in love she was. Perhaps because it was all so eminently *right*, because everybody at the studio from Papa Mayer down was tickled about it and feeling it was so fine for Judy—perhaps she just couldn't quite believe it. I thought it was a little tough on Mr. Minnelli to have everybody approve of him to such a terrific extent, because girls are very funny about that and sometimes they don't think it is altogether romantic to have fallen in love with a man that the family cheers for. I went away with a feeling that maybe nothing would come of this romance, that maybe it would be smothered by well-wishing friends and family and studio.

But then Judy called me and I went over to lunch. We sat there talking about a lot of things and then Judy picked up the telephone and called the commissary. She was right fussy about Mr. Minnelli's lunch. His coffee had to be hot and were the veal chops nice or had he better have chicken and did they have any cottage cheese salad? There was a great deal of consultation before she decided on the veal chops.

The veal chops came with piping hot coffee and all was set out on the small table under Judy's eye—and she reset it twice, and got a little vase of flowers, and stood off and looked at it. We talked some more and still Mr. Minnelli didn't arrive. Judy got up and wrapped a napkin around the hot coffee and peered under the lid at the veal chops. "Do you think they'll be ruined?" she said. "I expect they will. Cold gravy is awful."

After a while she went to the phone and called Mr. Minnelli's office. "He's supposed to be here," she said, with a chuckle. "He never knows what time it is. It's wonderful. He gets interested in his work or something and just forgets everything."

The door burst open and Vincente Minnelli came in talking a mile a minute.

It is very difficult to convey his charm on paper. I thought—but he is very young—very young to be so successful. He can't be so young as Judy, of course but—he has that same quality of youth. (As a matter of fact I found out later he is thirty-four.) He's what I call an attractive ugly man—or at least for the first few minutes that was what I thought. Then I decided that he was attractive and then I forgot all about it, and just knew that he was utterly real and unselfconscious and full of that rare enthusiasm for living that makes everything and everybody around him come to life.

He was born in Chicago of Italian parents and his earliest ambition was the theater. So as soon as he could he went to New York and that swift understanding and enthusiasm carried him on a wave into some of the best musical shows New York ever had, as a stage director. Before he was thirty he had done half a dozen of them—and then he came to Hollywood.

The other day in the projection room I saw a picture called *The Clock*. It stars Judy Garland and Bob Walker, was written by Paul and Pauline Gallico, adapted to the screen by Robert Nathan and directed by Vincente Minnelli. *The Clock* has a sort of charm and honesty and reality beyond any other picture I have seen in a long time; it has a poignancy that reaches out and touches your heart. It's one of the greatest and most moving love stories I have ever seen on the screen.

When I saw it I couldn't quite explain it—but after I met Vincente Minnelli I could. Also I could understand him better.

"Your lunch is probably cold," Judy said, beaming upon him. "Did you forget about us?"

"Forget?" said Mr. Minnelli, "but, darling, I am quite early. I was over in Cedric Gibbons's office. It seems that I want too many sets. Or they are too expensive or something."

"I expect you got them just the same," said Miss Garland.

"Well yes—I did, as a matter of fact," said Mr. Minnelli. His dark eyes twinkled at her. "I explained about them you see and then he understood how necessary they were."

"Anybody who starts listening to you explaining," said Judy, "is nuts. Eat your lunch. Is the coffee hot enough?"

It was stone cold, but Vincente smiled brightly and said it was splendid.

I looked at them and thought they were a very fine pair of typical and representative young Americans. Judy sat in a straight chair with one foot under her. The stiff little white shirtwaist with a severe black bow and the straight tailored skirt of black and white checks gave her a trim, neat look—an oddly feminine look. Minnelli, in worn and sloppy tweeds with a sweater instead of a shirt, sprawled at ease on the big divan, never taking his eyes off her. Every move she made, every word she said, seemed to give him a real and evident delight.

We talked about the dialogue—which is so all-important to pictures. Minnelli said that he was in favor always of as little dialogue as possible. We talked about that classic made by the Army Air Force, *The Memphis Belle*, and of the simplicity and power of the real things the crew said to each other in the midst of battle.

"When you see a thing like that," said Vincente Minnelli, "you get on your toes and wonder if even Shakespeare could equal the sheer drama of reality."

They were excited about a concert they had heard with Yehudi Menuhin at his best—and about a new Tommy Dorsey recording—and about house furnishings. Vincente said, "Judy is a very remarkable woman. She knows that chairs should be comfortable to sit in. Oddly enough, very few women know that."

It came over me all of a sudden that here were two people not only very much in love but presenting that oneness, that unity of purpose and intent that is so reassuring. You could see them supplementing each other, supporting each other, maybe fighting once in a while, but meeting shoulder to shoulder the many problems of a Hollywood star's marriage. You could see there would be gaiety and tenderness and maybe pain in their lives—but always that oneness, that unity. So that things would draw them together instead of driving them apart. You felt glad that there was such equality between them, this brilliant young director about whose future everyone is so enthusiastic and the young star everyone loves.

So that the people who love Judy Garland on the screen can all say, as I did—this is right, this is all right—and wish them the happiness and the progress together that I saw so plainly between them.

HALFWAY TO HEAVEN

ROBERTA ORMISTON | October 1945, *Photoplay*

Five days past her twenty-third birthday, and just one day after completing *The Harvey Girls*, Judy married Vincente Minnelli in an intimate ceremony at her mother's home in Hollywood. Unlike her marriage to David Rose, this union was Metro-approved, with Louis B. Mayer giving away the bride. The newlyweds departed that evening on the Super Chief "Train of the Stars," destined for a New York honeymoon. During their stay, Judy threw a bottle of pills into the East River in declaration of new beginnings, promising Vincente she would rid herself of all medications.

Toward the end of their stay, Judy found out that she was pregnant. Phoning her mother she announced, "I'm going to have a baby, Mama. Do you mind?" Baby Minnelli—Liza May—was born March 12, 1946, at Cedars of Lebanon Hospital in Los Angeles, weighing 6 pounds, 10 ounces.

Judy and Vincente would tell you—that a honeymoon in a penthouse is a modern version of the old-fashioned paradise.

Crowning a beautiful building on the ultra-fashionable Sutton Place in New York City there is a triplex penthouse. The beautiful rooms on all three of its floors open on lavishly furnished terraces where trees and gardens grow fabulously in painted tubs.

A guest, standing on the upper terrace of this penthouse during a party recently, looking down at the city lights far below and then up at the stars, said: "More than halfway to Heaven ..."

An amusing remark this but also something of an understatement. For it was here, through the long summer, that Judy Garland and Vincente Minnelli honeymooned. It was here they found their way to the same quick and sensitive understanding as man and wife that they have enjoyed this last year as star and producer.

From the first there was a creative affinity between Vincente and Judy. It would, of course, take a man as sensitive and shy and also as brilliant and as much fun as he is to comprehend a girl as wholly the artist as she.

Vincente says of Judy proudly, "She's the most responsive actress I've ever worked with. When we have rehearsed a scene I have only to say, 'Judy, I wish you could do it more—' and before I have finished I know by her eyes she understands. And when we do the scene, then, it has just the essence I wanted for it."

Judy, in turn, says of Vincente: "We have known each other for about four years, but not well. Vincente was the producer for *Ziegfeld Follies* [*of 1946*], *Meet Me in St. Louis* and *The Clock*. But it wasn't until *The Clock* that we began going out together.

"Everything about that picture was wonderful. We had such fun making it—Vincente and Bob Walker and I working always so close—that we didn't know how the dickens it would come out. Seemed almost as if we were enjoying it too much."

A long time ago Judy and Vincente worked together too. When she and Mickey Rooney were doing those old Busby Berkeley pictures Vincente designed many of their production numbers.

"Only I never knew it," Judy says. "After all I just got a script and it never said who had sat at a desk in one of the offices and planned what went into it . . . .

"But when Vincente told me the numbers he had worked on I realized that even then—before we met—he understood me better than anyone else. For the numbers he worked on always were my favorites."

Judy and Vincente, as you know, planned to be married in New York. Manhattan really is his home. He has many dear friends there; all the theater people and writers and musicians and charming cosmopolites who have adored him ever since he produced the delightful Music Hall shows and presented Bea Lillie and Bert Lahr in his own production, *The Show Is On*.

With a New York wedding in mind, Vincente, busy in California, telephoned Mr. John of John Frederics in New York to ask if he knew of an apartment. John offered to look around. Finally he called Vincente back. Martin Block, the radio star and producer of *Make Believe Ballroom* would lease his triplex penthouse, ringed with terraces and furnished with a French decor.

John went on, in effect: "You enter an L-shaped corridor, Vincente. On that floor is a guest room and bath and a master bedroom and bath and dressing room. Also, at the end of the corridor there's a dining room, kitchen, pantry and servants' quarters . . . A curving stairway leads to the second floor and the living room, about fifty feet by twenty-two . . . The third floor is smaller, has a playroom and bar, including a slot machine . . ."

"We'll take it!" Vincente decided promptly.

When at the last moment Mrs. Garland was unable to come east for the wedding, Judy decided to be married in her mother's house. This also meant that Louis B. Mayer could give Judy away. Often Mr. Mayer must have wished, together with all those who love Judy, that somehow she might find the happiness and fulfillment personally she knows professionally, even though this is not too often given the true artist. For there's an excellent chance that Vincente, another true artist, as her husband may bring the same bright magic into her life that he has, as her director, given her pictures.

Certainly the few close friends who saw them married, heard their quiet steady voices making their vows, saw the deep tenderness of their marriage kiss, believed it was a happy day.

Judy wore a pale blue-gray jersey dress that had a little bustle and that was embroidered with pink pearls. A La Boheme bonnet sat far back on her reddish gold hair. She carried pink peonies almost as big as herself. There was a bride's cake, three tiers high, which Judy and Vincente cut with an old silver knife tied with gardenias and white ribbon. In the garden they posed for color pictures for *Photoplay*. Between time everyone must admire the black-and-gold wedding band, set with tiny pearls, which complemented the pearl engagement ring, set in gold and black enamel, which also was Vincente's design. Then they were off for New York.

"When we arrived the apartment was waiting," Judy said. "Vincente had thought to have it filled with flowers. And right away we did as we had planned—just moved in and pretended to be New Yorkers . . ."

A cook and a maid were waiting too. And when Judy and Vincente had bathed and changed, breakfast was served on the upper terrace, so very high that only a few of Manhattan's tallest spires stood between them and the blue dome of the sky.

"It's all been wonderful," Judy says. "Especially this chance to meet Vincente's friends who love him . . . And, of course, I keep hoping, in time, they'll be my friends too . . ."

"Whenever I came to New York before," Judy says, "I lived in a hotel— for two weeks perhaps—and rushed, rushed, rushed. I had to cram about one hundred and sixty three things into that time—shows, mostly. Now we go to the theater two or three times a week and take our time about it."

It wasn't, of course, completely idyllic. Nothing ever is. The second day they were in New York the cook and maid moved out, displeased over what neither Judy nor Vincente have the least idea. For five days after that they had no one to help them. They called every agency. Like a thousand other New Yorkers they would have packed and moved to a hotel if they could have gotten accommodations. Then, through an advertisement in the *Times*, they interviewed a maid. "I'm the luckiest person in the world," Judy insists. "She's a wonderful woman, this maid! And the selfsame day she arrived I went downstairs and in the lobby was a woman waiting to see me. She's now our most magnificent cook, a Creole, and she has agreed to go back home with us!"

Also, in typical New York fashion, Judy and Vincente have weekended all summer in the country with friends and have also visited Nick Schenck at his Long Island villa, where the talk of pictures and the theater and actors and artists and writers is the talk both Judy and Vincente dearly love.

The very week they arrived, Nick Schenck took them shopping in Tiffany's.

"Metro wants to buy you a wedding present, Judy. Pick out something you like."

Hesitantly, Judy chose a simple gold brooch.

"Nonsense!" exclaimed Mr. Schenck. "You must choose something much gayer."

After considerably more hesitation, Judy selected a bracelet of square diamonds and emeralds and a companion pin that broke into two clips—all so beautiful that they left her breathless.

Then Mr. Schenck insisted that the groom choose a wedding present for himself. After some demurring, Vincente selected a handsome gold wristwatch as his gift from Leo, the Lion.

Speaking of weddings, Judy's mother, appropriately enough, gave them a clock. "Such a beautiful, old, rare clock—from England," Judy explains. "It will sit on our bedroom mantel or bedside table. It strikes with beautiful chimes. And on either side of the face are porcelain figurines, a little boy and a peasant girl.

"It's the sort of thing you want to pass on in your family—to your children and their children ... ."

She spoke of her prospective children several times. For in spite of a foolish newspaper item, she and Vincente have no idea of adopting a baby. "We expect," she says, "to have a baby of our own someday. And another. And another. Until we have a good-sized family. For what could be more exciting than having children and watching them develop and grow and helping them on their way? That is something that would last for always."

The party the Minnellis gave—one of a very few—was to honor Judy's sister [Jimmie] on her birthday and the eve of her opening at La Martinique. Unwilling to trade on the name Garland she is known professionally only as Miss Dorothy.*

Many of the sixty-odd guests were Dorothy's friends, many more were Vincente's—so many were strangers to Judy. With sweet naturalness,

---

*Born Dorothy Virginia Gumm, Judy's sister "Jimmie" (also known as Virginia Garland) worked at M-G-M as a script clerk and appeared as an extra in several films. Abandoning the Garland moniker, Jimmie became "Miss Dorothy" (a stage name dating back to her days in vaudeville) when she embarked upon what was a short-lived run as a musical-comedy solo act in the mid-1940s. Judy and Vincente were in New York when Miss Dorothy opened at the La Martinique nightclub on July 4, 1945.

therefore, she made no attempt to introduce people or to call them by name. But she moved from group to group with simple friendship. Even if Judy hadn't been a famous star, eyes would have followed her the night of that party. For she was lovely in a pale blue brocade hostess gown with a tight bodice, low square neck, long sleeves, flaring peplum and wide trailing skirt.

At one end of the lantern-lit terrace stood the long buffet table. And in the center stood a chocolate cake, Dorothy Garland's favorite, ablaze with candles.

Throughout the party there was a fine musician at the piano. And the Merry Macs moved from group to group, serenading. Dorothy sang, too, while Judy stood half-hidden and applauded, if possible, even more enthusiastically than all the rest.

Finally Judy sang, too. "Embraceable You" came first. Then, with the Merry Macs as background, she sang "The Trolley Song." And always her eyes sought Vincente and always her voice as well as her eyes turned warmer to answer his smile.

"Vincente forgets to be shy when he looks at Judy," an old friend said. "Because he completely forgets himself. It's such a wonder he ever found her. Men like him—charming and gay and kind, with his elfin humor—are so likely to marry women who aren't able to share their interests. Judy looks up to him. You might almost say—if they weren't such friends—that she is terrifically impressed by him. So Vincente is stimulated. And they're both happy."

Soon now, when Judy and Vincente return to California, they'll live in his house. "I like it so much I didn't want to go to a new place," Judy says. "However, since it was a typical bachelor house and not large enough for two we bought the lots on either side. Now we're building on a little bath-dressing room for me. And when we can get priorities we'll put a dining room on the other side."

The Minnelli house sits on top of a high hill midway between Beverly Hills and Hollywood. You travel winding roads to get there. But the view, looking out over trees and gardens and town and sea, is unbelievable. The house itself has the feeling of houses in Mediterranean countries. It's seashell pink outside and predominantly dark green inside. Vincente has furnished it with the beautiful eighteenth century pieces he's collected for years. And it's done in bright colors and quilted chintzes and pale rugs, with lovely pictures, rare porcelains. It presents a quaintly dignified facade to the road. But on the other side terraces furnished and gardened luxuriantly lead to the badminton court which is a gathering place for the wittiest and the most brilliant and charming people in all Hollywood.

At night, at the Minnellis', when the lights come on in the town below and the stars come out overhead, you seem to be suspended between two skies. All of which bears out the prophecy of Judy's and Vincente's friends that even when the honeymoon is over they'll go right on living halfway to heaven.

JUDY GEM
On Diversity

"When you get to know a lot of people you make a great discovery. You find that no one group has a monopoly on looks, brains, goodness or anything else. It takes *all* the people—black and white, Catholic, Jewish and Protestant, recent immigrants and Mayflower descendants—to make up America. It just wouldn't be *our* kind of America without any one of them."
—*Speaking for America*, Scholastic Magazines, 1946

THIS IS WHAT I BELIEVE

JUDY GARLAND | October 1946, *Screenland*

Judy shared her views on life, death, war, and spirituality in this piece written during the first half of 1945 while in production for *The Harvey Girls*.

Here's Judy, herself—no frills, just a nice, honest girl speaking her mind on the really important things

When *Screenland* asked me, on the set of *The Harvey Girls*, to talk about what I believe about life, love, religion, happiness and immortality, I was flabbergasted by the immensity of the subjects covered. But after I caught my breath, I was glad that I was given this chance to express my ideas. Usually an actress is asked about nothing more vital than whether she prefers coffee with sugar or without, crystal ashtrays to silver ones or blondes to brunettes. I realize that this subject takes a great deal of thought, but I will try my best to put on paper what I believe.

Life? I believe that happiness can be achieved if you don't get in your own way. You should always keep your sense of perspective, both about yourself and about things outside yourself.

I believe you should be critical of yourself but not overcritical. The latter inhibits you too much. You avoid realism and wrap yourself in a cloud of misery. If another person is in a bad mood, you think it's because of something you have done, when actually he or she may have had a quarrel with someone else and is not thinking of you at all. Or if you're in a bad mood, you expect the whole world to share it, and take personal offense at everyone else who seems reasonably happy. You say to yourself, "Nobody cares how I feel."

Such a perspective is completely distorted and selfish. Being over-critical of yourself brings it on. I remember between the ages of 14 to 20, I went through such a stage. I was particularly sensitive about my nose and teeth. My teeth didn't all grow at the same time. I thought I was snaggle-toothed, and often used to put my hands over my mouth to hide my teeth. I was like the girl in the ads who was afraid to smile.

Perhaps every girl goes through a period in adolescence when she is overcritical of her own looks. That viewpoint is just as bad as being too conceited. Actually it's a form of conceit and selfishness because it means you're concentrating too hard on something about yourself that isn't really terribly important.

An actress is apt to suffer from this oversensitiveness. The average girl can look at herself in a mirror, and by picking the angle, see what she wants to see. But in the movies, your face is magnified, every little defect shows up multiplied a thousand times. So being an actress is a terrific test of your ego. No matter how your face looks on the screen, however, you have to remember that people are going to judge you by your personality and the way you act, as much or more than by your looks.

Certainly the girl who isn't an actress is going to be judged more by her personality than by her looks. A boy once told me that when he goes to a dance he never tries to pick out the prettiest girl at the party or dance; he just picks out the one with the nicest smile.

Death? I don't believe that dying is the end. There is too much prepa-ration in life for something else.

Immortality? I believe that there is such a thing as personal survival. I don't believe that there are golden streets in Heaven and that gingerbread grows on all the trees, but do believe that there is something afterwards. I find it hard to believe that there is such a place as hell in the afterlife.

Prayer? Prayers are important, particularly in wartime, and a great comfort to people at all times. When I was little and said my prayers every night, I once got the idea that if I prayed for somebody else each night I would appear unselfish. So I asked for nice things for other people, always adding, "But I don't need anything," and hoping that I would get nice things as a bonus for my supposed unselfishness. Perhaps I shouldn't tell this on myself, but once I didn't get something which I wanted badly, and then I stopped praying for a while. Of course, I resumed my prayers again later. Now I don't say bedtime prayers, but pray at other times. I know now that some prayers are answered affirmatively by God and others are answered otherwise, because it's God's will, but however they may be answered, there is still comfort in the prayer.

Religion? I believe that the real expression of your religious beliefs is shown in the daily pattern of your life, in what you contribute to your surroundings and what you take away without infringing on the rights of other people. I don't disapprove of people who make a habit of focusing all their thoughts on religious ideas, unless they let religion become an opiate with them and do harmful things to other people. No one should feel that because he goes to church every Sunday he can do cruel things which people are not ordinarily supposed to do and that God will overlook his bad behavior.

I like going to church at Christmas, Easter and when I'm not working, because it is peaceful there and a place of goodwill, where some of the nicest people in the community congregate. But real religion is in your mind and heart, and can't be judged by the number of times you go to church.

War? You can drive yourself crazy trying to figure out why God allows wars. Once I heard a group of women discussing this and one of them (not myself) said, "How can there be a God when these terrible wars go on? How could He permit it? My own attitude toward war is fatalistic. I feel that human beings create the machines of destruction; we make the troubles that cause wars. True, people are dragged into war who have no control over it, but man, not God, is responsible. We haven't progressed far enough from Neanderthal man to permit all craving for violence to disappear. Some day in the future, when human beings are born without tonsils, which we probably don't need, and without appendices, which we certainly don't need, our physical brains may be developed to the point where all savagery has disappeared. But at the present time there is still something in man's nature which permits the violence of war.

So much for my larger beliefs. All our lives we wonder about these things but we'll have to wait for that afterlife in which I believe to find the answers. However, there are some things we all seek—success, love, and friendships, about which an actress can speak up boldly, since every one of us tries to achieve these things.

I believe that success is fun, but can be a burden if it is not handled right. If success is won along one line, that automatically requires the successful person to achieve it along other lines.

Successful people are often very versatile. Vincente Minnelli, my husband, for instance, besides being a fine director, paints exquisitely. Of course, I may be prejudiced, but I wish you could see the painting which Vincente did of a set he designed for Beatrice Lillie's play, *At Home Abroad*. That painting hangs in my dressing room, and captures an atmosphere which is just as authentic as the family atmosphere captured by Vincente in *Meet Me in St. Louis*. Of all the pictures I have ever made, I think *Meet Me in St. Louis* is my favorite, because I felt that was the nicest family I ever met in pictures. They all fought together and had disagreements, but you knew that in time of trouble they would all stick to one another. I've been very lucky in my family life, I must say, both on and off the screen!

The man or woman who achieves a successful career must be successful also in his handling of his own mentality and ego. Being an actress is the most grueling test for the ego, for the success of being an actress floods you. When you are a success in some other line, your intimates know about it and the people in that line, but the world as a whole doesn't necessarily make a fuss about you. An Einstein, whose success is actually much greater and whose work is much more important than that of any actor, isn't followed by crowds of admiring fans. The success of an actress is seen. Her work is constantly exhibited. So if she loses her sense of perspective, she may begin thinking how great she is, when actually her success may be just a matter of luck and a few pretty close-ups. But that kind of success doesn't begin life as a member of a family; you go on as a member of a family; then eventually, if you're lucky, you have a chance to start your own family. The kind of person you are throughout your whole life depends to a large extent upon the kind of person you are as member of a family group. In a family you learn selfishness or unselfishness, consideration for others or lack of consideration—why, your whole future is mapped out by the way you treat your family and the way they treat you. That, I believe, is our American way of life.

We learn in our own families to see the other fellow's point of view. In *Meet Me in St. Louis* the *Smiths* were all upset at first when *Alonzo Smith*, the father, decided on a move to New York. To be sure, he was just trying to make things nice for the family, but they began to think he was just a selfish tyrant, because they had so many ties in St. Louis. *Esther* didn't want to leave her beau; *Rose* was afraid she wouldn't make friends in New York; *Tootie* couldn't bear to leave her snowmen. It was selfish in a way, but it was all so natural. There was a lot to be said for *Mr. Smith*'s point of view, and a lot to be said for his family's.

After a while, they began to realize he wasn't being a monster of selfishness, and peace reigned again in the family. Then, after they understood his point of view, he began to grasp theirs. And so he called the whole family down into the dining room, and told them he had decided to stay in St. Louis after all.

It's significant, I think, that in the Fascist countries, where the family unit was not considered important, where the state was all-important, cruelty and brutality crept in. So let's be thankful we live in a country where we can be sentimental about our families. And let's be thankful, too, we live in a country where we can achieve success through our individual efforts and not through regimentation.

However, no matter how wonderful your family is, no matter how much success you achieve in your career, you won't be a really happy person unless you also achieve success as a woman. And for most women, that includes a happy marriage.

I believe that it is possible for a woman to have a successful career and a happy marriage, too. In the case of a career woman, marriage requires more patience, thought, and understanding. But it can be done, as witness the case of Helen Hayes who is one of our finest actresses, and a great success as a wife and mother, too.

I imagine that it's hard for a man to be married to an actress. He can't feel, as most men like to feel, that everything depends upon him. He knows his wife is financially independent. She must therefore make him feel that even though she can stand on her own feet financially, she is emotionally dependent on him, that everything else in her life—even her work—revolves around him. I believe that she shouldn't keep any part of her life to herself. Since she can't give her husband the satisfaction of feeling that she needs him financially, she must make him feel needed and wanted in every other way, and in no way shut out from her life.

I think women get themselves mixed up by making too many promises. There is something so romantic about promising your heart forever and ever to a person. Men are more honest about those things. Women often wind up with guilty consciences because they have made too many promises to the men they love. They get carried away with themselves.

It's always better to promise less and do more. So I believe in making as few promises as possible, even to myself. I'd rather do this than wind up with a guilty conscience because I hadn't carried out all my plans. Make plans, certainly, but don't be upset if something happens to make it impossible to carry them out.

We hear a great deal about love at first sight, but I believe that a person is safer if love develops gradually. If people marry after knowing each other only a short time, they have to make all their adjustments afterwards. In the case of people who have known each other for some time, many of the adjustments can be made before they marry.

We knew that a great many hasty war marriages have taken place, and often mistakes, then forget the past. That you should live not for yesterday, but for today and tomorrow. Old people, they say, live too much in the past. So if you don't want to get old before your time, don't dwell on your past mistakes.

We all want friends. No matter whether you want one good friend or many friends, you must be willing to give your time and sympathies to them. Some people who think they want friends really just want to use them—to cry on their shoulders and to have someone in whom to confide. Real friendships are a matter of give and take. You must not merely want to cry on their shoulders but be ready to listen to their troubles when they want to cry on yours.

Sometime the best of friends grow apart through acquiring different interests or because events in their lives are not synchronized. When that happens, you mustn't feel too badly. You must learn to let go and accept what is happening now, rather than try to cling to outworn interests. I don't mean that you should ever just drop old friends, but if you do grow apart in your interests, you mustn't grieve about it. Change is inevitable; and if you change in one direction and a friend changes in another, your interests sometimes do grow far apart. It may not be the fault of either one of you, just the pattern of events.

I believe that if you are lonely sometimes, you should accept it, without feeling that life has treated you badly. There are lonely moments in all lives. Even when you are in a crowd, a feeling of loneliness can wash over you. Remember that other people in the same crowd may be feeling the same way. If you're a wife with a husband in the service, remember other wives with husbands overseas know the same loneliness you feel.

To sum up my beliefs: I believe that no matter what happens to you in life, if you retain a sense of perspective, both about yourself, and life in general, you'll be able to meet situations gallantly and wisely. It won't be easy, ever, to face real tragedy, but as time goes on a sense of perspective can help.

JUDY GARLAND HAS HER SAY

JACK HOLLAND | December 1948, *Silver Screen*

Easter Parade paired Judy with Fred Astaire, who was summoned from his retirement when planned costar Gene Kelly broke his ankle. "Judy Garland dances as if she had been Fred Astaire's partner all her life," announced the *Hollywood Reporter*. "On her own, she sings and performs with irresistible Garland charm. The exquisite Technicolor shows off her fresh, youthful beauty." *Easter Parade*, "Metro's finest musical of the year," was released in July 1948, and this interview was conducted shortly thereafter.

This should settle once and for all the incorrect impressions that have arisen about Judy

No star has been the subject of so many rumors as Judy Garland, so to get the truth about this wonderfully clever little star, I subjected her to our lowdown treatment. The answers to the questions should settle once and for all the incorrect impressions that have arisen about Judy.

Me: You're not as interested in your career now as you once were?

Judy: More so than ever. And with each new year I find an increasing interest.

Me: You would prefer, for variety, to do some nonsinging, straight dramatic roles?

Judy: Not at all. After all, dramatic roles do not mean that the parts have to be nonsinging.

Me: You never like yourself on the screen and are very critical of your work?

Judy: I'm terribly critical, but sometimes I have liked myself. Not very often, but occasionally I like myself in my husband's pictures—and I kind of liked *Easter Parade*.

Me: Your favorite picture was *Easter Parade*?

Judy: No. One of my favorites. My pet was *Meet Me in St. Louis*.

Me: You were very frightened when you had to do the first dance with Fred Astaire?

Judy: No. He put me completely at my ease. He is a gentleman and he is lots of fun to work with.

Me: You drive yourself too hard when you're working?

Judy: Yes. I have a tendency to never let down during a picture. This is stimulating but can be very fatiguing.

Me: You carry your working problems home with you?

Judy: Naturally—and I discuss them all with my husband. We are partners in our home and in our work whether or not we are actually making a picture together. We share all problems with one another.

Me: You're an extremely nervous person?

Judy: So I've heard. I have moments of relaxation. The tension I'm under when I work at times makes for nerves.

Me: You have a hot temper and fly off the handle easily?

Judy: Not easily. It takes me a long time—but when I do explode there is no stopping me.

Me: You're inclined to dwell on your troubles?

Judy: I don't think so. I don't enjoy my troubles that much to dwell on them.

Me: You seldom find time for any relaxation and have no favorite way of relaxing?

Judy: That's right, except perhaps to read. I am an inveterate reader.

Me: You work with your husband well on a picture?

Judy: Yes. Extremely well. I have the highest regard for his talent and his integrity. I respect him.

Me: You have no idea what you would like to do if you were not an actress?

Judy: Not the slightest!

Me: You have no habits that annoy or tease your husband?

Judy: Well, he hasn't told me about them if I have.

Me: You're not, as a rule, a domestically inclined person?

Judy: No!

Me: Your health has been a subject of much batting about by columnists—and you're really very well?

Judy: Extremely well. And extremely strong. And the subject of my health has become a boring one.

Me: Your life is centered mostly on Liza?

Judy: On Liza and Vincente.

Me: You would like her to be an actress when she grows up?

Judy: Very much, if she wants to be.

Me: Since you began your career at the ripe old age of three, you'd have no objections if Liza got her start with the same difficulties you encountered?

Judy: I prefer that Liza wait until she is of an age where she can make a sound choice for herself.

Me: You're collecting things for Liza for when she grows up?

Judy: Yes. Linens, silver, certain pieces of jewelry, china, and various kinds of records.

Me: Your friends are mainly connected with the musical world?

Judy: No, not at all. Our friends are in all professions.

Me: There is nothing you do that could spoil Liza?

Judy: I'm not so sure. We'll have to wait for a while to see. If adoring her can spoil her, she's going to be spoiled.

Me: You like jewelry?

Judy: Yes, I do indeed. However, only antique jewelry. I now have a fine collection, what with the pieces my husband has given me.

Me: You're extravagant in many ways?

Judy: Not at all extravagant. In fact, I drive a 1941 Ford because it is so broken in, practically *broken down,* from my own particular style of driving!

Me: You're inclined to trust people too much and have, therefore, been hurt?

Judy: Yes.

Me: You like Hollywood society and go to many parties?

Judy: No. However, I have nothing against Hollywood society. I have found it attractive and at times very charming, but neither my husband nor I care for large parties.

Me: You dislike publicity and have been annoyed by stories about you?

Judy: Yes. "Annoyed" is putting it mildly; however, I realize that it is part of my work.

Me: You have no favorite type of music?

Judy: None. I like all music.

Me: You know of no one of whom it might be said you have a sense of hero worship?

Judy: No. That does not mean that I am overconfident of myself or of my abilities. It is simply that I believe people outgrow hero worship.

Me: You want to do a play in New York?

Judy: I'm not sure. I've thought about it often. Perhaps someday I will if just exactly the right thing comes along.

Me: You are afraid of doing radio broadcasts?

Judy: Yes. They have a tendency to make me nervous.

Me: You seldom give a thought to the future?

Judy: How can you have a child and not give a thought to the future? A daughter or a son represents the future.

Me: You have no time for hobbies?

Judy: I haven't found one I could be crazy about, except reading.

Me: You have no idea where you'd like to go or what you'd like to do if you got a real vacation?

Judy: Oh, yes! Lots of ideas that my husband and I share together. And Liza is included in all of them.

Me: You would handle your career the same way if you had it to do over again?

Judy: Yes, I am happy to say, yes!

And this should put the Judy Garland rumor factory out of business. Let's hope it has a quiet demise!

JUDY GEM
On Her Singing Voice

"Sometimes it's so loud it surprises me. But that's the way I've always sung. I've never trained my voice, possibly because I use the right muscles in my throat. When I was a kid in vaudeville, people would say I'd lose my voice before I got much older. That alarmed my mother, so she sent me to a vocal coach. The first lesson had me trying to blow off a piece of paper pasted on my forehead. 'Breath control,' she said. Next she had me singing with a pencil in my teeth. 'Poor diction,' she said. I told her I didn't usually sing with a pencil in my teeth. I think a lot of talent is dried up by too many lessons. If you've got it, it usually comes out anyway."

—To Bob Thomas, Associated Press, May 2, 1949

JUDY GEM
On Her Future Plans

"Now I want to have some fun. I plan to see all the plays in New York, then go abroad. I've never crossed the ocean. I never had time. I was always too busy working. Not until I read your column did I realize that I had done 30 pictures since I was 12. It's appalling. But I still want to work. Maybe I'll be able to play at the Palladium in London. I've been asked so many times, but being under contract to a studio, I've been unable to accept any outside engagements, and that goes for radio. During the past six years I could have made a fortune on the air, but, except for occasional guest spots, I couldn't appear on radio. It was against studio policy. If I do get to work at the Palladium and am a success, I'd like to do a play. Maybe I could do the Mary Martin role in a second company of *South Pacific*. Oh, how I'd love that. I want to prove to my studio and to myself I can succeed on my own. I may be wrong, but I think I have talent enough to take me anywhere I wish to go."

—To Hedda Hopper, June 26, 1949

PART III

THE 1950s

JUDY WRITES A LETTER

JUDY GARLAND | September 1950, *Motion Picture*

It has been well documented that, as the 1940s drew to a close, Judy was dependent upon cyclical doses of uppers and downers, and overworked to the point of exhaustion. She underwent psychotherapy and was even admitted to sanitariums on several occasions. Tensions between Judy and Vincente were at an all-time high when the two announced their separation on March 30, 1949. They briefly reconciled later that year, but their marriage was nearing its end.

From 1948 through 1950, Judy completed *Easter Parade*, *Words and Music*, *In the Good Old Summertime*, and *Summer Stock*, but the press focused on her dismissal from other productions, namely *The Barkleys of Broadway* and *Annie Get Your Gun*. "I don't know [when I'm going back to work]," she told Hedda Hopper one evening at the Mocambo nightclub in May 1949. "I'm suspended so high I can't even sit down!"

Motion Picture announced in the summer of 1950 that Judy's film career seemed at its end, which alarmed its readers, many of whom responded with letters of concern, disbelief, and sympathy. "Could it be true?" asked one reader. "How sick is she?" asked another. "For how long will she be out of picture making? Those questions we want answered. Not from her press agent, but from Judy Garland herself. We are tired of the gossip and we want the truth."

It is apparent Judy was fed up with the gossip, too, given that she responded to the magazine personally in a letter addressed to *Motion Picture* editor Maxwell Hamilton. This brazen dispatch signified the arrival of an unrestricted Judy, one clearly breaking free of the Metro publicity machine. That the letter was written and published without the studio's consent, or even its knowledge, spoke to the strained relationship between her and the studio.

Judy was shattered when a third suspension came down on June 17, 1950, on the set of *Royal Wedding*, in which Judy had recently replaced a pregnant June Allyson. Two days later she attempted suicide.

We said in our June issue that Judy Garland would never make another picture, that she was under constant guard. Judy denied our story in the letter you'll find on these pages. Judy's shocking attempt on her life, however, proves we knew what we were talking about!

In the June issue of *Motion Picture*, we published some pretty ugly, but well-founded, rumors about Judy Garland, to the effect that she never would make another picture. Judy denied our story and, on her own behalf, wrote us the letter printed on these pages, a letter we felt—and we told Judy so—was one of the frankest, most honest we've ever received from a star. Then, on June 20th, came the shocking news that Judy had attempted to take her life. We still think you'll want to read this dramatic letter, written, as we know it must have been, while Judy was under the strongest of emotional strains. For, to us, it paints a vivid picture of Judy Garland, the *one* picture which perhaps shows Judy as the truly beloved star she certainly has been.
The Editors.

Hollywood, California

Dear Mr. Hamilton:

Although I don't believe in answering Hollywood gossip about myself, whether to deny or affirm it, your article in *Motion Picture* seems to call for some sort of word from me. So I take up the challenge:

First of all, let's talk about the reason I don't act the same way I did when I was 14 years old and "skip about the M-G-M lot like a gay ragamuffin," to quote you. The answer is simple. That was fourteen years ago! I'm quite sure everyone in the world changes rather radically between the ages of 14 and 28 and, if they don't, they should. Certain responsibilities, raising a child, running a home—all add up to changes; very normal ones, but changes nevertheless.

May I emphasize the word *normal*? You see, I'm so tired of reading articles in newspapers and magazines in which I'm described as neurotic, psychotic, idiotic, or any "otic" the writer can think of—and also that I am, as I've read too often, a desperately sick woman (Ah, the drama of it all), with everything from falling arches to possessing at least two heads. Allow me to start pulling you writers and columnists down to earth. Whether it makes for good reading or not, I'm sorry to have to tell you I'm hopelessly normal; normal enough to get tired once in a while, normal enough to rest when this happens (No, dear, *not* in a sanitarium—just some place dull, like Monterey Beach, where I'm writing this), normal enough after I rest, to go back to work and make a *hit* picture and normal enough to get damn mad at the junk you boys and girls have written about me.

This is my first answer but not my last. I've kept quiet until now because to try to answer seemed to be giving dignity to pure rot. However, enough is enough. So here we go—

Of course I'm not quitting pictures. Are you kidding? I love my work, and I am looking forward with great anticipation to doing *Show Boat*, my next assignment, in which I play the best part of my career, the role created by the beloved Helen Morgan, the role of Julie.* Before this I'm going to take a trip to Europe with my husband and daughter, as the studio won't be ready to start production for several months. In the meantime, Vincente will go to Paris to shoot his next picture and he is taking his family with him.

Next, how I felt about not doing *Annie Get Your Gun*—this was not a tragedy to me. It was a very good part, but there are a lot of good parts. I just finished a fine one in *Summer Stock*. The preview last Thursday night was the most successful I've had in five or six years. The audience seemed to love it. This thing you wrote about my having a doctor or, as you put it, a *guard* on the set with me, is simply fantastic. My physician (most people have one, you know) wanted to see how pictures were made and asked if he could visit my set. I said "Of course." Result—you make it sound as though I was shooting the musical version of *The Snake Pit*.

And what is the prize remark you quoted as mine? Oh, yes—"The only real happiness in life is found in unhappiness." Wow! That's not only heavy, it doesn't make any sense! If I wanted to convey a Chekhovian philosophy, I'd word it better than that.

If I tried to answer all of the many weird and baffling things that have been said about me it would fill volumes. Let me tell you how it's affected

---

Show Boat was not to be. Studio executives felt that Judy's recent weight gain left her unrecognizable and said she was not photographable "in her physical condition."

me. I'm unscathed, unscarred, unembittered and it's left me with a better sense of humor than before.

At first it was uncomfortable having a few people in Hollywood peer at me as though I were either Lon Chaney in full makeup or a walking Charles Addams cartoon. But my good friends laughed long and loud, and I heartily joined them. It's good to be able to laugh at yourself—and I don't think it's considered neurotic!

I have the public, my warm and loving friends, to thank for setting me straight. They seem not even to be aware of all the printed nonsense; they still treat me with deep affection. Their love is constant, mine for them everlasting.

There's my answer, Mr. Hamilton. Print it as I wrote it, and you'll be doing me a favor. If you don't, I suppose it will be because my letter lacks in dramatic weightiness. But come on, all of you writers, radio commentators, gossip reporters, columnists, editors:

Let's keep it light!

Judy Garland

AN OPEN LETTER FROM JUDY GARLAND

JUDY GARLAND | November 1950, *Modern Screen*

On September 29, 1950, Judy Garland parted ways with Metro-Goldwyn-Mayer. Legend has it she was fired, but in truth it came down to a mutual dissolution. The studio deemed her to be a liability; she was no longer cost-effective. But Judy reached a point where she just wanted out, and by 1950 her doctor demanded it. "It is with great reluctance that Judy's request has been granted," said Louis B. Mayer in his official statement to the press. "We wish her all the success and happiness in the continuance of her career." Recalling the split, he later expressed, "She had to go; it broke my heart."

"I was a very tired girl," Judy announced in a public response, "and now maybe Metro realizes that. . . . I feel like I've shed a suit of armor." But the pressure and anxiety quickly began to mount. Sixteen years and more than two dozen feature films after having signed with Metro, she found herself out of work and, to quote much of the press at the time, "unemployable" at the age of 28.

Judy expresses her gratitude to Modern Screen's *understanding readers*

Dear Friends,

This is a thank-you note.

At a time when I've been gossip's victim and the target of a thousand lies, you people have stood by me. I won't ever forget that.

You've judged me not on the basis of headlines, rumor and innuendo but on my performances as an actress and entertainer.

Ever since the release of my last picture, *Summer Stock*, thousands of you have had the kindness to write me. You've congratulated me, encouraged me, and pledged me your support. And for all this—let me repeat—I'm eternally grateful.

Inasmuch as it is impossible for me to reply individually to your more than 18,000 letters, I'm using this space in *Modern Screen* to answer those questions most frequently asked.

I have a responsibility to you friends. Rather than let you be misguided by the flood of nonsense printed about me by reporters and uninformed writers who know none of the facts, I intend to fulfill my responsibility by telling you moviegoers the truth.

I am not quitting motion pictures. Movies are my life's blood. I love making motion pictures and always have ever since I was a little girl.

I do not intend, however, to make any films for the next six months. I'm just going to relax, take things easy, and regain my peace of mind.

For a while I expected to go to Paris with my daughter, Liza, and my husband, Vincente Minnelli—but his studio has decided to film all of *An American in Paris* in Hollywood, and since he is directing that picture and plans shortly to direct the sequel to *Father of the Bride*, we all plan to remain in California.

I love to work, I love to sing, I love to act—I get restless when I don't—and it's entirely possible that I will do a few broadcasts with Bing Crosby or Bob Hope before six months are up.

My health is fine. As I write this, I've just returned from a vacation in Sun Valley and Lake Tahoe. I'm suntanned, I weigh 110 pounds, and my outlook on things is joyful and optimistic.

Many of you have written and asked what was wrong with me in the past.

The honest answer is that I suffered from a mild sort of inferiority complex. I used to work myself up into depressions, [and] thought no one really cared about me, no one outside my family, that is.

Why I should have ever gotten depressed, I certainly don't know. You people have proved to me that I've got thousands of friends the world over, that you care about my welfare and my career.

It's perfectly normal for people to have their ups and downs. I know that now, but a year or so ago, these depressions of mine used to worry me, and the more I worried about them, the lower I felt.

Anyway, all of that is gone and done with. The slate of the past is wiped clean. Insofar as I'm concerned, the world is good, golden and glorious. My best years and my best work lie ahead of me, and I'm going to give them everything I've got.

Many of you have asked if I realized how closely you followed my career and behavior. I certainly do, and that's why I want all of you to know, especially the youngsters, that I'm not in the slightest embittered about Hollywood and that I still think a motion picture career is one of the finest ambitions any girl can have.

It means hard work and it has its pitfalls but so has every other occupation.

If my daughter, Liza, wants to become an actress, I'll do everything to help her.

Of course, being a child actress and being raised on a studio lot is not the easiest adjustment a young girl can make. You don't go to baseball games or junior proms or sorority initiations, but every success has its sacrifices, and these are the ones a very young girl must make if she wants a career at a very early age.

The girl who finishes her schooling, however, and then wants to become an actress is facing a thrilling, rewarding career.

If I had to do it all over again, I would probably make the same choices and the same errors. These are part of living.

A lot of fanciful stories have depicted me as the victim of stark tragedy, high drama, and all sorts of mysterious Hollywood meanderings. All that is bunk.

Basically, I am still Judy Garland, a plain American girl from Grand Rapids, Minnesota, who's had a lot of good breaks, a few tough breaks, and who loves you with all her heart for your kindness in understanding that I am nothing more, nothing less.

Thank you again.

Judy Garland

MY STORY

JUDY GARLAND AS TOLD TO MICHAEL DRURY | **January 1951,** *Cosmopolitan*

Judy's first major print feature after the split with Metro came in the form of this "as told to" piece for *Cosmopolitan* in which she recapped her life story and, for the first time, made mention of a dependency on sleeping pills. She also addressed her highly publicized suicide attempt of the previous year, and announced career plans for the future.

"People will believe anything, good or bad, about movie stars. You get used to it, of course, but it can still shock you."

All my life I have tried to do whatever was expected of me, and now sometimes I think that isn't very smart. Sooner or later something inside of you kicks. It has taken me a long time to find that out, because I am a born trouper. My father used to say, "It won't make any difference what Judy does for a living, she'll tear the house down getting there," and he was right. I would have trouped in a shoe factory.

As it happened, I got into a business where trouping counts. One snowy Christmas Eve before I was three years old, I began singing and dancing on the stage in a little town in Minnesota. I poured my heart into five straight choruses of "Jingle Bells," and I would have kept it up all night if Dad hadn't carried me off, kicking and yelling like an Indian. I don't know whether I actually remember that or whether I've heard people talk about it so much that it seems as if I remember, but I do know this: I took one look at all those people, laughing and applauding, and I fell hopelessly in love with audiences. After twenty-five years, I still love them, and it has been a serious romance.

I wanted it that way. My mother is a strong-minded woman, but she was never a "stage mamma." During those vaudeville years, my sisters and I, while standing in countless wings waiting for our cues, used to hear other mothers threatening their children, saying things like, "You go on out there or I'll break your head," and it made us kind of sick. Nobody ever talked to me like that or forced me in any way. I drove myself—but it was my own doing.

Why I felt compelled to do it, I don't entirely know. It wasn't to forget my troubles—I've never been able to lose myself completely in my work the way some people can—but so much of the time acting was the only reliable thing I knew, the only place where I felt like a useful person, where people said, "Fine, you did a good job. Come again," and everybody needs to hear those things.

When I was about fifteen, I went back to see Grand Rapids, Minnesota, where I was born. I found a gracious little town, full of trees and porches and people who know how to live in simple goodness. I think I would have liked to grow up there, carrying my schoolbooks in a strap and having a crush on the milkman's son. At least it made me feel good and somehow comforted to know that that was where I had my roots. That's the kind of roots I'm trying to provide for Liza, my little girl. While we were in New York last October, Liza wanted very much to go home for Halloween. She had her costume planned, and she'd been invited to a party where there would be popcorn and apples on a string. I let her go. Not just because we could afford it, not to spoil her, but because I felt it was important for her to have that memory to cling to.

My father, Frank Gumm, was a wonderful man with a fiery temper, a great sense of humor, and an untrained but beautiful voice. He met my mother, Ethel Milne, when he was singing in a Wisconsin theater where she was the pianist. They toured vaudeville together as "Jack and Virginia Lee, Sweet Southern Singers," until their first baby was coming, and then Dad bought the movie theater in Grand Rapids, and they settled down in a two-story white frame house with a garden behind it.

By the time I came along, Susie was seven and Jimmie was five. My parents were hoping for a boy, and I understand they tried to wield a little prenatal influence by referring to me as Frank, but I don't think they were deeply disappointed when they had to revise it slightly to Frances. Contrary to what some people seem to think, I wasn't a tomboy. I had great vitality, but I never took it out in athletics, and to this day I hate exercise of that kind. I play tennis a little, but that's all, and we don't own a swimming pool.

I adored my father and he had a special kind of love for me. In the evening before he went to the theater, while I sat on his lap in a white flannelette nightgown, he used to sing "Danny Boy" and "Nobody Knows the Trouble I've Seen." He lived to know that I had signed a contract with Metro-Goldwyn-Mayer, but not long enough to see any of my pictures.

Being the daughters of show people, Sue and Jimmie were already a song-and-dance team for all community affairs, and I was full of infant fury at being left out. At Christmas, Mother and Dad did some of their old numbers, so the whole family went to the theater. The first two Christmases, I slept in a dressing room, but when the third one came, I was all eyes and ears. They told me to sit quietly on a box—they should have known better. I marched out in the middle of my sister's performance and launched into "Jingle Bells" at the top of my voice. After that, there were three Gumm Sisters in the act instead of two.

Nobody ever taught me what to do on a stage. I have never had a dancing lesson or a singing lesson in my life, and I still can't read music. In those days, that wasn't so unusual; vaudeville was full of people who taught themselves to dance and sing, made up their own routines, and even sewed their own costumes. You could either do it or you couldn't. It was as simple as that. But today it sometimes gives me the rocky feeling that I don't know what I'm doing. I'm never sure how I've done till I see the final pictures—and I do see them. Seeing your own movies along with an audience is the only satisfaction you get; it's the only way to tell whether you've "sent" just yourself or whether you've let the audience in on it.

In 1927, Dad sold the theater and bought another in Lancaster, a little town in California, on the edge of the Mojave Desert. We lived there for nine years, and I wasn't happy any of that time. It wasn't anybody's fault.

Life in those desert towns can be rough; the land is barren, red-brown and harsh, and the people come to be a lot like it. I started school there, and I should have made friends outside my family, but other children found me difficult, I imagine, though I didn't intend to be.

I was never fond of school, really. The only teacher I felt attracted to was Miss DuVal—I never knew her first name; I don't suppose I even thought she had one. She taught the kindergarten and she also managed all the school plays. She liked me, and thought I was talented. When she put on *Goldilocks and the Three Bears*, she gave me the lead, which impressed me because my hair was neither golden nor curly. Shortly thereafter the school board dismissed Miss DuVal—I still think it was because she had too much imagination!—and after that the leads in plays were handed out according to grades. You can imagine where that left me: in the third line of the chorus. Alas, people with high grades don't always make the best actresses.

At Halloween, our house was a brief center of attraction because we had an attic full of old stage costumes. Kids came around and let Mother sew them into some of our most cherished outfits, but they rarely gave me much of a chance to make friends. I wasn't very happy.

But we were away a lot, because by that time we had started to tour, and the work, as always, had meaning for me. Mother played the piano and chaperoned, while Dad stayed home and ran the theater. I think he and Mom were as happy as most couples, but she was part of an era that was hard on women. She wanted so desperately to be a person in her own right, and I can understand that. If I weren't in a business that has always accepted women as people, that would have been one of my battles, too. Mother *had* to succeed in whatever she undertook, and I don't think there's any denying that part of success is money. Once when we were engaged to play at a civic banquet in Los Angeles, it looked like our big chance. Mom dyed materials in the bathtub and stayed up nights making costumes on an old treadle sewing machine. We knocked ourselves out, and we knew they liked us, but the man paid us a total of a dollar and a half. Mom put her curly gray head down on her arms and wept.

As a family we were never poor, but as a vaudeville act we were frequently broke. There was always a manager who couldn't pay us, or a downright cheat who wouldn't, but Mother never wrote home to Dad for money. Once, in Chicago, we found ourselves working for a mob of real gangsters, and when, after six weeks, Mother tried to collect what was owed us, they told her to shut up and stay healthy.

It was in Chicago, too, at the Oriental Theatre, that we were billed on the marquee as "The Glum Sisters." We protested to the master of ceremonies, whose name was George Jessel, and he said bluntly that Gumm wasn't much better. "It rhymes with crumb and bum," he said, "and in this business that isn't good. Why don't you change it?" He suggested we call ourselves Garland after a friend of his, Robert Garland, then the drama critic of the New York *World-Telegram* and now with the *Journal-American*. I doubt if we knew what the *World-Telegram* was, but drama critics were all right when they were on your side, and we adopted the name.

About the same time, I acquired "Judy" from a Hoagy Carmichael song. At first my family continued to call me Baby, my name since infancy, but I wouldn't answer until they said Judy, and in about three weeks they gave up. Inside of a year, people in Hollywood were even addressing my mother as Mrs. Garland.

We went home to see Dad and then got a call for a season's work from a man we knew, named Bones Remer. He ran the Cal Neva Lodge at Lake Tahoe. That's the place where the state line runs right through the middle of the dance floor. At that time, if you sat on one side of the dining room, you paid a sales tax; on the other side, you didn't. During our act, Jimmie and I would wave to each other from different states. We got a big bang out of it.

We had been lukewarm about going. I was glad to be with Dad, and Susie and Jimmie had discovered the opposite sex. But Bones always paid us, so we took the job.

It wasn't very eventful, and when fall came, we left, with Mom driving the old car, which was packed to the eaves. We had got about two miles down the mountain when Jimmie let out a yelp—she'd forgotten a big hatbox with all our headgear in it. We had to go back.

I ran into the dining room to get the box. Bones and some other men were in there, sitting around a table. Bones asked me to sing for his friends. I told him my mother was waiting with the motor running, and anyhow, there weren't any musicians. One of the men stood up and said he could play a little piano. What would I like?

In my earnest way of trying to do what was requested of me, I said, "Well, I guess it's okay. Can you play 'Dinah'?"

He grinned. "I can manage. I wrote it." He was Harry Akst. I was flabbergasted, but I sang, and when I got back to the car, I caught a scolding for taking so long to get the hatbox.

I've heard about twenty versions of what happened next, some of them pretty wild. One story has it that M-G-M signed me without making a screen or sound test. Nothing could be farther from the truth. We went home to a house we'd taken in Los Angeles, and a few days later Lew Brown, the songwriter, who was also an executive at Columbia Pictures, called up and asked my mother to bring me to the studio. He'd been at Bones's table with Harry Akst. Of course we went, and I sang for some people there, but nobody was impressed. Lew Brown told an agent named Al Rosen about me, and Al towed me all over Southern California. I think I had an audition at every major studio, but everyone kept saying, "She isn't any age. She isn't a child wonder, and she isn't grown up." Nobody had ever heard of *Junior Miss* or [*Meet*] *Corliss Archer* then. A teenager was regarded as a menace to the industry and fit only to be stuffed in a barrel until she could be made into a glamour job.

By a process of elimination we arrived at Metro where Jack Robbins agreed to hear me and got Louis B. Mayer to come in, too. When they told me, I asked, "Who's Mr. Mayer?" I guess they nearly dropped their teeth. Nobody said a word, but he couldn't have been mad because three days later my mother phoned me at school and said Metro wanted to put me on the payroll.

In the beginning, nothing changed. We kept living in the same house, and I didn't buy a lot of clothes or anything. I didn't expect much because I had certainly never planned on being a movie actress. I went to school in M-G-M's little red schoolhouse, which happens to be white. There were a half dozen other children there, all much younger than I, and there was also Mickey Rooney, bless him.

Several years before, I had met Mickey at Lawlor's School for Professional Children. Now Mickey took me in hand and showed me the ropes. He was tough, generous, gifted, and loyal. He told me not to be afraid of anybody on the lot, great or small, and never to do anything I didn't want to simply because other people said I must. It was good advice, and I wish I'd taken it; he'd had a heartbreaking time of it himself. Mickey and I have had a good, solid relationship over the years, not like a brother and sister because it was never that intimate, and not—to the disappointment of moviegoers, I guess—in any way romantic. Professionally and as a person, he respected me, and I him.

Hollywood is a place where it's easy to think the world revolves around Hollywood. You love it and live it, your friends are mixed up in it, your leisure time is dogged by it, everything you do is measured against it—will this be good or bad for your career?—you never get wholly away from it, no matter where you go or what you do. Don't misunderstand me; I love acting and if I couldn't do it anyplace else, I'd act on a street corner and collect pennies in a hat.

It's hard to keep your perspective in a world like that. When you grow up in it the way I did, it's hard to acquire a perspective in the first place. I wasn't a baby when I went there, but at fourteen was impressionable, excited, and eager to make good at any cost. I had missed the gentle maturing experiences most girls have, and I was supercharged with the kind of physical energy that spills out all over the place. People like me don't grow up easily; they bounce. One day they're adults with a head full of wisdom, and the next day they're stubborn children who have to be led by the hand.

Remember that girl in the book *Kitty Foyle*? She said her father was wonderfully wise—he knew when to treat a fourteen-year-old kid like a woman and when to treat her like a baby. I often thought of that because I needed my own father so much, but he died of pneumonia [*sic*] a few weeks after I went to work at Metro. I did a radio show with Al Jolson [*sic*] the night before my father died. Just before we went on the air, the doctor, who was Dad's best friend, telephoned and asked me to do a specially good job because Dad would be hearing me. I knew then that Dad was dying; he was too sick to have been allowed a radio otherwise. I sang my heart out for him. By morning, he was gone.

About six months after Metro signed me—I had begun to think they put me under contract just to send me to school—another girl my age walked into the schoolroom. Her name was Deanna Durbin. Nobody had ever looked so good to me. We were the only adolescent girls on the lot, and we promptly formed a coalition and became fast friends. Eventually somebody discovered they'd hired us, and we made that awful two-reeler together called *Every Sunday Afternoon.* Then she went to Universal and became a really big star, long before I got anywhere at all. I was never jealous of her. I had no reason to be; we didn't do the same kind of work, and anyway, I liked her.

It was Mickey Rooney who gave me my first real insight into acting. I'd been in vaudeville ten years, and I'd never read a line; I only sang and danced. When at last I got some parts at Metro, in *Pigskin Parade* [on loan to 20th Century Fox], *Thoroughbreds Don't Cry*, and *Broadway Melody* [*of 1938*], I had to look at the results sideways to make them seem bearable. I thought that I was bad. I had tried too hard. I thought I overacted something awful.

Then came my first Andy Hardy picture, with Mickey clowning around, but doing a brilliant job. He was so easy, so natural. Just before our first scene together, he took my hands and said, "Honey, you gotta believe this, now. Make like you're singing it." And all at once I knew what I had been doing wrong. Good singing is a form of good acting; at least it is if you want people to believe what you're singing. If you can make yourself *believe* what you're saying—and you have to say some pretty silly things in musicals—everything else falls into place. Your timing, your gestures, your coordination, all take care of themselves. I learned to relax, and I found I could do a lot better.

The next big thing I learned about acting came six years later when I beat my head against my first scene in *Meet Me in St. Louis.* Because of my photographic memory, I was known on the lot as a one-take girl—two at the most. Nobody directed me very much; I just went out there and did what came naturally. So I hadn't reckoned on Vincente Minnelli. We had met before, but I had never seen him at work or worked under him. He made me do that first scene in *Meet Me* twenty-five times. I couldn't believe my ears. I was baffled and scared cross-eyed. When I went to my dressing room for lunch, I told my maid something dreadful had happened between my last picture and this one; I'd lost all my talent. I cried all over my makeup, and she almost had to push me back on that set. But then on the first try, it went off smooth as cream. Suddenly I knew what he had wanted all along; I saw that if I was ever going to be any good, I had to let go of myself and *be* whatever character I was portraying.

Vincente drove the whole cast, and in the end, I was more pleased with *Meet Me in St. Louis* than with anything else I had done up till that time.

I was to receive still another lesson in acting two or three years after that when I went to see *The Glass Menagerie* on Broadway. To be sure I'd have tickets, I wrote ahead for them before I left the [West] Coast. When I got to New York and picked up the tickets at the box office, a little note from Laurette Taylor, the play's star, was enclosed, asking me to visit backstage. I was touched and surprised, because we'd never met, and of course I went, my face still streaked with tears after her exquisite performance.

In general, visiting actors backstage is unsatisfactory. They're tired and hungry, or there's a brawl, with too many people. But Miss Taylor welcomed me as if into a drawing room. She washed her face and put on an old cotton robe, and then talked to me for two hours. I sat with her, drinking in her words, learning more about my own profession from her, perhaps, than from all the rest of my experiences, put together. I can't put into words what she conveyed, but I came away feeling as if my head were full of stars and I could do anything. Some months later I heard with shock that she was dead.

One day, years before *Meet Me in St. Louis* and my visit with Laurette Taylor, Mr. Mayer called me into his office and told me Mervyn LeRoy was going to produce *The Wizard of Oz* and wanted me to play Dorothy. It was my first big break. I got a special Academy Award for that film, and I wheedled my mother into letting me wear long white gloves to the reception, and a little white ermine cape I still have and still wear. Later, when

Mickey and I made *Babes in Arms*, I got my first long dress, white and *bouffant*. Other girls get their first evening dress for proms; I got mine so I'd look right when I put my feet in the wet cement at Grauman's Chinese Theatre.

Then everything did change, and very fast. I had obtained permission to go back to public school, and I attended Bancroft Junior High my whole last year, and graduated. It took me a while to convince the other kids I really wanted to be one of them, but when they decided I meant it, they took me right in and I lived as they did, with football games and gym lockers and all the rest of it. Then I tried to go to Hollywood High, but I lasted only six weeks.

People more astute than I have tried to understand the relationship between movie stars and fans. An actress not only holds a certain job, but in a sense she *is* that job; the fans like her and resent her job, if that makes sense. I'll never forget the first time I found myself in a mob of any size. Mickey and I went to New York for the opening of an Andy Hardy film, and there were about five thousand people in Grand Central Station to meet us.* I was terrified. It's one thing to be part of a happy mob like that, but it's something else to be its focal point. With the best intentions in the world, such a mob could kill you.

One of the most amazing things about all the trouble I've had lately is that people no longer want to paw me. People I see on the street, total strangers, look at me differently—as though they realize almost with amazement that I, too, have feelings.

I have lived hard and worked hard. I have never stopped to ask myself where I was going. There wasn't time, and the present was too exciting for me to worry about the future. Ordinarily it takes an actor two or three months to do his part in making a picture, but because of all the music and dances and rehearsals, a musical requires nearly six. I've worked in thirty-five pictures in sixteen years, only one of which was entirely without music—more than two a year. It was possible only because I am blessed, and cursed, with a photographic memory. I look at anything once—phone numbers or lyrics or music—and it sticks in my mind. I

---

*The enthusiastic reception at Grand Central Station actually took place on August 14, 1939. Judy and Mickey arrived in New York City to promote *The Wizard of Oz* and *Babes in Arms*.

have never studied a line of dialogue in my life. If I'd had to, I probably wouldn't have been an actress, because I don't like studying. While I'm getting my makeup on, I read a scene over—and that's it. I can remember as much as nine pages that way, sometimes for years.

When I was nineteen, Dave Rose and I eloped to Las Vegas, if you call it eloping when your mother goes along. I don't know how to explain that marriage; there wasn't any real reason for it. I was much too young. Probably nobody should be married at nineteen, but you couldn't have made me believe it then. Mom tried to tell me; so did several other people. I thought my superficial knowledge of the world was all there was to know.

I was in a cocoon emotionally, and Dave needed a certain kind of a girl that I wasn't. He's a talented man with an inner strength that makes him live a little apart. He enlisted in the Army without telling me till afterward. He didn't do it to be mean; he was just accustomed to fighting his own battles and making his own decisions. He and I were among the first entertainers to go into Army camps and put on shows. We worked hard at it, and we made records together, but music wasn't enough. And I was awfully young. It was something only time could do anything about.

I ran into Dave on the street not long ago. He's married to a lovely girl, and they have a baby daughter. I'm glad for him. We're each kind of content about the other. To feel no ill will toward a person you once were married to is a special kind of blessedness, and I'm grateful for it. During the time our marriage was running out, though, I was despondent. I didn't want to make a botch of my relationships with people. Nobody wants that, really, not I nor anybody else. The only thing I did well, it seemed, was work. That is not always a blessing.

Paul Gallico had written a story especially for me, and Robert Nathan adapted it into a screenplay called *The Clock*. It was my first and only crack at a completely nonmusical movie, and I loved that story. It was a delicately balanced thing about a soldier and a girl who met in wartime under the clock in Pennsylvania Station. They got separated in a crowd and didn't even know each other's names so they went back to the clock and found each other again. They were married in an ugly civil ceremony, with an elevated train drowning out the words. But they went into a church later and made their own service and their own beauty, and the next morning the soldier had to go away to war.

It had to be done just right. Robert Walker played opposite me, and he's wonderful, but somehow it didn't go together. After a while, the studio shelved it. I wasn't happy about that, and I kept going over it in my mind. One day I went to the studio officials and told them I knew what the picture needed—Vincente Minnelli.

"That man?" they exclaimed. "Are you crazy? He's the guy you were always getting so mad at."

"Yes, I know," I said, "but he got the best work out of me I've ever done, and I know he'll understand this story."

I got him, and we did the picture. It just missed being great. The critics said it proved I could hold up my end without a forty-piece band, and that was gratifying. From my personal point of view, it was a triumph because it was during *The Clock* that I looked at Vincente one day and something hit me. I thought, here was a man I could know for years and still find fresh interest in. We started going out together, and about six months after my divorce was final, we were married in my mother's house.

We took three months off for a honeymoon in New York and then went to Boston for the opening of one of Vincente's pictures. It was the first time in more years than I could remember that I just relaxed and had fun and let somebody else take care of me. By the time we got back to Hollywood, I knew the baby was coming and I felt happy and loved.

We were wild over Liza from the first moment we laid eyes on her, but I fretted over not having the calm and serenity I thought I ought to have. I wanted deeply to be a good wife and mother, and I was a little scared. In an effort to learn why I had never been able to get closer to people, I took a series of psychoanalytical treatments, and I have never regretted anything more. I'm sure psychoanalysis has helped a great many people, but for me it was like taking strong medicine for a disease I didn't have. It just tore me apart.

I went back to work and lashed myself as I always had. The friction of personalities in the movie business is something fairly severe. I've never worked in an office, but I think it's like office politics, magnified a hundred times by money, by fame, by the lopsided idea that only movies mat-

ter. I don't want to hurt anyone, and obviously I won't name names, but
there have been people in Hollywood who sometimes made it extremely
hard for me to do what I was so desperately trying to do—find myself. At
least I felt that way.

Actors live in a queer sort of double world. Not many of us have the names
or identities we were born with. I don't associate Frances Gumm with me
—she's a girl I can read about the way other people do. I, Judy Garland,
was born when I was twelve years old. When a studio puts you under
contract, its publicity department starts turning out news copy about you
that you read with astonishment. You think, can this be me they're talking
about? They don't really manufacture untruths, but they play up whatever makes interesting reading, and then a columnist adds his own little
embellishments and another adds to that until there's a whole body of so-
called "facts" floating around—almost like another you—that simply isn't
real. It isn't a lie, but it isn't real, either.

It's as if people were confusing you with some role you'd played on the
screen. As a matter of fact, people did that with me and Dorothy of *The
Wizard of Oz*. It took me six years to convince even movie people that I
wasn't permanently twelve years old, wearing my hair in pigtails; I'm still
trying to convince outsiders. You can't very well go around denying the
stories your studio releases when it is doing everything it can to make you
a star, and sometimes you get to doubting your actual personality.

When I was still a little girl, I found out people will believe anything
about movie stars, often without any evidence at all. They will believe
good things and bad things, often in equal measure, if it is just printed
somewhere, or maybe merely rumored. You get used to it, of course, but
it can still bother you a good deal. And it isn't just the bad things that can
be bothersome—sometimes you read or hear something wonderful about
yourself that has no basis in fact. Then you begin to wonder what kind of
world it is that you live in, and you begin to wonder sometimes what kind
of person you really are. Since childhood, I have always been on what I
suppose would be called the "sensitive" side, and I can have more than the
average share of "nerves" on occasion. And I certainly have been bothered

often with sleeplessness. Being unable to sleep is a pretty terrible situation, as anybody knows who suffers from this condition. At times I have been pretty much of a walking advertisement for sleeping pills. This is hardly something unknown to friends and acquaintances. But some people have exaggerated the habit, and twisted it around with words, and it is that sort of thing that can get a gal down, even if she has a lot more stability than I have. Taking sleeping pills is hardly a good habit. Nobody knows that better than I, but this inability to get a good night's rest has nagged me since childhood. And even though pills come on doctors' prescriptions, as mine did, they can be a tremendous strain on the nervous system. I was having my share of troubles with the studio and, there's no doubt about it, my physical condition didn't help.

And while I was in this condition, I became very concerned about Vincente. He is a calmer person than I have ever been, he's brilliant and temperamental, as he should be, and I got to thinking that a proper wife for him should be placid and always on an even keel. It was pretty plain that I was never going to be just that. In justice to him, I felt we ought to call things off, and he, trying hard as he always did to do whatever was best for me, finally agreed.

At the time, I was up to my elbows in *Annie Get Your Gun*. I'd made five pictures since Liza's birth, and started the ill-fated [*The*] *Barkleys* [*of Broadway*]. My dearest desire—to know and love another person as I never had been able to do—was blowing up in my face, and one day I walked smack off the set and didn't go back. I wouldn't have cared if a truck had hit me. The studio promptly suspended me and then, anxious to help, financed an eight-month stay at a Boston hospital where I went for rest and recuperation. The best thing about that whole trip was patching it up with Vincente. I found out he wanted *me*, not a hypothetical creature I thought I ought to be. He and Liza came to Boston to see me, and we stayed, the three of us, in the same suite of rooms in which Vincente and I had spent part of our honeymoon. I returned to Hollywood, rested, full of hope and courage, and eager to work.

I made *Summer Stock* with Gene Kelly, who is a dear. You can work in pictures with some people and never really get to know them, but Gene and I have been friends ever since our first film. I was partly responsible for getting him out there. I had seen him on Broadway in *Pal Joey* and had told Metro what a fine thing it would be if they put him into movies.

We got through *Summer Stock*, but not without a struggle. Gene encouraged me to forget what people might be saying, laughed with me, helped keep down the friction. I was late—I've been unpunctual all my life—and there were fights over that. I hate fights. I can't stand ill-feeling. I was wobbly and unsure, and desperately trying to prove, not to the world but to myself, that I was making good as a person.

My relationship with the studio for several years had been a little like that between a grown-up daughter and her parents. In some ways, they regarded me as their personal property, and they couldn't seem to realize I wasn't a child anymore. There was constant tension.

In such a mood, we went into rehearsals for *Royal Wedding*. At the end of two weeks, I was jumpy and irritable and sleeping very little. They were jumpy, too, and I couldn't blame them; they had put a million dollars into *Annie* before that day when I walked out blindly. On a Friday afternoon, I canceled a rehearsal, and in a matter of hours, I was out of the picture and indefinitely suspended.

It's hard for me to talk about what happened next. I felt humiliated and unwanted, and I was faced with the bitter knowledge that I'd come to that unhappy position by my own actions—it's true they were actions I couldn't seem to help, but they were my own. All my newfound hope evaporated, and all I could see ahead was more confusion. I wanted to black out the future as well as the past. I didn't want to live anymore. I wanted to hurt myself and others.

Yet even while I stood there in the bathroom with a shattered glass in my hand, and Vincente and my adored secretary, Tully, were pounding on the door, I knew I couldn't solve anything by running away—and that's what killing yourself is. I let them in and tried to make them understand how sorry I was.

It wasn't a good experience, but I think I'm better for it: You're always better for the tough things if you can get through them. The terrible tension broke, and I've had time for reflection. When *Summer Stock* came out, people liked it, and that made me happy because I've begun to see that it isn't nice to hurt the people you love, and I still love audiences. Metro and I parted amicably, which was fine of them and good for me. I had been at the same place for sixteen years; it's healthy sometimes to make a change.

I'm going to try my fortune now in radio and on television, and I hope to appear soon on the Broadway musical stage. I find I'm acquiring a certain philosophy and that, I think, is the one thing I've needed above all others. I'm not religious in the ordinary sense, but I have a growing faith in God. I send Liza to Sunday School because I want her to get acquainted with Him early. I'm learning to let go and stop forcing things, stop trying to meet life in a head-on crash. Nobody can wipe out his mistakes; you can only learn from them and go on from there. And so, perhaps, I have at last grown up. I'm learning to take myself as show people know how to take others, the good with the bad. I'm people, too. If I can remember that, I'll be all right.

RADIO INTERVIEW

ART FORD | September 1951, *Milkman's Matinee* (WNEW, New York, NY)

Judy's final reconciliation with Vincente Minnelli was brief. "I was just too lonely," she told a superior court judge on March 22, 1951. "I couldn't go on. . . . When we were first married, we were very, very happy. We had many interests together, our work and our friends. We enjoyed living. Then suddenly, without warning, my husband became withdrawn. He secluded himself. He wouldn't explain why he went away so often. I had to appear alone at parties and many places and it was very embarrassing to try to explain why he wasn't along. I was nervous, very nervous and ill. I had to call the doctor many times."

Recently released from the confines of M-G-M, and soon to be freed from her broken marriage to Vincente, Judy was essentially a free agent. Encouraged by Michael Sidney Luft, her new love interest, she took a daring step in the direction of independence in the spring of 1951. Judy set out on a professional journey that would establish and define the future of her career as an entertainer. With a monthlong gig beginning April 9 at the London Palladium, the city's preeminent variety house, she returned to her home on the stage and began concertizing. "I came full of fear; I left full of hope," Judy told the British press at the time. "I have found where I belong—out there under the limelights singing for my supper. . . . Out there, under the lights, I suddenly knew that this was the beginning of a new life . . . no performer can experience the Palladium 'roar'—that Niagara of noise rolling cross the footlights . . . without being shaken."

Following a triumphant tour of the British Isles that took her to Liverpool, Dublin, Glasgow, Edinburgh, and Birmingham, Judy returned to the United States determined to bring her live variety show to Broadway. "Now I know I can do it," she told Hedda Hopper. "I'm going to pick up where I left off. I've had enough trouble. Now I'm going to see to it that everything is right." It was soon announced that Judy would headline a scheduled four-week engagement—an all-star "two-a-day" bill—at the legendary Palace Theatre in New York City's Times Square.

In the days of the Gumm Sisters, "playing the Palace" was the dream of every vaudevillian, but by 1951 the once-sacred showplace was a dilapidated RKO movie house. Prior to her October 16 premiere, Judy participated in this interview for *Milkman's Matinee*, a popular all-night radio show on WNEW.

Art Ford: A few years ago, we were standing outside of Loew's State's stage door. A whole bunch of kids were waiting around because a very talented young lady was making a personal appearance there. They were waiting for her autograph. We were just watching to see what was going to happen. All of a sudden, a little kid came running down the street, tearing down at about ninety miles an hour, and sort of made her way through the crowd of kids that were waiting for their autographs and said, "Gee, kids, I'm awfully sorry but I've got an awful lot to do! I'll see you after the show!" Well, of course, the little girl was Judy Garland! And she had a lot to do; she's done a lot and she's gonna do a lot more, starting October 16th. It's our pleasure to have in front of our microphone tonight, Judy Garland, to tell us about her plans for her opening at the Palace Theatre here in New York. But before we do that, I'd just like to say hi!

Judy Garland: Hi!

AF: How are you?

JG: Fine.

AF: How was London, Judy?

JG: Oh, London was *wonderful*! It was very exciting. It was hard work, but it was certainly gratifying. The people were lovely to me.

AF: The Palladium didn't frighten you too much?

JG: Oh, of course it did! [*Both laugh.*] It scared the heck out of me! But it really was quite exciting!

AF: I walked in there one afternoon when it was empty and just stood on the stage. And I know what you must have felt when you walked out and looked at that place, because I don't think I've ever seen a more frightening theater from the stage anywhere in the world!

JG: It's *terrifying*!

AF: It looks ten times bigger than it is!

JG: I know, I know!

AF: The reception that the English gave you is now a matter of record. But I'm curious to know what songs did the people in London like that you did in the show?

JG: Well, they seemed to like the songs that I've done in pictures before. They were especially fond of "Over the Rainbow" and several other things I've done in pictures. "The Trolley Song" and "The Boy Next Door," and those kinds of things. They have a certain nostalgia about them, you know?

AF: Who played for you? Did you have a big pit orchestra or did you use a piano?

JG: No, we had a pit orchestra [led by] Woolfie Philips. He's a very talented man. Then I had a pianist, too . . . Buddy Pepper. He was onstage with me and he was very good.

AF: How long were you onstage at each show?

JG: Well, about fifty-five minutes.

AF: Wow! You had to work in London. You didn't have a vacation at all! [*Judy laughs.*] Did you see much of England? Did you do any shopping in London?

JG: I didn't do much shopping in London, no. I was working too hard. But I did some in Paris.

AF: How did you like Paris, Judy?

JG: I love Paris! I think it's one of the most beautiful places I've ever seen. I think it's really a woman's town because of all those beautiful clothes and . . .

AF: All those beautiful women!

JG: And all those beautiful women, you're right! [*Laughs.*] No, I thought it was enchanting and I did adore it.

AF: Are you gonna go back?

JG: Yes, whenever I can.

AF: I don't blame you. How was the food in Europe? Did you like it?

JG: I didn't mind it.

AF: Well, you didn't have a chance to enjoy it in London and I suppose in Paris you were too busy shopping. You've had a lot of big moments in your career, and you've had too many big moments. You've had so many big pictures and so many wonderful records, it's not even fair! And now here you come along with October 16th, which I guess is just about the biggest day of all, isn't it? Opening at the Palace Theatre, two-a-day. Those are words that might have been taken from the front page of an issue of *Variety* or a story about American show business. And I guess that if you really stop and think about it from the point of view of just plain artistry, you couldn't bring your songs and your work to an audience in a more perfect spot than the Palace Theatre.

JG: Do you think that, really?

AF: I think an awful lot of people are gonna be watching you that day, Judy. Not just the people in the orchestra, but all the great names of vaudeville who've played the Palace will be up there looking down and saying, "Well, look [at] that kid! How did she get there? And I bet she's having a wonderful time!" What tunes are you gonna do at the Palace? Do you know yet?

JG: Well, I'm going to do practically the same program that I did in Europe, with a few added things. I'm going to do the tramp number from *Easter Parade*, and lots of the things that I've done in pictures, and also some added ones that people haven't heard.

AF: What about the quick costume changes? In Hollywood you can take all the time you want for a change, but in a show like this, for example, changing into the tramp thing, you have to run backstage and it's really show business again, isn't it? You really get to work!

JG: Yes, yes! Well, I don't think we're going to run offstage to do that because that's too much of a stage wait. I think we're going to just dress right onstage. You can put that great big silly costume on over your dress, you know? And rather than have a stage wait, I think it's better. And also I think the audience would like the idea. It sort of lets them in on it. You don't go off and make a big mystery of it every time you change.

AF: I understand that you're heading out to California. Is that to prepare for the appearance at the Palace?

JG: Yes, it is. I'm leaving in a few days. And Roger Edens, who is . . .

AF: Your right hand!

JG: [Roger's] such a talented man. He's with M-G-M. And Bob Alton and Chuck Walters. They're all going to help me.

AF: Speaking of Roger Edens, Judy, here I am on a record show, I see a record in front of me which reminds me of Mr. Edens. He was the chap, I think, who did the arrangement on "You Made Me Love You." That sort of helped things go for you, didn't it?

JG: Yes, that's right!

AF: Gee, that was a wonderful record! Do you remember the time you cut it, or, rather, the time you played the scene? Was it in front of a mirror you were writing a letter in *Broadway Melody* [*of 1938*]?

JG: I was writing a letter in front of his picture.

AF: Oh, Clark Gable's picture. Gee, I guess every kid that has ever heard that record and for those of us who were fortunate enough to see that picture, sort of find that that was the personification of hero worship and fan worship. I wonder if we can take time out from our interview right now to have you play, Judy, your own wonderful record of "Dear Mr. Gable."

JG: Well, if you can listen to it, I can!

In the backyard of her Bel Air home on Stone Canyon Road, 1940

With Terry the cairn terrier, "Toto" in *The Wizard of Oz*, November 5, 1938

With classmate Mickey Rooney during the production of *Thoroughbreds Don't Cry*, 1937 INTERNATIONAL JUDY GARLAND CLUB

At home in Hollywood with sisters Jimmie (left) and Susie (center), circa 1938
INTERNATIONAL JUDY GARLAND CLUB

Frances Ethel Gumm,
Chicago, 1934

Age thirteen, late 1935

M-G-M's *Ziegfeld Girl*, 1941

Presenting Lily Mars glamour portrait session, fall 1942

On the backlot at M-G-M with "boy next door" Tom Drake from *Meet Me in St. Louis*

At an M-G-M party celebrating the fifteenth anniversary of *Modern Screen*, 1945

Publicity portrait for *The Harvey Girls*, 1945

With costar Gene Kelly on the set of *The Pirate*, 1947

An elegant pose from one of Judy's last portrait sessions for M-G-M

During a recording
session for Columbia
Records, April 3, 1953

With Sid Luft at the world premiere of *A Star is Born*, September 29, 1954

Preparing for a Luft family photo, 1956

In concert at London's Palladium, 1960

February 19, 1961, in Dallas, Texas, where she would perform two days later

On the cover of Hugh Hefner's short-lived magazine, *Show Business Illustrated*

In rehearsal, April 25, 1962

Visiting with the London press in her hotel suite, April 1962

With Jack Paar, 1962

With Liza, Joe, and Lorna on her 1963 Christmas show, episode No. 15 of *The Judy Garland Show*

With Gypsy Rose Lee on San Francisco television, August 1965

With Mickey Deans, December 1968

At the *Valley of the Dolls* press conference, 1967

With children Lorna and Joe at Disneyland

Backstage at Copenhagen's Falkoner Centret, March 25, 1969

Judy Garland, New York, January 7, 1963

AF: "You Made Me Love You," Judy.

[*Plays "Dear Mr. Gable (You Made Me Love You)."*]

AF: We're auditioning a young lady disc jockey here tonight in our special salute to Hollywood. Her name is Judy Garland. Frances Gumm. [*Judy laughs.*] And that record, of course, needs no comment. And I'm sure that, as I am, many of you are very curious about Judy and her appearance at the Palace Theatre. Judy, I know that you did some dancing around the stage at the Palladium. Are you gonna dance at the Palace?

JG: Well, as a matter of fact, I didn't dance at all at the Palladium, but I want to dance here at the Palace. I want to try to incorporate as many things as I can do . . . you know, comedy and a little acting.

AF: Are you going to do a scene or a little bit?

JG: Yes.

AF: Oh, wonderful! Gee!

JG: Yes, and dancing and so forth.

AF: Do people in London and places that you go still associate you with Mickey Rooney and say, "How's Mickey, Judy?" Do they remember the Hardy series? Did that make an impression on them?

JG: Well, I imagine they do. I don't particularly recall that, but I'm sure they do, you know.

AF: That was such a long series and such a wonderful one. Say, how's Liza, the Judy Garland of tomorrow? How's she doing?

JG: Liza? Oh, Liza's fine!

AF: I hear she's one of the reasons you're heading back for the coast.

JG: That's right! She's *wonderful!*

AF: Did she want to go to Europe?

JG: She *was* in Europe.

AF: She did go to Europe. You sent her back to the coast.

JG: Well, it was too hot here, you know.

AF: I agree!

JG: And she had to get back to school, too. She's a big girl now. She's a young lady. She's going to school.

AF: What about your apartment hunting in New York? Have you found a place? Are you going to stay in a hotel, or what are you going to do?

JG: Well, I don't know yet. I'm looking like crazy for a place to live because I expect to be here for quite some time and I don't want to stay in a hotel.

AF: Do you do your own cooking, Judy?

JG: My own cooking?

AF: Do you ever cook?

JG: Are you kidding?

AF: [*Laughs.*] I don't know!

JG: Not me!

AF: Not you? [*Laughs.*] Well, I knew you were a little bit busy to be cooking.

JG: No, I just don't know how! I've just been a real dope about it. I just don't know the first thing about it.

AF: Well, now here's the first girl I've met to have mentioned . . . Most of them say, "Oh, you'd be surprised" or something if they don't cook. But here Judy just comes right out flatly and says "No!" You know, another thing, Howard Dietz was telling me a few minutes ago that this filling the last half of a two-a-day is something that has been done by very few people. I believe he said that Nora Bayes did it at the Nora Bayes Theatre, and Joe Cook did it. I suppose that it'll sort of go down as a record once you've finished this engagement. The show is divided into two parts: the act that precedes you and your part, which is the end. Is that right?

JG: That's right.

AF: And who's going to play piano for you in New York? The same fella you used in London?

JG: No, I'm very fortunate. Hugh Martin is going to play piano for me.

AF: Hey! How'd you get him to want to work that?

JG: Well, he wanted to do it. And you know we're very good friends and he felt a certain amount of sentiment about it. And the excitement of going into the Palace. He just wanted to do that for me, and I think that's very fortunate for me because he's one of the best accompanists in the world, besides being such a fine composer.

AF: Well, you can't kid me, I know! When you played Loew's State, you used to have Roger Edens down in the pit for you, and you just want to have a good time backstage when you're not on. You don't want to be bored, and I don't blame you. I don't see how you could be bored with this particular engagement. How long is this for? Is it two weeks? Three weeks? Four weeks?

JG: Well, it's for *four* weeks, but with an option to go longer than that if anybody comes to see it! [*Laughs.*]

AF: I'll be there to see it! What about motion pictures now? I know that they must be calling you up every day and asking you to come and work for them. Have you been submitted any scripts to consider?

JG: Yes, I've been delivered a lot of scripts and I do want to go back into pictures because I like them very much. I like making pictures, but I just haven't found quite the right thing. And besides that, I'm having so much fun doing what I'm doing now, you know, so I want to sort of go along with this for a while and then, when I find just the right vehicle, I'll go back and do a picture.

AF: Well, you'd better. That's all I can say, because you've had too much fun playing to just people. You've got to reach the world again, and of course motion pictures is the way to do that. Judy, I wonder if we could play this record I have over here, which sort of is, I think, an acting record as well as a singing record.

JG: What's that?

AF: It's "Sweet Sixteen" from one of the Andy Hardys.

JG: Oh, my goodness. That was 108 years ago!

AF: No, it wasn't. It's a wonderful record. And here she is now, Judy Garland, playing her own record of "Sweet Sixteen."

[*Plays "Sweet Sixteen."*]

AF: And there you have Judy Garland and "Sweet Sixteen." Well, I think one of the nice things about Judy is, as you can tell from speaking with her, and I think you sort of feel that you are tonight, audience, because I know that I feel that she's talking to you, not to me. And that's the way she's always been in pictures and in the way she's always sung. She's sung to each and every one of us, whether playing to a small group or playing to herself. So I think all we've got to do with Judy is say we wish her all the best of luck, because I think any one of us would hate to walk out there that first night at the Palace and start the two-a-day going again. But who else can do it besides Judy? So I know that you and I feel very close to her and we're going to see her while she's in New York. And start pestering the Hollywood boys to make sure she gets the right picture and gets back on the screen there, because most of the country wants to see her again, too.

JG: Oh, that's very nice of you! Are you gonna come to the show?

AF: I'll be there the very first day. Opening day. I'll be right in the first row, because that's where I watched you at Loew's State with Roger Edens playing away in the pit. And that's where I'll be at the Palace Theatre, Judy. And any time you get tired with this thing, feel free to come back and become a disc jockey and join us.

JG: All right!

AF: We like you. I don't care if you are a star, we like you! Good-bye, Judy Garland.

JG: Good-bye. And thank you very much.

AF: Thanks for being with us. And good luck to you at the Palace Theatre.

SOMEONE TO WATCH OVER ME

JOAN KING FLYNN | May 1952, *Modern Screen*

What began as a four-week engagement at the Palace quickly turned into a triumphant 19-week record-breaking run of 184 performances grossing nearly $800,000. In March 1952, Judy was presented a special Tony Award for her "important contribution to the revival of vaudeville." She and Sid Luft took the Palace show on the road for four-week stints with the Los Angeles Philharmonic and at the Curran Theatre in San Francisco, but further tour plans came to a halt when Judy discovered she was pregnant. She and Sid were married on June 8 between shows in San Francisco.

"A woman needs a man to protect her and love her," says Judy. And it looks as if she's found him—at long last

For Judy Garland, the past few years have been filled with frustrations and unhappiness, but the nightmare was blotted out by the cheers and bravos of a tear-swept audience one April night last year at the Palladium. In the wings, the man she loved stood proudly by. The presence of Sid Luft made her happiness complete.

He was standing by her side again a few weeks ago on Judy's closing night at the Palace Theatre. In her dressing room, in one of her rare interviews, the twice-divorced star told this writer why she had chosen Sid Luft to be her husband.

"Any woman who's a real woman wants a man to protect her and love her," she said. "That's what Sid Luft does for me. We have accomplished so much together."

The facts are there to prove it.

Directly over her brown head, as she spoke, was a new but permanent fixture on the wall, a gleaming, gold plaque which read:

THIS WAS THE DRESSING ROOM OF JUDY GARLAND WHO SET THE ALL-TIME LONG RUN RECORD OCT. 16TH, 1951 TO FEB. 24TH, 1952, RKO PALACE THEATRE.

For 20 exciting, song-filled weeks, the star who had tried to end her life in despair before she met Sid Luft had made show business history. Not only had she become the world's highest-paid performer, but she was acknowledged by all to be tops in her profession. Sophie Tucker, the grand old veteran of song, had wept on opening night at the comeback drama of the glorious Garland voice and sense of showmanship.

Looking back over those satisfying weeks, Judy said, "This whole thing at the Palace has been magical." Huddled in her cotton dressing gown, she looked youthful and slender once again.

"Sid has done it for me," she said simply.

He reentered the room which he had left when Judy started to discuss her feelings for him.

"That's my fella," she praised as she watched him adoringly through the dressing-table mirror. Brown-haired, brown-eyed, with much the same coloring as Judy, the soft-spoken Luft is tall, slender and handsome.

There is no inordinate display of affection from this couple in love. Just a quiet acceptance and understanding of what each means to the other.

The telephone rang. It was for Luft, who was arranging some last-minute details for a closing-night party in the theater. Judy had been disappointed earlier that they might not be able to hold it in the Palace, but Luft with deft, able management had smoothed out the wrinkles, much to Judy's pleasure.

He explained to her in amusing detail how he had accomplished it. Her upturned nose crinkled in gleeful delight at this recital, and she doubled up in joyous laughter.

The happy secure girl was far different from the frightened, bewildered, overweight creature she had been before Luft and love changed her life.

Before they first went out together, each was living a day-to-day existence. Luft, too, was at loose ends.

The romance between Judy Garland and Sid Luft was almost over before it began.

It happened like this:

"Judy Garland, please. Sid Luft is calling."

"Just a moment, sir. I'll see if she's in." The New York hotel switchboard operator left the line. When she returned, she said briskly: "Miss Garland has gone out."

Disappointed, Sid Luft hung up the telephone. Perhaps he hadn't been definite enough about the date he had arranged for that November night in 1950. Maybe Judy misunderstood or maybe she was just kidding a few evenings before when she agreed to go out with him. They had met at a party. Later when the group went to El Morocco, he and Judy had danced together and laughed together, too.

"Well," Luft reasoned as he walked away from the phone, "I guess it's just one of those things."

The same unhappy thoughts were sifting through the mind of singing star as she paced the living room of her hotel suite. In a wall mirror she caught her reflection, all dressed up and obviously not going any place.

"You might as well take your hat off, Judy," she told her shining self. "You've been stood up."

It might have ended there except that a few nights later, the two met again at a New York party, this time a bit frostily. But nobody can be indifferent for long when Judy Garland's around.

"What happened to you the other night?" Luft got up enough courage to ask her.

Judy's famous cascading laugh rang out. "What happened to *me*?" I like that. "What happened to *you*? *I* was there!"

In the midst of relieved explanations they made another date and kept it.

The Garland laugh, which had been stifled too long in the months of personal tragedy and turmoil, rang out more often after that and it was no coincidence that she laughed longest and happiest when Sid Luft was at her side.

The sparkle was back in her deep brown eyes, her voice and her smile. Judy Garland was in love!

Her millions of fans who sat in judgment on everything she did took a dim view of this new man in her life.

"Did Judy do the right thing in divorcing her director-husband, Vincente Minnelli?" they asked querulously. "Should she have terminated her contract with M-G-M? Will this Luft, Lynn Bari's ex-husband, break her heart?"

The valiant singing star heard these rumblings. In the hectic years before when she was a public puppet whose talent and destinies were pulled and tugged at by many, she might have listened, but in her own emotional upheaval of maturity she had broken the strings that had made her bow and sing and dance to others' biddings.

At long last, she was a free soul.

"Judy and I never had any doubts," Luft told this writer.

"I love Judy. I want to protect her from the trauma she once knew. I don't want her to be bewildered or hurt again. I want her to have happiness. She knows now what she wants and that's to be free to make her own decisions, not to be tied down to any studio. I, nor anyone else, can never force her to do anything she doesn't want to do. When she was a child and a star, everyone was telling her what was good for her. She listened. The only security she knew was that she had a talent, one that she takes for granted because singing is as much a part of her as breathing. She has no desire to retire because she always has to sing."

Whenever Judy enters a room, even if it's filled with glamorous women in jewels and furs, somehow Judy involuntarily takes over the room. That's the magic of her talent.

It was in London, where Judy had cabled Luft in Hollywood to join her "for moral support," that the star asked him to manage a tour she was to make in the English and Scottish provinces. He realized that physical health and exercise were as essential to her well-being as emotional security. In Scotland, Luft, a good golfer, introduced Judy to the game that originated there.

"Her fourth time on a golf course, she shot a 48 for nine holes," he recalled with pardonable pride. "In Glasgow I had a set of clubs made to her measure—she's not very tall, you know, and needed special clubs. We had a little set made for her daughter, Liza, too, with her name on them."

After her endurance test of 20 record-breaking weeks at the Palace theatre, Judy proved she is in top condition again.

That last night as she sat in the dressing room and discussed her plans, she admitted with a peaceful, gentle smile that for the first time in many years she had no problems. She was no longer the puppet on the string. No one was tugging at her.

Her future had been planned at her own bidding; marriage to Luft at a then-undisclosed time and place, and a sunny sojourn in Florida with rest and golf her prime requisites.

In the latter part of April, she said, she was scheduled to appear at the Philharmonic Auditorium for four weeks in her show, which carries the credit line, "Production under Supervision of Sidney Luft." After Los Angeles, she planned to take her act to San Francisco. In late fall, she hopes to make her first movie since *Summer Stock.*

"None of this would have been possible," she said glowingly, "without Sid. He and I have accomplished so much in the last year. He's the kind of person you can lean against if you fall down. He's strong and protects me. I respect him. And most important, I like him as much as I love him."

JUDY GEM
On *The Wizard of Oz*

"That entire production is precious to me. It aroused my imagination and it all seemed like a fairy dream come true. Also, it is ever the reminder of the most sensational moment of my career—the night of the Academy Award dinner when Mickey Rooney presented me with the golden Oscar. The lump in my throat was so big when I sang 'Over the Rainbow' that I sounded more like Flip the Frog than the most excited girl in all Hollywood. And I'll never forget how Mickey came to my rescue, for I was so nervous I thought I'd faint. He practically held me up through the second chorus."
—To Maude Cheatham, *Movie Life*, August 1952

JUDY GEM

On Her Absence from Films

"I think I've become much better since then. I know it sounds awful to say, but I never really liked myself on the screen before. But now I go to the rushes and I actually enjoy them. I even cry a little at the sad scenes. The four years have done me a lot of good. I got out and met the people and sang before live audiences. It improved my timing, and my voice is better, too. I think I look better. I don't have that 'little girl' look anymore."

—To Bob Thomas, Associated Press, November 9, 1953

JUDY GARLAND'S MAGIC WORD

LIZA WILSON | **September 26, 1954, *The American Weekly***

By the time the Lufts welcomed baby daughter Lorna on November 21, 1952, everything seemed to be on track for Judy's return to films, a musical remake of *A Star is Born*. She and Sid formed their own production company to co-produce the film, which took several years to make and more than nine months to shoot. The result of the $4.8 million Warner Brothers endeavour was nothing short of phenomenal, a unanimous success, with *Time* calling *Star* "a massive effort. Judy Garland gives what is just about the greatest one-woman show in modern movie history. . . . A stunning comeback."

Variety concluded "the tremendous outlay of time and money is fully justified. It is to the credit of Jack Warner that he kept his mind and purse strings open and thus kept the project going." But it was Jack's brother, Harry Warner, that sliced and diced *A Star is Born* to pieces shortly after its promising premiere. He ordered nearly a half hour be cut from its run time, seriously compromising its continuity. Judy never got over the hack job that many felt cost her the Oscar that year. In private she was known to call him "Horseshit Harry," exclaiming that he "cut *A Star is Born* with his gums!"

"Timpani!" may not mean much to you—but it set the stage for one of Hollywood's greatest comebacks

Judy Garland and Sid Luft, two young people very much in love, sat close together in their parked car on a promontory of Lookout Mountain. Below them glittered the lights of Hollywood.

"It's beautiful," said Sid, "isn't it?"

"No," said Judy in a strange, frantic voice. "It's ugly. I hate it. I want to get away, Sid. And I don't ever want to come back."

"That's only because you've been badly hurt, honey," said Sid, drawing her closer to him. "You're unhappy and confused. But you're one of the biggest names in show business. You can make thousands of dollars in radio, in theaters . . . you can make millions in—"

"By the way," Judy interrupted, with a tense little giggle. "I'm dreaming of a beautiful steak."

"Sorry, honey," said Sid. "I haven't any money."

"Neither have I," said Judy. "I'm broke."

Almost four years later, Judy Garland had occasion to remember that night on the mountaintop when they had to borrow enough money for a hamburger at a drive-in. It was July 29, 1954, and the last scene of *A Star Is Born* was finished. Cast, crew and Warner Brothers executives gathered around to kiss Judy and slap Sid on the back. As the Lufts left, someone called after them, "You've got a wonderful picture. You'll make millions."

"The last time we were making millions," said Judy with a laugh, "we couldn't even afford a steak. Now we have a beautiful baby, a lovely home and a good picture." Affectionately she brushed her cheek against Sid's coat sleeve. "But I couldn't have made the picture without you, Sid. When I fell in love with you I'd lost all confidence in myself. I was a silly, frightened girl—but your love gave me faith in myself again. Remember opening night at the Palladium in London?"

In the spring of 1951, Judy had borrowed money from her agents to pay for her tickets to London. Sid went with her as her manager. It was her first public appearance since she had become emotionally confused and despondent over her career.

"I was sick with fear, that opening night," she recalls. "Five minutes before curtain time I told Sid I couldn't go on.

"Sid shook me so hard I heard my teeth rattle. 'You silly girl,' he said, 'those people out there love you. You're not going to fall flat on your face.'

"So what do you think I did? I fell flat on my face. I sang three songs. The audience applauded. I started to take a bow. My poor trembling knees buckled—and down I went.

"I managed to get offstage and had no intention of going back—ever. But Sid made me and the audience was warm and friendly."

After the Palladium came the Palace in New York. Sid was still busy bolstering up her ego. But a member of the Palace management, who shall be known as Mr. X, was just as busy breaking it down. He wouldn't paint her dressing room or hire extra ushers. ("Gotta save money. You won't be here long. Won't be many people coming to see you.") But when he refused her a timpani (a member of the kettle drum family) for the orchestra, it broke what little spirit she had left. One of the musicians said he'd be glad to lend her a timpani.

"No," said Mr. X. "We haven't room in the orchestra for a timpani. We'd have to take out three $4.80 seats—and they are all sold for opening night. We'll need every cent we can make. I don't expect this show to last long."

Came 2:30 in the morning—the morning of the opening. Judy had finished a rehearsal, a rather sad, dispirited rehearsal. She and Sid lingered on the bare stage after everyone else had gone.

"Sid," said Judy, "I just can't do the 'Get Happy' number without a timpani. I'll be a flop."

Sid patted her hand. And then, across the stage, he saw a box of tools a carpenter had left.

"Shall we?" said Sid, pointing to it.

"Let's," said Judy.

They unscrewed three seats from the first row of the orchestra and dumped them backstage. They called the musician who'd offered to lend them the timpani. They took a taxi to his apartment in the Bronx. By 5 that morning, the orchestra had a timpani. Well, that night Judy sang "Get Happy" as it never had been sung before and her opening night at the Palace made theatrical history.

Judy, you'll remember, played the Palace for 19 weeks, a sensational engagement that broke the records of such headliners as Kate Smith, Eddie Cantor and Georgie Jessel. On Sundays she liked to drive in Connecticut with Sid. One Sunday Sid said to her, "I've got a picture in mind for you."

"I've got one, too," said Judy. "What's yours?"

"No," said Sid. "You tell me yours first."

Suddenly she became quite shy.

"For years I'd wanted to do *A Star Is Born*," says Judy. "When I suggested it to Metro, while I was under contract there, they laughed at me. I was afraid Sid would laugh, too. So for 15 minutes we drove along, each waiting for the other to say first. And suddenly we both shouted simultaneously, '*A Star Is Born!*'"

During the pre-production days of the picture, Judy as star and Sid as producer had many problems. ("Sid had most of them. I was busy being pregnant.") Sid wanted the best, no matter what the cost. George Cukor to direct. Moss Hart to write the script. Harold Arlen and Ira Gershwin to do the music. Irene Sharaff to design certain sets and costumes. [Richard] Barstow to direct the dancing. The studio—one eye on the cash register—tried to offer substitutes. But Sid got what he wanted.

"Timpani became our rallying cry," says Judy. "To us Timpani means: Nothing is impossible. Often I was depressed and willing to compromise, but Sid would shout 'Timpani' and I'd rally for battle. I'm sure Jack Warner thought we were crazy."

One morning, a few weeks after the picture started, Judy woke with a headache. Her phone rang. It was Sid.

"Judy," he said, "what's the matter? We're waiting for you on the stage!"

"I have a headache," said Judy. "I think I'll stay in bed today."

"Timpani," said Sid, and hung up.

Judy was on the set in an hour. Strange what love, and timpani, can do for a girl.

HOW *NOT* TO LOVE A WOMAN

JUDY GARLAND | February 1955, *Coronet*

It has been well documented that Judy's personal life was full of highs and lows. She relied heavily on the strength and stability she found in Sid, but the Lufts' relationship was rocky, to put it mildly. Their marriage flourished and then faltered to the point that Judy filed for divorce on several occasions during the latter part of the 1950s, but each time the couple quickly reconciled. Whether qualified to offer relationship advice or not, Judy provided fascinating insight into her marriage when she addressed the audiences of both *Coronet* and *Reader's Digest* (May 1955) in this essay on the art of being a subservient wife.

A great actress tells frankly the single thing a man must know to make a woman happy

Millions of words have been written on how a man should love a woman. But I have been looking in the mirror and thinking backwards. And I would like to give you my reflections on the things a man should *not* do in loving a woman. Perhaps I am wrong. You will know.

Don't yield your leadership. Don't hand us the reins. That's the main thing. We would consider this an abdication on your part and quicker than anything else, it will fog the clear vision of mutuality which made us love you in the first place.

It would confuse us, it would alarm us, it would make us pull back.

Oh, we will *try* to get you to give up your position as Number One in the house. That is the terrible contradiction in us. And you must realize that we can't help it. It will be a mistake on your part if you blame this contradiction on us and get furious at its very existence. You will have to understand that it *does* exist, because you're the one who's going to get us over it, if anybody ever is.

We will seem to be fighting you to the last ditch for final authority on everything for a while. But in the obscure recesses of our hearts, we want you to win. You *have* to win. For we aren't really made for leadership. It's a pose.

If you can't teach us that, I think it would be better for you to leave. I really do. It means we really can't be women at all. Or at least we don't intend to be women for you.

And some woman *will* mean to be for you. There have always been plenty of fish in the sea and there always will be. Just don't stay around and be licked; that's no way to love a woman. And that's no woman for you to love.

I think this first bid to get you down, to domesticate you, to make you give up your leadership, is a test we simply must put you through. For, at heart, we are dreadfully insecure. And we must know, beyond doubt, that we're safe with you. That you can take it, that you are not bluffing about your strength. And most of all, that you *care* enough to win.

Yes, that's it. *That you care enough to win.* It isn't that we're testing you just because we're biologically vulnerable—are going to bear the children. That's not it at all. We're brave as lions (no matter how much we snivel at our "fates") when it comes to our biological destinies. Or your economic ups and downs. Or earthquakes or floods or anything real and tangible like that.

What we're really scared of is that your love will go dead on us; that you will leave us. And, being women, being the natural born "passive" ones, that we won't be able to lift a finger to stop it, that being the "followers" means ceding our rights to fight for what we want to keep. To fight for *you.* And that's why we fight *with* you, why we struggle; until we're totally reassured that it's all right to stop trying to tame you, to beat you to a pulp, to a nonresister who will never leave us. And whom, at that point, we wouldn't love anyhow.

You may say you don't like it that way. You like a woman who knows her own mind. Whom you can depend on. Who's clear, definite and so forth. You don't want a child bride with a flower-mind cluttering up the landscape.

Well, that's all right, too. We will be what you want us to be. We will be Miss British Tweedy with horsewoman's stride and a stentorian voice. Or we will be Miss Sunshine Efficiency of 1955 with a house in apple-pie order, the children as quiet as mice and your slippers waiting. Or we will be Miss Roundeyes Switch-hips with a champagne giggle and a come-hither leer twenty-four hours a day. *We will be anything you want.* That's the point. As long as you want it, and make it clear that you do.

And you? What do you have to do to get this paragon of giving womanhood? Well, don't worry about the details if you really love to have us around. It'll show. We'll know. It doesn't matter if you don't help with the dishes if you think it's demeaning. It probably is, if you think so. And it doesn't matter if you're terrible at odd jobs around the house, rebel at our long phone conversations with girlfriends, get furious at our pampering of the children, bring us to heel about money. Oh, if you only knew how much it didn't matter. *If* we know, know, *know* that you're Number One and love the role.

Oh, maybe some *little* things matter. How and how often you get it over to us, spontaneously and in your own way, that the intense secret of our love is on your mind, causing you to think about it. But never mechanically. The mechanization of love we dread more than anything. It means death to us.

I know a husband who sent two dozen roses a day to his wife. Every day, every day in the year. In the end the routine arrival of the flowers, such a lovely gesture at the beginning, became a horror to her. Her "thank you darlings" became phrases to choke on, her pleased smile curdled on her lips.

"What did I do?" he asked bewilderedly when she sued for separation. Well, he hadn't done anything terrible. But yet he had.

Gift-giving, we know intuitively, is one of the chief ways you have of telling us about your feelings for us. It is only meaningful to the woman if she recognizes that subtle essence of wanting-to show-your-feelings in the giving. The gift? Our hero would have done far better to have given one rose a month, interspersed with an occasional set of inexpensive earrings or box of chocolates than to have indulged his monotonous fantasy to the extent he did.

And, for heaven's sake, don't trust when we tell you what we want directly. We don't *want* a new mop. We don't even want a washing machine. We want something from you that is exclusively for us. A five-dollar bill, even a one. If you say something *right* with it, something you mean: "Run wild with this, darling" or "But yourself five ice cream sodas."

"Why should I buy five ice cream sodas?" we might ask hopefully.

"Because I want to think of you having a big binge in an ice cream parlor tomorrow and getting out of this child-infested madhouse."

Pretty silly, isn't it? Of course. But you don't know what it does for us that you're silly. Silly with us. It means you are still silly about us.

And one more little thing, perhaps the same thing as gift-giving. Or perhaps even more important. Showing that you want to be alone with us. At a party saying: "C'mon out into the kitchen with me while I mix them some drinks—they'll get along by themselves," meaning the guests of course. And they will; and you'll find us such a flashing hostess when we come back from that four-minute exclusive excursion with you that you'll wonder what got into us.

Or, at a picnic in the country, saying: "You kids stay here. Mother and I are going for a walk alone for a while." And then taking our hand. Just a little walk. Just a few minutes. Just to show us we're not all mother, all helpmate.

We lose our identities quickly in what we're doing, we women. And you give it back to us when you show us that we're basically your sweetheart—not just the mother of your children or your economic collaborator. The kids will never have seen such a motherly mother in their whole lives as we will be when we get back from that little walk.

You see the point? We become unsure, get nervous about our real meaning, unless you affirm it to us. And this brings me to the problem of arguing and fighting.

Nobody (who knows) will say that an occasional brisk encounter, verbally of course, will do any harm to either of the combatants. In fact, it's a specific for certain forms of material doldrums. Minor discords are like flat stones: they can pile up. Or like a fog: they accumulate. And a good tiff can be like a breath of cool breeze to a valley mist, blowing it away, clearing the atmosphere. So don't be afraid of a fight with us. We're not made of glass.

But when we must have an argument with each other, don't yell at us. Not unless we become *utterly* impossible and you simply can't help it. We suspect a yeller. And it isn't because the loud voice frightens us. It's that we know at once, someplace deep inside, that your voice-raising means weakness. That somehow, we have scared *you* and by raising your voice, you are admitting it.

Do you know how to stop a yelling woman? Just be silent until we are. Because we're being absurd and childish, and we know it. If you don't share our childishness, you'll win the argument every time that it has any importance at all. For of course, we want you to win it. That noise you heard just before you made us giggle at ourselves with your well-timed silence was a tiny, tiny thunderclap in an infinitesimal teapot.

So, you see, you have the Indian sign on us. But never doubt it. Just remember the beautiful passage from Ruth that always brings tears to a woman's eyes. Remember? "Whither thou goest, there will I go; and where thou lodgest, I will lodge. Thy people shall be my people and thy God my God." We weep at it because it is such a beautiful description of woman as a follower. And therefore, you and you alone must be the leader. If you are not, nothing else really matters—not money, not brains, not beauty. No, not anything.

JUDY GEM

On *A Star is Born*

"I'm a little tired of being the patsy for the production delays on this picture. It's easy to blame every production delay on the star. This was the story of my life at Metro, especially when I was a child actress. When some problem came up that they couldn't lick, the delay, no matter what caused it, was always blamed on the star. Whoever was responsible figured that the star could get by without a bawling-out, they couldn't. . . . I caused three days delay in one year—and it was illness, not temperament."

—To James Bacon, Associated Press, February 17, 1955

JUDY GEM

On Television

"Oh, dear, this television is a monster. I'll be lucky if I live through it. I'm in a daze most of the time. That four-eyed color camera just throws me. They tell me to look right in the lens, but I don't know which one. I guess it's the little hole on top. . . . It's a new medium—another form of show business. I've wanted to try it, to reach a new kind of audience."

—To Associated Press, September 19, 1955

JUDY GEM

On the London Palladium

"Standing in the wings, waiting to go on, I became paralyzed. My knees knocked together and I walked on like a stiff-legged toy soldier. After a while, without knowing how it had happened, I found myself, not standing on the stage, but sitting on it. It was said I tripped over a wire or a loose board. That's not true. I didn't fall at all, really, I just collapsed. The fall happened after I had sung two or three numbers. I was trying to take a bow. I just went 'Ugh' and sat down. I sat there and thought, 'Damn this.' I looked up at Sid, who was hanging out of a box, screaming, 'You're great, baby, you're great.' Somehow I got back on my feet, lurched back to the wings. I remember thinking, 'That's it. Judy falls on her can and that's the end of the great comeback.' I was ready to quit, but my old friend Kay Thompson was waiting at the side of the stage. She screamed, 'Get back there. They love you.' Then she gave me a hug and a shove that carried me back almost to center stage. Instead of giving me the bird, those wonderful British people clasped me to their hearts. I unlocked, and everything I wanted to do came surging out. All the bad years went. It was like being reborn. It was like being given a new life to start all over again."

—To Joe Hyams, *Photoplay*, January 1957

JUDY GEM

On the 1955 Academy Awards

On a March night in 1955 when the Academy Awards were given out, everyone in Hollywood seemed to think it was a race between Grace Kelly for *The Country Girl* and me for *A Star Is Born*. Like just about everybody else, I wanted an Oscar and I wanted it badly.

Of course I knew there was a good chance I wouldn't win, and anyway an event that meant a lot more to me was coming up in my life. I was going to have a baby. According to the radio and television people, any woman can have a baby, but only one woman a year can win the top Oscar. So the National Broadcast Company conducted a full-scale invasion of my hospital room.

Outside my window they built a platform big enough to launch a rocket. It was three stories high, and the idea was for the cameras to shoot through the window the minute I learned I'd won.

Then, just twenty-four hours before deadline, Joe was born. There I was, weak and exhausted after the battle to bring him into the world. He was very frail, and the doctors were giving him only a 50-50 chance of survival.

As I lay there in bed, the door burst open and in came a flock of TV technicians. I already had a television set in my room, but they dragged in two more huge ones. When I asked why two sets, I was told that I would have to talk back and forth with Bob Hope, who was master of ceremonies at the awards, and they couldn't take a chance on one of the sets not working properly. Then they strung wires all around the room, put a microphone under the sheets and frightened the poor nurses almost to death by saying, "If you pull up the Venetian blinds before they say 'Judy Garland,' we'll kill you."

Outside the window I could see the cameramen on the tower getting ready to focus on me in bed. Then someone turned on the TV set and Bob Hope came on. We listened to the whole ceremony, the excitement building up. Then Bob announced the winning actress. It was Grace Kelly.

I didn't have the time to be disappointed, I was so fascinated by the reactions of the men. They got mad at me for losing and started lugging all their stuff out of the room. They didn't even say good night.

—To *McCall's*, April 1957

JUDY GEM

On Concert Venues

"I'm a little nervous about the great honor of appearing at the Met, but I've been dreaming about it since I was a little girl. There is no firm line anymore between popular and classical performers. Classical artists like Helen Traubel, Lily Pons, Patrice Munsel and Lauritz Melchior have all made good in TV and nightclubs. Now I think it's time some of the popular entertainers turned the tables and seek new audiences, too. Nat (King) Cole and Frank Sinatra could be great successes in concert halls. This is a big step for me, and harder than nightclubs in a way. But appearing in concert halls has one advantage. You only do one show."

—To Vernon Scott, United Press International, March 25, 1959

PART IV

THE 1960s

JUDY GARLAND
FAR FROM HOME

ART BUCHWALD | October 2, 1960

Judy recorded and performed concerts around Europe for much of 1960, taking up residence in London, where she and the family spent Christmas before returning to New York City on New Year's Eve. Humorist Art Buchwald, a Pulitzer Prize-winning author and columnist, interviewed Judy by phone from France for his syndicated column.

PARIS—Among the Hollywood stars who have moved to Europe is Judy Garland, who has taken up residence in London. Miss Garland's press agent asked us if we would like to interview her by telephone and we said we would like to. It was the first interview ever done across the English Channel with Judy Garland.

It went like this:

"Hello, Judy? How are you?"

"I'm fine."

"What are you wearing?"

"A red dressing gown. I'm going to have a cup of tea."

"What else?"

"Cucumber sandwiches."

"No, I mean what else are you wearing?"

"White slippers."

"Is your hair up or down?"

"Down. How are you, dear?"

"I'm fine. I'm wearing a black tie and a . . ."

"What else?"

"Nothing else. I'm not going to have any tea."

There was a pause. Apparently, she was eating a cucumber sandwich. We asked her: "What happened? Why did you leave Hollywood?"

"Well, you see I've been there for so many years and I like it very much, but I decided it would be nice to live in England—you know, because I wanted the children to go to school in Europe and I'd like to be around with them.

"Liza, my 14-year-old one, is having trouble, though. The educational system in Southern California is behind the English schooling system— it's even behind the New York schooling system, and Liza has to have tutoring before an English school will take her."

"What are you going to do over here?"

"I'm going to do concerts and probably make a film or two."

"That will take a year or so?"

"Over a year. I don't know how long I'll stay. It's funny—the papers in America have been writing a lot of mean things about me moving over. They seem to think that I'm a traitor or something."

Sound Angry

"They'll soon be calling you a runaway movie star."

"Yes, and they sound very angry, but they shouldn't be. After all, I'm going back there."

"They say most Hollywood movie stars who take up residence in England are not driven home by bad publicity but because there is no central heating."

"We're staying in Carol Reed's house. He doesn't have central heating, but there are stoves in every room. It's real nice and warm.

"Eddie Fisher and Elizabeth Taylor are still looking for a house over here. As a matter of fact, they looked at this one before we did, but they looked at it on a dreary, rainy morning and none of the heaters were on, so they turned it down. When Eddie came over the other day all the heaters were on, and he was mad as hell he didn't take it when he had a chance."

Miss Friends?

"Do you miss your Hollywood friends?"

"Yes, I miss them, but I have friends over here."

"You'll miss the elections."

"I have an absentee ballot, so I'm going to vote."

"Kennedy?"

"Natch."

"Would you go out campaigning for him if you were in the United States?"

"Oh yes. But it probably wouldn't have meant anything one way or another."

"Maybe you could make a record over there."

"That's an idea. Something like 'Even in Kensington I think of Kennedy.'"

Renting House

"Are you renting your house in Hollywood?"

"Yes. But I let my staff go. This European trip gave me a good excuse to fire them. I didn't have the nerve to do it before. I think it was good to get away just to give me a chance to get rid of all of them."

"How's the English staff?"

"Very nice, very English. They belong to Carol Reed. The cook is wonderful."

"How's the butler?"

"There is no butler."

"No butler? No wonder Eddie Fisher didn't want the house."

JUDY GEM

On Tragedy

"People think of me as a neurotic kid, full of fits and depressions, biting my fingernails to the bone, living under an eternal shadow of illness and collapse. Why do people insist on seeing an aura of tragedy around me always? My life isn't tragic at all. I laugh a lot these days. At myself, too. Lord, if I couldn't laugh at myself I don't think I'd be alive."

—To journalist Herbert Kretzmer, 1960

JUDY GEM

On Birthdays

"I don't remember having any birthdays as a child. My mother was always afraid the studio would decide I was too old to play child parts. So we just ignored them."

—To George and Helen Matthews, *Redbook*, August 1960

JUDY GEM

On Belting

"[They] nicknamed me 'Little Leather Lungs.' I hated that but I loved to sing. There is something wonderful about belting a song across the footlights, clear and true, and feeling it bounce off the top balcony. I can't explain it. There's nothing like it. It seems to be a kind of a female thing, this business of singing a song straight from the belly. I don't know of any male singer who does it, but Sophie Tucker, Ethel Merman and a lot of other great women singers have that quality in their delivery."

—To George and Helen Matthews, *Redbook*, August 1960

JUDY GEM

On Living in London

"In Hollywood, my daughter came home from school and said the child of a star told her I was 'nothing but a fat has-been!' She told him that's more than his father is—a never-was. Imagine the difference here. My children go to school and no one pays attention. One English child told Lorna she had heard one of my records and thought it was all right. A nice downplay and that is what I've found. I can go shopping and be absolutely unnoticed, like anyone else."

—To Tom Reedy, Associated Press, January 21, 1961

JUDY GEM

On Audiences

"You stand there in the wings, and sometimes you want to yell because the band sounds so good. Then you walk out and if it's a really great audience, a very strange set of emotions can come over you. You don't know what to do. It's a combination of feeling like Queen Victoria and an absolute ass. Sometimes a great reception—though God knows I've had some great receptions and I ought to be prepared for it by now—can really throw you. It kind of shatters you so that you can lose control of your voice and it takes two or three numbers to get back into your stride. I lift my hand in a big gesture in the middle of my first number and if I *see* it's not trembling, then I know I haven't lost my control.

A really great reception makes me feel like I have a great big warm heating pad all over me. People en masse have always been wonderful to me. I truly have a great love for an audience, and I used to want to prove it to them by giving them blood. But I have a funny new thing now, a real determination to *make* people enjoy the show. I want to give them two hours of just *pow*!"

—To Shana Alexander, *Life*, June 2, 1961

TV INTERVIEW

HELEN O'CONNELL | June 23, 1961, *Here's Hollywood*

Following a seven-year hiatus from films, it was announced in January 1961 that Judy Garland would return to the screen in Stanley Kramer's upcoming film *Judgment at Nuremberg*. Given her reputation in Hollywood, the decision was one that Kramer agonized over for some time, but he eventually offered $50,000 in exchange for her portrayal of German hausfrau Irene Hoffman Wallner.

This interview with singer-turned-host Helen O'Connell was filmed in Los Angeles on the set of *Nuremberg* in March 1961. *Here's Hollywood* was produced by Desilu and ran for two seasons on NBC-TV.

Helen O'Connell: And now for a special treat we're visiting Universal Studios via monitor, where Judy Garland is busy appearing in the Stanley Kramer production *Judgment at Nuremberg*. This is a milestone in her career because it marks her first picture in six years, and we're very anxious to talk to her about it. Judy, now that you've appeared in the film *Judgment at Nuremberg*, the inevitable question is . . . how does it feel to be back before the cameras?

Judy Garland: Well, it feels . . . it feels very nice. I'm enjoying it a great deal. I had forgotten how much detail and how much work actually goes into movie-making, but I am enjoying it.

HOC: The particular role you play in the film is different from anything you've ever done on the screen. How did it happen that you chose this as your first picture in six years?

JG: Well, I think it's a terribly important picture—I think what it has to say is important—and also the opportunity to work with marvelous actors and to work with Mr. Kramer was very tempting and I couldn't resist.

HOC: This is a Stanley Kramer picture. Now, how do you like working with this producer?

JG: I think I could be the president of his fan club [*laughs*] because I find him imaginative and exciting and he knows exactly what he wants and what he wants is inevitably right. And yet he's still very calm. He's very gentle. There's no tense feeling. He's marvelous. I would love to work with him again. Also, the little that I do is quite good, you know. I mean it's written well. I don't know whether I do it well. It's written beautifully. It's very explosive.

HOC: How would you describe the part?

JG: It's the part of a German woman who during the Nazi regime is put into prison for not participating in a Nazi plot to execute a Jewish man.

HOC: I see. It sounds very interesting, and it has a big cast—Spencer Tracy, Burt Lancaster, Richard Widmark, Marlene Dietrich, Maximilian Schell, Montgomery Clift—you work with all of them?

JG: Yes. I work with Mr. Widmark in the apartment and then I work with . . . Well, as a matter of fact, I have no scenes with Miss Dietrich or Mr. Clift. But in the courtroom Spencer Tracy is the presiding judge and Richard Widmark is the prosecutor and Burt Lancaster is the chief defendant. Is that how you'd say it? The defendant? And Maximilian Schell is the prosecutor. And I'm surrounded by rather good people, I'd say.

HOC: There's been a lot of talk about actors being cast in pictures requiring them to play roles that, although quite brief, are very potent. Now, how do you feel about this, Judy?

JG: Well, I think it's a good idea. They do that in England a lot, and I think it's good for an actor. I don't mean just a little cameo role where you sort play yourself in your own setting, but if you actually play a character part, no matter how small, if it's good, I think it's interesting for an audience and it sort of keeps your own work interesting doing that. That's the most involved answer I've ever heard!

HOC: [*Laughs.*] How do you regard yourself? As an actress or as a singer?

JG: [*Hesitates.*] I don't know. I suppose I'd be called an entertainer, I think.

HOC: I know that Mr. Kramer and other producers have called you the world's *greatest* entertainer. I don't think there's *any* argument about that. What are your plans now?

JG: I'm going to do a concert tour in the East, and I'm going to play Carnegie Hall in April, and I'm looking forward to that. Then, after that I'm going back to London and I'll probably work there. I have a movie to do there.

HOC: In this role, a tremendously dramatic one, you do an outstanding job. Is there any thought of your concentrating on dramatic roles in the future, do you think?

JG: No, I wouldn't stop singing, you know. I think that I would like, though, to only do a good story, and if there's music with it, that's fine. And if not, that's fine, too. Just keep working. [*Laughs.*]

HOC: Judy, thank you very much.

JG: You're very welcome.

JUDY GEM
On 1961

"This is the best year of my life. I'm well again—can you believe it?"
—To Jane Ardmore, *The American Weekly*, October 1, 1961

JUDY GEM
On Anxiety

"I had so many anxieties, so many fears. I'd had them as a child and I guess they just grow worse as you grow older and more self-centered. The fear of failure. The fear of ridicule. I hated the way I looked.

"I cried for no reason, laughed hysterically, made stupid decisions, couldn't tell a kind word from an insult. All the brain boilers gave me up. I staggered along in a nightmare, knowing something was vitally wrong, but what? It got to the point where I was a virtual automaton—with no memory! I played some very big dates in '58 and '59. . . . I don't remember any of it."

—To Jane Ardmore, *The American Weekly*, October 1, 1961

JUDY

JAMES GOODE | **October 31, 1961, *Show Business Illustrated***

Judy was named "Show Business Personality of the Year" for 1961, as well as "Female Vocalist of the Year," and awarded "Best Popular Album of the Year" by *Show Business Illustrated*, a short-lived publishing venture by *Playboy* proprietor Hugh Hefner. With flair and sophistication, the magazine showcased the best in film, theater, music, nightclub acts, television, and books. The first copies of the biweekly surfaced in the summer of 1961. "It will do for show business what *Time* does for news and *Sports Illustrated* for sports," Hefner told the press. But *Show Business Illustrated* turned out to be a costly flop for Hefner, and he sold the publication to a competitor after only six months and eight issues.

During the magazine's short lifespan, journalist James Goode accompanied Judy Garland on tour and penned this fascinating trilogy focusing on her rejuvenated career and life back out on the road.* Goode went on to serve as executive editor for *Playboy*, *Playgirl*, *Penthouse*, and *Viva* in the 1970s, and was credited with having created the popular *Playboy* Interview.

In 1997, Hugh Hefner was asked to recall *Show Business Illustrated*. "I kind of wish I would've stayed with [it]," he replied. "*Show Business Illustrated* is *Entertainment Weekly*."†

Miss Garland of the built-in sob is once again over the rainbow and on first-name terms with the universe. Here is the beginning of a three-part love song to America's apparently indestructible girlfriend.

---

*Part II of the feature appeared in the issue dated November 14, 1961, with Part III following on November 28.

†From "Playboy Interview: Hefner on Branding," *Advertising Age*, November 3, 1997.

Last summer, at an unrecorded point, but most likely the Fourth of July, Judy Garland became a national monument. America's on-again off-again love affair with the girl-next-door-grown-up was stabilized at last. Judy Garland was back on top again, apparently for good. What is more, she was happy, and her resurgence proved that she had been in our national subconscious all along (with such forgotten virtues as speaking your mind, turning the rascals out, and freedom from fear).

Things came to a head at the Garland concert on April 23 at Carnegie Hall in New York, which became a mass demonstration of love shortly after the first note. It was plain that Judy had emerged from the doubts, fears and gloom of a long illness to find a delightful world, and everyone had wanted her to be happy for so long that when she was, it was more than they could stand. Overnight, one of our potential liabilities became a national asset. Edward R. Murrow, anxious to convince Latin America of our goodwill, asked Judy if she couldn't learn her songs in Spanish. A Broadway director, Jack Cole, said that it plainly didn't matter, that she could sing "Rock-a-Bye Your Baby with a Dixie Melody" to an audience of Russians and they would understand. It was all in the voice, not the words.

Judy Garland had started a wave of public love that spread faster than she could sing, beginning last winter in Miami Beach and moving on to Dallas, Houston, Buffalo, Washington, obliterating two hip New York audiences in Carnegie Hall, building to ever-larger mass demonstrations at Forest Hills, the Music at Newport Festival, Atlantic City, and finally carrying her to San Francisco and a record audience at the Hollywood Bowl.

After Forest Hills, riding back to New York in a limousine with her managers, Judy laughed in disbelief about all of the small intimate places she might play: the Hollywood Bowl, Madison Square Garden, the Golden Gate Bridge. But the joke became a reality as the Hollywood Bowl (not big enough for Garland) sold out in ten days after the announcement that she would appear. It was plain that there was a crying (or shouting) national need for Judy Garland. She could easily have walked across the country singing to people lined up on either side of the road.

The only new recording made by the resurgent Garland (*Judy at Carnegie Hall*—Capitol, $10) has sold over 100,000 copies since its release at the end of July. What she was saying in the Carnegie record, from the opening attack on "When You're Smiling," in a voice as clear as a million gallons of spring water, was: "I love you, this is a romp, and let's go." The applause began at total acceptance after the overture and became compulsively vocal as one skeptical Garland-lover after another in the predominantly show business audience conceded that what they were hearing was really true.

Judy talked some of the lyrics, was best at full volume, did not always have ultimate control, and was working with a pickup band that occasionally played slower than God. It did not matter. She could have sold strawberries off the stage and charmed them all. She wasn't working, she was just talented. After the 21st song at Carnegie, the audience began to shout requests. Judy said, "I know, I'll—I'll sing 'em all and *we'll stay all night*. I don't ever want to go home. . . ."

Carnegie Hall had one advantage. It was a relatively small box and, unlike the outdoor appearances, Judy could bounce the notes of pure Garland emotion off the sides and even the top, but she sang as well everywhere else.

"The concerts were the formal part of her life last summer, but she was just as happy offstage, spending her time with her children and her friends, and vacationing at Hyannis Port, Massachusetts.

Even though Judy Garland had already signed a contract to write her autobiography long before this resurgent period, the publisher now had to resign himself to a long wait. As Judy said, "It's too soon. I have too many things I want to do. I have a feeling that I am just about to do the best things I've ever done. There are things I haven't really tried."

Judy was simply recognizing the fact that she had already had two careers, each of them as sensational as any in her profession, and that she would like to pursue a third, without distractions. After the current phase, she would probably settle for something simple, like producing shows on Broadway, or dictating her life story. For the moment, the best technique for grabbing Garland and putting her on paper seemed to be to recapitulate the basic facts of her life as briefly as possible and zero in on the 1961-model Judy.

Furthermore, the conventional terms "biography" and "life" do not seem to apply to the astral history of Judy Garland. Some of us remember

20 or 30 events in our lives that have had great emotional impact or professional significance, and some of us have only been touched by three. Judy has had significant visits from fate hundreds of times.

Judy Garland was born, if not with a caul, with inexhaustible energy, superior intelligence, a talent for every form of entertainment, a strong body and, most important, an overwhelming compulsion to keep trying and keep going. This formidable combination has used up everybody and everything in her 39 years except Judy herself, and even that has been close.

With only three or four pauses while she pulled herself together, each "pause" being billed as utter tragedy or complete collapse by professional crepe-hangers and oversolicitous fans, Judy managed to marry three times, bear three children, and make and spend $6,000,000. Meanwhile, she appeared in 31 motion pictures (as the star in most), grossing $250 million for M-G-M, and entertaining audiences totaling upward of one billion persons. Besides movies and TV she made better than 750 personal appearances, including benefits, USO shows, nightclub dates, theater presentations, and concerts before audiences ranging from 1,000 to 15,000 persons.

Some of the historically great motion-picture stars made no more than nine or ten pictures; some popular entertainers are content to work three or four weeks a year in nightclubs, or to star in one or two television shows a season in order to maintain a career; and some singers have made a national reputation with one song. Judy Garland, in addition to her movie career, which is far from over, has averaged one personal appearance each week for the past 12 years, including a record-breaking (19 weeks) run at the Palace Theatre in New York City; thereby, she has stamped her own name on over 100 songs. Anyone else is free to sing them, but they do so at their own peril. The resulting comparisons are likely to be rather odious.

If the above record is not enough for any five human beings, consider a childhood on the stage, the early loss of a father, a six-day week at M-G-M for 14 years (from age 12 on) with frequent 18- and 24-hour shooting sessions, and a completely public life, without normal friendships, until the age of 19. Add to this the strain of working closely and intensely with a large and shifting complement of other professionals over the years; not only the 200 persons involved in each of her 31 motion pictures, but also some 300 others—doctors, lawyers, agents, press agents, producers, entrepreneurs, secretaries, arrangers, composers, accompanists, conductors and dancers. You would have to be a very strong elf indeed to survive.

Judy was and is. Born Frances Ethel Gumm in Grand Rapids, Minnesota, on June 10, 1922, she worked first as a professional at 2½ years old, when she broke into two impromptu choruses of "Jingle Bells" during one of her sisters' acts on the Rialto Theater stage in Grand Rapids during Christmas week. The family moved to Lancaster, California, shortly thereafter, and her mother (who created the act, wrote the arrangements and played the piano) took Judy and her two older sisters to Los Angeles. There Judy, at five, became one of the Meglin Kiddies (an organization composed of a great quantity of flopping blonde curls, ruffles, bows, tiny tapping patent leather shoes and very little talent). Dressed as Cupid she appeared with them at a downtown Los Angeles theater, where she sang "I Can't Give You Anything But Love." After Judy finished this inauspicious single, their mother revived the sister act and took the Gumm girls to Chicago, where they were erroneously billed as the Glum Sisters at the Oriental Theatre. To avoid such unfortunate mistakes in the future, George Jessel, also on the bill, suggested they change their name. He came up with "Garland." A 1934 run at the Wilshire Ebell Theatre in Los Angeles was their last appearance together (Judy's sisters are now housewives, one in Las Vegas, the other in Dallas). M-G-M spotted Judy at the Wilshire and the result was an audition before Roger Edens, a member of M-G-M's music staff.

Edens today recalls: "Her mother brought Judy to me to audition. Her mother played the piano and she sang 'Zing! Went the Strings of My Heart.' I knew instantly, in eight bars of music. The talent was that inbred. She sang it exactly as she sings it today, her mother's arrangement. I fell flat on my face. She was just so high and chubby, wearing a navy-blue middy blouse and baby-doll sandals, with lots of hair and no lipstick. I really flipped. I called Ida Koverman, L. B. Mayer's secretary, and she called Mr. Mayer, and he called the lawyers and she was signed to a contract that day. It was like discovering gold at Sutter Creek. Mayer took her all over the lot that day and made her sing for everyone.*

"She started the next day to school on the lot and also worked two hours a day with me, never on scales, just singing and working on the arrangements that I wrote for her. Out of these sessions, Mrs. Koverman chose her to sing for Clark Gable at a birthday party for him in the commissary. During lunch, I wrote the verse 'Dear Mr. Gable' to the song, 'You Made Me Love You'; and Judy got her first important chance, singing the same song in *Broadway Melody of 1938*. She was a hit.

"For the first two years at Metro, she worked with me two hours a day, six days a week. Then Metro sent her to New York to appear at Loew's State. I went with her and took her to the top of the RCA Building before the opening and told her, 'This is all going to be yours someday.' Metro had told me to buy her a dress for the opening and we went to Best's and picked out an organdy one. The opening was at noon. There was this unknown 15-year-old girl alone for the first time on an enormous stage, nervous and singing much too loudly. The audience was coughing and a baby started crying. People laughed at the baby and Judy stopped her song, laughed and started again. That one thing steadied her and she wrapped that audience up from then on. She has been able to handle an audience ever since."

The next 13 years of Garland is very familiar contemporary history, and an argument for stricter child labor laws in California. Besides the required three hours a day of school on the M-G-M lot, Judy spent two hours a day working with Edens, and only then began the exhausting work before the cameras, often finishing at four or five AM. Judy appeared first in a two-reeler, *Every Sunday*, with Deanna Durbin, was loaned out for *Pigskin Parade* with Stuart Erwin, established herself with "Dear Mr. Gable" in *Broadway Melody of 1938* and then starred in a succession of box-office smashes, ranking as one of the 10 best money-making stars in the Motion Picture Herald-Fame Poll in 1940, 1941 and 1945.

Her pictures, which are as much a history of M-G-M or life in the United States as they are of Judy Garland's career, were: *Thoroughbreds*

---

*Edens recollections here seem foggy and somewhat abbreviated, and other sources within this volume seem to offer a more reliable timeline for Judy's arrival at Metro.

Don't Cry; Everybody Sing; Love Finds Andy Hardy; Listen, Darling; The Wizard of Oz (for which Judy was given a special, not a regular, Academy Award); *Babes in Arms; Andy Hardy Meets Debutante; Strike Up the Band; Little Nellie Kelly; Ziegfeld Girl; Life Begins for Andy Hardy; Babes on Broadway; For Me and My Gal; Presenting Lily Mars; Girl Crazy; Thousands Cheer* (in 1943, Judy's first grown-up role); *Meet Me in St. Louis; The Clock* (Judy's first straight dramatic role); *Ziegfeld Follies of 1946; The Harvey Girls; Till the Clouds Roll By; The Pirate; Easter Parade; Words and Music; In the Good Old Summertime;* and *Summer Stock.* She ended her association with M-G-M in 1950. Since then, she has starred in *A Star Is Born,* for Warner Brothers, and most recently played the role of a German Hausfrau in *Judgment at Nuremberg* for Stanley Kramer.

Judy married musician David Rose when she was 19, divorced him four years later, and immediately married director Vincente Minnelli. A daughter, Liza May, was born the first year and Judy was divorced again, after six years of marriage, in 1951. She married Sid Luft, who also became her manager, in 1952, and began the series of concerts and appearances that are still going on. A second daughter, Lorna, was born that year, and a son, Joseph, in 1955. Last summer in the midst of her concert appearances Judy announced, for the second time, that she was separated from Sid Luft.

So much for the Judy of history. Now for the 1961 model, who protests "I paid thousands and thousands of dollars to psychoanalysts and I couldn't tell them a thing. Why should I talk to you?" And suddenly she gives in. "What the hell, why fight it any longer. I'll tell everything and hope that it comes out all right."

The performance began with a drink at The Carlyle on New York's Upper East Side. For those interested in fashion, Judy was wearing a green silk coat over a green silk dress and she looked very well indeed.

She entered with David Begelman, one of her two managers. The other, Freddie Fields, was in California. There was a little trouble. David was carrying a bottle of Blue Nun Liebfraumilch for Judy and an officious bar manager would not allow her to drink it. He didn't have any wine like it but he didn't want her to drink her own. The problem is that Judy's doctors only allow her to drink Blue Nun and one other label of Liebfraumilch, since a recent hepatitis attack.

Finally the manager of the hotel was called and gave her dispensation to drink. Judy began to talk about life in show business. "It's when you believe the romantic thing that you get in trouble. I know some people who have lost their way. You can wind up a triple schizophrenic." We left the Carlyle and hailed a cab for the West Side. Familiar with New York cab drivers, Judy asked David when we got into the cab to ask the driver to go slow. The driver immediately put the cab in gear and roared toward the entrance to Central Park. Judy asked David to tell the driver to let us out.

We hailed another cab. David asked the driver to go slow. The driver took off like the outside chariot in *Ben-Hur*. Judy huddled back against the seat, not terrified, just realistically frightened. Life was precious to her, the mark of a happy person.

Back at her apartment, David Begelman left us and Judy talked about *Broken Blossoms*, a 1919 D. W. Griffith masterpiece starring Lillian Gish and Richard Barthelmess, which she had seen on television the night before. Judy said that Barthelmess had been so beautiful, made up as a Chinese, but that the subtitles had been ridiculous. Lillian Gish at one point had said to Barthelmess, "Why are you so good to me, Chinky?" Judy laughed as she repeated the line and then described a scene in which Barthelmess tried to stop a fight among three sailors. They had stopped fighting each other long enough to beat up Barthelmess, the Chinese peacemaker, and Judy thought that was *very* funny.

Judy asked me if I liked David Begelman. She said that she calls Freddie Fields and David "Loeb and Leopold" because they are so bright. "It's not like the usual artist-manager contract. We're partners; they see that the lights work and the curtain goes up. They found schools in New York for the children and they found this apartment."

We arranged to meet again that night to see a motion picture, *The Guns of Navarone*, that had just opened on Broadway. Halfway through, Judy turned and asked if I wanted to see the rest of it. I replied that we had invested so much time in it already that we should stay to see the guns blown up. She agreed, somewhat reluctantly, but couldn't help turning sideways, averting her eyes and muttering at the screen as the story slowly unreeled, "The nerve of that director to come back and show those German soldiers in their underwear!" Judy said that she had been hoping all along the Germans would win.

The next evening, after dinner, Kay Thompson, the author of *Eloise* and one of Judy's oldest friends, brought a new song "How Deep, Deep, Deep Is the Deep Sea?," loosely based on "How Deep is the Ocean?," to play for Judy. Liza Minnelli, 15, Judy's oldest and Kay's godchild, sang with Kay, who played one of two grand pianos ferociously. Then we all tried it, from the top. I couldn't keep up and listened with Liza while Judy and Kay sang an incredible Thompson arrangement of "The Thrill Is Gone." The fast, loud, intricate delivery went on through "Great Day" and Liza squealed with delight on "Lift up your head and shout" and "It's so far away."

Kay sang "Some, somebody must love me, I wish I knew who it was . . ." and then "On the Atchison, Topeka and the Santa Fe," from *The Harvey Girls*, and that set off a chain of stories about M-G-M, where they had first met, Judy as a child star, and Kay as an arranger and coach. Liza sang, on request, "Jamboree Jones" with a great deal of her mother's talent, and then the three sang "Bob White."

Liza imitated the singing of Lorna and Joe, the two younger children, who were asleep at the other end of the apartment. "Everyone in the family is musical," said Judy. Lorna and Joe had learned the scores of *Bye Bye Birdie*, *Gypsy* and *West Side Story*, and sang them unerringly and relentlessly. Judy had taken Joe, then only four, to see *Gypsy* and had held him on her lap in a front-row seat. Joe had been quiet until Ethel Merman began to sing "Some People." In his baby way Joe began to sing along with her: "He was saying to me, Wose," and by the climax, Joe's "but not Wose" could be heard right along with the powerful Merman voice.

In England, a year ago, Judy had been anxious about showing her children and her home to the notoriously ruthless British press, but it seemed to be called for and a group of reporters were invited for tea. They came in to hear Lorna and Joe singing, innocently, the words from *West Side Story*, "Officer Krupke, you're really a square . . . my father is a bastard, my ma's an s.o.b. . . . goodness gracious, that's why I'm a mess . . ."

Judy wanted to end the evening singing some quieter songs: "Joey," which she described as a singer's song, and "Never Will I Marry," which she was about to add to her rigid concert list.

It was obvious that the alchemy she practiced in the concerts was only a part of her own happiness. Singing was her life, never work nor an exercise, and she sang, I discovered, with as much delight and meaning to her friends and children at home as she did at the concerts.

With several days free before her concert July 1 at Forest Hills, Judy wanted to see a new motion picture every night. After writhing through *The Guns of Navarone*, which she called *Navarone Sunday*, we attended *La Verite*, with Brigitte Bardot, whom she liked as an actress, and *Rocco and His Brothers*. Waiting in the lobby of the Paris theater on West 58th Street for the beginning of *La Verite*, she saw a copy of Bosley Crowther's book on L. B. Mayer in a small showcase. She wondered whether Crowther had understood Louis B. Mayer.

Despite Mayer's reputation as a despot, she said, "He had moments of kindness and he followed them. I had just been thrown out of Metro, after 16 years. I was ill and I didn't have any money to go into a hospital. I went to L. B. Mayer and asked him if the studio would lend me some money. Mayer hadn't wanted to throw me out and he called Nick Schenck (the chairman of the board) in New York while I was in the office and asked if they could loan me some money. Schenck told him that they were not running a charity institution. Mayer hung up and said something strange and kind of marvelous: 'If they'll do this to you, they'll do this to me, too,' and they *did*, as you know. He lent me the money himself and I paid him back. Crowther doesn't say anything about his kindness or the marvelous movies he *did* make. It's stylish to knock L. B. Mayer."

About her own frankness and honesty she said, "Maybe it's because I've reached a point in my life when I must be accepted for what I am, and not for some preconceived pattern. You want to please, but you want to please on your own terms. I think good manners and thoughtfulness are important, but, aside from that, that's the best I can do."

I asked Judy whether she wanted to go back to Hollywood and she shuddered. "I hate the sun. For 36 years I looked out the window every morning and there it was, always the same. And I don't like swimming pools. But I stayed there and I don't know why . . . perhaps because I thought it was my home. Many times it's much better to cut loose. I'm getting practical. I'm just beginning to realize the value of money, for example. I was surrounded by people who said, 'That's all right,' and I never looked into the finances. Now I see it all. If you have children who depend on you, you can't be facetious or romantic."

Judy's children, she claims, are the most important part of her life: "There isn't anything else but that. Everything else comes and goes but your children are there. And if you're smart, and give them enough respect and love, they will be there. There's no better insurance against loneliness than that."

The discussion was resumed over supper. I asked Judy how she kept going on tour; did she read? Bobby Kennedy ("He's the most disarmingly honest man I know") had lent her his car in Washington, complete with air conditioning, radio-telephone, and a copy of Irving Stone's book on Michelangelo, *The Agony and the Ecstasy*, but she found it hard to concentrate: "The day after a concert I'm mentally weary from remembering all of the lyrics.

"This last tour, oh my God, it was fun. For one thing, it was successful, and *that* can make anything fun. And there were three of us, David and Freddie. They can make me laugh all day long. I would have been dead a long time ago if I hadn't been able to laugh. At every crisis in my life, some Mack Sennett situation has come up that saved the day. You suddenly start to giggle in the middle of a tragedy.

"I'm very lucky, because something very funny will come along, and thank God I can recognize it.

"Right now I think is possibly the best time of my life. I'm terribly healthy. I have three marvelous children, and I think I have a brand new career opening up. There's lots I have to do. I haven't ever really acted. I've done things I liked, though. It's very difficult for a woman alone in this particular business. You arrive at the conclusion that you must be what you are. If you're not too bad and don't need too many changes, you'll be all right. I don't feel like taking a swipe at anything. I feel terribly fortunate and very lucky."

Judy then departed into one of her curiously charming nonsequential observations. She evidently felt that we had gotten too serious and wanted to bring me into her own world of candid humor: "Did you ever realize, as long as you're writing for this entertainment magazine, that all dancing teams beat each other up after every performance? They do the most beautiful things on stage, and as soon as they come off, the stagehands have to interfere to keep them from killing each other. I knew a man who danced with a midget girl. She couldn't have weighed more than

60 pounds but he beat her up if she had too much for lunch, complaining that she was too heavy to lift."

The next evening we went to the opening of *Rocco and His Brothers* at an Upper East Side art house. Shortly after the beginning of the picture, the mother of Rocco and his brothers began yelling in Italian at her sons for a full and horrible 10 minutes to wake them up to shovel snow. She drove Judy out into the street along with the sons, and we missed what was supposed to be one of the best pictures of the year. Even though she obviously hated the mother ("What could she have done with a more important event, like a death in the family?"), Judy was too polite to tell the manager why we were leaving so soon.

Judy didn't know why she couldn't tell him: "I'm terribly conventional, I suppose, a bit of a square, but at the same time I don't live in a stuffy way. When we were leaving the theater, I couldn't say anything to that man. When a show is in the making, I may see reasons for change, but after it's open, when nothing can be changed, I see no reason for saying, 'What the hell did you do that for?' You have to be pretty presumptuous to say something to Noël Coward about a show."

We were eating dinner at Danny's Hideaway, a famous show business nest, and a long line of people came by the table to talk to Judy: Arthur P. Jacobs, who runs the publicity firm that handles Judy; songwriter Adolph Green; and a young lady who wanted to take Joe Luft to a children's party the next day. Judy was the focus of attention during dinner but took no notice of the stares. She held up an arm to show me a present from Sid Bernstein, who was producing the 1961 Music at Newport concerts. It was a gold bracelet, with a pendant in the form of a girl singing in a tent, all in diamonds and rubies.

"I look like *Tess of the Storm Country*. I have a theory that I cheapen furs and jewelry. Diamonds turn to rhinestones and mink turns to squirrel. Did I tell you I got a wig for the concerts? I discovered that my one great expense on tour was carrying the hairdresser around. They were *all* expensive. The only way out, I thought, is to invent a really good wig. I called Kenneth (the best hairdresser in the country), at Lilly Daché and I said, 'Now, who can make the best wig?' He sent over a lady with head calipers to measure my skull, and also lots of little swatches of hair. The wig finally arrived in Detroit. You've never seen such a gray wig in all your life, and it cost hundreds. A great clump of hair came loose in the back. I put it on for everybody and I thought I'd die. They finally got it to a fairly good color but it came so low on my forehead I looked simpleminded."

As we left Danny's Hideaway, where the last thing you could do was hide, we turned in a half bottle of Blue Nun to Danny, who keeps a bank of half-finished bottles of wine for Judy. As we reached the door, a drunk selling balloons got into a fight with the doorman. When that was over, the driver of the rented limousine reported that the battery was dead. It was 12:30 AM and Kay Thompson was rehearsing some songs in a CBS studio not far away. We got into a cab and found Kay in a deserted broadcasting booth running through "How Deep, Deep, Deep Is the Deep Sea?" with three male singers. Kay and Judy sang "Great Day" and the three boys looked as if they had just seen into the Great Beyond. They countered with another run-through of "Deep Sea," which Judy had never heard in a complete arrangement. She was just as impressed with them as they had been with her and refused to sing again, saying, "I can't follow that."

Judy and Kay went back to the apartment to play the Carnegie recordings, which had just come in that day.

Judy said that the sound of the band while she was performing was most important to her. "I happened to walk by the brass section that night, before the Carnegie concert, where this Capitol recording engineer was telling the trumpets to take it easy. I said, 'Oh, no, this is my night' and the poor fellow went home with migraine." Judy listened to "Just You, Just Me" and told Kay, "This was great in Buffalo. You should have heard the band."

The Carnegie audience was the best of all, though. Judy quoted David Begelman: "The ins applaud the beginning notes and the squares wait until the opening words, 'the night is bitter.'" Kay imitated Judy singing "The Man That Got Away," with her arms flailing out in all directions, and said that the whole front row at Carnegie looked like a dentist's ad, except Roger Edens, who somehow had never seen a Garland concert, and was crying from happiness.* And Judy told Kay that Kay had behaved like Mrs. Meglin with her Kiddies, saying, "Smile, baby."

---

*Edens had, of course, seen and taken part in numerous concerts given by Judy, so Goode's remark is puzzling.

Kay asked Judy if she was paid from the receipts after each performance. Judy said there was always a check before she went on. "In Texas it is different. They pay you in cash, and you don't know how big $20,000 can be until you hold it. It was like Charlie Chaplin in *Monsieur Verdoux*. What to do with the money? I had Gertrude Palmer, my secretary, with me with a bag. I said, 'Just stand there in the wings where I can see you and don't put the bag down.'

"There are going to be 14,000 people at Forest Hills," she added a little apprehensively.

"Not enough," Kay returned jovially. But the hour was late and the Forest Hills concert was only two days away. It was time to go back to work.

In the next issue James Goode takes Judy Garland step by step through one of her big nights, describes in intimate detail what happens before the spotlight catches her and after it lets her go.

PART II: Garland performing is Garland at the moment of truth and triumph. Here is a play-by-play account of one of the Garland love-feasts that are becoming legendary in the annals of recent show business—the preparation, the delivery, the aftermath.

The Garland-Fields-Begelman corporation, inactive for the five weeks since their second Carnegie concert, went to work again on Friday, June 30. At 9:30 Friday evening, David Begelman and Freddie Fields arrived at the Garland apartment in a rented gray Rolls-Royce limousine and drove Judy to the Forest Hills Tennis Stadium on Long Island to check the lights and the special platform and "to get the feel of the place" for the next night's concert. Nothing was ready and the three-man amusement corporation turned around without a whimper and cheerfully returned to town. There Fields called Forest Hills again and three hours later they were on their way back to Long Island.

In the clear moonlight Judy stood in the deserted stadium, looked out at the rows of empty seats and commented, "It seems all right, but the stands look frightening and far away." When I asked Judy why two

90-minute round trips were necessary for just a brief glimpse, she said, "In my business every night is opening night."

"JE REVIENS, I RETURN"

David Begelman picked up Judy in the Rolls again the next day at 2:30. They drove through Central Park and, pretending not to see him, passed Freddie, who was waiting at the corner of 57th Street and Park Avenue. "He's running after us," David said, looking through the rear window, "like an abandoned unwed mother." After they circled round and picked him up, Judy found a small bottle of perfume left in the Rolls by a previous tenant. She read the label, *"Je Reviens*, I return. I got it for the comebacks. It's a perfume company, owned jointly by Gen. Douglas MacArthur and Judy Garland. David, what are we going to do about the airplanes? [The Forest Hills stadium, open to the skies, was directly under the flight patterns of La Guardia and International airports.] I've been trying all night to think of airplane jokes. . . . God, that was marvelous in the stadium last night, the moon and the cool air. I'm wondering whether I should talk at all in that big place. . . . At seven, I woke up for the children, and at 10 I was hit by a sledgehammer and the next thing I knew it was 1:30 and Emmy was waking me up. I said, 'I don't care, what day is it?'"

Freddie Fields told the most unrelaxing story he could think of, about a macabre restaurant in Hong Kong where the guests are invited to pick out live animals from a pit and watch them boiled alive for dinner. There was no response other than muffled horror and he adjusted his cuff links. Judy told him that they had gone out of style five years ago. David forced a boisterous "Ha . . . ha . . . ha." Judy laughed at David and asked him to do it again. He refused, saying, "Judy, you know how nervous I get just before a concert."

The Rolls turned into a Howard Johnson's restaurant when Judy and David decided they wanted ice cream cones. Judy said, "I'm hungry. I looked in the cupboard this morning and there was nothing but cat food from when I had Bluebell." On the way in, a lady asked Judy, "Are you who I think you are?" Another lady passed David at the entrance wheeling a baby carriage and David shouted after her into the crowded room, "Take your hands off my child." We bought ice cream cones and drove on to Forest Hills.

Judy and her luggage were checked into a suite at the Forest Hills Inn, where Stevie Dumler of the Freddie Fields office and her hairdresser, Mr. Kenneth of Lilly Daché were waiting.

We settled down for the long wait till showtime. Fields tried humor: "Ronnie Roye [the local entrepreneur] can't get the sun to focus. I'll tell you right now the stage has to be moved forward 15 feet." David looked at Judy, who had changed into a frilly, diaphanous robe. "You're too good to be out here, for Christ's sake, singing for these people with grease under their nails." Freddie: "We're putting the band around you so there won't be any chance of not hearing them." Judy: "I'm wondering about catching my heels on the grass going over to the stage." Freddie: "On 'Over the Rainbow,' let's take the blues and reds out and leave just a spotlight, so you can get on and off without people watching you climb those steps." David mimicked Judy, who has a fear of falling everywhere but on stage, walking down the steps onto the tennis court. David said they could put up a screen at the steps.

JUDY TALKED ABOUT SOAP OPERAS

Mr. Kenneth, impeccable and quiet, was watching television, and Judy began talking about soap operas, saying that the similarity of characters, plots and dialog made her think she was lost in a world of heartbreak where 70 people led hopelessly entwined and tragic lives. "You really get a little mixed up," she said. Judy then passed the time signing checks that Stevie had brought along to pay the musicians' and hairdresser's bills and her own allowance, $100 a week.

Judy wanted to sleep for a little while so Fields and Begelman drove over to the stadium to look at the stage. Fields' first look of anguish was at the piano, which was sitting in the bright sunlight, covered by canvas. Fields spoke to the head grip: "You shouldn't have done that. It will be a full tone off by tonight. Is a tuner coming?" The man replied that he had already been there, and Fields explained that the heat from the sun would change the tone, asking if they could put the piano somewhere in the shade. They could not.

Fields and Begelman directed the placement of the tiers for the 28-piece band, while the band itself rehearsed under an awning at the rear of the makeshift stage. Fields explained that the thin hardwood flat that extended under the band was installed to bounce the sound of the band to Judy as she sang. "We really use dynamics. Judy is one of the few singers with orchestrations that use dynamics, varying intensities of volume."

Fields conferred with Myles Rosenthal, a young New York sound engineer dressed in Bermuda shorts, who had installed what he called the "first split-stereo sound system for a concert."

A QUESTION OF VOLUME

In a semicircle on the grass facing the audience were 16 James B. Lansing high-fidelity speakers arranged in four clusters. They carried individual and separate sounds from microphones set at intervals through the band and also from Judy's own microphone. Fields and Rosenthal walked the handheld Garland mike forward while the system was turned on, speaking into it at intervals to see whether she would get an echo, or "feedback," if she should walk past the speakers on the grass during the concert. There didn't seem to be any feedback, but Rosenthal was nervous. He asked if Judy sang with great volume. He was told that she did. Fields cautioned him not to change the volume level during the concert because it might throw her off.

Fields, an old MCA hand now on his own, rhapsodized about his latest client. "Besides pure entertainment, Judy is an emotional experience. The Carnegie audience all ended up on the same level, enraptured. She brought the humanity out of everyone. Carnegie was pure strength, never a moment when she wasn't a giant. She never broke the spell. When she walked on that *Nuremberg* set [Judy had recently finished her role in *Judgment at Nuremberg*] all the stars there were a little bit smaller. If we've done anything, it's to make her career a business. You wouldn't run Macy's with lackeys or relatives."

Freddie was interrupted as Judy walked onto the tennis courts for a rehearsal. She was dressed in turquoise slacks, a dark green shirt, white loafers, and she wore a pair of dark glasses. Freddie put his arm around her as she sang "Never Will I Marry," in a low voice, rehearsing the song for the first time with the band. Judy then opened up so that she could be heard over the band without a mike. David said, "I've heard of warming up, but this is ridiculous." Judy turned to leave, and David admonished Howard Hirsch, the bongo player, "Play the hell out of them tonight, Howard."

Judy walked out onto the makeshift stage and slid her feet back and forth on the varnished wood, to see whether there were any rough edges. Then she tried the mike. Myles Rosenthal smiled at the strength of her voice and said to Freddie, "I see what you mean." Judy then tried the mike out on the grass, walking forward, beyond the speakers, again despairing at the size of the enormous stadium that she had to fill with sound that night. She told Myles not to take the mikes away from the brass section. Remembering that she once had swallowed a moth during an outdoor concert, she asked Freddie if he had brought a bug bomb.

Judy and David went back to the Forest Hills Inn so that Mr. Kenneth could start on her hair. It was now six o'clock, two and a half hours until the concert would begin. Mr. Kenneth had set up an elaborate dressing table and had unpacked a portable hair dryer. Judy asked him, "What will we do with my hair tonight?"

"I don't know," he said. "I thought we might try glue."

David called room service and ordered Judy's dinner: two lamb chops, a side order of mashed potatoes, lima beans and a tossed salad with Roquefort dressing. A teenaged rock 'n' roller performed silently and lasciviously on the television set, while Mr. Kenneth set Judy's hair before turning on the dryer.

The long hose attachment and the blower at the other end gave Judy a Martian appearance which she didn't like. "Kenneth, we've got to do something about that wig so I won't have to go through this. Couldn't we take a tuck in here and there?" Mr. Kenneth was obdurately watching the television set, which had switched from the rock 'n' roller to the last 30 seconds of an old Henry Aldrich picture.

A CHAT WITH HER CHILDREN

Stevie Dumler called the house that Judy had just rented at Hyannis Port, on Cape Cod, to find that Liza, Lorna, and Joe had arrived safely that afternoon. Judy's voice was warm as she talked to her children. "Liza? How is the house? Do you like it? Do you think we're going to have fun? Lorna? Hi, baby, how are you? Did you like it? You got a swim in already?" The voice grew still more affectionate as Joe came on the line: "Hello, darling, how's my baby? . . . The cold icy water? I miss you, Joe. I miss you very much."

In a few minutes Judy and David were laughing again, about some silly names they had invented for business people: "George Gross, Ned Net, Tim Tax, Sam Subpoena, Leonard Lien," and Judy added, "Freddie Foreclosure." It was getting late, and dinner had not arrived. David called room service and got special treatment. Dinner was wheeled in and Judy looked at her watch. "Dare I eat? I won't be able to breathe!"

David said, "Even if you don't breathe, you're still the best singer around." Judy laughed. "I wonder if Marguerite Piazza has as much fun as *we* do?" Judy trifled with her dinner, then napped under the hair dryer. Mr. Kenneth couldn't watch television any longer.

Judy woke up. "What do you think, Kenneth? Shall we finish my hair?" Mr. Kenneth did, and Judy began to make up for the concert, now only a half hour away. "These are my 14,500-people eyelashes." She was referring to her three sets of false eyelashes—for small, average and large audiences. Forest Hills would require the longest ones. "I have a line on my head from the dryer, Kenneth." Mr. Kenneth, wryly: "I like it." Judy: "It looks like a skull operation." Mr. Kenneth: "Didn't you know what I was doing?" He combed her hair and Judy was almost ready.

I asked Judy whether she thought about a performance before she went on. "Every once in a while I think about it. I find too much concentration isn't good for me. It may be good for the Method people, but I have a general picture and I try to let things happen spontaneously. I never know what's going to happen anyway. The mike may blow, or *anything*. I used to suffer awful stage fright. Now it's such a relief to be without it, I enjoy every part of the day. My God, it used to be agony. Now I get an exhilarated feeling from the audience and the singing. I *do* like to sing. It's a lot of fun, you know, with good orchestration. The whole thing is kind of a romp, which it should be. It comes through much better. You have a feeling everybody likes you. Why else are they there?"

Mr. Kenneth interrupted: "Do you think I'll ever get to do the president's wife?"

THE JUDY GARLAND KIT

Judy laughed and asked if she had told me about the Judy Garland kit that David and Freddie had invented to sell at concerts. "It consists of one long eyelash, a tear-soaked handkerchief, a tiny bottle of Liebfraumilch, a used Life Saver and a baby fan." David burst into the room. "You don't know what's going on outside. The whole town is agog." He went to a closet to get a dress for Judy. "How did this get in here? Judy, you can have your choice. Kenneth's jacket or any one of these costumes." Mr. Kenneth: "She can wear it if she'll autograph it afterwards." Judy: "There was a ridiculous woman who came up to me in a dining car and said, 'Would you sign this piece of toast for me?'"

It was time to go. Stevie and Mr. Kenneth packed all the clothes, the makeup table and the hair dryer, and everyone moved downstairs to the Rolls to drive one block to the West Side Tennis Club which, since there was no adequate dressing room at the stadium, would be Judy's base during the concert. Judy took over the ladies' room of the club, and a guard was posted outside to keep people away. It was dark, and the stadium lights facing the club illuminated a wide green lawn and the tennis courts. Judy was dressed in a black sheath and a sequined jacket, and we climbed into a small English convertible for the short drive down a private walk to the stadium. Mr. Kenneth and a photographer rode on the fenders of the car.

Mort Lindsey, the orchestra leader, greeted Judy with a kiss, and Judy asked, "Where do they let the lions out?" The bandstand was brightly lit but the audience sat in total darkness, making the stadium look even larger than it was. Jeff Hand, of the Fields office, handed Judy some Life Savers. Freddie said, "Go tell Mort we're ready." David said, "Nobody can find him." A phone rang in the lighting booth at the left. Freddie was nervous: "That's not going to go on during the concert, is it?" He called Rosenthal in the sound-control room, as the band began the overture. "Jack it up really high," Freddie ordered.

"...DO I WALK TIPPYTOE...?"

Judy listened: "You do lose the impact of the orchestra outside." David called for a flashlight so Judy could walk down the short steps to the stage. Judy asked, "Have they got the sound up? Is there a runway out there or do I walk tippytoe like the wolf in *The Three Little Pigs?* Is there a handkerchief?" The band had reached "Over the Rainbow" in the overture, and Judy began to walk on, to deafening applause, and sang "When You're Smiling." Halfway through, a plane flew over, cutting half of the sound, but Judy didn't stop until after the first song, and said to the audience, "A small, intimate room." There was laughter and a voice in the top rows shouted "Louder! Sing louder!"

Judy said, "Sing louder? I've got a frog in my throat." Then, as more planes began to fly over the stadium, "Here they come! I'll be right back. Mill around." She walked off to their laughter to get a glass of water to clear her throat and was back in seconds, asking, "Now, can you hear?" She began "Almost Like Being in Love" with a slight throaty quality, and was completely relaxed as she sang "Do It Again."

The banks of 54 red and blue lights dimmed down by prearrangement, leaving a single pin-spot as she sang the words "Turn out the light" from "Do It Again." The darkness was broken only by the spot and the occasional flare of matches in the audience and then the quiet spell was shattered as Judy began the loud cha-cha-cha arrangement of "You Go to My Head," taking the mike from the stand and doing quick little cross steps over the stage.

Judy stopped again to talk to the audience and catch her breath. A man's voice behind me said, "She's terrific, she really is." Judy looked up at the man running the big spotlight who couldn't seem to find her on the stage. "Have you got trouble up there?" she asked. Then Judy started to talk about her hair, just as if she were back in the hotel suite. "I have this friend. She's darling. She's so chic you can't stand it. She sent me to her hairdresser. He clipped and cut and it got higher and higher. I tried it at a concert, looking like an overweight Balenciaga model. I walked on balancing my hair. I get very warm when I work and it started to fall. I looked Neanderthal. The varnish was running . . ." Her voice trailed off and the crowd laughed at her story. Judy cued the band and sang "Alone Together," reaching the words "to cling together" just as another plane came over. It didn't matter. People were standing, shouting "Bravo, bravo!" and the applause lasted for several minutes. Judy spoke: "I think that last 707 went right down my throat."

She introduced the next number, a medley that featured nine jazz musicians from the band: "I'm known mostly for marching songs. I like to sing jazz but they won't let me. We have nine marvelous men in the band. Would nine marvelous men come forward?" She began to help the drummer move his equipment down onto the stage and chased away a stagehand who was trying to help. "Have you got everything you need? You have so much equipment. Have you got your clothespins on your music? I'm supposed to conduct this. What is it? One . . . two . . . one, two, three . . . it works . . . 'Who cares if the sun cares to fall in the sea?'" She was off, one arm shooting up on the words "*You* care, *baby*, for me . . ."

Listening to the jazz group before she began "Puttin' on the Ritz," she said, "You moan, don't you? What tempo is this? A striptease tempo? I don't do it, I just talk about it." She finished the medley and the lights came on, to show Judy helping the drummer back onto his stand with his equipment, singing "What Is There to Say?" softly to herself. She turned and told another story: "I've got to tell you something while the plane comes over. Wouldn't it be awful if one saw the lights and landed here?

COMMENTS ON THE ENGLISH PRESS

"The English press . . . is just horrible. You can sue and they pay and then say something awful again. You sue and they pay again. I didn't want to meet them but I was told I must. There were 20 reporters and 20 photographers jammed into this airless room. One young girl came up to me and said, 'You look absolutely marvelous,' and she kept coming up and saying it for two hours. You know, by the end of the party I kind of liked her and I offered to give her a ride to her flat. I wanted to hear more. The next morning I read the paper that the girl worked for and there was a headline: JUDY GARLAND ARRIVES IN LONDON, and further down was this girl saying, 'I met Judy Garland last night and she's not plump, she's not chubby, she's *fat!*'"

The band swelled into the opening bars of "The Man That Got Away" and the stadium echoed with applause that drowned out the music.

The laughter was real, the tears were real, and the words were real: "When you're smiling the whole world smiles with you . . . All the music of life seems to be like a bell that is ringing for me . . . Life is one long jubilee . . . I know how Columbus felt finding another world . . . The world is a stage, the stage is a world . . . We're in or we're out of the money . . . I believe in doing what I can, crying when I must, laughing when I choose . . . but I believe that since my life began, the most I've had is just a talent to amuse, heigh ho, if love were all . . ." Finally, there came the strongest public image of all, the little girl who wants escape: "If happy little blue-birds fly beyond the rainbow, why oh why can't I?"

Also in the Garland repertory were a few effervescent expressions of pure joy, where style and virtuoso talent eclipsed meaning, songs like "San Francisco," the last number before intermission at Forest Hills. She began it with an arch verse in a nasal twang. By the time she had thrown her head back for the last iron-lung delivery of the words "San Francisco," the audience was roaring in delight. She kicked off her shoes, left the stage, and wandered barefoot on the grass, bowing to applause that didn't stop until after she finally walked into the backstage darkness.

David and Freddie met her at the stairway next to the band and hustled her into the little English car, to take her back to the tennis club for a half-hour rest. Judy took off her clothes and sat in a dressing gown on the cool tile floor of the ladies' room. A huge fan sent a torrent of air through the open door of the room.

Mr. Kenneth rebuilt Judy's frayed and soaked hair: Stevie helped her into black trousers and another bright, jeweled jacket, and it was time to go back to the lions. In the car, Judy had a premonition: "My voice is going. It's the fresh air, David says. I get sick from too much of it." She laughed weakly.

Judy delivered the fast "That's Entertainment" and then stopped to let another plane go by. "Let's let him go over. They always come over on the ballads." She started her slow, quiet, "I Can't Give You Anything But Love." She was alternately aggressive, loving, wise, despondent and gay, explosive and despairing through "Come Rain or Come Shine," "You're Nearer," "If Love Were All," "A Foggy Day," "Stormy Weather," and "Zing! Went the Strings of My Heart." An impulsive voice from the top of the stands shouted, "That's my girl," and other voices said, "That goes for all of us."

She then asked if anyone liked "A Foggy Day" and they did, even more so after she sang it. Then, "There's a lovely song that Noël Coward wrote for *Bitter Sweet*. I can never remember the words so I have to look at them," and she did. It was "If Love Were All." In "Zing! Went the Strings of My Heart," Judy became athletic, dancing, leaping, kicking and bouncing across the stage. At the end you felt that there was nothing she or her voice could not do.

Judy began a medley of "You Made Me Love You," "For Me and My Gal," and "The Trolley Song." The people in the aisles and the first rows began to spill out onto the grass to be nearer Judy, and policemen lined up in long rows to keep them away from her. The crowd continued to desert their seats and to press forward. Judy started her last number, "Rock-a-Bye Your Baby with a Dixie Melody" to a swelling roar of applause that drowned out everything. She stomped on the hardwood with each beat of "a million baby kisses I'll deliver" and exploded at the final "melody." The audience answered explosion with explosion.

Fields, Begelman, her press agent John Springer, and the cordon of policemen watched anxiously as Judy took her bows again and again, walking close to the growing mass of Garland-lovers on the grass tennis courts. Springer said, "This is where the madness starts," as if the audience reaction up to this point had been calm. Judy walked back to Freddie and David and they led her slowly back to the stairs, while she caught her breath in gasps. A minute later she shook her head like a prizefighter after a nine-count, and broke loose to return to the frenzied audience.

Judy sang "Over the Rainbow" for her first encore, hiding her exhaustion, and walked around the field again in a small spotlight, blowing kisses during the applause. The crowd on the edges of the field was growing larger with each song, many of them taking pictures. The policemen had to hold hands to keep them back as Judy sought out Freddie and David for a second breather. The roar of applause never stopped from the end of "Rainbow" to the beginning of "Swanee," as she came back again, determined, asking David for the "hat, hat, hat" she needed for her second encore. She clapped it on her head and rolled through "Swanee," building to her biggest note yet on the ending.

This time the noise and the surge of uncontrolled fans *was* madness, as Springer had predicted. You could not tell whether the crowd was clapping, shouting, screaming, laughing, or crying. The sound suddenly had no character. It was just an expression of total approval and acceptance. The audience closed in until there was only a small open circle. The policemen tried but couldn't stop one lady, who broke through and kissed Judy. Judy herself was completely exhausted, winded, and hardly able to walk once she was out of the spotlight. But she mopped her face, took her familiar deep, deep breath, straightened her shoulders, and went back for the third round on will alone.

Fields said, "You know what creates panic? Cops. If we left her alone, they'd never touch her." Judy was off and into the most demanding song of the concert, "Chicago," with apparent ease. As she sang "You will never guess where," the audience answered spontaneously "Where?" and Freddie yelled, "Go, go." Another voice yelled, "Come on, Judy," and the audience began to clap with the beat. The concert had become a religious rite. She strutted as the tempo built, and when it was all over, at last, and Freddie walked in to pick up the pieces, she became playful and pulled Freddie back to the spotlight, pirouetting. Freddie walked her back to the car. Even though the professionals there knew that there weren't any more songs, they felt that Judy wanted to go back again.

A boy that she recognized leaned into the car and kissed her. She told him that she had seen him on the sidelines during the performance. The audience had impressed her: "They were so sweet . . . Look at my hair . . . I'm sweating gallons . . ."

Back in her decompression chamber, sitting again on the tiled floor of the dressing room, Judy told Freddie, "I missed doing that. I'm no good without a particular date to look forward to. I think I got a little out of shape. You need a concert to do a concert."

Half an hour later, she was ready to go back to the hotel, and the entourage pushed its way through the fans outside the tennis club. At the street, where the Rolls stood waiting, three young men burst into a parody of a song from *Bye Bye Birdie,* "We love you, Judy, oh, yes we do, we love you Judy, we love you true, when you're not with us, we're blue . . ." Judy stopped Freddie and asked the boys to sing it again. She was charmed. In the car, Judy cried with happiness: "You two are the luckiest thing that ever happened to me," and Freddie replied, "You're the best thing that ever happened to me." Judy sobbed again, "What a terrible thing. What if I turned out to be a sentimental slob?" Freddie dispelled sentiment with some practical news. Forest Hills had brought in 13,704 paid admissions for a gross of $54,621, over twice as much as either of the two Carnegie Hall performances.

It was nearly midnight by the time Judy was dressed for dinner and went downstairs to the hotel's sidewalk café to celebrate yet another Garland victory. Judy, David, John Springer, Abby Mann, the screenwriter who had written *Judgment at Nuremberg,* Rowland Barber, a freelance magazine writer, and myself sat at one table. Next to it were Freddie, Dorothy Kilgallen, and some friends. The hotel dining room trio, consisting of a guitar, a bass fiddle, and an accordion, came out to serenade Judy and she sang along with them, giving them requests, just as if she hadn't sung a note since the day before. The two tables, led by Judy, sang for three hours, without a pause for dinner, running through 38 songs, starting with "Just in Time," and finally ending with "The Party's Over," Judy, Freddie, and David sang loudest when they came to "No more doubt or fear, I've found my way" in the first song, looking at each other and smiling.

Finally Freddie said that it was 3:30, and the G-F-B Corp. collected their mountain of luggage and settled into the of the Rolls. Just as they were leaving, a very proper lady put her head in the window and said with great emotion, "Judy, Forest Hills *loves* you."

NEXT ISSUE: In Part III Judy conquers a reluctant Newport; she neighbors with the Kennedys at Hyannis Port, and elucidates the Garland philosophy of life.

Part III: "For the ending I fall off the stand" • "What are you doing tonight? Would you like to see a movie at the Kennedys?" • "I could never cheat on a performance, or coast through. My emotions are involved" • Judy in the sun at Newport • Judy across the street at Hyannis Port • Judy and friends discussing how she stays on top.

Judy's afternoon concert at Newport July 3 did not have the compelling emotional quality of Forest Hills and Carnegie Hall.

It was not that Judy gave less than she had before: if anything, she worked harder to compensate for unfortunate physical conditions. The *Music at Newport* concerts, their popularity undermined by the riots the year before, were held on a football field, the folding chairs of the audience strewn along its length. There was a tiny square bandstand, 10 feet high, at one end. Loudspeakers, a changing complement of jazz performers, and two hot-dog stands constituted *Music at Newport*. It might have been a political rally in Indiana.

There was no sound quality, not even that provided by the stadium shell of Forest Hills which held the sound briefly and took some of the curse from an open-air performance. Judy sang facing into the sun, and each song was marred by a breeze that was picked up by the microphones hanging above the band. Technically it was a disaster, but Judy won her audience. If not so completely as at Forest Hills, the crowd was nonetheless hers by the end of the first act. That afternoon 7,650 people attended, but an equal number of empty chairs at the back and the generally undisciplined audience, half of them modern-jazz addicts who roamed aimlessly through the rows during the performance, made it look more like a sales convention than the worshiping congregation that Judy usually commanded.

Judy spoke frankly between songs: "What have they got this fence here for, to keep me from getting to you? What baby, you *want* to? You'll be deported if you do. ... I've never seen so much wandering around in an audience. Well, it's a moving audience and we'll just have to keep moving with them. . . . Are you supposed to sing over the top of this thing? . . . . I must get a stagehand's union card. Did you put that there, darling? Was it to *help* me? My goodness, it's funny in the daytime, isn't it? . . . . For an ending, I fall off the stand. . . . Let's do the Noël Coward if it hasn't blown away. . . . This show is not without incident. . . . [Then, reading from a slip of paper handed to her] This is an emergency, a Dr. Victor Madeiros is wanted in the Pinkerton tent. . . ."

It was over, but not too soon. As far as Judy was concerned, the only good thing about Newport, aside from the money (a $25,500 gross for the afternoon), was the house trailer that Sid Bernstein, the 1961 *Music at Newport* producer, had given her for a dressing room. After the concert, 50 old friends stood outside the trailer and filed through, two by two, emerging through a door at the other end as if it were a mobile-home exhibit.

Yul Brynner's young son Rocky, just over from Europe and traveling alone, dropped in to pay his respects to Judy. Judy said, "Liza's in Hyannis Port. What are you doing in Newport?" Rocky: "Seeing you. You murdered them. It's unfair to do that to an audience." Judy said that she had learned backstage behavior from Laurette Taylor. "If people didn't come back to see me, I'd feel very bad because I'd think they didn't like the show."

Anxious to see her children after a three-day separation, Judy was driven alone late that night in the chauffeured Rolls to the Hyannis Port house she had rented for the rest of the summer. She also wanted to spend some time with her friends in the Kennedy clan across the street. There was not a concert in sight until Forest Hills again, nearly four weeks later.

In Hyannis Port, Judy fell into the life of a summer resident, emulating the wealthy Boston women who had fewer responsibilities, hiring a couple to cook and take care of the house, visiting the Kennedys and Shrivers, renting a convertible which she drove into Hyannis on shopping trips, spending long hours with her children, Lorna and Joe, avoiding the sun and the beach assiduously, and occasionally visiting daughter Liza, who was working a 14-hour day, seven days a week, as an apprentice at the Cape Cod Melody Tent.

Judy wanted to see [Frederico] Fellini's celebrated *La Dolce Vita* to round out the informal Garland film festival that had begun in New York, and we found it playing in a drafty bubble-shaped steel theater, with canvas chairs, outside Hyannis. But the picture was so good that Judy would have looked at it upside down. At dinner afterward, she saw a parallel in the unpretentious quality of the better foreign films and what she had learned about performing: "Isn't it marvelous to see something that is truly moving? Ten years ago I went to the Palace in New York and then to the Met with eight or 10 chorus boys, choreography and another act. My show was really *produced*. When I got to London finally, I asked about doing a concert. I knew I could. I felt too good. [This despite the fact that she was recovering from a severe bout of hepatitis.] If I had believed any of the doctors I've met, I'd be a hopeless invalid.

"I said I'm just going to go out and do nothing but *sing*, by myself. Just get a good band and I'll sing for an hour, then 10 minutes intermission, then another hour. Elaboration on a good theme isn't necessary. Perhaps it distracts an audience to see all of the trappings, like chorus boys. Even though I'm working twice as hard as I did at the Palace, I get much more satisfaction, an *exultant* satisfaction out of this. It was fun to go out and sing and celebrate afterward at Forest Hills.

"Funnily enough, the first 10 minutes at Newport threw me. The lack of a spotlight is funny to a person trying to create an emotional thing. Then I got into their spirit. . . . I really do live for talent. A movie like the one tonight, a moment that takes you out of yourself into . . . a how do you say it? . . . something you have no control over . . .

"I wish that the arts were appreciated, but that's stupid, they're damn well appreciated. Anybody with a deep talent will keep on. I don't think there have been many undiscovered geniuses. I think Fellini has it—along with pure genius, a driving desire to be heard. No great artist is content to sit back and say, 'Nobody understands me.' For me, George Gershwin was a genius. I had an awful fight with Ernst Lubitsch, who said, 'They are coming along but there is just no American music.' What did Gershwin write? He simply discovered a certain style that typified American music."

Judy called the next day: "What are you doing tonight? Would you like to see a movie at the Kennedys'?" I drove to Judy's house and was stopped at the street corner by a uniformed policeman and two Secret Service men. I told them I was going to Miss Garland's, gave my name and was waved on. I picked up Judy, said good night to Lorna and Joe, put the familiar bottle of Blue Nun *Liebfraumilch* in my outside coat pocket.

We went down the street to the same Secret Service men who had accosted me earlier. They expected Judy and walked with us to a driveway that served three or four white, two-story frame houses, most of them on the beach facing the Atlantic. The scene was pure Norman Rockwell: children, bicycles, cars, dogs, grass relieved by an occasional hedge, and lighted dining rooms and kitchen windows where all manner of Kennedys and their staffs were having dinner. We walked toward the farthest house, passing one last lighted room, where the seated figures of the president, the first lady, the attorney general and his wife could be seen, dimly, at dinner.

We entered the last house, which I was told belonged to Joseph Kennedy Sr., and met R. Sargent Shriver, head of the Peace Corps, and his wife, Judy's friend, Eunice Kennedy Shriver.

We looked at the rather quiet Kennedy collection of old English furniture, talked about seeing *La Dolce Vita* the night before, and descended into the basement. The projection room seated about 30 people, and by the time the picture started it was filled with an informal, happy and talkative group of similar-looking Kennedys, their dissimilar mates, and children and some unidentified men. The president and Bobby Kennedy and their wives did not appear.

The picture began, and before long it was apparent that Judy had gotten herself into a situation where she couldn't walk out. It was the late Gary Cooper's last film [*The Naked Edge*] and also starred Deborah Kerr; but neither of them could save it. Judy tried very hard not to say anything, and did not, but the fingers of both hands opened and closed rapidly and nervously for the awful duration of the film.

Upstairs at last, we couldn't talk about it. Ted Kennedy and Shriver couldn't either, and shortly afterward I took Judy home. Judy said she liked the Kennedys' informality and she thought they were a wonderful example of how to raise a family in wealth and still give them great ambitions.

The next meeting I had with Judy was back in New York City at Voisin, a fashionable restaurant Judy chose because of its chocolate *soufflé*. We walked in bravely, carrying the Blue Nun, to find Richard Rodgers and his wife, old friends of Judy's, at the next table. He stood up and kissed Judy, telling her the truth, that she looked marvelous, but, he said, running his hand over his head, he was losing his hair. Judy said, "With your talent, you don't need hair."

We settled down next to them and discussed world affairs for a while. "If men could only sit down and say, 'Let's talk, *correctly.*' Men have honor without understanding," said Judy. "Men destroy and women preserve."

For the rest of the evening Judy answered questions and went a long way toward explaining the current Garland boom.

"What are you saying when you sing?"

Judy: "Just tremendous love. 'Come along with me and let's enjoy this.' I have a tremendous desire to please. I have a quite sincere love for people who pay for tickets, drive to theaters, park cars and sit in uncomfortable seats. I do wish people would feel everything I sing, hear the words and be affected by them. You must remember that over the years, multitudes of people have shown me a great deal of love and loyalty, a very, very deep love. The papers have often given me bad publicity. Some writers said I was through but, by God, the audiences came and bolstered me. What they were saying was, 'We don't give a damn what the papers say, we love you.' That's why I could never cheat on a performance, or coast through. My emotions are involved."

"Do you mind the invasions of privacy in show business?"

Judy: "The only thing is that I don't like to be watched when I shop or walk. It never enters my mind that they're saying, 'There goes Judy Garland.' I think they're saying, 'My God, isn't she awful?'"

"Which song do you like best of all?" Judy: "'Through the Years,' by Vincent Youmans."

"If you had it all to do over again, would you have gone to work at the age of 12? If Liza wanted to go into show business, would you allow her to?"

Judy: "What do you mean, 12? I was two. The only reason I'm letting Liza do this now is because she has been longing to do summer stock. When summer's over, she'll go back to school. I think it robs a youngster of too many things. It's too competitive. I don't think children should be thrown into that at all. They should have proms and football games and all of the fun of growing up. I was on stage from the age of two. I don't regret it, I learned a lot, and I've been successful. But I do think I missed a lot. It's a very lonesome life.

"I've come through it just fine. I have three lovely children, but there were moments I wouldn't want any children to have. I have no ambitions for my children except for them to be happy and well adjusted. I don't want to push."

"You said something weeks ago about the Mack Sennett situations that keep happening in your life. How do you explain them?"

"I just think people are terribly funny. I don't mean that in a deprecatory way. I'm hilarious. I'm really a joke to myself. And I can't take people too seriously, either. I can love them, but the overall thing is kind of funny. It really is."

On this philosophical note, which may well be the essence of Judy Garland, I ended the movie-going, the socializing, the interviews and thanked Judy for her candid cooperation. But Judy had only partially answered the most important question of all: What does she do to an audience?

The two ranking authorities on the question were her discoverer, Roger Edens, and her friend and former musical coach, Kay Thompson. Edens began: "It's right down deep inside. Good, solid, raw talent creates excitement. That was the charm of the Carnegie Hall concert. I had never seen her on [that] stage before. I still don't believe anything like this could happen. She practically burnt the house down. She said, 'Let's do it,' as though she had never done it before. It's there and when she touches it, it emerges. It's alchemy."

Kay Thompson harmonized: "She's saying 'Here I am and there you are, so shall we begin?' It's as if she belongs and the audience belongs. There is an instant point of contact, and at that instant something opens and takes place, both parties giving everything. There is some connotation or fragrance of rain or shine. There is an intimacy, a sharing of emotions for two hours. I don't think she ever realized what she could do until now."

The Garland fever continues. At the Hollywood Bowl on September 16 she set an all-time attendance and dollar record. The Bowl sold its 18,000 capacity plus an additional 600 standees, for a gross of $75,400. But that was not all. "At 8:25 PM, five minutes before the show started," Freddie Fields relates, "it started to rain. Those people out there are not accustomed to rain. We rushed Judy on stage before anyone could leave and she held them there in the rain for the entire show. Not *one* of them moved. They put up umbrellas and pulled coats over their heads but not *one* of them moved. They even made her sing "San Francisco" again, after "Chicago!" We built a ramp out over that 40-foot pool in front of the stage and she sang out there in the rain."

Suddenly, every producer and every entrepreneur in the United States, and a scattering of foreign countries, wanted Garland in one medium or another. Judy was booked for so many different things so far in advance that her chances of becoming a Scarsdale Guinevere in the new home she has just rented outside New York were rather slim.

The schedule for the months after the Bowl appearance included 10 concerts, at Denver, Boston, Montreal, Newark, Pittsburgh, Miami, Philadelphia, White Plains, Rochester, and San Francisco. Wedged in among these were a benefit in Los Angeles and the most off-beat use of the Garland talent yet devised, a sound track for a full-length UPA cartoon, *Gay Purr-ee,* for which Judy would sing six brand-new Harold Arlen–Yip Harburg songs, as Mewsette, a cat who leaves her farm in the French provinces to discover the joys and sorrows of Paris.

On December 11, Judy will fly to the Berlin premiere of Stanley Kramer's *Judgment at Nuremberg,* if both Judy and Berlin are still holding up. Immediately after the Berlin ceremonies, Judy will return to Hollywood to start rehearsals for the Garland television special with Frank Sinatra and Dean Martin as guests. It will be taped January 1–8 and be shown Sunday evening, March 11, on CBS at 9 PM EST.*

After more concerts, Judy will costar with Burt Lancaster in January in a Stanley Kramer production, *A Child Is Waiting.* Then she will go to London in March to film *The Lonely Stage,* based on the original television

---

*Judy's special with Sinatra and Martin aired February 25, 1962.

play by Robert Dozier, to be produced by Stuart Millar and Lawrence Turman for United Artists. At the moment, Judy has three additional films under consideration, all of them starring roles, one for the Mirisch Brothers, one for Ross Hunter and, bringing her full circle, an M-G-M musical.

Show business for all its sentimentality is frequently cynical, a condition that derives from broken or unfulfilled promises over the years. When anything or anyone is successful, the first question is always whether the success will last. This is especially true of Judy Garland. Somewhere, there's a someone who does not like Judy Garland; but that individual at the moment seems to be in hiding.

In the absence of any overt detractors or enemies, Judy must rely on her friends for misgivings about her continued career. Her friends would like to believe that Judy will go on forever, but they are also professionals who know the terrible demands of what she has committed herself to do, and there are a few intelligent reservations about what is humanly possible.

She is a highly emotional woman, which, happily, allows her to give everything she has to an audience. It also means that she is totally vulnerable each time she walks on a stage. These two factors, and the physical demands of the concert tours, may eventually have their effect.

The occasional break to make a motion picture, tape a television show, or to record an album is necessary for Judy's own well-being and is also the variation that could prolong the present near-mystical Garland craze indefinitely.

Mystical, mysterious, mystery—there is indeed a certain mystery which divides the great artist from the technically accomplished or merely "talented" performer. No artist of our time has shared her gift with such complete, almost thoughtless abandon. This sharing is at the center of Judy's mystery, and it is for this that the American audience loves Judy so much.

A *REDBOOK* DIALOGUE: NOËL COWARD & JUDY GARLAND

November 1961, *Redbook*

What originated as a reporter's tape-recorded interview with playwright Noël Coward became a fly-on-the-wall look into a fascinating friendship. It was during the week of August 11, 1961, that Judy traveled with Kay Thompson and publicist John Springer to attend a preview of Coward's *Sail Away* at Colonial Theatre in Boston. Peppered with various exclamations by Thompson (the woman responsible for introducing the two), the conversation between Judy and Noël was taped the following day and later edited for *Redbook*.

They seem poles apart: America's Judy Garland, who can warm 50,000 hearts singing familiar songs in a huge, open stadium, and England's Noël Coward, who acts, writes and directs his own sophisticated plays and musical comedies. But they are devoted friends, and deep admirers of each other's talent. They are equally outspoken about the theater, the public, and life backstage, which they discuss with unusual honesty in the following dialogue tape-recorded in Boston shortly after the opening of Coward's new musical *Sail Away*.

NOËL COWARD: Let's just—before we start talking—decide what is interesting about you and me, Judy. I'd say it's first of all that we're very old friends, so that takes care of itself. What is interesting about us both is (a) you are probably the greatest singer of songs alive, and I . . . well, I'm not so bad myself when I do my comedy numbers, and—let's see, what else?

JUDY GARLAND: And (b), Noël, is that we both started on the stage at about the same age, didn't we?

NC: Yes. How old were you when you started?

JG: I was two.

NC: Two? Oh, you've beaten me. I was ten. But I was—

JG: What were you doing all that time?

NG: Oh . . . studying languages! No, I started at the age of ten in the theater, but before that I'd been in ballet school. I started in ballet.

JG: You were going to be a dancer?

NC: Yes. I was a dancer for quite a while. Fred Astaire designed some dances for me in 1923. I was older than ten then, of course.

JG: How marvelous! I didn't know that! Did Fred—

NC: I don't think he was very proud of the dances, because I don't think I executed them very well. There was a lot of that cane-whacking tut-tum-ti-ti-tum in them.

JG: But, to go back, where did your theater . . . Did you have any background? Was there anyone else in your family at all that was—

NC: Theaterly?

JG: That's it . . . theaterly.

NC: No theater. Navy.

JG: No theater? How—

NC: We didn't know anything about it. My father's attitude was always one of faint bewilderment. But my mother loved the theater, you see, and she took me to my first play when I was five years old. It was my birthday treat. Every sixteenth of December I used to be taken to a theater. And then I was given a toy theater for Christmas.

JG: By your mother?

NC: By my mother. She adored—she loved the theater, you see.

JG: Yes. Yes!

NC: And I was wildly enthusiastic about it and so that's how it all started. I had a perfectly beautiful boy's voice, so I was sent to the Chapel Royal School, where I trained to be ready for the great moment when I gave an audition for the Chapel Royal Choir, which is a very smart thing to be in. I did [Charles] Gounod's "There Is a Green Hill Far Away," and I suppose the inherent acting in me headed its ugly rear, because I tore myself to shreds. I made Maria Callas look like an amateur. I did the whole crucifixion bit—with expression. The organist, poor man, fell back in horror. And the Chapel Royal Choir turned me down because I was overdramatic.

JG (*laughing*): That's divine!

NC: Then Mother was very, very cross and said the man who had turned me down was common and stupid anyway. After that we saw an advertisement in the paper that said they wanted a handsome, talented boy, and Mother looked at me and said, "Well, you're *talented*," and off I went to give an audition. That's how I got on the stage.

JG: Divine! But it was different for me. I came in with vaudeville. I . . . You know, it was sort of rotten vaudeville, not good vaudeville. I told you this once before, I think. I came in after the real great days and before television. Really, it was awful vaudeville, you know, so there was nothing very inspiring. But my children are being exposed to all the best.

NC: Of theater?

JG: Yes. I want them to be exposed to it. I think it's rather stupid to be involved in making movies or whatever, and just leave your children every morning—

NC: "Mother's going out now."

JG: Yes, and say, "I'm going to work now, but you mustn't know where because I don't want you exposed."

NC: Well, also the children might adore being exposed. Why not enjoy themselves?

JG: So I take them along with me. They have been on movie sets. They have been backstage in the wings. They know what I do when I go to work. Sometimes I think that actresses who say they don't want their children exposed to publicity and don't want their children photographed . . . Well, I have a strange, uncanny feeling that maybe Ma doesn't want any attention taken away from her, you know?

NC: You can't have secrets from them. If your mother happens to be an actress, you've got to take it on the jaw and understand that you're the daughter of an actress. . . .

JG: And you know, it isn't a bad atmosphere. It's fun for our children to go to the theater. And I think that as long as I have a good relationship with them and our home life is a good one, the entertainment world can't possibly hurt them. I don't know whether any of them will become entertainers or not. We'll see. My oldest daughter, Liza, is talented and sort of stuck on the business.

NC: I'd love to see Liza.

JG: She started to dance when she was five.

NC: And you encouraged it?

JG: Yes. And she's a brilliant dancer, really. But now she has grown up with the best of—of talents. She has seen you. Her father, who is a very, very talented man, has exposed her to the best of the theater, so she does have taste and she does have a talent. Now she's in summer stock. My other daughter, Lorna—she's eight—is the Gertrude Lawrence of Hyannis Port. She's just impossible, and the most beautiful creature who has ever lived, I think. And she's so shocking and bright and cunning and hep. She's such a great actress that we don't know what we're going to do with her. We really don't. I'm sure she's going to turn into something important. I don't have any idea at all what it will be, but it will be startling and flamboyant and— But I'm taking over the whole darn conversation.

NC: No, darling, you should.

JG: It's funny how Liza is so much like me, a quietness much of the time, a little sedentary, and Lorna is just the opposite, a mercurial child.

NC: When I saw you first, Judy, you were a little girl, although you talk about the vaudeville and all those things . . . But of course, that is the way to learn theater, and not acting school—playing to audiences, however badly.

JG: Trial and error. Trial and error.

NC: Whenever I see you before an audience now, coming on with the authority of a great star and really taking hold of that audience, I know that every single heartbreak you had when you were a little girl, every number that was taken away, every disappointment, went into making this authority.

JG: Exactly. Exactly, and it's all—it sounds like the most Pollyanna thing to say, but it is truly worth it—the heartbreak and the disappointments— when you can walk out and help hundreds of people enjoy themselves. And this is only something you can learn through trial and error.

NC: Nobody can teach you . . . no correspondence courses, no theories, no rehearsals in studios.

JG: No, you can only learn in front of an audience.

NC: And if there are people who cannot withstand these pressures, and if they are destroyed by these pressures, then they are simply no good and are just as well destroyed.

JG: Do you really mean that, darling? What do you mean?

NC: Well, my dear, the race is to the swift. In our profession the thing that counts is survival. Survival. It's comparatively easy, if you have talent, to be a success. But what is terribly difficult is to hold it, to maintain it over a period of years. You see, nowadays, when everything is promotion and the smallest understudy has a personal manager and an agent rooting for her and a seven-year contract with somebody, they don't take the time to learn their jobs. Then after their first success they run into difficulty—they have personal problems. And when public performers allow personal problems to interfere with their public performances, they are bores.

JG: Yes, and if they're haunted and miserable off stage, they are still bores. Because they are entertainers, and entertainers receive so much approval and love—and for heaven's sake, that's what we're all looking for, approval and love. And they receive it every night and in every way. If they are good, they receive adoration, applause . . .

NC: Applause, cheers, flowers.

JG: And if they insist on leaving the stage and going—Well, I did this for many years. I was the most awful bore. I went offstage and I'd go into my own little mood and remember all the miserable things and how tragic it was—and it wasn't tragic at all, really. I was just a plain bore. And I think anybody who clings to this tragic pose is a *poseur*—a phony.

NC: Self-pity.

JG: It's self-pity, and there's nothing more boring than self-pity.

NC: And it's a very great temptation—particularly when you're a star and you know that you have an enormous amount of responsibility, you are liable to fall into the trap of self-pity. If somebody doesn't please you or something goes wrong, you fall into the trap—you make a scene, which is quite unnecessary. If you're an ordinary human being working in an office every day, you wouldn't behave like that. No, an entertainer has to watch his legend and see that he stays clear and simple.

JG: But you've always done this, Noël. Now, I've known you for years. You've always done this. You are a terribly wise man who in spite of many facets of talent and brilliance and so forth has kept your mind in complete order and your emotions in order. You have great style and great taste. Weren't you ever inclined to fall into a sort of self-pity?

NC: Oh, yes, yes, yes.

JG: Oh, good. It makes me feel much better, because I really did it for a long time.

NC: After all, Judy, darling, I'm much older than you.

JG: Not much anymore, darling. Nobody is.

NC: I've been in the theater fifty-one years, and all my early years were spent in understudying, in touring companies and everything. But then I had my first successes, and they came when I was terribly young. I was only in my early twenties. *The Vortex* opened in London on my twenty-fifth birthday. After that I went through a dangerous phase. Suddenly everything I did became a great success. I didn't realize what danger I was in. I had made this meteoric rise, I had five plays running, I was the belle of the ball—and they got sick of it. And I got careless. I thought it was easy to be a success, and it's never easy.

JG: No. No, it never is.

NC: I wrote one or two things that weren't so good. And at the age of twenty-seven I found myself booed off the stage by the public on an opening night, and outside the stage door someone spat at me. That was a shock. It didn't hurt me, though. I was rather grateful for the bitter experience, for being shown I wasn't quite as clever as I thought I was.

JG: You were grateful to the public?

NC: Yes, they judge what they see—and it's up to me to make them see what I want them to see. Now, for instance, last night [the Boston opening of Noël Coward's new play, *Sail Away*] they came into that theater and they got a first impression. I had everything on my side. I had an extremely good cast, very good orchestra, wonderful choreography—

JG: And very good music and very good material, darling.

NC: Which I'm very proud of. But what was wrong with it—and I know this—was, there are certain moments when it needs tightening. There are certain numbers that occur *here* when they should occur *there*. The first part of the play goes too long without an up number. There are a whole lot of lines that might have been hilariously funny but didn't get over, and

I've seen it now with two good audiences. So now those lines will be cut, that's what.

JG: Gosh, I didn't—I may sound stupid, but I don't remember a good line that anybody missed.

NC: There wasn't a *good* line that anybody missed. It was the *bad* lines. (*He laughs.*)

JG: I don't remember a bad line.

NC: Tonight I shall sit in that theater with my secretary and make a note of every line I'm going to cut, and I should think there'll be over fifty. I've already cut four scenes and three big numbers.

JG: My God, you're a pro! And that's what's important. You have to know how to make people feel how you want them to feel. That's the challenge. That part that I took in *Judgment at Nuremberg* is a wonderful, wonderful role. It will probably last only about eight minutes on the screen, but what happens in those eight minutes is important, and it was challenging. The whole feeling was challenging—Stanley Kramer, the director, and Spencer Tracy, and a great script. I've always wanted to work with Stanley Kramer. I have a great admiration for him. Why does an actress take a part like that? Because the correct people are involved. Much more important than billing and starring.

NC: Billing and starring are the two most boring words in the lexicon. As long as when you're up there you do it right.

JG: You were certainly the star last night [at a party for cast and friends after the opening of *Sail Away*].

NC: Thank you, darling. There were far too many people there. But I was slightly proud that they had taken that picture of me looking like a very old bull moose and put it up in place of the portrait of George Washington. In Boston, of all places! Considering the Boston Tea Party, this was really very kind of them. I imagine they've forgiven us for that now.

JG (*laughing*): At least you've been forgiven.

NC: I was absolutely exhausted. I've been working frightfully hard these last few weeks—we had been rehearsing during the day—and then opening night. The first night is always an ordeal. However successful you are, you're always nervous that first night. But it went wonderfully and I was very happy. I came back to the hotel, washed my face and hands, had a drink and then I thought, Now, this must be done properly because everybody is coming to the party. It's my turn to give a performance—at midnight. Then you came. And you stopped being Judy and became *Judy Garland.* And I was no more Noël. I was *Noël Coward,* debonair, witty, charming and . . .

JG: . . . and I was Dorothy Adorable.

NC: And you were just Dorothy Adorable, and we smiled and we took the show. And there we both were, together with a lot of people who stood around waiting for us to be charming and clever and entertaining. We were such good sorts. My dear, going on being such good sorts in public for a long time is very wearing, because we weren't feeling really in good sorts at all. What we wanted to do is get away and . . .

JG: and put on some slacks and sprawl out on the floor.

NC: . . . put on some—take off our shoes and have a drink and discuss show business. That's what is really interesting. In all the concerts I did for the troops during the war, the only thing I dreaded was the party given after the show by the commanding officer. I might have done five concerts in a day in the heat of Burma, but the officers would still expect me to come to their party. And then, after giving me a couple of drinks to help me relax, they would come out with it: "How about giving us a few numbers?" You want to clobber them. You're dead. But you say yes.

JG: You do it. You do it.

NC: You do it. And you go home screaming.

JG: I'm getting so [old] I wonder why I do it anymore. But I still do. I suppose it's something we never—

NC: We're show people.

JG: I suppose. Once in London, I remember, I was invited to a party. First I had to do some recording, and it took hours. I had five or six recordings, and you know that means doing them over and over—and I sing terribly loud. It was late, and I called and said I'd be late for the party. When I finally arrived, I found that everybody had already eaten and just the leftovers were still on the table—you know, awful bits of cold ham and wilted lettuce. I was so hungry that when the hostess brought me a miserable-looking plate, I started eating. "Now," she said, "Kay [Thompson] is at the piano, and everybody's been waiting for you to sing." I said, "I've just been singing for five hours, you know." But what could I do? Kay and I sang for another three hours. Then we went home on our hands and knees. Just so tired. But the people really were standing like statues and they had been there all evening.

NC: They get it for nothing. Getting it for nothing. They say, "Wouldn't it be wonderful if we could persuade her to sing?" That's all right. That's fine. But what is irritating is to be taken for granted, when they expect you to perform come hell or high water. With or without an accompanist, whether or not you've just finished working, you are expected to sing. And as soon as you start—everybody starts to talk.

JG: Oh, darling, they don't do that to you too!

NC: I'll tell you one little story that happened during the war. I came back to Cairo after a long, hot day entertaining in one hospital after another, and I found a message saying King Farouk was giving a party that evening and would I please come? So I obediently had a shower and got into a white dinner jacket and went off to one of the most boring social affairs imaginable. My eye caught a very nasty-looking upright piano, and I thought, Hello, hello—this is it! And King Farouk, covered in medals, came up and asked me very courteously, "Mr. Coward, would you sing us a few songs?" I thought it discourteous to say that I don't like playing for myself while I sing, so I agreed. I went to the piano and sang a number and everyone was fairly attentive but restless. Then I started on "Night and Day"—I can play it well and I've got a good arrangement. And I did the drip-drip-drip of the raindrops and all the rest, with everyone quiet except King Farouk, who was busy impressing the lady next to him. He was so rude that I lost my temper. So I got to the chorus and sang, "In the roaring traffic's boom" and then I went, "In the SILENCE!" He stopped dead, and there was a terrible hush, and then I continued blithely, "of my lonely room, I think of you."

JG *(laughing)*: Lovely!

NC: In the old days, when we entertainers were considered rogues and vagabonds and we weren't received socially—which of course saved us an enormous amount of boredom—we were bloody well paid for performing. We might be shown in through the servants' quarters, but that was all right. You'd sing your song and get five hundred quid for it.

JG: When I was at Metro—I don't think I was much over twelve years old, and they didn't know what to do with me because they wanted you either five years old or eighteen, with nothing in between. Well, I was in between, and so was little Deanna Durbin, and they didn't know what to do with us. So we just went to school every day and wandered around the lot. Whenever the important stars had parties, though, they called the casting office and said "Bring those two kids." We would be taken over and we would wait with the servants until they called us into the drawing room, where we would perform. We never got five hundred quid, though. We got a dish of ice cream—and it would always be melted.

NC: But I'm talking about the . . . the big stars now—not kids. In the old days the big stars were common trash, however big the star.

JG: With certain groups I still feel that I'm being taken up as a kind of— you know, sort of, oh, it's fun with Judy Garland. She's *fun!* She sings! You feel you're being used as a kind of foolish court jester who'll be dropped next season when the newest property comes in.

NC: Oh, yes, and after you've done your number, darling, without any rehearsal and no lighting and no rest, someone says, "My, doesn't he look *old.*"

JG *(laughing)*: Or fat.

NC: But, of course, it is no use ever expecting society to understand about show business or entertainers because they never do, do they?

TV INTERVIEW

MIKE WALLACE | December 1961, *PM East/PM West*

Despite warnings from several German extremist groups, Stanley Kramer secured Berlin's Kongresshalle as the venue for the world premiere of *Judgment at Nuremberg*. A press junket costing upward of $150,000 brought in hundreds of journalists from around the world. Among them was a pre–*60 Minutes* Mike Wallace, who conducted this stimulating sit-down interview for *PM East/ PM West*, the host's bicoastal late night syndicated talk show produced for the Westinghouse Broadcasting Company.

Mike Wallace: Judy, why do you come on a junket like this? Is it because it's in your contract with Stanley Kramer or is it something that you enjoy?

Judy Garland: Oh, no, it's not in my contract with Stanley Kramer. I come on this junket because I feel the picture is terribly important.

MW: Now, I've heard you say that a half a dozen times and the reporters have asked this question, why you've done this picture.

JG: Yes.

MW: And you say you feel this picture is terribly important. Why is the picture so important to *you*?

JG: To me?

MW: Yes.

JG: Because it represents a time in my life. The time of the Nuremberg trials was the most important time in my life, and I think it's important that my children see the clarification that *Judgment at Nuremberg* brings about. It's a pairing of certain issues and I think it's one of the most adult pictures ever made. I think the issues have been presented correctly, and I feel it's important from *that* viewpoint . . . from the viewpoint of young people learning from our era.

MW: Mmm. Now, on a junket like this, with two hundred or three hundred newspapermen following you around and throwing question after question, is this something that you enjoy or is it truly a chore for you?

JG: Well, no, I didn't come to Berlin to . . . I consider this a job to do, you know? But it's a pleasure to do anything that will help to prove my point of view in doing this picture. And it's also a pleasure just doing this for Stanley Kramer because I respect him so.

MW: Even after [seven] years, your first film when you come back, your first part is that of a sort of a *drab* character.

JG: Yes, very drab. Yes. Very drab. But a hausfrau. A German woman. And I'm only in the film actually seven or eight minutes.

MW: I know.

JG: But what I have to say is important, I believe. At least I hope it turned out that way.

MW: It certainly did turn out that way. Tell me, why . . . I don't know if you've thought about this . . . but why do you think within the last year or two there's been such a resurgence in the Garland career?

JG: I don't know. I was asked that a minute ago. It's a matter, I think, of working very hard and very diligently and being at your best whenever you do work, you know. And in order to do that, you have to enjoy your work. You have to enjoy what you're doing and believe what you're doing. And then there's always an element of luck and timing, and I seem to have gotten caught up in a lovely whirlwind that is quite invigorating.

MW: Well, I would say, every once in a while in show business this kind of thing happens. It's not really a comeback, but it's an exciting thing that happens to a performer that has happened to you, as I say, over the past year [or] year and a half, and it is a tremendous amount of satisfaction to you, I suppose.

JG: Oh, well, it's *most* satisfactory. It's the best thing that's ever happened to me, you know, because things went quite slowly for a long time. And I thought that that was all right. It was all right. I'd worked for so many years anyway. But then all of a sudden when this just started to roll, and all the concerts were successful in Europe, and I lived in London and I got back to America and there was so much work to be done. Well, it's a marvelous thing to sit and say "How am I going to get time to do this, that, and the other?" instead of having too much time on your hands.

MW: What do you work *for*, Judy?

JG: I work for, I suppose, what we all work for. We work for a monetary value, of course. Then, beyond that, I work for . . . you see, I worked for so many years that it would be rather foolish to say I never want to work again, you know, at this age. Neither could I afford to financially and emotionally. I'm not prepared for that right now. I work for the satisfaction of knowing that I've worked hard all my life and that at least I'm making people happy sometimes during the day or night.

MW: Do you feel very successful? Do you feel that you are a successful person, a successful performer, and a successful human being?

JG: Yes, I do. I do, I have to say. I don't mean to sound egotistical when I say that, but I'd be rather neurotic if I didn't feel that. It's been proven to me, and I have my children, who are very attractive and happy and warm. So I, obviously, am doing very well as a person and my work is going well.

MW: Bless you.

JG: Thank you, Mike.

MW: And you have never seen the *real* Judy Garland until you have seen her on a charter plane [*Judy laughs*] at 5:00 in the morning in green tights and a blue silk nightgown. And Kay Thompson's dog along with her.

JG: [*Laughs.*] Oh, Mike!

MW: Thank you, Judy.

JG: Thank you! [*Laughs.*]

JUDY GEM

On Crying

"Why do people *cry* over me? Darned if I know. I sing something happy like 'Zing! Went the Strings of My Heart,' and I feel it's going over great and everybody out front should feel as happy as I do, but then I look down, and someone there is bawling. I'd like to set something straight. *I do not cry.* People are always writing that I'm bursting into tears. The only thing I ever burst into is a good song . . ."

—To Rowland Barber, *Good Housekeeping*, January 1962

JUDY GEM

On Carnegie Hall

"[During the overture,] I kept thinking of who was out front, and kept telling myself 'This ain't Dallas, kiddo! This is Carnegie Hall. New York City—and it ain't [Jascha] Heifetz or [Arthur] Rubinstein. . . . [Once onstage,] I decided right away that they liked me and I loved them, and we had ourselves a ball."

—To Rowland Barber, *Good Housekeeping*, January 1962

JUDY GEM

On *A Child is Waiting*

"Retarded children are realists. They know what it is to be rejected, because they have been rejected many times. . . . These children want affection, yes. But most of all, they need to be accepted as human beings. They need to feel useful. People don't want to face such things. Human beings hate things that are mysterious to them. But I think shining a spotlight on such things can make people understand and want to help."

—To Bob Thomas, Associated Press, February 1962

JUDY GEM
On Stage Fright

"I'm a victim of the most awful stage fright. I always get sick right before I go on the stage. It's such a lonely feeling. But no matter how frightened you are, you have to do it. I figure if people have gotten in their cars and driven there and paid to see you, you just bloody well have to go on."

—To Rick Du Brow, United Press International, February 23, 1962

JUDY

JACK HAMILTON | April 10, 1962, *Look*

For this prominent cover story in *Look* magazine, a popular biweekly, Judy sat down with the publication's senior editor, Jack Hamilton. Hamilton later co-authored the popular book *They Had Faces Then: Annabella to Zorina, the Superstars, Stars and Starlets of the 1930s*.

Judy Garland concluded her now-legendary one-woman-show tour of 42 cities last December in Washington, DC. When the sound of unrestrained *bravas* had died away, she told the people waiting for her in her dressing room, "This is the first time I've ever felt a sense of accomplishment from a job really well done. I'm free now. For a few days, even my voice is my own. I feel like sitting in a draft in a wet bathing suit!"

But Judy's backbreaking work schedule ("I'm so strong now that I can make my muscular husband say 'Uncle' when we wrestle") went rolling on. After a few days' rest, she flew to Berlin for the world premiere of *Judgment at Nuremberg*, her first film in seven years. On her return, she began taping a TV spectacular, *The Judy Garland Show*, with Frank Sinatra and Dean Martin. When that was done, she went before the cameras again, as Burt Lancaster's costar in *A Child Is Waiting*. She plans to go to Spain with her husband, Sid Luft, for a month's vacation and then to England for another movie, *The Lonely Stage*, a "drama with music."

This is a time of triumphant vindication for Judy Garland, after what she calls "seven years of rotten luck." She says, "Isn't this pretty good for somebody Hollywood thought was too old, too fat, and too undependable to offer a job? For an 'undependable,' I certainly made a lot of pictures. The only time I was undependable was when I was ill and couldn't work. Everybody is undependable when they're ill."

Today, she is a wryly humorous, still-complicated woman who has, after much bludgeoning by "rotten luck," worked out a new appraisal of herself as a human being. What happened this past year to bring her and her career back to life? Judy answered our questions without hesitation and with fresh candor:

"Now is the first time in my life I've felt like a mature woman, and I'm damned near 40 years old. Some people never reach maturity, and I'm lucky I found it at 40, instead of at 70. I was raised in a film studio and had no normal school or family life. I didn't see anything of life beyond the studio, and I think that's the reason I was so slow in growing up. Maybe it was just *me*—I still don't know.

"All my life I refused to accept the love that people wanted to give me. But after the satisfaction of my work this past year, I at last can understand and evaluate my abilities. I know I'm a kind person. I know I'm a good mother. I know I'm a good actress and singer. I realize now that people like me. I'm always afraid of sounding conceited, and this is the first time I've ever talked this way. But it's better than the years and years when I thought of myself in the most negative and destructive way.

"It was my long bout with illness and near death, and the thoughts that went with them, that forced me to take stock. I knew I couldn't go on the disastrous way I was headed when I was at the Metropolitan Opera House in 1959—giving a terrible concert. I behaved like an automaton. Everybody was saying, 'Well, she's always been *strange*, anyway.' I collapsed and gave in to being ill.

"What I had had all this time was hepatitis, and nobody had diagnosed it. A young doctor, a liver specialist, finally told me that this was my illness. He said, 'I think you're going to make it, with luck. But you'll have to adjust yourself to the fact that you'll be a semi-invalid for the rest of your life.'

"My first reaction to this was, 'You couldn't have told me anything better. I've worked too hard all my life anyway.' But even when he was talking, I knew, subconsciously, he was wrong. I knew I would be able to sing again someday. I just needed a long rest to get away from the pressure of set engagements. Pressure alone can bring about fears and breakdowns.

"I finally got well for good and felt strong enough to work. The real reason I got well was for my children. I couldn't be a semi-invalid, or die. I had to live to protect and to love them. My first breakthrough, as a worker, was my new format of concerts, which my husband and I conceived in Europe, and, later, Freddie Fields managed in America. Then Stanley Kramer asked me to play a part in *Judgment at Nuremberg*. He never looked at me with a doubtful look and never asked questions about me. He treated me as a working actress. This was the final vote of confidence I needed.

"I no longer dwell on the bad years. I feel no vengeance against anybody. If you have the intelligence, you try to go on to better things. I don't even 'hate' the people in Hollywood who wouldn't give me a job by accusing me of being 'late,' among other things. I was always at work on time for years.

"My children are the most special thing in my life. They are very portable. I've uprooted them, dragged them from one country to another, because I'll never leave them in the care of servants. They are happy only as long as their mother and daddy are with them. You try to keep them as long as you can and prepare for the day when they'll leave. You have to be ready not to be an idiot about it when they do leave, because they will. They must have a life of their own.

"But, right now, we're just a family of baggy-pants comedians. We have lots of fun, lots of love. Even at our lowest moments, we are really very funny together. The kids are even amused by Momma's bad Irish temper. They think it's funny when she explodes and apologizes the next minute. At least, I don't sulk and get ulcers.

"Liza is 16. I've always known she was a marvelous dancer, but she dazzled Sid and me with her performance as Anne Frank at school. She was very professional about rehearsals, took direction only from her director and wouldn't let Momma butt in with free advice.

"Lorna is nine. She looks like a rose, and she's destined to be an actress. She has an actress's mind, with its imagination, fiendishness and curiosity.

Joe is six, and he's going to be interested—like his father—in machines. He's also interested in music, although he goes to sleep halfway through my concerts. He may go to MIT and then decide to be a symphony conductor after all. He knows every note of the orchestration of *West Side Story*.

"My children never play my records at home. They aren't too interested in my career. Little Lorna once, quite sharply, told a patronizing English newspaperman, who had asked her if Judy Garland sang lullabies to the children at bedtime, "No, she doesn't, and we don't call her Judy Garland, just Momma."

Judy's role in the movie she is making now, *A Child is Waiting*, has a particular meaning for her. "It's a story of the problems of retarded children. I wanted to role so badly because I've done work with troubled children and I know a bit more about them than most people. A disturbed child once helped me to get well.

"In 1949, I had a nervous breakdown and went to the Peter Bent Brigham Hospital in Boston. Next to the hospital was another for children. I visited these children one day, all alone. Later, I started daily visits. There was one particular little girl, a disturbed child, who aroused my curiosity. She was six years old—my son Joe's age now—and she hadn't talked for many months. She had come from a family that had obviously mistreated her. She was punishing them and the world by refusing to speak.

"I stopped by every day to talk to her especially. For some reason, I was smart enough to know I shouldn't ask her any questions. I just *told* her things. I told her about Dorothy in *The Wizard of Oz*, about Mickey Rooney and Clark Gable and about my family's old vaudeville act. Once in a while, she'd smile, but she would never say a word to me.

"After eleven weeks, I was well enough to go back to Hollywood, and my manager came to get me. I went to the children to say goodbye. They gave me flowers. My own little special friend was waiting for me, with flowers she had crumpled and torn in her nervousness. I sat down with her and told her I had to go home because I was well now, and I told her how much I would miss her. She began to cry. Then, for the first time in months, she spoke: 'Don't go, don't go away!' She began to scream, and people ran over to us, astonished. My manager came and said, 'We'll be late for the train.' I told him we'd have to take a later train, because I wanted to have a long conversation with my friend. Then she talked and talked and talked to me. She told me some of the things that were troubling her. I made her promise to tell these things to the doctors and nurses after I had gone, and told her they would do everything to help her.

"This was one of the greatest triumphs of my life. She had helped to make me well, and I had helped her."

Kay Thompson, Judy's longtime friend from the old M-G-M days and a consultant on her recent TV show, says, "Most people still think Judy is helpless, with people waiting on her and doing things for her. She not only conceived and selected her own concert program, but she made all the musical arrangements, designed her own clothes, and supervised the lighting. She has an executive's mind. She goes in, gets the thing done and leaves."

About this, Judy says, "If I didn't know how to do these things, I'd be pretty dumb after all these years. It's a protection for me to have technical knowledge. It makes other people around me happy, because they don't have to worry about *all* the millions of details.

"I design all my own clothes because I got bored with couturiers poking at me and murmuring, 'We understand your fitting problem.' I can never wear the expensive dresses they create. I put them down in the cellar. I don't flatter myself. I do my best to overcome my basic problem by my own designs. For one thing, I'm so short that I should wear a narrow skirt. I choose the material and send my designs for suits and dresses to a good tailor."

As for the spell she casts on audiences, one of her musicians says, "She sends out yoga waves. She has every heart with her. One of the reasons is that she's a real musician. I respect her so much I'd work for her for nothing."

Judy herself says she "hasn't a clue" as to her mesmerism. "It *may* be my power of concentration. I really mean every word of every song I sing, no matter how many times I've sung it before. But then in Paris and Amsterdam, I didn't sing in French or Dutch, and the same audience uproars took place. So I really don't know what it is. Something wonderful takes place between me and all the people out there. It's like a marvelous love affair. All you have to do is never cheat and work your best and work your hardest, and they'll respond to you. Such satisfaction can't apply to many other things in life."

In Berlin, for the premiere of *Judgment at Nuremberg*—for which she received her second Academy Award nomination—she was trailed by photographers and fans, gave a mass interview to the German press. "There's a trick about handling crowds," she says. "If you try to push your way through in a panic, they'll mob you. The psychology is to walk very slowly, talking and joking as you walk. Then they are nice and sweet, nobody gets hurt or pushed, or mad at you—and we all end by loving each other."

In takeoff from Toronto, after two concerts there, Judy sits next to her husband, praying and clutching photographs of her children. "I'm just a sentimental and superstitious old Irish biddy at heart," she says. Between travels ("It's the traveling that knocks me out"), they live mostly in the East, in New York City and Scarsdale, NY. Last summer, they lived in Hyannis Port, Mass, in a house near the Kennedys' (they are friendly with President Kennedy). "I'll never live in California full time again," she says.

With director Norman Jewison, Judy watches a playback of her recent TV show. She performed each number in one "take," without mistake or mishap, as in her concerts. When she struck a note she wasn't pleased with, she'd joke, "I sound like Andy Devine or the Andrews Brothers." But she was exultant that her show "really catches the live feeling of being in a theater."

After the last concert of her tour, in Washington, Judy and her husband threw a party for her musicians, later played poker ("baseball") all night. Judy often has trouble sleeping and, at home, spends her sleepless hours reading and cooking. "When my body becomes immobilized from too much reading and sitting," she says, "I get up in the quiet of the night and cook something delicious—which I never eat. I put my marvelous concoctions in the icebox to surprise the children in the morning."

"It's a great thing to lose fear. I had an unreasonable block against television, and I had to break through this final block in my life. My previous TV shows were utter chaos to me, because I was so frightened. In those shows, I'd blow up like a fish—you know, the kind of fish that expands if you tickle its tummy?" When someone called her the greatest entertainer of her time, she said, "Oh, no. What about Jolson and Sinatra?"

RADIO INTERVIEW

WILLIAM B. WILLIAMS | April 23, 1962, *Make Believe Ballroom* (WNEW, New York, NY)

The *Make Believe Ballroom* was a mythical venue debuting in 1935 on WNEW 1130 in New York. Williams B. Williams took the reins as host in 1958 and was known to buck the mainstream top 40 trends fueling other popular stations. He remained focused on and faithful to pop standards and the music of his friends, which included everyone from Frank Sinatra and Tony Bennett to Duke Ellington and Ella Fitzgerald. Judy was also among Williams' esteemed list of friends, and joined the host to play selections from her Carnegie Hall album in this "ballroom" setting for what proved to be a wonderful hour commemorating the first anniversary of her 1961 Carnegie triumph. A month later, on May 29, 1962, *Judy at Carnegie Hall* was awarded an astounding five Grammy awards, including Best Solo Performance by a Female and the prestigious Album of the Year.

Judy Garland: This is Judy Garland. Welcome to the *Make Believe Ballroom*. Tonight, here at the *Ballroom*, we'd like to take you back exactly one year to Carnegie Hall and we'll recreate musically what happened when I walked out on stage and began the Carnegie Hall concert of April 23, 1961.

[*Plays "Just You, Just Me."*]

William B. Williams: That was some of the excitement attended to the Judy Garland concert a year ago, and we're going to re-create the concert for you here tonight at the *Ballroom* exactly one year later. Judy, before we get to some of the music of exactly a year ago, I wonder—first things first—a lot of people have called in and written in and are worried about how you're feeling. How do you feel?

JG: I feel *fine*. I was never sick, I just went in for a good rest. I was just there a few days.

WBW: I'm sure you are aware of the kind of loyalty your fans have. You have fan clubs dotted all around the landscape around New York. And we've been receiving calls all week worrying about you.

JG: Oh, how silly. Well, I've been working for two years without letup and I thought it might be a good idea to just go into the Presbyterian—

WBW: Columbia Presbyterian—

JG: Columbia Presbyterian Hospital and get a few days' rest and a checkup at the same time. Therefore, I couldn't answer phone calls. It was good for me.

WBW: You look fine. You look well rested.

JG: I am.

WBW: In doing this concert again, we're letting a lot of people in on what some 3,145 people witnessed a year ago. What were your feelings? Was that the first night of the concert engagement?

JG: No. You mean of the concert tour?

WBW: Of the tour itself.

JG: No, that came, actually, in the middle of the tour. I don't remember the exact date we started the tour. I know it was in February. Was it in February? Yeah. It was in February and this was in April, so it was sort of in the middle of the tour. And you asked me how I felt?

WBW: Mm-hm.

JG: Well, I don't think I've ever had a more *marvelous* evening for *me*. I hope the audience felt the same way. I had a great time, and the response was so gratifying. I had never seen Carnegie Hall. I'd never even been inside of Carnegie Hall.

WBW: Well, Carnegie Hall has known—through the years—concert artists, classical artists, violinists, pianists. I wasn't there that night, but people who were there said the love of the audience for you was almost a tangible thing. It was almost something you could *feel* come out of the audience.

JG: Where were *you*? [*Laughs.*]

WBW: I wasn't there that night because, frankly, I couldn't get a ticket. Tickets, as you probably know, were at a premium.

JG: I'm just fooling you, Bill.

WBW: I wonder, can you as a performer feel that kind of love when it erupts from an audience?

JG: You mean, something, as you say, something tangible?

WBW: Yeah.

JG: Well, I don't . . . It sounds rather difficult, without sounding egotistical. I do feel *love*, yes, and they show me love. You know, they demonstrate their love by applause and by saying lovely things to me. And, yes, I *can* feel it. I can feel it. I hope they feel the love that I have for them.

WBW: Do you notice a difference in cities? Are there any cities that are tougher to get audience response from than others?

JG: This last concert tour was . . . I don't know why, because I've done tours before and I've been on the stage before, but this somehow, chemically or whether it was the programming of the songs or the timing, whatever, created a lot of excitement wherever we went. Some audiences, naturally, were a little slower getting started and you had to work a little harder, but they all wound up quite successfully.

WBW: I think the rapport that exists between you as a performer and an audience is something to behold. I know of no one else who has it. Let's get to some of the music of that concert. We're not going to follow the program as it happened that night. Right now, for example, this tune is by Noël Coward. It's called "If Love Were All." I remember reading an interview recently that contained dialogue between Mr. Coward and yourself about show business.

JG: Yes.

WBW: I think it was in *Redbook*.

JG: That's right. Yes. We're very good friends.

WBW: Do you ofttimes do Noël Coward tunes? How do you select, for example, why did you select this particular Noël Coward tune?

JG: Well, I think that it's a lovely lyric. It's one of the most interesting and one of the most poignant lyrics that I've ever heard. It's a beautifully constructed melody, and magnificently constructed lyrically. It's always been one of my favorites. The first time I did this concert was at the Palladium in London, sort of off the cuff, actually. I didn't take much time to prepare it, but I wanted to sing one of Mr. Coward's songs, and this happened to be the one I chose because it's one of my favorite songs.

WBW: Here then, in concert at Carnegie Hall—staid old Carnegie Hall, I might add—Miss Judy Garland, as she did one year ago, Noël Coward's "If Love Were All."

[*Plays "If Love Were All."*]

WBW: Our guest in the *Ballroom*, Miss Judy Garland. Judy, we're going to pause now and catch up on late news and weather and then continue with our concert, the re-creation of it, of one year ago.

JG: All right.

WBW: All of that here at WNEW in New York, AM and FM.

[*Station break.*]

WBW: Our guest is "Miss Show Business." Who first dubbed you "Miss Show Business," do you know, Judy?

JG: By golly, I can't remember. I think it was Alan Livingston with Capitol Records.

WBW: Uh huh.

JG: Yes.

WBW: Incidentally, speaking of Capitol Records, the concert is on Capitol Records and has sold as well as any album this size has ever sold, I think. It's a great tribute to *you*, I think, as a performer, and also to the recording technique. I think they have captured all of the excitement that was there that night.

JG: Yes, it was quite extraordinary that they could do that, you know, because under the conditions being in the theater—and actually giving a performance and not—I, as a matter of fact, forgot that they were recording. I was too caught up with the evening and the excitement, and probably, if I'd remembered they were recording, it wouldn't have been any good. I'd have been so busy with my pear-shaped tones that don't come out well at all. But I think they did a marvelous job, technically, you know.

WBW: For example, on this next tune—I think it's a Harold Arlen–Johnny Mercer tune, "Come Rain or Come Shine"—all of the things that were in the original recording, they captured, I think, at Carnegie Hall. Did Nelson Riddle do this arrangement for you?

JG: Yes, he did. He did the orchestration. Roger Edens did the vocal arrangement.

WBW: Uh huh. And this is Judy in concert with "Come Rain or Come Shine."

[*Plays "Come Rain or Come Shine."*]

WBW: In the *Ballroom* this Monday evening, our guest: Miss Judy Garland. The occasion: the first anniversary of Judy's concert at Carnegie Hall. You've taken that concert tour practically all around the world.

JG: Well, we've gone lots of places with it. It started in England and we've played many towns in England, and we took it to France and then Holland and let me see … then I came back to America and we played forty-two cities.

WBW: I would be remiss, as far as your fans are concerned—and, gosh, they're in the hundreds of thousands in this area—if I didn't determine from you whether you're going to work in New York or the environs in the near future, in concert or whatever.

JG: Well, I've got to go and do a movie first in London. I'm leaving in a few days. As a matter of fact, I'm making another album on Thursday night.

WBW: This Thursday?

JG: Yes. Before I go. For Capitol. And then I'm off to London. I imagine I'll be there three or four months. It takes that time to make a picture.

WBW: You just completed a film out on the coast, too.

JG: Yeah, yeah. That was a straight, nonsinging part, you know.

WBW: You mentioned the name Roger Edens earlier, Judy. Am I correct, is my intelligence correct, didn't you do your original audition for Roger Edens? Or wasn't he in on your original audition at M-G-M?

JG: He was at M-G-M, yes. Mm-hm.

WBW: And you did "Zing! Went the Strings, [of My Heart]" was it?

JG: Well, I didn't audition for him. He was, at the time, just a pianist. He had been Ethel Merman's accompanist here in New York, and then he came out to Metro and nobody paid much attention to him. And he got sort of dragged in to hear this little girl—many years ago, need I say—sing. [*Laughs.*] He accompanied me because my mother, you see, who used to accompany, was ill and couldn't be there. So he came in to accompany. I was about twelve and from then on we've been working together.

WBW: Was the tune "Zing! Went the Strings of My Heart"?

JG: Yes.

[*Plays "Zing! Went the Strings of My Heart."*]

WBW: If you're within the sound of WNEW Radio tonight, you're in great luck. Our guest in the *Make Believe Ballroom*, Miss Judy Garland, and we're playing some of the tunes from the Carnegie Hall concert of one year ago. The album title: *Judy at Carnegie Hall*. We'll get back to chatting with Judy and some more excerpts from that album after this word.

[*Station break.*]

WBW: You're with WNEW in New York, AM and FM, in the *Make Believe Ballroom*. Our guest, Miss Judy Garland. Judy, you mentioned earlier going to England to do another movie. It's seems you have conquered just about every field of communication available. Do you have any frustrations as a performer? Anything you'd like to do that you haven't done?

JG: Well, I've never done a play on Broadway, and I've thought of that. I don't know, really, whether I'm geared for that every-night thing. I think I would like it, though, if it had good music and a good story. It's rather tempting. That's the only thing I haven't done. I finally conquered my [*laughs*] fear of television, and I do adore television now.

WBW: The special you did recently with Frank [Sinatra] and Dean [Martin] was just great.

JG: Did you like it?

WBW: Yes. Norman Jewison.

JG: Yes. He's terribly good, by the way. He's just marvelous.

WBW: Speaking about talented people who surround you, the young man who conducts for you, Mort Lindsey.

JG: Yes.

WBW: I'm a big fan of Mort's. I've known him for a long time, and he does wondrous things, I think, for you.

JG: Oh, he's *marvelous*. He's just marvelous, and we got him sort of on a *fluke*, actually.

WBW: How so?

JG: Well, when I came from London I was supposed to work, do concerts at one of the hotels in the Catskills, and the conductor came down to New York to rehearse my music. And the music is quite difficult to play. You know, Nelson Riddle and millions of high trumpet notes and bongos and all those things. And he just said that he didn't think that he wanted to take the responsibility. So I forget whether it was David Begelman or Freddie Fields picked up the phone and called Mort Lindsey. Luckily he was home. He, I think, was about to take a year off, wasn't he, just to write music? He wasn't going to conduct anymore. He wanted to write. So we finagled him to come to the rehearsal, and he rehearsed the whole show with the band and I don't think it took any longer than two hours and we did the concert and we've been—

WBW: He's been with you ever since.

JG: Yes. I think he's absolutely marvelous.

WBW: This tune "Chicago" that we're going to hear now, whose arrangement is this? Do you know offhand?

JG: You mean the orchestration?

WBW: Yeah.

JG: Or the vocal arrangement?

WBW: The vocal arrangement.

JG: Well, it's Roger Edens' vocal arrangement and it's . . . let me see . . . I don't know. I think my brother-in-law, Jack Cathcart, made the orchestration to "Chicago."

WBW: Alright, here then, again, in staid old Carnegie Hall, exactly one year ago, Judy Garland and a tribute to Chicago.

[*Plays "Chicago."*]

WBW: At exactly 7:00 PM, that's Miss Judy Garland, with us here at the *Make Believe Ballroom*, and we're re-creating that memorable concert of exactly one year ago. Judy, we're going to pause once more and check up again on the very latest news and weather, and then more excitement with "Miss Show Business," Miss Garland, here at the *Ballroom*, here at WNEW in New York, AM and FM.

[*Station break.*]

WBW: In the *Ballroom* this Monday evening we are very pleased to welcome as our guest a young lady who a year ago was working very hard—a little later on tonight, it would have been [a year ago]. The concert started, I guess, about 8:30 that night, didn't it?

JG: I think it started at 8:45.

WBW: You had a lot of notables in the audience, among them Rock Hudson and Dore Schary. A lot of visiting celebrities and of course people who just love you. I wonder, Judy, in watching an audience react to you, have you figured out or do you take the time to figure out or *should* you figure out why you communicate so well with them and, let's say, some other performer may not? Have you figured out what it is?

JG: No. I haven't a clue. I don't know what it is. Maybe it might be that I feel a genuine affection and love for people who pay money to come and sit and watch me sing. I have great respect and I also believe in never cheating an audience because they have been kind enough—

WBW: They've spent their money and—

JG: Yes. It might be that. Otherwise, I don't know. I really don't know. All I know is it's very nice.

WBW: Speaking about that kind of thing, as far as performers are concerned, do you see any performers around today whom you particularly like? You know, newcomers coming up? As far as singing is concerned, for example, if you were locked in a room and had to listen to some albums, what albums would you choose? What singers? What performers?

JG: Well, I think there are a lot of good singers, really. Very good singers. They're not newcomers. I'm too old now to know about all the newcomers [*laughs*], but I'm sure some of them are marvelous, I just haven't heard them. But I do think that Tony Bennett is marvelous. Of course Frank Sinatra. I—

WBW: May I interrupt you for a second? You say, "Of course Frank Sinatra." Any singer you talk to says, "Of course Judy Garland" and "Of course Frank Sinatra." Now, let me ask you. As far as Sinatra's concerned, what is it? The way he feels a lyric?

JG: I don't know. I don't know. I can't answer you any more than you—than I could when you asked—

WBW: I figured I could kind of trap you there and get the ... [*laughs*]. As I say, I wonder sometimes because singers say, almost inevitably, you ask one hundred singers, ninety-nine of them will say, "Of course Judy," and "Of course Frank." I've wondered, in looking at Frank's work, what it is. Whether it's his lyric interpretation—

JG: Well, I think it's his lyric interpretation and the quality of his voice. And also, he does cast an almost hypnotic spell, you know. He really does. You just don't look away when he's entertaining or singing, you just listen to what he has to say. I think Peggy Lee is a marvelous singer. I like the girl named Kay Starr. I think she's a wonderful, wonderful singer. [There are] many, many fine singers.

WBW: I wonder, talking about singers of today now, the kind of background that a singer like you have had in working vaudeville, movies, television, I don't know that the singer of today can get that kind of background. A singer today, a youngster, can get a hit record and suddenly be put on a television show and have forty million people sit and watch in judgment.

JG: Yeah, that's kind of rough on them, I think. Because I came from vaudeville, originally, and then went into movies, I was lucky enough to have had that kind of background. Therefore, I learned by trial and error, you know, how to entertain, how to sing, and so forth. It's rather a rough go on young kids now because they're—

WBW: They don't have the basic training.

JG: Yes, but if they're good they'll last. I have a theory that basic, good talent is not unfounded. Somebody always finds a person—young person or whoever—if they're *really* talented they'll be found. They'll find a way to be found.

WBW: Speaking of talent, let's get to Judy in concert again and "That's Entertainment."

[*Plays "That's Entertainment."*]

WBW: You're with WNEW in New York, AM and FM, [with] Miss Judy Garland, and we're re-creating as best we can some of the wonderful contagious excitement that attended Judy's Carnegie Hall concert one year ago. Judy, again, in reading in magazines like *Cosmopolitan*, *Redbook*, and in interviews, I know the great love you have for your children. Do they show any signs of becoming performers?

JG: I'm afraid so. Yes. [*Both laugh.*]

WBW: Why "afraid so"?

JG: Well, you know, I went along with the theory for a long time that they shouldn't be exposed to this—

WBW: Horrible world of show business.

JG: But I'm afraid they're stuck with it. My sixteen-year-old daughter is *terribly* good. She's a magnificent dancer and also an awfully good actress. And she's very pretty. And my nine-year-old girl is the Gertrude Lawrence of Scarsdale! [*Both laugh.*] There's just no holding her. My little boy, Joe, he's seven. He doesn't know quite whether he wants to be a conductor or a mechanic. He takes everything apart, you know, the way boys do. And yet, he knows the whole score—the *background* music—of *West Side Story* and conducts it when no one's watching. If anybody's watching he just stops immediately. He thinks that's, you know, he doesn't want to be caught at it. So I think they're sort of . . . I don't know what they're going to do. They can do what they want. But *thank God* they're talented! Wouldn't that be awful if they wanted to be onstage and had no talent?

WBW: I don't think there'll be any problem. I remember, again, seeing some still shots of your eldest daughter and she's a *beautiful* girl.

JG: Yes, she's lovely.

WBW: She's sixteen?

JG: She's sixteen. Yes.

WBW: And she's been studying ballet from—

JG: She's been dancing. She's been studying dancing since she was four years old. She just wanted to go to dancing school and she has a sort of a natural, marvelous grace and coordination for dancing. This last summer we spent in Hyannis Port. She went into summer stock and was an apprentice at the Melody Tent, which means you paint scenery and all this stuff. They finally thought she was so good they gave her several acting roles. She never talked to me about it, and I did the best I could to not look [*laughs*] like I was being shut out. But she finally explained to me, very kindly, that she didn't think she should ask me anything about acting [and] that she should wait for the director to tell her. And she was quite right. But I went and saw her. She's a *wonderful* actress.

WBW: Are they severe critics, for instance, when you work a concert? Do they come to your concerts and then offer critiques afterward?

JG: No, they come to the concerts and they've heard me sing, so they sort of like the excitement and sometimes there are celebrities there. They couldn't care less about me and my thing. You know, I am just mama. They've heard me sing on the stage and they're kind of bored with it. And I'm glad! [*Laughs.*]

WBW: Let's get to another tune you did in concert a year ago. [On] this particular tune, "When You're Smiling," it seemed to me that in listening to it on the Capitol recording that the audience was really at this point as . . . I guess you'd call it a fever pitch. And when you start . . .

JG: Well, that was the opening number, wasn't it?

WBW: Was "When You're Smiling"?

JG: Yes.

WBW: Well, that shows you. I didn't know that. They were at a fever pitch in *front* then because I noticed that as you started the song, there seemed to be a swelling of applause and—

JG: It was marvelous, wasn't it? Oh, I wish we could go back a year and do it all over again.

WBW: Well, as I said, from the reaction of people around New York, they're waiting for you to appear. Anyway, here's Judy at Carnegie and "When You're Smiling."

[*Plays "When You're Smiling."*]

WBW: This is the final segment of the *Make Believe Ballroom* and our guest, Miss Judy Garland. Judy. We were speaking before about acting. You were up for an Academy Award as a result of *Judgment at Nuremberg*.

JG: Yes.

WBW: Is this going to be an extended part of your career now? Dramatic parts?

JG: Well, I don't know. If the role is dramatic, doesn't call for singing, I enjoy that. I must say, though, I would rather do something that includes music because music [and] singing makes me very happy. I enjoy singing. However, I'll take a good dramatic role if it comes along.

WBW: What's the picture in England?

JG: It's a picture called *The Lonely Stage*. It's quite a good story but with music.

WBW: Given the opportunity, is there any role that you have read or any book you've read that is the kind of a role you'd like to do? Does one strike you offhand?

JG: I don't know. I really don't. I read a lot of books. No, I can't think of anything offhand.

WBW: Because you mentioned earlier about trodding the boards on Broadway. Is there any particular vehicle you had in mind?

JG: No. No. I was just speaking in general, you know.

WBW: Because I have a sneaking hunch—and I'm not that conversant with agentry and all that—but I don't think you'd have any problem getting a play on Broadway if you really wanted to do one. [*Both laugh.*]

JG: No, I don't think so. At least I'd hope I wouldn't have any trouble. But I haven't been able to give that much time to thinking or choosing anything. I've been going like a *whirlwind*, you know, working.

WBW: You worked out in the open, as it were, in Forest Hills last year. The night I saw you they had a few planes flying over. [*Judy laughs.*] That must be kind of distracting.

JG: Well, yes. They only flew over on the ballads, too. [*Laughs.*]

WBW: Speaking of ballads, let's get to a ballad out of the Carnegie Hall concert. I have heard "I Can't Give You Anything But Love" done in every conceivable way. I don't think Jimmy McHugh has ever had it done as well as you do it in this.

JG: Do you like it?

WBW: *Beautiful.* You did it on your TV special, too.

JG: Yes. I think it's a pretty song and it's usually always been done at sort of a flapper-age tempo. And I think it's a lovely song.

WBW: All right. Well, here then is Judy Garland with Jimmy McHugh's "I Can't Give You Anything But Love."

[*Plays "I Can't Give You Anything But Love."*]

WBW: I guess, again, we would be remiss if we didn't include "Over the Rainbow." When you did "Over the Rainbow" in [*The*] *Wizard of Oz*, am I correct, I think Harold Arlen—I did an interview with Harold once—and it seems to me that he told me the tune was originally not going to be in the movie.

JG: Well, they shot the song. They recorded the song and I sang it, and then they shot the scene. And then when the picture was finished, you know, they take pictures out and preview them; sneak previews here and there in different towns. And they didn't think that it was a very good idea to have the song in the movie. They seemed to feel that it would hold things up. So I think after possibly four or five previews with the song *out* they finally thought, *Well, OK, we'll leave it in.* [*Laughs.*]

WBW: On the chance that it might go.

JG: Yeah. [*Laughs.*]

WBW: Because, obviously, this song, as we mentioned earlier, is—you *own* the tune as a singer and as a performer. Harold Arlen, I think, is a brilliant writer.

JG: He is.

WBW: He writes things that, first of all, when you marry your performance with that kind of a tune, it's brilliant.

JG: He is an *amazing* man, you know, because he can write "Over the Rainbow," which has a childlike, wistful quality, and a new song he's just written called "Little Drops of Rain" that's in this UPA feature-length cartoon. And that has the same qualities as "Over the Rainbow." And yet, he can then turn and write "Come Rain or Come Shine."

WBW: Great blues.

JG: Or "Stormy Weather" and then also write "Get Happy." So he's an amazing man.

WBW: One thing I've noticed in your concerts and in the album, for example, you utilize—I guess you'd call the tunes—most of them are standards. Do you do any current songs?

JG: Well, I do. Not in this album. After this was recorded I put in "Just in Time" and also a song from *Greenwillow*, I think it was.

WBW: The Frank Loesser song?

JG: It's called "Never Will I Marry" and that's about as current as we've gotten. I haven't done any of the brand-new songs.

WBW: One quick question before we hear "Over the Rainbow." What is your reaction to current pop music?

JG: Well, what *kind* of music do you mean?

WBW: Well, the music—if you were driving in a car or listening at home—that you would hear on radio stations around the country The so-called "top 40" records. In other words, what the youngsters are being exposed to today as the big hits of today. Do you have any feelings on it?

JG: Well, no. You mean twist music or rock 'n' roll?

WBW: Rock 'n' roll. Whatever.

JG: I've never liked rock 'n' roll very much. There are, strangely enough, a couple of good twist songs, you know. It's a shame that the composer had to make twists out of them [*laughs*], but I think youngsters now are being exposed to the kind of songs we grew up with, from what I gather. I'm sure you're doing that and I think it's a good idea.

WBW: We managed to survive. All right, here's Miss Judy Garland and Harold Arlen's "Over the Rainbow."

[*Plays "Over the Rainbow."*]

WBW: Judy, I thank you very much for taking time out—this is a phrase I'm sure you've heard before—from a very busy schedule or I think in England they say "shed-yoo-ul."

JG: Well, either one, I think it means the same.

WBW: Yeah.

JG: I'm not sure! [*Laughs.*]

WBW: A very busy schedule and spending your first anniversary of Carnegie Hall with us here at the *Make Believe Ballroom*. On behalf of—and I'm not exaggerating—*millions* of people who didn't get a chance to see you at Carnegie and who hear the album and who love your work, I thank you very much.

JG: I thank you, Bill, and I think it's a wonderful thing. I'm very flattered that you're playing the album.

WBW: Good night.

JG: Good night.

JUDY GEM

On Liza's Career

"I'm an absolute imbecile when I see her perform. I cry. My little girl!"

—To Sheilah Graham, March 4, 1962

JUDY GEM

On Her Own Career

"I love my career. I want to say this because I'm always being painted a more tragic figure than I am, and I get awfully bored with myself as a tragic figure. I wouldn't have been anything but an entertainer. With all the troubles, with the stumbling and falling on the way, the rewards are still so great. If you happen to be a success, you meet writers, politicians, people in the arts. People with stimulating ideas in many places. It's a marvelous opportunity to lead a broad existence. As a performer, I love the enthusiasm audiences have shown me. You can't blame me—we all want to prove ourselves, and I've had an appreciation shown to me in the most inspiring, spontaneous ways."

—To Associated Press, August 26, 1962

TV INTERVIEW

JACK PAAR | December 2, 1962, *Jack Paar Program*

Airing December 7, 1962, Judy's dazzling appearance on Jack Paar's show solid-
ified her viability as a television personality. Not only did she look slim and radi-
ant, she was sharp-witted, and exhibited an energy and warmth that communi-
cated effectually through the broadcast medium. Whether truthful or tall tales
exaggerated for effect, Judy's anecdotes were hysterical and well received by
both studio and home audiences. "I liked myself for the first time on television,"
she later recalled. "I thought I was kind of funny. Jack made me show off."*

As Paar later recalled, "Everyone knew of Judy the singer . . . but what I
discovered was her ability as a conversationalist. On Judy's first TV appearance
with me, we talked more than she sang, and that was a side of her which was
my discovery. I often had her on the program where she never was allowed to
sing. I only wanted to hear her talk. Judy was very funny offstage as well. Never
bawdy, it was rather a grand manner that she had, and at times you would have
thought she came from a high social background rather than her 'born in a trunk
backstage' upbringing."†

Variety took note, declaring Judy to be "a picture of mental and physical
health," and calling her appearance "a highly rewarding and gratifying display."
Soon after, reports that a television deal was in the works were confirmed when,
on December 28, 1962, Judy entered a four-season, $24 million contract with
CBS for a weekly Garland variety series. As she told the press just a few months
later, working on a series would allow her to remain close to home and family,
and also promised financial stability. "You know how I look on this series?" she
asked. "As a secure way of living. I can get up in the morning and go to work and
come home at night to things that are familiar and mine. I'm so tired of being on

---

*Judy Garland, "Judy Garland's Own Story: There'll Always Be an Encore," *McCall's*, February 1964.
†Jack Paar, *P.S. Jack Paar*, Doubleday, 1983.

the road. The concerts have been marvelous for me, but I've been living in hotels now for the last three years and I've had it."*

Jack Paar: I've learned in show business: the greater the talent, the smaller the introduction. I shall never forget the time I saw Red Skelton in a supper club. I've seen him several times, but the house lights dim and a voice simply says, "Ladies and gentlemen, one of America's clowns," and the simplicity of that introduction I shall never forget. And if that be true, then Judy Garland needs no introduction at all—except to say that she's pure magic. So . . . abracadabra: Judy Garland.

[*Entering to "Over the Rainbow" and one-minute-long standing ovation, Judy takes a seat next to Paar.*]

JP: And I'm crying. I don't know why. I'm very touched by things like that.

Judy Garland: Oh, you're very sweet.

JP: Well, let them have a look at you. That's what they want to see. They want to see Judy Garland. You know all of us have given our hearts to you so many times that you have permanent possession of it. Can we talk tonight about anything? Silly little things?

JG: Sure! Yes, anything you want. Anything you want.

JP: Someone's gonna review this show and call it "Punchy and Judy." Now watch, they'll do that. [*Judy laughs.*] I know those cats, you know. But anyhow . . . What a great laugher. She laughs, boy, at red ties, they say.

JG: [*Touching his tie.*] I laughed at *this* one! [*Laughs.*]

JP: C'mon. Boy, you sure got over Norman Maine in a hurry. [*All laugh and audience applauds.*] Ha-ha! Oh boy. Hey, listen. She has the *greatest* stories and this is one of the great talkers in show business, but no one ever heard her talk, I mean no one professionally. Listen, tell them about

---

* Margaret McManus, "A Female Perry Como?" March 31, 1963.

the days at M-G-M . . . some of the stories about Mickey and Liz Taylor and those people. Just tell us the stories you want to.

JG: Well, I hardly know where to start.

JP: Tell them what you said about Liz.

JG: Well . . . [*audience laughs*] now it wasn't anything like that.

JP: No, no . . .

JG: Well, as you know, she's this marvelous sort of femme fatale.

JP: Yes.

JG: I can always just remember her as a girl with a lot of chipmunks and horses, and she was only about three feet high and two years old at Metro. I can't imagine this marvelous sort of [*with a grand gesture*] Cleopatra, you know. That shows *my* age.

JP: Well, Liz has grown up.

JG: Yes. [*All laugh.*]

JP: Oh, yeah. I laugh. She says she always thinks of Liz Taylor with chipmunks!

JG: Well, we had a pretty strange group, you know.

JP: Well, who all was in that group?

JG: Well, it was a terrible classroom in the first place, when you think of all of us in one group with Elizabeth Taylor in the schoolroom. You know, we went to school. We did, believe it or not. There was Elizabeth Taylor and Lana Turner and Mickey Rooney and Freddie Bartholemew and me and Deanna Durbin. [*Audience laughs.*]

JP: That was one room?

JG: One room! There was only one. And . . .

JP: Well, you all turned out swell. [*Judy laughs, makes a mocking gesture.*] What happened in Metro? What did they do?

JG: I don't . . . that was . . .

JP: Were you kids scared? Were you scared?

JG: No, *no*. [*Mocks shaking.*] Not at all! We were fine. Have you seen us since we've come out? We're a *very* peculiar group. [*Paar and audience laugh and applaud.*]

JG: Lana kept excusing herself every five minutes by having to raise her hand in school to go out and smoke. [*Audience laughs.*]

JP: How was Mickey?

JG: He went out and smoked, too. [*All laugh.*] We *all* did!

JP: How far did you go to school in that kind of system?

JG: We went to school clear through the . . .

JP: High school?

JG: Yeah.

JP: Is that right?

JG: Well, we got old enough and they finally *sprung* us. We didn't pass. [*All laugh.*]

JP: Did you kids know when you were that age that you were big stars or was that kept from you?

JG: Oh, *no*!

JP: Why were you frightened? 'Cause you were frightened . . .

JG: Yes, terrified.

JP: You were scared. Who were you scared of? Everybody?

JG: Everybody.

JP: Didn't you know you were big stars?

JG: No, no. No, they didn't let us know. We were kept under wraps.

JP: Who else do you remember? Listen, how'd you start? Did Jessel really give you your name?

JG: Yes.

JP: He says he [did]. Did he?

JG: Yes. Yes, he gave me my *last* name.

JP: Her name is Frances Gumm.

JG: Yeah.

JP: Frances Gumm, yeah. Isn't that right?

JG: Yes, that's right. Frances Gumm.

JP: Now, tell them about—were you good in vaudeville?

JG: We were terrible. Terrible.

JP: Yeah, who was in it?

JG: My two sisters, my mother, and myself. We were in rotten vaudeville, too. Not good Keith time or Orpheum time, okay, we were in *lousy* vaudeville. We were in between the switches where they'd show a movie you know and then throw on a lot of acts and then show the movie. We were part of that type work. We were terrible.

JP: Tell the story about Happy Harry.

JG: Oh . . .

JP: I know, I know. Come on. They want to hear all the stuff I hear.

JG: Oh, well we did this—my two sisters and I did it—tour throughout Washington and Oregon; all the rotten cities, all the little cities, not the main cities. But it was a tour so the acts stayed together for about six weeks. And we followed a *miserable* comedian—the most depressed comedian I've ever known—called Happy Harry. And he used to come on in "2." You know what that means . . . the curtain is quite a ways back so that there's a lot of room. And the music would start. His entrance music was sort of [*sings tune*] . . . There was only three pieces in the band—there *were*—piano, drums and some violin or trumpet. So there was an empty pit with just three pieces in it. Now Happy Harry would wait in back of the curtain. And the manager of the tour would make us wait all the way through Happy Harry's act to make sure we were ready, you know. So we watched this poor thing every night and they'd play [*sings tune repeatedly and with growing intensity*] and he'd break through and say, "Hello everybody. This is Happy Harry!" And, and he'd go on with the most *terrible* stories and we were [*bored gesture*] . . . Well, this one time . . . Do you still want me to go on?

JP: *Yes!*

JG: Well, this one town we hit, they put him in "1" instead of "2," which meant he only had that much space [*gestures*], you know, between the pit and himself. [*All laugh.*] We were in the wings, as usual, the Gumm Sisters, and the music went [*repeats tune*] and he went "Hello everybody, ah—!" and right into the pit. [*Audience applauds.*] But wait!

JP: Wait. It's more.

JG: He fractured his leg in three places very badly. And we were in the wings. Can I stand up?

JP: Sure!

JG: [*Standing*] We were in the wings just standing and the manager said, "Go on!" So we had to sing "Dinah." You know, we went [*singing and dancing*] "Dinah, is there anyone . . . " and this poor thing in the pit was going, "Owww! Owww! Owww!" [*Audience laughs and applauds as Paar wipes away tears.*] I wonder if he's still there!

JP: Oh, Happy Harry, he probably has his own show on the daytime nowadays, one of those quiz shows, I bet you. Listen, what was I going to ask you about? You weren't really a good act in the beginning?

JG: We were *terrible*. Even at the end we were terrible. We were always terrible.

JP: Were you jealous of Deanna Durbin? Would you kids get along?

JG: Yeah.

JP: Because you were both competitive like mad. [*Audience laughs.*]

JG: Yeah, I was very jealous of her.

JP: You were jealous of her?

JG: Yeah, not for long.

JP: Oh.

JG: Because we were [*audience laughs*] . . . the only reason I said that is she came to Metro originally, you know.

JP: From Universal?

JG: Yeah. No! She came to Metro first and then *went* to Universal. And when she came to Metro, I had just gotten out of vaudeville and I thought I was sorta hep. And in came this girl with [*gestures*] one eyebrow—never stopped in the middle—it went right across. Very low. And I thought, "Well she's nothing, really. Who's this?" [*Sings in operatic tone.*] And then they *fired* her and they were going to fire me because they didn't know what to do, actually, with thirteen-year-old girls [or] twelve-year-old girls. There was no such thing. You either had to be a munchkin or you had to be [*gestures to chest*] eighteen or something. [*All laugh.*] No, no in-between. So, they fired her and I thought "HA! Well, *you know*, that's all right, I'm going, too. They don't know what to do. Then they picked her up at Universal, and suddenly she was the most *beautiful*, glamorous girl and very talented.

JP: I liked you best, though.

JG: You did?

JP: Yeah.

JG: You just liked jazz, instead of opera.

JP: No, I don't like jazz much. No, no. I just, I just liked you.

JG: Did you, darling?

JP: You tear my heart out, you know? It isn't hard to tear it out, incidentally, but boy . . . No, there's a wail in your voice that just *moves* everybody.

JG: That's very nice.

JP: Oh it's very moving. I remember your first picture. You were in a band concert, right?

JG: Yeah.

JP: Is that true? Is that right?

JG: With Deanna Durbin. [*Audience laughs.*] It was "Opera Vs. Jazz" [and] called *Every Sunday.*

JP: Was she in it too?

JG: Yeah, *Every Sunday.*

JP: Well, I was in love with you.

JG: You were?

JP: Yeah. And that song, "Dear Mr. Gable."

JG: Yes.

JP: Yeah. And to me you'll always be Dorothy. Little Dorothy. Hey, tell the story about how those clowns tried to crowd you out in *The Wizard of Oz.*

JG: Oh, I don't dare. You're *terrible*!

JP: You knew that when I came on. Everyone knows I'm terrible!

JG: You mean Jack and Bert?

JP: Yeah, how they crowded you out.

JG: Well, you know they're my friends *now.* But then they . . . Well they are!

JP: How old were you?

JG: I was about twelve. No, no, I was older than that. I was fourteen [*sic*]. They tried to make me *look* twelve, in many different ways [*awkward gesture to chest*], but they didn't quite make it. [*Audience laughs.*]

JP: I'd know you're sixteen or more now! I just figured that out. You've got a lovely knee, do you know that? You've always did have lovely knees.

JG: Well, I've covered it a bit . . .

JP: That dress is becoming a blouse, isn't it? [*Laughs.*] Tell them about *The Wizard of Oz!*

JG: Well, we were . . . [*laughs*].

JP: Oh, I love her!

JG: I had to work with three very *professional* men, you know—Jack Haley and Bert Lahr and Ray Bolger—and they had so much makeup on. One was the Tin Man, and one was the Scarecrow, and one was the Cowardly Lion. And they were so busy complaining about their makeups, and each one was making bets as to which makeup was the most difficult. And they all gained weight all the way through the picture. And they all pretended they just . . . [*gestures fatigue*] and whenever we do that little dance up the Yellow Brick Road . . .

JP: Yeah, I remember that.

JG: I was supposed to be *with* them.

JP: They'd crowd you out?

JG: They'd shut me out. They'd close in, the three of them, and I would be in back of them dancing. [*Gestures dancing as audience laughs.*] I wasn't good enough, you know, to say "Wait a minute now!" And so the director, Victor Fleming, who was a darling man—he was always up on a boom—would say. "*Hold it!* You three dirty hams, let that little girl in there!" [*All laugh; audience applauds.*]

JP: Boy! I wish you'd come on this show every week and just tell stories. [*Audience applauds.*]

JG: I'd like to. I really would like to.

JP: I told you . . . Hey, look what I've done for Hugh Downs [Paar's partner/sidekick]!

JG: Yes.

JP: Oh, I got him already, didn't I? [*Judy laughs.*] We'll be right back after this message from Kimberly Clarke.

[*Commercial break.*]

JP: Oh, *peekaboo*! Listen, you gonna sing tonight?

JG: I would like to sing. Would you like me to?

JP: You know . . . [*applause*]. 'Cause if you don't sing, we're out those two guys holding up the cards out there. [*Judy laughs.*] There's a song . . . The people who wrote this *Gay Purr-ee*, the music, Hip Yarburg . . .

JG: No, no, no. Start again.

JP: Yip Harburg.

JG: Right.

JP: But what did it *used* to be?

JG: *Yip*! What was it, I wonder? Yip Harburg.

JP: I can't believe he changed his name from anything else.

JG: Well, he wrote the words. How could he write that name?

JP: Did he write "Over the Rainbow?"

JG: Yes.

JP: See, he wrote all of her great songs. And he's written some great songs in this new picture...

JG: *Gay Purr-ee*. Plug. [*Laughs.*]

JP: Yeah, *Gay Purr-ee*. But the song I like the *best*, I think, is "Little Drops of Rain." And I think it has the quality of "Over the Rainbow."

JG: It does.

JP: Did you hear about the producer who was fired . . .

JG: [*Interrupting.*] Also, you must hear, first, darling . . . [*touches Paar's face*]. Oh, forgive me for interrupting.

JP: You must never interrupt me. [*All laugh.*]

JG: First you must mention the man who wrote the music, too. Harold Arlen.

JP: Harold Arlen. [*Applause.*] Oh, I used to love him in all those airplane pictures. Oh, boy! Anyhow . . . [*all laugh*].

JG: That was *Richard* Arlen!

JP: Richard Arlen. Oh, yeah. Well, this song has all the . . . Did you hear about the producer who wanted to work with you and got fired because he wanted you to open with "Over the Rainbow?" He wanted you to walk out, sit down, and open with "Over the Rainbow." That's an inside joke. And I see it stayed inside!

JG: Yeah . . .

JP: Anyhow, this is a great song, I'm telling you. Don't fool around when I say something. You know that. "Little Drops of Rain." You ready?

JG: Yes, I'm ready.

JP: All right!

[*Lights dim as Judy sings "Little Drops of Rain" in her seat alongside Paar, who leads a standing ovation at song's end.*]

JP: I know you've never done this song before, publicly, but I'd like for you to do it for me: "Paris is a Lonely Town."

JG: What's that again?

JP: "Paris Is a Lonely Town." [*All laugh.*] Will you do it for us?

JG: Surely. But do you mind if I go over and make sort of a production of it? [*Strokes his cheek.*]

JP: [*Enamored.*] I don't care *what* you do!

[*Judy sings "Paris Is a Lonely Town" to an enthusiastic audience literally yelling for more by the song's conclusion.*]

[*Commercial break.*]

JP: Listen, tell them that crazy story about Orson Welles.

JG: Oh . . .

JP: She's got the greatest stories in the world. I'll let her talk.

JG: Oh, no. You mean the one about the opening in Washington? Well you . . . do you want me to?

JP: *Sure* I want you to do it! [*Audience applauds.*]

JG: Orson Welles. Orson Welles is a great friend of mine, and when he first started in the theater he did weird, weird plays. *Wonderful* plays. But he used platforms that came up out of nowhere, and revolving stages and all kinds of things that hadn't been done before. And they were doing some *very* extravagant play. I forget . . . I think it was a Shakespearean play. As a matter of fact, I think it was a combination of *three* Shakespearean plays. And at one point . . . [*laughs*] at one point he had fifty soldiers with crusade outfits, you know, with the [*gestures*] helmets, march onto the stage with bows and arrows, you know, and they pulled their bows and arrows and shot the arrows into the wings where there was a big board. And it had gone all right, you know, all during rehearsal. And they opened in Washington. [It was] a very formal opening, with lots of senators and little old ladies, and it was black tie. And these fifty soldiers . . . I have to stand up . . . [*stands*]. Fifty soldiers came marching up and they stood and pulled their bows and arrows. And just as they pulled the bows and arrows, somebody pushed the button to turn the revolving stage and *fifty arrows* went into the audience! [*Audience laughs.*] You've never *seen* such people saying, "Let's get *out* of here!" [*Audience laughs and applauds as Judy returns to her seat.*]

JP: He's a marvelous talent.

JG: Oh, he's marvelous. Yes, I remember one. Can I tell one more? Oscar Levant. You know Oscar?

JP: Oh yes. I do. I've had the pleasure to . . . [*laughs*].

JG: Oscar Levant came to Paramount Studios to make a movie, and he always wears a blue suit that he's worn for about 108 years. The same blue suit and same dark tie. Black tie. And it was his first day at Paramount and he was sort of shuffling around with his pigeon toes and wondering what stage to go to and so forth. And he saw in the distance, a great big man come out with a Hawaiian shirt on, white pants and sandals, and big black glasses. Eight scripts under each arm, and a bunch of secretaries in back with papers just flying left and right. And as this group drew nearer to Oscar, he realized that it was Orson Welles—you know with the Hawaiian shirt and the girls—and he didn't say anything. He just looked. And as Orson passed Oscar, he looked at Oscar and said, "Hello, Oscar. I hear you've gone Hollywood!" [*All laugh and applaud.*]

JP: Hey, tell us some of the stories about the concerts you've done. The crazy things with the microphones and all. Like tonight.

JG: [*Laughs.*] Yeah. Well, let's see. Well, you know I did all those concerts. I did forty-three concerts in forty-three towns, and so it got to the point where you just got into town and hit the hotel. And I would lie in state like Stalin, you know, and not talk. And then hit the theater and sing and get *out*, you know. Before they caught us. But we did one thing I think you want to hear. We played Houston. And we had curtains that parted in the middle, you know. And there were two stagehands *walking* the curtains, you know, how they have to walk the curtains out around the bandstands. And this little old man . . . He didn't like me or anything 'cause he wanted to play gin, obviously, with the rest of the musicians. Oh, sorry! The rest of the *stagehands*. Oh my! And he was standing, waiting to walk the curtain. I'd finished part of my show, the curtains had closed, and he was standing waiting to open them again. I said, "Open them, open them." He walked back and somehow he managed [*stands and turns*], as he was walking, to get caught [in the curtain]. And he just kept rolling up and rolling up and rolling up, and he got all wrapped up in the velour! I didn't see him and I had about three more numbers to do, and David Begelman and Freddie Fields, my *darling* managers, were backstage and they . . .

JP: The man was yelling, wasn't he?

JG: The manager, the manager . . .

JP: Wasn't he yelling? Wasn't the old guy yelling?

JG: No, no, no. We couldn't hear him. Well, I couldn't hear him. I guess he could.

JP: You didn't hear him, but he was yelling.

JG: He was in three feet of velour.

JP: He was all wrapped up.

JG: So they rushed up to David and said, "How much how much longer is she going to be on?" And he said "Not too long, not too long. Don't worry about him. He'll be all right," you know. Terrible. And I sang for about thirty-two minutes and I went off. I looked down and there were these little feet and one hand. One hand. And just a voice going, "Mmm-mmpppphh." [*Audience laughs.*] And I said, "What the *heck* is going . . ." And they said, "Never mind!" Needless to say, at the end of the concert we unfurled him. We flew him out by unwrapping the curtain.

JP: How old a fellow was he?

JG: Oh, he was about sixty-eight.

JP: Probably the best action he's had in a long time! [*All laugh.*] Even at sixty-eight he's a little *velour*! You know, it's *something*! Oh, dear. [*All laugh.*]

JP: We'll be back after this message . . .

JG: [*Laughs.*] You wanna *bet*?

[*Commercial break.*]

JP: There's a boy backstage growing older . . . [*audience laughs and applauds*] I was telling Judy, you know, with his hair, that great voice, and this marvelous personality, and all that curly hair, and he's got skin like Lillian Gish, as she pointed out . . . [*all laugh*].

JG: He's so darling. He's *dreamy*.

JP: Why can't he have a few pimples? Just to give him . . . [*all laugh*]. Ladies and gentlemen, one of the nicest guys in the show business, Bobby Goulet. [*Audience applauds as Goulet enters and kisses Judy.*]

JG: Oh, you are a pretty one!

JP: Did you think we weren't ever going to bring you out?

Robert Goulet: I wasn't sure!

JP: [*To Judy.*] He's a handsome devil, isn't he?

JG: He's murder.

JP: And I think it's obscene, don't you?

JG: I don't . . .

JP: Don't you have any crooked teeth or *anything*?

RG: I've got a pimple here I thought I'd grow for you.

JG: [*Laughs.*] Where? I wanna see it! [*Audience laughs.*]

JP: And he's a real nice man. Real nice man. And you're gonna open in Boston . . .

RG: Yes, I go to Boston this week sometime. I'll be opening the night that we play this [*Jack Paar*] show . . .

JP: I'm glad you brought that up.

RG: Did I? [*All laugh.*]

JG: That's what he's here for, honey.

JP: Let's try it again! Hey, I hear you're going to open in Boston.

RG: Yes! [*All laugh.*] It's funny you should ask. Yes, I'm going to play in at Blimstrom's in Boston, yes. Very soon.

JP: That'll be about the same time this show is playing.

RG: As a matter of fact . . . [*all laugh*].

JP: In the picture *Gay Purr-ee*, there is a song called "Musette." Would you do that?

JG: [*To Goulet.*] You want to? [*Audience applauds.*]

JP: It's a wonderful ending for us tonight.

JG: I don't know. Do you think we can remember the words?

RG: I don't know. It's been so long since I've done it.

JG: [*Purposely ignoring Paar.*] And by the way, are we supposed to sing or anything when we go around to all these places?

RG: No, no, no. But the thing that irks me is that we have to go to all these places [*laughs*] and theaters.

JG: What are you going wear?

RG: I don't know.

JG: You don't? Are you going to wear a black tie?

RG: I think I'll wear a black tie.

JG: Oh, will you?

RG: Yeah.

JG: All right.

JP: [*To audience.*] Do you feel I've lost the ball? [*All laugh.*]

RG: Why don't we sing, Judy?

JG: [*Laughs.*] Yes . . .

JP: Watch yourself at all times! [*Audience applauds.*]

[*Judy sings "Musette" with Robert Goulet.*]

JP: And now a refreshing scene from Menthol Newport Cigarettes! [*All laugh.*]

[*Commercial break.*]

JP: [*Breathless.*] In many, many years of crazy, wild, informal, unwritten, scriptless teases, this was the most enjoyable night I've ever had. [*Applause.*]

JG: Oh, Jack . . .

JP: [*Looks at wristwatch.*] We're late! [*To Goulet.*] May you be a big smash at Blimstrom's . . .

RG: Thank you, Jack.

JP: And Judy Garland, I'm indebted to you for coming on this show. I don't even belong in the same *building* with you.

JG: Oh, don't be *silly*, darling!

JP: Good night, sweetheart.

JG: I loved it. I loved every moment.

JP: Good night!

JG: Good night!

JUDY GEM

On Her Weekly Television Show

"It was a big decision, but a wonderful decision. I don't think of it as so formidable. I'm going to be a female Perry Como. I'm going to take it easy, and have wonderful guests, and share the spotlight. I'm not going to try to carry the show every week all by myself. . . . A weekly show isn't anything like a 'special.' On a 'special' you feel so pushed, so responsible. You only have one chance. It's concentrated chaos. Everything depends on it. If you're on every week, you can relax. If you are not absolutely great one Sunday, there's another Sunday coming right up. . . . I want to keep the show very simple. In television, you are in a room, not on a stage, so you don't get too fancy."

—To Margaret McManus, syndicated columnist, March 31, 1963

JUDY GEM

On Liza's Career

"One day I heard Liza was being asked to sing in a cartoon version of *The Wizard of Oz* [which eventually became *Journey Back to Oz*]. I thought they were just exploiting Liza to use my name. But when I finally read the contract, it stated that she was to be billed under her own name. They wanted Liza [Minnelli], not Garland. I was out—and I didn't mind!"

—To Jack Ryan, *Family Weekly*, May 19, 1963

BEHIND JUDY GARLAND'S FRANTIC DRIVE FOR SUCCESS IS THIS FERVENT PRAYER: PLEASE . . . SOMEBODY . . . LOVE ME!

EMILIE FRANKS | November 1963, *TV Radio Mirror*

Judy's return to television meant her return to the fan magazines. One of the few remaining in 1963 was *TV Radio Mirror*, which brought its readership up to date with the new TV star's personal life in this feature with its dramatic, pleading headline. There's a mention of Judy's on-again, off-again marriage to Sid, as well as their history of disputes and quarrels. Although Judy filed for divorce in August 1962, the couple reconciled in concurrence with the new television deal, and delayed the dissolution of their marriage for several more years. Nevertheless, the Garland-Luft union came to a bitter end several years later, and their divorce was made final in May 1965.

"When I was a child," Judy Garland once said, "more than anything else I wanted to be loved by my parents. It seems to me my greatest responsibility as a mother is to give my children all the love I have.

"As a child I lived in a lot of houses, but what I wanted most was a home. And a home is what I'm trying to give my children."

Judy Garland, born Frances Gumm, has never come out flatly and blamed her parents for the insecurity and unhappiness she has suffered all her life—but there's no doubt that deep in her heart she holds them responsible.

Judy never had any real childhood. She went on the stage [by the time] she was three and, because in those days show-business folk were not considered "desirable," Judy found it tough going. Many mothers wouldn't even let their children play with her.

"The only time I felt wanted when I was a kid was when I was on stage, performing," Judy recalls. "The stage was my only friend—the only place where I felt alive and comfortable and safe. Later, when I broke into movies, I felt awkward, plump and unwanted. I've never had any formal training, and my lack of stage education gave me an inferiority complex which I've never lost. I never knew when I was doing a thing right—and I still don't. Each time I get before an audience, I'm suffering inside, certain I'll goof. And when I hear the audience applaud and feel that they mean it, I want to cry, the happiness hurts so. But today, the only time I really feel happy and alive is when I'm with my children."

When Judy Garland met Sid Luft, her present husband (with whom she is battling in an on-and-off marriage), she was in one of her "nobody loves me" stages. He said that he loved her. He made her feel wanted and needed. The little girl whose father had died before she reached the peak of her career finally found the father image she was looking for. After two unhappy marriages, to two good, fine men whom she still admires ("I had good taste," she says in recalling David Rose, composer-conductor, and Vincente Minnelli, director-producer), Judy felt she had found the answer. So far, the record would seem to indicate she hasn't. After umpteen separations and two filings for divorce, Judy and Sid still can't seem to make up their minds if their union was made in Utopia or in hell.

The only thing that is certain in Judy's private life is that she's determined her children will come first, last and always. And she can't be knocked for that.

"My children are the most important things in my life, far more important to me than career, success, marital happiness or anything else," Judy insists. And even costars who have had reason to quarrel with her and doubt her sincerity—and there have been many of them—agree it's one area in which she's telling the truth.

Judy works hard at her career. Backstage, sipping wine from a tumbler, spraying her throat, drinking soda water and lemon juice, wiping away perspiration with a bath towel, she is like a fighter . . . a bantamweight . . . who follows a regimen of preparation for the ring, leaves it stumbling and drained, to be helped to her dressing room by a corps of devoted seconds.

Even when the crowd screams for more, Judy herself, full of mixed pride and uncertainty . . . "as always" . . . is half-telling, half-asking, "I did it again . . . didn't I?"

But even when she's working hard, as she is now on her weekly CBS-TV series, Judy's thoughts are never far away from her trio of young 'uns—Liza, 17, Lorna, 11, and Joey, 8.

"I have three lovely children," says Judy, "but I have no ambitions for them other than that they be happy and well adjusted. Isn't that what every child—every adult—should want from life? What does the other stuff—the so-called success—add up to? I remember the night I was up for the Academy Award for *A Star is Born*. Little Joe had been born just a day before.

"TV cameras moved in for what I now jokingly call 'the kill.' They were to be there if I won. I didn't. Grace Kelly did—and why not, she'd done a good job. When her name was announced, all the technicians packed up their equipment and moved out—without even saying good night, let alone they were sorry I didn't win. They seemed annoyed at me for losing. Well, I don't want that for my children. If they want careers, fine—but first I want them to learn, to get an education, to have something else to fall back on if show business doesn't work out for them. Also, and most important, I want them to understand that family, friendship, love, and many other things are more important than careers."

How successful has Judy been in keeping her offspring out of show business? Judging from the success of her eldest, Liza Minnelli, not at all. But analyze it further and you'll see she's been completely successful in her aims. Liza took New York City by storm in an off-Broadway production of *Best Foot Forward*. Her reviews and her pubic acclaim were nothing short of sensational. But Liza is no Frances Gumm turned into a fictitious Judy Garland. Liza Minnelli is very much herself. Liza had the advantage of growing up feeling very much wanted and secure. Her mother had her physical custody, but her father, Vincente Minnelli, also took a great interest in her life and her future. He and Judy discussed all problems concerning Liza. They were friends and speak well of each other to this day. Liza was never turned against either parent. She loves, respects and admires them both.

It was her own decision to enter show business. After finishing high school, she won a scholarship to the Sorbonne in Paris—no easy feat. But she wasn't happy. She got her feet wet in show business at fifteen, when she worked a fourteen-hour day, seven days a week, as an apprentice at the Cape Cod Melody Tent. She painted sets, scrubbed the stage, ran errands, and did all the other menial work of an apprentice. Judy and Vincente had hoped it would discourage their daughter. It did not. It only made her hungry for more show business. So, when she was offered a chance in *Best Foot Forward*, how could they refuse?

When old-timers in Hollywood meet Liza they are amazed that she is so well-adjusted and happy. How, they ask, has such a delightful girl come from a household of strife and discontent? The only answer would seem to be that she *knows* she is loved. No matter her problems, Judy has always kept her children as close to her as possible—and not in a matriarchal sense.

"I know my children's lives can't be normal because of the way I live," Judy explains, "but I do try to make things as normal as possible. They have traveled all over the world with me. Yet I believe they have been helped by the security of being with their mother. That is better than the best boarding school, or a home full of servants and no mother. True, Sid and I (Sid fathered Lorna and Joe) have had our quarrels, but I've tried to keep the children out of it. My problem is with Sid —Sid's problem is with me. Lorna and Joe are loved by us both, and it's important that they know it."

But the fact remains that Judy's parting—or rather, partings—with Luft have not been amicable, as were her previous ones from David Rose (by whom she has no children) and Minnelli (Liza's father). Her career has been more on the downgrade than the up since she wed Sid, and her battles with him have made many headlines—something both Rose and Minnelli tastefully avoided. She reportedly attempted suicide on several occasions—though she emphatically denied it, claiming all the instances were "accidents." During one period, she fled to London to avoid Luft's claiming custody of the children and asked that they be made wards of the court. Her on-and-off marriage with Sid is bound to have some effect on Lorna and Joe, no matter how hard she tries to protect them. Even if the quarrels do not take place before them, it doesn't matter—Judy and Sid always end up making headlines, and not pretty ones, at that.

Thus far, Lorna and Joe would seem to be happy—though, since Judy keeps them as cloistered as possible, no one knows for sure. They do not, however, have the security of Liza, whose father Vincente Minnelli, says of Judy, "She's a great, great talent. I'm proud to have had a daughter by her." Instead, unless Judy and Sid change their tactics, they will be reading in the papers once again of bitterness and strife between their parents. The one thing that can save them is love—and their mother knows it. Judy speaks of them with pride and devotion, and every minute she works, her heart is with them. She wants the public to scream: "More, more, more!" But most of all, she wants her children to love her.

"It's wonderful how different my three kids are." says Judy. "Liza and Joey are the most like me—outgoing, affectionate. But Lorna! She's independent. I know what my problem is. I mustn't let myself become too dependent on my children. And I mustn't let them become too dependent on me. I'm not permissive with them. Not at all. I'm strict, but my kids aren't afraid of me. We respect each other.

"The one thing I pray is that my children can help themselves through what they learn. I couldn't—at least, not until now. I had to suffer years first before I learned that pills, screaming and other crutches didn't solve the problem. Now I know it's in yourself and love for others—particularly your children."

JUDY GEM

On Her Public Image

"I hope I'm endangering my public image. I'd like to do away with it! I'm a cheat. That's what I am. Public image: it's a phony! My public image isn't anything like me. People think I'm either a breakable Dresden doll or a wide-eyed Kansas teenager. I haven't been a teenager for a long time, and if I were breakable, I wouldn't be here now."

—To Edgar Penton, *ShowTime: The Colorful World of Entertainment* (syndicated column), November 1963

JUDY GEM

On Her Weekly Television Show

"You really want to know why I'm tackling a television series? Because CBS is letting me be myself—letting me be a whole, total, complete person. I can sing anything I want to sing. 'Old Man River'—I've never sung that before. I don't think any woman has. But I'll sing it in one of our shows. And I want to talk, just talk. Not come out and say, 'I'm Judy Garland and that's that and now I'm going to sing a song.' Not just that. I want to carry on a conversation with someone. You know, I'll bet before the series went on the air that a lot of people had no idea I could carry on a conversation without having someone write the script.

—To Edgar Penton, *ShowTime: The Colorful World of Entertainment*,
November 1963

JUDY GEM

On Her Weekly Television Show

"I touch. I've always touched people. All the time I touched. It's a habit. It isn't nervousness. It's pure affection. I'm a woman who wants to reach out and take 40 million people in her arms, but I've been told [by CBS brass] that I must watch myself. . . . CBS knows more about television that I do. All they want for me is a smash."

—To Howard Tuckner, *Newsweek*, November 4, 1963

JUDY GARLAND: 97 POUNDS OF HEART

LLOYD SHEARER | December 15, 1963, *Parade*

The Judy Garland Show premiered on September 29, 1963. As detailed in this feature for *Parade*, there was trouble brewing from the start, as CBS never established a clear plan for the series. A succession of three executive producers—each with varying approaches to properly presenting Judy in this medium—worked on the show, but none of their perspectives were shared by the network. The biggest obstacle was the show's time slot (opposite *Bonanza*), and CBS president Jim Aubrey and his network cohorts sentenced *The Judy Garland Show* to death when they refused to move it to another night or time.

Each Friday night at 9:30 a little left-handed lady with large luminous brown eyes and a throaty, vibrant voice, larger than life, slithers onto stage 41 at the CBS-TV studios here.

For an hour and a half she sings, reminisces, sips tea, chats lightly, and cavorts with such guest stars as Lena Horne, Count Basie, Mickey Rooney, Mel Torme, Barbra Streisand, and, on occasion, her own children.

From these carryings-on, her producer and editor put together 52 minutes of videotape eventually telecast on Sundays as the *Judy Garland Show.* For this one-hour package, sometimes stirring and memorable, other times mediocre and old hat, Judy Garland is paid $150,000—or about half of what CBS gets for the time and program.

Of her $150,000, Judy pays her cast and crew approximately $100,000, sometimes more. This leaves the tiny singer (5 feet tall, 97 pounds) with $30,000 to $50,000 each week, making her, along with Danny Kaye, probably the most highly paid star in TV.

Judy's basic deal with CBS calls for her company, Kingsrow Productions, to turn over to the network 30 one-hour shows at $150,000 per show. In addition, the network guarantees to rerun eight of these shows at $75,000 each.

"The best part of Judy's deal, however," explains agent Freddie Fields, who negotiated it, "is that Judy owns the tapes, and they're worth at least three to four million. She can release them over and over again. She can sell the syndication rights, the foreign rights, anything she wants. For once in her hectic life, this little dynamo is going to be financially secure. And it's about time.

"Judy," he goes on feelingly, "is 41. She's done everything there is to do in show business, from vaudeville to one-night stands. She's earned fortunes for other people, but she's been victimized over and over again. Before we made this deal with CBS, she was practically broke. But television is going to give her what it's given others much less talented than she— security. These shows are going to bring in money so that she doesn't have to sing her guts out in concerts night after night to support her kids."

A STORM IS BREWING

Judy puts it more gently. "It's nice to think," she says, "that these shows will make me rich."

Even nicer to see is Judy Garland—after all the professional and domestic crises she's weathered—happy, healthy, relaxed and seemingly at peace with the world, especially while a storm brews 'round her lovely head.

This storm concerns *The Judy Garland Show*. Through no fault of her own, Judy's is not a commercially successful television program.

At this writing it has a Nielsen rating of 18, which means that of the 50,000,000 television families in America, approximately 18 percent, or 9,000,000 families, watch *The Judy Garland Show* on Sunday nights. Admittedly that's a large number of families. But *Bonanza,* slotted by NBC against Judy at the same time, has a Nielsen rating of 35, which means that twice as many families prefer watching the Western to viewing Garland. Also opposite Judy on Sunday nights is a third program, *Arrest and Trial,* telecast by ABC. *Arrest and Trial* also has an 18 rating. In fact, its rating is a fraction higher than *The Judy Garland Show,* so as of this moment, Judy's show is running last in a race of three.

In a sentence, the *Judy Garland Show* is in trouble.

The fault is not Judy's, and she knows nothing about this rating abracadabra. The man who goofed in this particular case is Jim Aubrey, the CBS chief who placed the show into the Sunday night 9:00 to 10:00 PM time slot opposite *Bonanza.*

He made the judgment, and the audience figures have proved him wrong.

Judy Garland—and this is the opinion of the men who have produced her show (she has had three producers to date)—should be spotted on Monday nights from 10:00 to 11:00, or even on Sunday nights from 10:00 to 11:00.

"She is basically," says Norman Jewison, who produced eight of her shows, "a sophisticated performer who appeals to sophisticated, intelligent, and literate people. She is definitely not the girl next door. She will never attract the mass meat-and-potatoes audience that *Bonanza* does, and it's foolish even to let her try."

George Schlatter, a talented producer who was removed by CBS from Judy's program after he had done the first five shows, operated on the following concept: "Judy Garland is someone special, one of the great, electric, incomparable talents of our time. I can't tell you," Schlatter says, "how cooperative Judy was when I worked with her. She did everything I asked, and more. She was prompt, tireless, painstaking. She worked like a Trojan. All this baloney about her being temperamental and high-strung— she showed none of that.

"In her first five shows—and these haven't been telecast in sequence— I framed her as someone very special with a background of elegance and

TV FINANCE

Television is primarily an advertising medium, and only those shows which prove profitable to a sponsor remain on the air in prime time (7:00 PM to 11:00 PM, with minor variations).

For an advertiser, *The Judy Garland Show* is reputedly one of the most expensive programs in television. Before it went on the air this past September, the show had six commercial minutes to sell. CBS sold them to four sponsors for $56,000 a minute.

The four sponsors who shelled out $336,000 for the time and talent on *The Judy Garland Show* were led to believe by their advertising agencies that this was a good buy, a wise purchase, that the show would attract a tremendous audience. It does not do so in terms of cost.

Unless CBS lowers its asking price from $56,000 a minute to something like $20,000, or makes other concessions, Judy's sponsors will probably cancel. The current word in advertising circles is that CBS has already lowered its asking price drastically. Thus, *The Judy Garland Show* continues, but the $64,000,000 question is: for how long?

incomparable talent. I framed her performance as an event, because I think it is."

The CBS program chiefs—and let's not get into names here—feel that what Judy's show needs to gain a wider audience is a family of regulars such as Garry Moore offers. They feel strongly that the show should have two or three performers who appear every week.

Judy, who knows relatively little about television, is willing to listen to anyone. She went back to New York a few weeks ago and was advised by network executives that she must stop touching her guest stars, that people complained about such physical intimacy; so she has stopped. She was also told that she must talk to TV editors throughout the United States, so she has arranged an elaborate setup of long-distance conference calls whereby she talks simultaneously to 10 or 12 reporters throughout the country.

I was at her house one recent afternoon—a one-story, modern, eight-room Brentwood job worth $250,000, pool included—when she was giving out with such an interview.

Here are some of the questions and answers:

Q. How do you like TV compared to other media you've worked in?

A. I like TV better than any of the other jobs I've had in the past. It's hard work, but we've got it down to a pretty good routine now. I work four days a week and have Saturday, Sunday and Monday off. It's inspiring and fun and not too much work.

Q. I thought your television show was supposed to originate in New York. That was the original announcement.

A. I know, but we decided it would be better to do it from out here. After all, it gets so hot in New York during the summer. I would have had to take an apartment in Manhattan and my children would have had to be out on Long Island. This way we are all together. And besides, I have such a pretty new house. Oh, yes, my children watch the show. They come to the studio on Fridays when I tape it, and I must tell you this. The other week they were sitting down front, and they fell asleep while I was doing the show. My daughter, Liza—yes, she's out here, in fact, she's so busy I have to make an appointment to see her—I've done one show with her, and I'm doing the Christmas show with my other children, too.

Q. Is it true that CBS didn't like the first concept of your program and is now changing it?

A. Well, they're thinking along the family concept right now, that I should have a group of regulars, a Judy Garland family of performers, so that the program doesn't look like a spectacular each week.

Q. Judy, I've heard some people say that you look like a little old lady on television.

A. Well, I am a little old lady.

Q. Is it true that you won't allow people to watch you in your dress rehearsal?

A. I don't like a lot of people sitting in the audience during rehearsals because I'm too hammy and I wind up singing to them. I entertain the visitors, and then when it comes time for me to tape the show I'm dead.

Q. All the girls in my office want to know how you managed to diet so much—you must have lost 100 pounds.

A. That's my secret. Seriously, I just stay away from food. I drink tea.

Q. What do you do when you're not working?

A. I stay at home with my children. I play a little golf. I wait around for Tuesday and work to begin.

As all her fans know—and most of them are 30 or over—Judy Garland has not lived a particularly happy life to date. Child movie star, poor picker of husbands and lovers, bedeviled and bewildered by agents and advisers, wracked by illnesses physical and mental, this great talent, this living legend, has somehow managed to generate from her own essence enough fortitude, enough determination, to fight herself out of life's defeats.

It is ironic at this point, when she is healthier and happier than she's been for years, that Madison Avenue and the advertising fraternity should interpret Judy and her show in the light of disappointment.

Heretofore, Judy Garland has never failed in any avenue of show business. If her weekly TV series ends in statistical failure because it has been incorrectly targeted by network masterminds, at least Judy will have the satisfaction of winding up with three or four million dollars to balm her low Nielsen.

JUDY GEM

On Kindness

"We have a whole new year ahead of us, and wouldn't it be wonderful if we could all be a little more gentle with each other, and a little more loving, [and] have a little more empathy? And maybe next year at this time we'd like each other a little bit more."

—*The Judy Garland Show*, episode II
(taped October 18, 1963, aired January 5, 1964)

JUDY'S STORY OF THE SHOW THAT FAILED

VERNON SCOTT | May 2, 1964, *TV Guide*

As predicted, CBS canceled *The Judy Garland Show*. The network allowing Judy to make the announcement herself meant she could exit from the ordeal somewhat gracefully, but more importantly for CBS, they wouldn't have to take the blame for the show's demise.

Judy's made-up resignation to James Aubrey was released to the press on January 22, 1964. "I am most grateful for the support that I've had from CBS these past months, both personally and professionally," the letter read. "I have found my experience on weekly television a most gratifying one and a part of my career that I will always remember as exciting and fulfilling, as well as challenging. Now, however, in spite of all this, I have had to make the decision not to continue after the production of my twenty-sixth program. I have found the involvement that I must give to production and performing these programs to be incompatible with the time and attention that I must give to family matters."

Aubrey made his own ingratiating public response. "Although I can appreciate the compelling reason for Miss Garland's action, I would like to say how genuinely sorry all of us at the network are that she has reached this decision," he said, going on to praise her talent and even extending an invitation for future collaborations. "We look forward to her return to television—hopefully on the CBS Network."

No one was fooled by the underhanded activities at CBS. Critics and astute viewers alike knew the network's disregard for the show was to blame for its demise. As Terry Turner observed in the *Chicago Sun-Times*, "They hired Judy because she was a star, and then they wouldn't let her be one."

She tells of her triumphs, frustrations and mistakes, and vows, 'Never again.'

"I don't blame people for watching *Bonanza* instead of *The Judy Garland Show*. It was a natural choice."

The only thing remarkable about that statement is that Judy Garland made it. She was perched on a chair in the living room of her Brentwood, Cal., home, sipping a vodka and tonic and casually performing a post-mortem on her series. It had been trampled every Sunday night in the ratings by the galloping Cartwright clan, and systematically dismembered by the critics.

Judy was neither distraught nor angry about her year on television. The show had failed, true, but she didn't believe she was a personal failure. Her mood was clinical.

"I wasn't disappointed that we didn't get higher ratings," she said. "I don't think we deserved them. The time slot was impossible. After four or five years of loyalty to *Bonanza*, I can understand why viewers did not switch to my show."

She added proudly, "But I did prove to everybody that I was reliable. They said I'd never answer the bell for the second round. But we turned out 26 shows. And some of them were damned good, too. Especially the last five we did."

It wasn't until she'd completed the first 19 segments that Judy insisted on a concert format, a move she desperately wishes she had made earlier: "I wanted to do concerts from the beginning because of the success at Carnegie Hall. It's what I do best. And I wanted guest stars who also sang. There was a philosophy at CBS that I couldn't do a *special* every week. They said a concert was a special. But if I ever come back to television, it will be for a group of concerts.

"My year on television was very enlightening—and funny. It was instant disaster. Sometimes instant success. It was that way every week, one way or the other. By the time we discovered where we were going, it was too late."

She sprang to her feet and pirouetted across the deep shag rug, holding her highball daintily aloft. She did it well. "The network wanted me to be sort of the girl next door," she piped in a falsetto version of *all* the girls next door. "But they couldn't find the right house, or the right door. I've never been the girl next door."

"I didn't want to do a variety program, either. I thought we could use movie techniques to get away from pure television quality. But everyone kept telling me, 'This is television, Judy. It's not like movies or concerts. You have to get used to this medium. Just take our word for it; we know what we're doing.' And I took their word for it. I believed they *did* know what they were doing."

Judy sat down, tucking her frail legs beneath her. She wore a gray sweater and white Capri pants. Her fragile appearance—she now weighs 95 pounds—cloaked an inner strength compounded of instinct and a will to survive. Her enormous eyes seem to work almost independently of her thought processes. They tell you things she cannot, or will not, say herself.

As she spoke, her eyes revealed that the failure of her show was less a professional disappointment than a personal blow. Judy needs to be loved. Indeed, she dies a little without it.

The absence of an overwhelmingly large and impassioned audience for her show was a new experience in her 39 years of show business. (She started at age 2.) She had given everything. And for the first time the affection of the concert halls did not come rushing back to her. This plaintive longing to give and receive became apparent on the show, resulting in mass hysteria on the part of CBS brass.

"They told me I was a *toucher*," giggled Judy. "They sent me back to New York and called me on the carpet for kissing my guests and for touching them with my hands.

"The room was full of executives. Dozens of 'em. Maybe even some from NBC. They said, 'Don't touch the guest stars.' I explained that I've always been demonstrative. Some of the guests were nervous and I'd give them a pat of reassurance or hold their hands. But the executives showed me letters from viewers accusing me of being either drunk or nervous or both. They even wrote that there were supposed to be some sexual implications.

"So I said, 'OK, I'll be absolutely sterile. I won't touch a soul.' But on the very next show Zina Bethune kept touching *me*. So did Vic Damone. They were nervous I guess. And so was I, for fear I'd touch them back."

George Schlatter, the Garland show's first producer, says: "Judy's physical reaching-out was an extension of the emotional reaching she does every day to friends, and sometimes strangers. It's not a quality that lends itself to television. The camera gets in the way; it comes between Judy and the viewer. The audience remained untouched."

But if Judy was baffled by her inability to transmit her warmth to viewers, she was fantastically rewarded financially. *CBS paid her more than four million dollars.* The money went to her production company, which paid for production costs and salaries. The network provided the airtime. Judy spent freely, giving each segment an expensive, dressed-up polish. But she banked a fortune too, and owns all 26 tapes outright. Profits from reruns are all hers.

There were crises and clashes, and nervous calls from the insomnia-plagued star at 3 and 4 AM. People were fired. There was a procession of four producers, two directors and nine writers. But, to a man, they worked in awe of Judy Garland.

Says producer Gary Smith, who lasted 21 shows (longer than anyone else): "Everyone was afraid of Judy. I was, too. We checked with her before making decisions. Judy gobbles up people emotionally and intellectually. She wears everybody out. But she is a magnificent performer and she adapted herself beautifully to the weekly TV format."

Judy's emotional peaks and valleys are well known. But, says Smith, she managed to be *up* for every show: "She's a *red-light* performer. When the camera's red lights blinked on, she was at a peak and ready. We had some disastrous dress rehearsals, but the same material came alive the minute we had a studio audience for Judy to react to."

Smith was fired; he presumes by Judy. But, like the others, he has only praise for her. "She's a great creative star and an awesome personality."

A note to Judy from CBS-TV president James Aubrey illustrates the network's regard for her—or, at least, its technique in handling stars: "It has been a tremendous thrill working with you. The tube will not shine as brightly with you off the air. . . . No one has ever fulfilled a commitment with more dedication or more integrity. I look forward to the future when we work together again."

"Is it Ned Nielson?"

Judy is less sentimental. She looked for the amusing elements of her video experiment. "I'd really like to know who this guy Nielsen really is—and what's his first name?" she said. "Is it Ned Nielsen? I don't think there is such a person! I think there's just some guy who didn't make good with a network once and then just named himself Nielsen and became very important somehow.

"I don't know about ratings. But I *do* realize you don't do a weekly show for pure art's sake. You go in for the money, too. And if you accept as much money as I did, then you do your best.

"We made some mistakes, like the expensive turntable stage. It had a lot of noisy machinery under it and turned in a full circle so they could build back-to-back sets and swing me around. But I suffered dreadfully from motion sickness. I'd get violently ill. Or the table would come to an abrupt halt and I'd lose my balance. Once I stepped off while it was still going and staggered around like I'd jumped off a train or something. We quit using the turntable after seven shows.

"They'd edit the tapes without my knowledge. So a song with a guest star would pop up in a completely different show. My hairdo and wardrobe would mysteriously change from scene to scene."

Jerry Was Miscast

Jerry Van Dyke, woefully miscast as "host," and the tea-pouring ceremony with guests were other goofs.

"The network wanted *familiar spots* like those on *The Garry Moore Show*, something people could look forward to. That's where the tea party came in. Jerry was supposed to help give a *family* feeling to the show.

"But we had nine different formats. We spent four or five weeks drifting around on the air looking for a format. They never consulted me about changes. They didn't want to upset me, they said. I followed orders until I began to listen to my own instincts."

One thing her instincts told her was that the music was hideous.

"We had bad audio problems from the beginning," she said, her tone serious once more. "Half the time I couldn't hear the orchestra because it was off to one side. I was told it was a unique television technique. It left the stage free for sets and backgrounds.

"I got tired of the *television look*. And I wanted to hear the music. So I yelled and they finally put the band on stage behind me. I also insisted on a hand microphone because I can control a hand mike. Nobody could turn a knob somewhere to balance out the sound."

Judy poured another vodka and tonic. Her television problems seemed far behind her. She was happy and talkative.

"I'll miss CBS Television City. It must have been built by the same guys who designed the fun house. I could never find anything in that building. I had to get there 45 minutes early every day so I could get lost for a while. I went on the sightseeing tour with the crowds three different times just to find out where my office was."

Judy rehearsed only two days a week, Thursdays and Fridays, taping the shows Friday nights. Often last-minute changes were made after dress rehearsal, throwing the crew of 40 into mild panic.

"I remember once we were doing a Japanese version of *My Fair Lady*, and 15 minutes before taping began, I told [producer] Bill Colleran that I thought the number was too long," Judy recalled. "Bill hollered, 'It's not long. It's out!' So I had to learn a couple of extra songs in a big hurry.

"Vic Damone and I never did rehearse our *West Side Story* songs. We pre-recorded them and went right on the air. A couple of times I learned the music as I sang it on the show, reading the words from idiot cards. I don't know how to read music. Never have. But we got by. How? Black Irish luck, I guess."

Judy will return to her concert tours, grateful to television for exposing her to new fans, and hoping they I will come to hear her sing in person.

She winced when I asked if she would do another series.

"No," she answered. "All in all, the show was a good thing to have happen to me. I learned a great deal. But if I had known what I was in for, I would never have tried a weekly series. Not ever."

TV INTERVIEW

GERALD LYONS | May 11, 1964, Sydney, Australia

With the television series debacle only a couple of months behind her (the final episode aired March 29, 1964), Judy was booked for several concerts in Australia "to clear up some of my financial problems," she explained. Earning a reported total of $52,000 for three shows, she was said to be the highest paid entertainer that country had seen to that point, and her reception in Sydney was deemed superior to that given Queen Elizabeth II a year prior.

Judy gave this interview to local television news personality Gerald Lyons the day she touched down in Sydney, and participated in several others during a press conference welcoming her to the city. The response to her shows was overwhelmingly positive, with *Variety* claiming, "Miss Garland won the greatest audience ovation in the history of Australian showbiz. She had the audience in the palm of her hand from the moment she stepped on the rostrum." And a reviewer for Sydney's *Sun Herald* asserted that "The Beatles may come and go, but the past week belongs to Judy. The little figure under the lights conquered all."

Judy's travel companion on the Aussie tour was new boyfriend Mark Herron, thirty-three, whom she had met at the very beginning of 1964 at a New Year's Eve party. The two traveled by train to Melbourne, where the response was a stark contrast to that she had received in Sydney. Judy's medication had been confiscated upon arriving in Australia, so she was trying to adjust to another variety and hadn't slept for several days. Struggling medicinally and vocally, she arrived more than an hour late (exactly sixty-six minutes, according to one reviewer) for her sold-out concert at Festival Hall. Unaware of the reasons surrounding her tardiness and unusual behavior onstage that evening, members of the restive audience became aggressive and some even shouted insults at her from their seats. Halfway through the show, while singing "By Myself," Judy began to weep and soon bolted from the stage. She did not return.

"The legend of Judy Garland was sadly and brutally shattered," wrote Raymond Stanley for *Variety*. "She talked and aimlessly wandered about the stage and the last thing she seemed to want to do was sing. Her total time on stage was sixty-five minutes, and she refused to take any bows or encores." A gathering of two hundred ill-wishers convened at the Melbourne airport for a send-off when Judy and Mark fled for their next stop: Hong Kong. She was terribly ill upon arrival and was asked by the local press what she was suffering from. "Australia," She responded.

The Australian tour was detailed by Judy in a self-penned piece that appeared in the August 1967 issue of *McCall's*: "I didn't know that Sydney and Melbourne are like Los Angeles and San Francisco. If you're a success in Sydney, you've got to be killed in Melbourne. And vice versa. I just went and tried to sing. Sydney was a tremendous success. But the Melbourne crowds were brutish, and so was the press. At my hotel in Melbourne, the press bored holes through the walls to spy on me. They'd taken the suite next to my bathroom and bedroom. So I went around with Q-Tips and stuck them through the holes. I heard screams on the other end where I'd jab the peeper in the eye. I think that is one of the reasons the reporters got mad at me."

[*Scene from* I Could Go on Singing *(1963).*]

Gerald Lyons: What Judy Garland is saying, in effect, in that scene is, "Here am I and there are you, so let's go," something she says before every performance and something she's probably saying right now, right at this moment in Sydney, as the Australian spotlights fall on her for the first time for her Sydney opening. That film is a widescreen production, a recent one, which hasn't been released here, and it's called *I Could Go On Singing*, which could well be the theme of Judy's troubled and brilliant career in show business. Well, this picture, then, her TV shows, and her many state appearances during the past three years have been a triumphant vindication or what Judy herself has called "seven years of rotten luck."

Now here are some scenes from another picture in which she co-starred with Burt Lancaster. It's a controversial story about retarded children called *A Child is Waiting*. In it Judy displays her talents as a dramatic actress.

[*Scene from* A Child Is Waiting *(1963).*]

GL: On her arrival in Sydney, Judy received and accepted, rather never steadfast, the full star treatment from press, radio, TV reporters, and curious fans, first at the airport, then at a lavish press conference in her hotel. Show business, for all its pomp and sentimentality, is often pretty cynical, a condition that derives from broken or unfulfilled promises over the years. When anyone is as successful as Judy Garland, somewhere there are people who are just dying to ask, and often do, whether all the success will last. Press conferences like this one, even with the meddling and influences of champagne and caviar can, beneath the surface, be quite savage personal intrusions. I asked Judy if the film on retarded children held any special significance for her.

Judy Garland: Well, I think it's a very important picture. I don't know whether people will be able to *bear* some of the truths in the picture, but it's a very fine cause, retarded children. I've worked with retarded children many years.

GL: You have?

JG: Yes. That's why I wanted to do the picture, and I was very flattered to be asked by Stanley Kramer to be in it.

GL: I believe, in 1949 you were in a hospital in Boston.

JG: That's right.

GL: And you met a retarded child.

JG: Yes, I met a whole hospital full and they really are so full of love and unquestioning affection. Many of them have very high IQs. The fact that the muscular coordination doesn't work sometimes doesn't mean that, in other words, they shouldn't be just shuttered away and be ashamed of. And I think the Joseph Kennedy Foundation is helping a great deal. I hope you like the film when you see it. I hope many people go to see it.

GL: Did it help you in your own case? I think you had a nervous breakdown at this time in 1949. Did this help you, getting to know a retarded child?

JG: Yes, yes.

GL: How did it help you?

JG: Well, it helped me by just getting my mind off myself. They were so delightful. They were so loving and good, and I forgot about myself for a change. And they liked to hear music. And they liked to display a kind of an unlimited approval of you; whether you approve of them or not, doesn't make any difference.

GL: You're quite a legend. A legend in what you do and what you're able to do with audience. Miss Garland, what is it you do to an audience? What do you give an audience?

JG: I just sing, so [*laughs*] I don't know. I just . . .

GL: No one else has quite been able to do this. Or very *few* people have been able to do what you do with an audience.

JG: Well, I like my audiences so much. I have great respect for them. I think anybody who'll sit in a chair and look at one person and pay money to see that, I think that's a great tribute. There's a kind of . . . a maybe a marriage between the audience and myself.

GL: Do you become very emotionally involved with an audience when you're performing?

JG: To a point. If I became emotionally involved I'd go sit in front and applaud, I suppose. Or else boo! [*Laughs.*] The only thing I can say is I'm involved to the extent of wanting to *please* my audience as much as I can.

GL: You've had many bouts of illness and you've made many comebacks.

JG: About a hundred and eighty-five up to now.

GL: A hundred and eighty-five comebacks.

JG: Yes, yes. [*Both laugh.*] I don't think I ever went anywhere, did I, really?

GL: You're always coming back.

JG: I'm just always coming back. [*Laughs.*]

GL: Well, this is how the press seems to treat it.

JG: I know.

GL: Does it worry you very much?

JG: No.

GL: Do you care very much about what you read about yourself in the press?

JG: I don't read too much about myself. I'm working too hard.

GL: You work hard. You work so hard that you become ill sometimes. You have been ill in the past.

JG: Oh, no, I haven't been ill for a hundred and eight years! [*Laughs.*] I've done every job they've thrown at me. [*Laughs.*]

GL: All right, why do you do it? Why do you drive yourself so much?

JG: Because I was born to do that to work and to try to entertain, take people's minds off their troubles for a while, if I *can*.

GL: And where do you derive—

JG: [*Interrupting.*] Why are you looking at me this way?

GL: Well, I can't see you any other way. [*All laugh.*]

JG: Just staring—you haven't blinked *once*! [*All laugh.*]

GL: I have, believe me. [*All laugh.*] What gives you satisfaction when you're singing and you have an audience?

JG: Their approval.

GL: Is this what you live for?

JG: Yes.

GL: Do you live for other things?

JG: Money.

GL: Anything else?

JG: I don't think so. No, what would you think?

GL: Your children?

JG: Well, that money's for my children.

GL: You've established a fund for the children, I believe, for your children?

JG: Oh, yes, yes.

GL: Do you want them to go into show business? One of them has been, I believe.

JG: One is an *enormous star*! Yes, she's a great recording artist and she's now understudying Barbra Streisand in a Broadway show.* And they're writing a show just for her to do. That's Liza, my oldest daughter.

GL: Does it make you happy they're in show business? That *Liza's* in show business?

JG: Yes, it makes me very happy. I think it's something to be very proud of.

GL: You started in show business yourself when you were about twelve. Or two and a half or something.

JG: *Two!* Two. Yeah. That's a bit young.

GL: Does it make life more difficult for you when you start at this age?

JG: No, no, no. I don't think so. I think the sort of climaxes and payoffs are much, much more important than any little minor difficulty that might happen, you know.

GL: What are you like as a person? Some people think you're rather temperamental and they're afraid of you.

JG: I know. I've always heard that.

GL: They're afraid if they rub you off the wrong way you'll run out of the door.

---

*At the time of this interview, Judy was under the impression that Liza was Streisand's *Funny Girl* understudy.

JG: Yes, I know. Well, it's just what you see here! [*Laughs.*]

GL: This, obviously, doesn't worry you.

JG: No, I don't know why they think that. I suppose they are told that by other people. Maybe they read it. In the papers.

GL: I think, somewhere, you said that you were a temperamental Irish biddy.

JG: No, I said I was just an Irish biddy. [*Laughs, puffing a cigarette.*]

GL: Are you superstitious?

JG: I don't *dare* be now that I'm flying. I didn't fly on airplanes till three years ago. I don't *dare* be superstitious. No, not really superstitious.

GL: What do you like doing when you're not performing? When you're not resting?

JG: I like to be with my children. Cook. I like to cook. I'm a good cook. I am quite a good cook.

GL: There's a story about you cooking for yourself at night, relaxing.

JG: Yes, it's good. It's a good thing.

GL: And you do this to relax after a show? You go home and you cook something?

JG: Yes, I make up recipes.

GL: Which you don't eat.

JG: No, I don't eat them.

GL: Who eats them?

JG: My children. I put them in the icebox. [*Laughs.*] Then they taste them, and if they like them I know that I'm a hit with the kids.

[*Scene from* The Wizard of Oz *(1939).*]

GL: With that song ["Over the Rainbow"], which she made, and which made *her* at the age of seventeen, and her chaotic years behind her, Judy Garland still seems to be looking for the rainbow. We're indebted to United Artists for *I Could Go On Singing*, for the extracts from that, and from the Burt Lancaster–Judy Garland movie, *A Child Is Waiting*, and to M-G-M for being allowed to show the extract you've just seen from *The Wizard of Oz*, which was done twenty-three or twenty-five years ago, I think.

JUDY GEM

On Performing at the London Palladium with Liza

"Wasn't Liza great? Don't write about me . . . write about Liza and how wonderful she was."

—To London *Daily Express*, November 1964

TV INTERVIEW

LAURIER LaPIERRE | February 7, 1965, *This Hour Has Seven Days*

Filling in for an ill Nat "King" Cole, Judy flew to Toronto on February 6 for a weeklong engagement at the O'Keefe Centre. The following day, she visited privately with Canadian broadcaster Laurier LaPierre before participating in a press conference at the King Edward Sheraton Hotel. Both discussions were edited into a segment for *This Hour Has Seven Days*, a television news magazine broadcast on Canadian Broadcasting Corporation.

John Drainie (host): Judy Garland rocketed over the rainbow to stardom when she was twelve. Now, three marriages, several breakdowns, and three hundred concerts later, Judy's still in there pitching with the same old magic.

Judy Garland: [*Closing eyes.*] Oh, dear.

Laurier LaPierre: But you have such lovely eyes. No, leave them open. And could you tell me what you feel as you walk on that stage and face all these thousands of people?

JG: I feel *marvelous*.

LL: Do they give you a feeling of accomplishment?

JG: They give me a feeling of love.

JD: But what are those times, Laurier wondered, when the audience may be hostile?

LL: Do you feel frightened of them?

JG: *Terrified.*

LL: Terrified. Completely terrified.

JG: Yes.

LL: But the courage amount—it must be amazing to carry on.

JG: Well, I've been doing shows for many years and it's my business, and so I have to kind of expect anything, you know. But I'm a very lucky woman.

LL: Madame—mademoiselle, rather—your daughter . . .

JG: Yes.

LL: The world has discovered the very great talent that she has, and I understand she's about to be in a new production [*Flora, the Red Menace*] directed by Mr. [George] Abbott and so forth.

JG: That's right.

LL: If you were to look back, Madame Garland, on your life, what sort of advice would you give to your very talented and very beautiful daughter Liza?

JG: I don't give her any advice. She's very wise. And she's seen my mistakes and my fears and so forth. And she has her feet on the ground all the time.

LL: Is the search for publicity a drive in an artist or does it come naturally that people would be interested in you? Or do you seek out [publicity]?

JG: No, I don't seek out . . . I'm quite shy, really.

LL: You're a quite shy person, aren't you?

JG: Yes.

LL: And you are overwhelmed, perhaps, by this? Angered?

JG: Not angered. I just I don't know what they yell about when I sing.

LL: But, for instance, you could not even have a love affair, you know, without the whole world knowing about it . . .

JG: Who said that?

LL: [You could not have a love affair] without the whole world knowing about it, madam.

JG: Well, *really*!

LL: I mean, you are capable of a love affair, no doubt, but without the whole world knowing about it?

JG: Well, that's all right. It makes it sort of *classy*, I think.

LL: It gives a certain tone to the love affair, which might not have happened otherwise. [*Both laugh.*] In your life, can you tell me a very happy, blissful moment you have had? Could you describe it?

JG: I've had many.

LL: But could you just think of one now and just tell us about it?

JG: Yes, I think being in love with Mark Herron is the best thing that ever happened to me.

LL: Being in love with Monsieur Herron . . .

JG: Yes.

LL: [It] has given a new dimension to your life? And to your life as an artist and as a person?

JG: Yes.

LL: Does Monsieur Herron manage your [career?]

JG: No, no, he's a wonderful actor.

LL: Of his own right.

JG: Yes.

LL: But he gives, from the height of his artistic knowledge, a certain thing to your career which was lacking before?

JG: He gives me just love.

LL: And that's enough, surely. Now, Madame Garland, I understand that there are a lot of other people who are waiting and who want to talk to you, and I simply would love if in the course of the week you would be so—

JG: [*Interrupting.*] Oh, by the way, I give him love, too. [*Laughs.*]

LL: I have no doubt about that. I was wondering, Madame Garland, whether if, let's say tomorrow, God forbid, all right, God forbid, that you…

JG: That I *die*?

LL: No, that you would retire from the stage.

JG: Oh.

LL: What would you do?

JG: I'd *cook*!

LL: But where did you learn to cook? At M-G-M.?

JG: Oh, no, I didn't have *time*! Actually, I had difficulty sleeping, so I learned to cook during the night.

LL: Instead of sleeping.

JG: Yes.

LL: Well, that's very productive!

JG: Yes.

LL: Most people, they toss around, and you get up and you cook.

JG: Yes.

LL: Do you remember any difficulties you've ever had cooking this way?

JG: Oh, good heavens! My youngest daughter has a pussycat who takes great pleasure in getting under my feet when I have a hot dish in my hands.

LL: Oh my. And what happens to the dish and to you?

JG: No, I kick the cat! [*All laugh.*]

JD: In the next suite, press, radio, television, and other unclassifiable inquisitors waited for their chance to try at some of those questions and a few new ones.

Press: Judy, what do you think that you most missed as a teenager?

JG: Eating! [*All laugh.*]

Press: Did you have to stay a certain measurement or something in those days?

JG: Yes, yes.

Press: Judy, what is the secret of your recent diet? You've lost a lot of weight and you look just fabulous, but how'd you do it?

JG: Thank you.

Press: But how'd you do it?

JG: I fasted. [*All laugh.*] I did. Really. For thirty days.

Press: No kidding?

JG: Yes.

Press: Judy, what feeling do you get when you walk onto the stage and get the acclaim that you receive, say, at the O'Keefe Centre?

JG: Oh, I feel great gratitude.

Press: Have you the vaguest idea why they feel the way they do about you?

JG: [*Shakes head no.*] No, I don't.

Press: Do you think they love you?

JG: Well, they make a lot of noise. [*All laugh.*]

Press: Judy, you've become a living legend. Do you ever wish you weren't?

JG: Isn't it awful? [*All laugh.*]

Press: Do you often wish you *weren't* a living legend?

JG: Yes, I do.

Press: Do you ever go to a town where you're not known? I mean, do you ever sneak into a town?

JG: [*Shakes head no.*]

Press: You can't walk down the street?

JG: No. Except when I was very fat. [*All laugh.*]

Press: Which do you enjoy doing more: television or screen?

JG: Or eating?

Press: Or eating! [*All laugh.*]

JG: I like screen better.

Press: Why is that?

JG: Well, because I can't find the cameras on television. [*Laughs.*]

Press: Miss Garland, if I was your fifteen-year-old daughter would you encourage—

JG: [*Interrupting.*] You may *be*! [*All laugh.*]

Press: Judy, what's your favorite song?

JG: "Over the Rainbow"! [*All laugh.*]

Press: Are you interested in politics at all?

JG: Sometimes. Sometimes, yes. I don't know too much about them, but I'm interested in world affairs, yes.

Press: You campaigned for Mr. Kennedy, didn't you?

JG: Yes, I did. In Europe.

Press: Who could vote there? The troops?

JG: Yes, the troops.

Press: The US Armed Forces.

JG: Yes.

Press: Have you any formula when you do get tired or you get depressed, as performers do? What do you do to pull yourself up again and get that marvelous gift that you have? People have called you or compared you to a phoenix, rising up.

JG: I slap myself on the hip. I do! In the wings. [*Slaps hip three times.*] Like an old pony.

TV INTERVIEW

GYPSY ROSE LEE | August 1965, *Gypsy*

Gypsy was a morning talk show hosted by Gypsy Rose Lee for San Francisco's KGO-TV. According to Noralee Frankel, author of *Stripping Gypsy: The Life of Gypsy Rose Lee*, "Gypsy chose a diverse array of celebrity guests. . . . Many revealed—or pretended to reveal—little-known aspects of their private lives. The show relied on informality and sexual humor, which suited Gypsy perfectly."

When Judy Garland taped the show in August 1965, the energy exuded from the banter between these two powerhouse talkers was inexorable. Although it is certain that the show was taped during the latter part of August 1965, there are discrepancies when it comes to the actual airdate. Some sources say August 30, 1965, while others claim September 13. The conflicting dates may be due in part to the fact that the show was syndicated by Seven Arts Television and likely aired on different dates and at different times throughout various markets.

Not included (but referred to) in this transcription was Gypsy's ambiguous introduction of Judy through a lengthy telling of having been introduced to Spencer Tracy on the M-G-M lot by Fanny Brice in 1937. After several minutes, and to the delight of her audience, Gypsy finally curtailed her rambling recollection: "At M-G-M, at the same time, there was the biggest star of them *all*," she said. "And she's our guest today."

Gypsy Rose Lee: Oh, hello. I'm so glad you're with us because I want you to meet my guest today. I'm so happy to have her. Judy Garland. [*Audience applauds.*] You see, that long story about Spencer Tracy really didn't make sense at all. I bet you thought I had Katharine Hepburn, didn't you? [*Audience laughs.*] See, I fooled ya! That's the way we do it around here.

Oh, deceptive people. During that intermission, we were talking about the film Judy was making at M-G-M at that time. Sophie Tucker was the big . . .

Judy Garland: Sophie Tucker owned the boarding house, and Mickey Rooney, I think, was a jockey, wasn't he?

GRL: He was.

JG: That's right.

GRL: But Fanny [Brice] wasn't in that picture, was she?

JG: Fanny wasn't in that, no. Just Sophie was in it. And *I* was in it.

GRL: Yes, I know!

JG: And there were a couple of *horses* in it. [*Laughs.*] Losers, I think. [*Laughs.*] I don't really remember. *Thoroughbreds Don't Cry* was the name of it, and I think that they'd arranged for it to be made with the leading child star at the time, who was Freddie Bartholomew. But Freddie's voice changed. [*Gypsy laughs.*] And he suddenly went [*sings high notes, then low*]. And so they got a new boy, Ronald Sinclair, I think his name was, and just put him in this starring role. It was kind of a rough go on him, I guess.

GRL: Oh, of course it was.

JG: Well, they ground him up into little bits of cement or something and no one has *heard* of him since. Not even as a *person*.

GRL: Nobody realized, I don't think, Judy, until you spoke of it one night on the *Jack Paar Show*, the terrible injustice that was done to *all* of you people, actually. You know, you think of someone being a great big famous movie star, how wonderful it is for her . . . But, *my*, when you realize they're pitting one of you against the other! They used Deanna Durbin to threaten you, didn't they?

JG: Well, no, they couldn't use us . . . we were on different lots, but they used, I remember . . . They got *mad*. Some of the executives had a fight, and Deanna Durbin and I were at an awful age when no one existed. You either had to be seven years old or you had to be twenty. You know, an in-between. There were no teenage . . . nothing. So we just hung around and sort of went to school and didn't know what we were there for. So finally they *fired* Deanna, and they were going to fire me, too, but Universal picked up her option, you see—or her contract, I should say—and then they made a star of her, and M-G-M got so mad at Universal they just said, "Well, we've got a girl that age, too!" So that's the only reason I really got a job. Because Deanna Durbin was a big seller. [*Audience laughs.*] And then, you know, they had these *backbreaking* hours that we used to work. Mickey and I would go to work, I would say, on a Monday morning we would check in about five o'clock. Well, I've got a funny story I must tell you. There was a man at the gate. He'd been there for a *hundred* years. He was really just like an old totem pole. [*Gypsy laughs.*] But you couldn't get into M-G-M without his letting you through, you know. So for a few years I had to walk through and he *always* stopped me. You know, I'd say, "Hello, my name is Judy Garland." He'd say, "Well, you're not on the list. [*All laugh.*] He'd say, "I'll have to call a couple of people." I'd think, *Well, I'm gonna be late for school and I already called a couple . . .* So I was always late. And finally, after being there for . . . sixteen years I was at Metro . . . I was absolutely terrified. Terrified! All sixteen years. It really was brainwash time. And they fired me and I was very happy about it, but I wanted to get a few things out of my dressing room. *Personal* things, you know, my own things. And I went back with my own car and I was wheeling in to Metro and he said, "Just a minute!" Same man. And I said, "Well, now, we've done this fandango for *so* many years. I'm not trying to get into a film. I just want to get in and get my things out of my dressing room. And he said, "You're not on the list." [*All laugh.*] And they really never let me in! They wouldn't, and I never got my things out of my room.

GRL: You never *did* get them?

JG: No, I couldn't get by that *man*! [*All laugh.*]

GRL: *Incredible!*

JG: I know! He was given orders to *shoot* at anybody . . . [*All laugh.*] I think his name was Dore Schary. He was in the uniform. [*All laugh.*]

GRL: Of course, I had such stars in my eyes in those days. The thought of just being in a movie, I didn't care *what* they did to me! They could put on a long, blonde wig, and change my name, and give me a peculiarly shaped mouth. And [they] loaded me down with clothes. They gave me everything I *didn't* need, you know? [*Judy laughs.*] But I didn't really care. I was just so happy to *meet* all the movie stars, you know, and I had three autograph books and almost full before they canceled me out.

JG: Well, I think that's *darling.*

GRL: I was working on my third autograph book . . . [*All laugh.*]

JG: Why don't you forge some?

GRL: You know, since then I've done that.

JG: Have you? [*Laughs.*] Certainly. I do with pictures around the house.

GRL: I did it with Shirley Jones. Shirley Jones left some pictures when she was on the show and they weren't autographed, and I was in there forging her handwriting on all of them. [*Laughs.*]

JG: Don't leave your checkbook behind! [*Laughs.*]

GRL: But it was so funny this morning before Judy got here. *Everybody* was in my dressing room cleaning up the place. They hid *everything*! They took all the Kleenexes and threw them away because Kleenexes, this is an ugly-looking thing, you know? It's utilitarian! They swept the floor, they cleaned the mirrors, they hid all my old clothes. [*Judy laughs.*] Finally they saw this list of pictures that belonged to Shirley Jones and they started throwing those away, and I said, "*Wait* a *minute*! After all, she *did* win an Academy Award, you know!"

JG: That's more than I did, you know. I've been . . .

GRL: If it'd been a picture of some naked girl sitting there or something that could have *offended* Judy. . . . [*Judy laughs.*] But believe me, this is the cleanest my dressing room has been since I've been up here.

JG: Really? Well, it's very clean.

GRL: I know, but they were squirting us with something to make it smell good and everything. Did you notice that? [*Laughs.*] It doesn't smell like that as a *rule!* [*Laughs.*] I mean, just at the last minute, somebody forgot and left that great, huge garbage can right outside the door! [*All laugh.*] And what do they do with the garbage can? They put it in the elevator and then Judy . . . [*All laugh.*] We'll be back in one minute.

[*Commercial break.*]

GRL: [*Laughs.*] No, but I was saying how we got everything all cleaned up and everything. I've known for about three days that Judy was going to be on the show, so I figured I am not going to *capitalize* on this, but I *couldn't* resist and I got on the phone and I called *everyone*. I called Hedda Hopper, I called the AP. I called the UP. Everybody I *know*, I telephoned! Then I started calling a few people I didn't know because I thought this is a great excuse. So I called, finally, New York to get the telephone number of Judith Anderson, who is going to be playing in *Medea*, and I thought, "Oh, how I'd love to have her on the show." So I thought, "What a good excuse, *you see*, to telephone her." So I said, "Hello, darling." I said, "I'm so hoarse. My throat [*coughs*] . . . But it *is* Gypsy Rose Lee. Remember, I met you twenty-seven years ago at a cocktail party? [*All laugh.*] And I said, "Please forgive me for being so hoarse, but I've been talking to Judy Garland. [*Clears throat.*] She's going to be on the show tomorrow. [*All laugh.*] I called my sister in New York. I called *everybody*! I was so excited about the whole thing. Then, of course, I must tell you the tragic thing. Last night, Mark Herron called and said, "Judy can't make it, she still has a cold," and I almost committed suicide.

JG: I had a *streaming* cold.

GRL: I know. Bless your heart . . . the fact that you came here at all, really . . . because, it's true, she did have a cold. She came up here [to San Francisco] to rest, really.

JG: And I'm appearing at that great big theater.

GRL: Yes! The Greek Theatre.

JG: No, right here. The Circle Star [Theatre in San Carlos].

GRL: Oh, Circle Star. That only seats about four thousand or five thousand people, but the Greek Theatre in Los Angeles seats sixteen thousand!

JG: Yes. And a lot of moths. [*Audience laughs.*] Can I tell you a story? [*Laughs.*]

GRL: It's outdoors, isn't it?

JG: It's outdoors, and really, I'm quite frightened of bugs and things that fly toward you, and when you're outdoors and entertaining and the lights are on you and bugs are attracted to you. So I'd gone through my whole show, and I was being sort of very pitiful and just darling, you know, and sitting on the stairs with the tramp makeup and I was singing "Over the Rainbow," and everybody was sort of going [*makes crying sounds*] and I was really just perspiring. Right in the middle of "Over the Rainbow" this moth flew right into my mouth. [*Audience laughs.*] Right into my mouth! Now, in the middle of "Over the Rainbow" you can't go [*makes spitting sounds*]. You can't do it! [*All laugh.*]

GRL: Oh, you didn't! You didn't!

JG: So all of a sudden I went [*gestures*] and parked him there, and he was with me all the way through! [*All laugh.*] It's absolutely true! And he flew and fumbled around and I just went on and sang . . . until finally the lights went out and it was such a spitting and stamping of feet. I just had to let him *stay* once he was there! [*Audience laughs.*] What do you do, spit it at 16,000 people? [*Audience laughs.*] I couldn't very well do *that*.

GRL: Have you ever done any of these [*coughs*] . . . I've laughed so hard . . . between the telephone and laughing, I've just ruined myself. I'll never sing tonight! [*All laugh.*] I hate to disappoint all those people at the Greek Theatre, too, but . . . [*laughs*] it isn't really the Greek Theatre, it's a Greek coffee shop where I'm doing belly dancing. [*All laugh.*] No, but this whole thing reminded me, when I was doing a number in Syracuse at a fair. Mike Todd was with me there. It was between jobs for both of us, you know, and somebody had to be working. And I dressed in the room where they curried the horses during the day, literally, and in order to get to the stage you had to cross the whole racetrack.

JG: How do you curry a horse?

GRL: With a curry comb. . . . you know, to get the bugs off and . . . horses are dirty, you know. Oh, of course they are. Anyway, it had rained the night before . . .

JG: I hit one once. I hit a horse once.

GRL: Oh, darling, please don't tell anybody because I don't want to have to report you.

JG: I did. I hit him in the nose.

GRL: I don't want to have to report you, Judy, to the ASPCA.

JG: He had a policeman on his back.

GRL: Oh, well, of course you're lying! [*All laugh.*]

JG: It was a good shot, anyway.

GRL: But I was in the middle of a field, all during my number, and it was a very quiet number. I tried to get the audience in the proper frame of mind . . . for me to take off my clothes . . . [*all laugh*] and there was a cow tethered—I think that's what you call it—right next to the ramp leading up to the stage, and all during the number he's going "mooooooo, mooooooo." [*All laugh.*] Trains are going by, the "toot-toot-toot...." [*All laugh.*] And then, as I lift my skirt to roll down my stockings, two great huge moths flew out! [*All laugh.*]

JG: Ooh! How *funny*! Really!

GRL: It was such a laugh, I wanted to keep it in the act, but I could never train a moth to do it again! [*All laugh.*] I tried doing it with those Japanese paper moths, but it wouldn't work.

JG: Yes, not the same.

GRL: No, it wouldn't work. It looked false. [*All laugh.*]

JG: Well, I bet they have moths around the Greek Theatre in Los Angeles that are as big as anything Bela Lugosi could dream up. Great big fat moths.

GRL: Moths are all around. They're talent scouts.

JG: Well, I shook hands with several of them! [*All laugh.*] Well, I'm going to miss that at this engagement here at the Circle Star. It's a very pretty theater.

GRL: Have you worked this sort of theater before?

JG: No, well, I did it once in Australia, which we won't even talk about. Australia—well, we might as well talk about it—was agony because no one told me if they like you in Sydney, they *loathe* you in Melbourne. And if they like you in Melbourne, they hate you in Sydney. If you just go there, two cents plain, and sing away, they go "*Yeah!*" in Sydney, and they just say, "*We don't like her!*" in Melbourne. And you come in and say "hello," and they say, "*GET OUT! GO AWAY!*" And you say, "Well, I can't get out until I've *sung*. Because I'm supposed to sing here!" [They say,] "We don't want you to sing, lady. Just get out." So then they all got loud and drunk because they'd closed the bars.

GRL: Talking about beers?

JG: Yes. Kangaroo beers, I suppose.

GRL: Oh, my God, that beer has *hair* on it! [*All laugh.*]

JG: And I carry a hand mic and some members of the press sitting along here would just take great pleasure in grabbing the cord of the hand mic, and I'd start waltzing across and all of a sudden, *BOOM* I'd get pulled back. So it was sort of a tug-of-war between the press and me. The press was saying, "Why don't you come down here and get drunk instead!" [*All laugh.*]

GRL: Oh, *really!* You know, before I went to Australia, they warned me. They said, you know, the Australians are sort of the Texans of the Pacific. Well, I never saw anything like that in Texas.

JG: Well, they're brutish.

GRL: But pretty healthy with all of it, you know.

JG: Oh, I didn't think . . .

GRL: You didn't think so. Of course, I was booked in Melbourne, but all I played was Sydney.

JG: Oh, Syndey's nice.

GRL: But they wouldn't book me anywhere else. They canceled me right after Sydney. I have no idea *why.* [*All laugh.*]

JG: No, seriously, Sydney is quite lovely.

GRL: But they loathed me so that they wanted to ban me before I ever went on the stage. So I said, "How can you ban me when you haven't caught the act yet?" So in all the newspapers were big front-page stories about "Are we going to allow this disgraceful thing to take place in Sydney, Australia," and of course when I went on stage it was such an innocuous act, you know, really. You see more on the beaches than I showed in my last encore. [*All laugh.*] And then everybody was so disappointed. They said, "Is *this* what they get all excited about in Los Angeles and New York?" I tried to explain to them that they didn't really get excited, that I just barely scratched out a living. [*All laugh.*] The only one who was excited was *me!* Oh, we have a commercial for just one minute. I was only kidding about Australia!

[*Commercial break.*]

GRL: I was just telling Judy Garland that I wish she wouldn't diet so much and get so thin. Not that you don't look wonderful on television, but even when you put on a little weight, your legs stay lean.

JG: Yes, well, I just *demand* that they stay lean. They have to get around so much. They're a moving target.

GRL: You have *wonderful* legs!

JG: Yes, well, they're straight. I think that's the thing. [*Laughs.*] They're just legs, you know!

GRL: No! Not really. Not really. I think that I saw the picture of you in the paper a few days ago and I'd talked to you on the phone and you said, "Oh, I've gained weight again." But you haven't gained that much weight.

JG: No, I've gained some.

GRL: You do remember, darling, you were *really* heavy when you played London, and that was one of the great big smash successes of your life.

JG: Yes, I was very heavy. It was quite a while ago, as a matter of fact, when I fell down at opening night.

GRL: Wasn't it wonderful?

JG: Wasn't it awful?

GRL: *Wonderful!* Oh, it was a buzz that just resounded all over the world.

JG: I was supposed to go out and sing three songs, and just bow slightly— sort of a curtsy—and go off and then come back and sing three other *outrageous* arrangements. They started to play my overture and my knees locked [*Gypsy laughs*], just like Frankenstein's bride. And they wouldn't bend! And I really walked on with two stiff legs, you know, and I just stood there in terror and sang the three songs. Then I thought, "Now it's time to bow." So I bowed and I just kept *going!* [*All laugh.*] I did one little curtsy and one nerve undid, and I just wound up sitting on the floor.

GRL: I thought what you did was trip and then you really took a real fall.

JG: No, I just, for no reason . . . if they'd had a wire going across or a rope or something, I could have made something of it. This way, I was just standing there and I simply sat down on the stage. I was trying to bow.

GRL: You know, there are some people at home that'd say, "Oh, Judy Garland. Oh, boy, she'll do *anything* to get her picture in the paper.

JG: A lot of people asked me if I did that on purpose, which flabbergasts me.

GRL: Well, you weren't here to see it, but there were headlines like *this*! [*Gestures.*]

JG: Yes, I know. Well, I hadn't made any for a long time.

GRL: If you had killed the royal family it couldn't have made a bigger splash!

JG: Yes, well, the only thing, once you fall . . . and I do fall a lot. My whole family has fallen. I have two sisters who fall down all the time, you know. I fall down. My mother was *always* falling down the steps. And my father fell. *Fall! Crack! Boom!* And we never get hurt, we just sort of get up and go on.

GRL: That's incredible! See, there you go talking about that ghost mother again! [*All laugh.*]*

JG: Are you gonna come to her rescue?

GRL: *No!*

JG: She can take care of herself!

GRL: So close to dinner time, too.

JG: Where's the gravy?

[*Commercial break.*]

GRL: Twenty seconds to say good-bye to Judy Garland. [*Audience applauds.*] She opens next week at the Circle Star Theatre and then the Greek Theatre in Los Angeles. Thank you so much, darling. And thank you!

JUDY GEM

On the Beatles

"[They are] great guys. Awfully nice young gentlemen. They're very intelligent. They *own* Liverpool now, don't they?"

—San Francisco Press Conference, August 1965

JUDY GEM

On Her Homosexual Following

"I couldn't care less. I sing to *people!*"

—San Francisco Press Conference, August 1965

---

*It is likely that Judy told a story of her mother during a break or a portion of the show cut from the broadcast.

"I'VE BEEN A FOOL"— BY JUDY GARLAND

COMER CLARKE | October 23, 1965, *Titbits* (UK)

This interview dates to Judy's run at the Thunderbird Hotel in Las Vegas, June 1965, just one month after her divorce from Sid Luft was final. Although the writer indentifies her to be "a young-looking 41," Judy had just turned 43. Liza was also interviewed.

Comer Clarke has met the biggest stars in show business and been in on their most intimate conversations.

He traveled more than 10,000 miles to meet them in their homes, on studio sets and backstage.

They confessed all—their secrets, fears, ambitions—exclusively for TITBITS.

Today Judy Garland tells how her daughter Liza saved her show business life . . . and Liza gives the secret behind her mother's flops.

It was two in the morning. The delirious, packed nightclub crowd sent wave after wave of cheers and applause surging across the floor. The beams of the spotlights spun again from their temporary resting place on the sweat-soaked band as the tiny, waif-like figure ran on the stage again and stood hands clasped and head bowed before the wildly excited crowd.

Then, in spontaneous unison, the audience rose to its feet in final, roaring tribute. Men threw roses from their buttonholes and women wept. Judy Garland, her sad, wistful, [brown] eyes brimming, too, with tears, took a last bow and ran back to her dressing room.

It happened in California. But, after Judy's brilliant, flawless, one-and-a-half-hour performance, it would have happened anywhere.

Later, Judy Garland, a little tired but smiling joyfully, told me: "At last I've found my crock of happiness and contentment. You know there have been many times when I've been in despair."

Then she admitted: "I've been a fool in many ways. I've let my hopes, my feelings and my fears get on top of me so many times.

"I know I have sometimes put on a show that wasn't good enough. That I have let my emotions run away with me. I couldn't help it."

For a woman who became a dazzling Hollywood star while still in her teens, it was a bitter confession. But it was true.

To most people Judy Garland has been one of the most puzzling of Hollywood's great stars. Few of her millions of fans throughout the world have followed the breakdowns and emotional crises which have marred her career without a feeling of sadness and pity.

Her successes were golden from the moment she captivated the world as the wide-eyed, wondering girl in *The Wizard of* Oz.

Many other achievements followed. Then, somehow, the rocket climb faltered. Her crashes were as painfully public as her successes. And they became more and more frequent. Within the last couple of years the emotional crises appeared to have deepened.

Near-collapses and seeming *uncertainty* on stage . . . *fluffed* lines . . . *failure* to hit the right notes . . . *late* appearances . . . inability to finish acts . . .

Judy's Australian tour last year seemed little short of disastrous.

Millions of British fans remember her performance in the TV show *Judy and Liza* from the London Palladium, when she several times failed to hit the correct notes and seemed to lean heavily on daughter Liza Minnelli. But, at the end she received a standing ovation, for few stars are as warmly liked as Judy.

This year, in Cincinnati, Ohio, some of her audience became angry when she unexpectedly stopped during her act, announced a surprise intermission and later walked on stage with her doctor, explaining that she couldn't continue.

Another time she was rushed to hospital for observation and it was explained she was "emotionally upset" after "allergic reaction to a drug."

Brilliant

Eleven days after, at Las Vegas, oxygen was rushed to her hotel cottage when she became ill.

The incidents were only a few of many. Fans watched with sadness and sympathy. The once dazzling star was becoming one of the fastest-falling stars in show business. A brilliant meteorite burning out and streaking to oblivion.

In the dressing room of that West Coast nightclub, I knew I was looking at a new Judy Garland. She said quietly and thoughtfully: "Yes, my daughter Liza and my two younger children saved me . . ."

She paused and then went on: "I suppose the song 'Somewhere Over the Rainbow' [sic] in The Wizard of Oz is what people most associate with me.

"But most people associate a rainbow with the fairytale crock of gold. I never sought for gold.

"What I have sought is what the little girl I portrayed in the film was searching for in that land over the rainbow—happiness, contentment and peace of mind. During these last few months, I seem to have found them."

She spoke these words with conviction. The change is immediately noticeable, and close friends and casual acquaintances have noticed it, too.

What has happened in Judy Garland's life during the past few months to bring about this zestful happiness where, for so long, there seemed to be only bleak despair?

"I guess I've always been the nervous kind," Judy said. "And I guess I've often worried and been upset when I didn't have cause.

"But much of my trouble has been due to the fact that my marriages have failed. For myself, this need not have been too upsetting, although, naturally, I regretted it. But it's different when you have kids. At least, it ought to be different, I think. It certainly had an effect on me.

"I was divorced from my husband, Vincente Minnelli, when Liza—she's 19 now—was only six. I know how much a girl needs her mother as she grows up.

"I guess that, as the years passed, I worried more and more about her. In show business, you're away from home a lot.

"Film and singing commitments seemed to take me all over the world. But, as often as I could, I worked here on the West Coast—in Los Angeles, San Francisco or in nearby Las Vegas—so that I wouldn't be too far away.

"I know the effect broken homes have on kids, particularly if they think parents don't care. Specially a mother."

Then Judy Garland fell in love with Sid Luft and they got married.

"Everything was happy for a while and we had two children, Lorna, who's now 11 and Joseph, who's now nine," said Judy. "But, as a producer, Sid was away a lot and so was I.

"Sid and I drifted apart. Showbiz is rough on kids, I guess. But neither of us knew anything else and that's the way it went. I had to earn my living."

Tortured

"I used to spend hours awake, when I should have been sleeping, thinking about the unfairness of it all to those kids.

"I tortured myself over and over again by asking, 'Judy, did you do the right thing having them?'

"I had to take pills to make me sleep. If ever I overslept, there were rumors that I'd taken an overdose.

"But I knew those kids needed a mother most of all, even though their parents had split up. I knew, too, that to gain custody, some dirty linen would be bound to be washed. Sure enough it was. The legal battles seemed endless."

Said Judy: "It all played on my mind. Every bit of tittle-tattle was a big headline. I knew the children would know. If you're a 'name' there's nothing you can do about it.

"And, you know, when you're going through a bad time, there are always plenty of people ready to help push you further downhill.

"They try to 'murder' you with all sorts of wild rumors. The worst interpretation is put on everything. When I was way out there in front of the footlights I often used to be thinking of my kids—and fluff my lines. And sometimes I was so distraught I just couldn't go on.

"Stupid? Maybe. But I guess that's how I'm made—a worrier."

I knew what she meant. For, earlier, in New York, I had talked to her beautiful and talented daughter, Liza.

Crumpled

"I have the best mother in the world," she said. "If she has faults, they are that she is warm and human. And that doesn't do in show business. It's easier if you're tough and hard.

"A lot of people have hurt her a lot of times and because she's thin-skinned and has taken lots of knocks in life, she's crumpled now and again.

"But, believe me, no children could have a kinder, more thoughtful mother."

Liza went on to tell me what she meant.

"One night, when I was studying in Paris, my mother phoned from Los Angeles after the first part of her show to see how I was. I think she guessed I was a bit 'down' and homesick. She's always really believed in that rainbow, you know, and that we all eventually find happiness.

"She said: 'You just go on believing, Liza.' And there and then started to sing me a lullaby she used to sing me when I was just a little girl.

"After a few minutes I went to sleep, still clutching the phone. That's what she means to me and that's the kind of woman she is.

"She was always scared I might be mixing with Left Bank drifters. Once, when I told her on the telephone that I was going out in a sweater and jeans, she sent a complete wardrobe out from the best shop in Los Angeles."

Worry

"With the clothes was a little note saying: 'Just keep the sweater and jeans for lounging about in the apartment, honey.'

"I guess she spent thousands of dollars on phone calls. Yet, when we went on tour together, I realized how great the toll of worry had been.

"Yes," Liza went on, "everyone is saying she's a new person now. It's all so wonderful."

Liza said of Judy's just-announced intention to marry her actor friend, Mark Herron, 29: "I think it's so marvelous. They are devoted. And we *all* get on so well together. We'll be a family again."

Back in her dressing room, Judy Garland, a young-looking 41, told me the real truth about the return after so long of the self-confidence and happiness which had once seemed to have left her.

She admitted, "Liza really saved me. Despite everything, despite the broken marriages and the upsets anxiety caused, she has grown into a self-confident young woman—a success in her own right and a fine actress.

"She says she's tougher than I am—and I'm glad. She says she doesn't want to be a great star—just to fulfill herself in life. That's what I lived and worked and worried to bring about for her and my two other children.

"I know," said Judy, "that every mother will understand what I mean. In these past couple of years, when everything seemed to be going wrong, it was Liza who was on hand.

"She used to say: 'Mother, you were there when I needed you.'"

Judy went on: "But, really, four wonderful things have happened within the last few months this year, and they are all things which have taken away the doubts and anxieties which have caused so much trouble in the past."

Judy counted them out on her fingers . . .

"ONE, Liza is a success in her own right as the star of the Broadway show *Flora, the Red Menace*. D'you know, she's just won a Tony—the Antoinette Perry Award—as the best musical actress of the year. Isn't that good?

"TWO, after so much legal back and forth, I'm finally divorced from my former husband, Sid Luft. I have always felt it better to cut completely if two people don't get on.

"THREE, I now have a full legal share of the custody of our two children, Lorna and Joseph. Sid had long fought for sole custody. I was scared to death I was going to lose them.

"FOUR, I'm going to marry Mark—Mark Herron. My three children adore him. So, at last, everything is wonderful all the way."*

---

*Judy married Mark Herron on November 14, 1965, in Las Vegas. Their union was brief, lasting only a few months

Judy Garland sat back in her chair and smiled.

"Now I have so much to live for," she said. "All those past problems are settled and the children of my marriages are growing up good and straight. I'm content."

I said good-bye and slipped out of the door as a messenger brought in another bouquet of flowers.

It really seemed that Judy Garland has, at last, found that long-elusive happiness that has lain all these painful last few years on the other side of her rainbow.

PRESS CONFERENCE: *VALLEY OF THE DOLLS*

LEONARD PROBST | March 2, 1967, *Monitor* (NBC Radio)

In arrangement with Twentieth Century Fox, Judy Garland participated in a much-anticipated press conference at the St. Regis Hotel in New York. There, alongside novelist Jacqueline Susann, she fielded questions relating to her casting as fictional Broadway musical comedy star Helen Lawson in the studio's upcoming production of *Valley of the Dolls*. "I don't think any actress could get a better role," she told the press. "I think there's a good chance to sing one song and yet I don't have to depend upon singing. I like to act, too, so I think it's going to be good. I hope I am good in it."

"The book deals with pills, to some extent," declared one reporter. "Have you found that prevalent around show business people?"

"Well, I find it prevalent around newspaper people, too," Judy quipped with a smile, much to the delight of those gathered.

Following the event, Judy accompanied Liza to a final fitting with wedding gown designer Annemarie Gardin. Liza's marriage to Peter Allen took place in New York City the following day.

Announcer: And now, *Monitor*'s Man on the Aisle, Leonard Probst, with the story of one of the legendary figures of show business.

Leonard Probst: New York looked like Hollywood last Wednesday—at least a small corner of it did. It reminded me of the old Hollywood when big studios did things in a big way. A movie studio had sent out telegrams the night before, alerting the press to The Event. If we would come to the Versailles Room of the St. Regis Hotel, a fashionable place on Fifth Avenue, we would see Judy Garland, the girl who had grown up in Hollywood, the girl who had played in *The Wizard of Oz* thirty years ago. Weekly news magazines, television, radio, and newspapers sent reporters. About fifty of us waited. Twenty-five minutes late, in she came with three press agents. Miss Garland was wearing a black dress with a yellow pillbox hat on her head. She looked thinner and tense. She carried an empty gold cigarette holder in one hand and occasionally fingered a triple strand of pearls at her neck with the other. She seemed frightened, but eager to be accommodated. She took a glass of water and said, "See, it *is* water," and then asked for orange juice. The story, which we all knew before we arrived, was that Judy Garland has been signed for a leading role in the film adaptation of *Valley of the Dolls*, a novel by Jacqueline Susann. "Dolls," Miss Susann confessed, was the name she had made up for pills, and the book is about people in show business who take too many pills. Although we didn't know she'd be there, Miss Susann entered the room and was followed by Judy. The first ten minutes was taken up by still photographers taking pictures of Judy and Jacqueline. Then they cleared off and the questions began. [. . .] The role Judy Garland will play in Hollywood is said to be based on a musical comedy star, Ethel Merman. How did Judy feel about that? As they used to say in Hollywood, *"Here's Judy!"*

Judy Garland: Well, I've heard many people say that it's Ethel Merman. Of course they say that about every book . . . not about Ethel [*all laugh*] . . . but, I mean, I don't really know whether Jacqueline had anyone in mind.

Jacqueline Susann: No, it's a composite picture. I've have people say, "Is it true Ethel Merman doesn't talk to you now?" And I say, "Well, we didn't talk *before* I wrote the book. We just don't talk louder! [*All laugh.*]

LP: Jacqueline Susann explained it was OK to play what at first might seem to be an unsympathetic character.

JS: You know a lot of people think that it's a brutal picture of a star. It's not. It shows how unhappy the star is up there with all the encroachments of success [. . .] It's a sad commentary, and there are so many stars, I think, who gets those telegrams being invited to every opening, every place, and then there's a mad scramble of "Where do we get an escort?"

JG: It's a funny thing, but I imagine a lot of people think, "Oh, we can't call her because she's obviously so busy," you know. So you just sit and stare at the phone wanting it to *ring*, even if it's the wrong number.

Press: I wouldn't want to hold you to a remark you made in '63, but you said, "Tragedies bore me. I don't want to have anything to do with them anymore. I'm interested in things that are fun." What changed your mind?

JG: I know that I'm not interested in being written about as tragedy's child as a person, you know. In a movie, if the role happens to call for a comedy, I can play that. If it calls for drama, I like anything like that. I think I was pretending how I like to . . . Having been written [about] for too long as just a woman who walks around *crying* all the time for no reason at all. Because I don't sing "Over the Rainbow" all the time! [*All laugh.*]

Announcer: The regular news conference ended and the star was then made available for a personal interview.

LP: Miss Garland, you were fourteen [*sic*] when you played Dorothy in *The Wizard of Oz*, and now at the age of forty-five you're about to play Helen Lawson, the tough, aging . . .

JG: I'll be forty-five in June. Let's not punch me up anymore, all right? [*Laughs.*]

LP: [You're about to play the] tough, aging Broadway musical comedy star in *Valley of the Dolls*. Is there any way to age properly in public when you're before the public eye?

JG: I think anybody can age well if they have a little intelligence and a little humor, whether they be in the public eye or not. It's a matter of balance, and the joy of the vines of life, and for your children. . . .

LP: Well, you're returning to Hollywood after a few years' absence, right?

JG: No, I'm returning to motion pictures. But don't say this is a comeback because, I must say, if [I do] one more comeback I'll have to just get *embarrassed!* I think I've done seventy-five so far! No, this is the first picture I've done in about two and a half years.

LP: Your daughter, by the time this gets on the air, will be married. Are you happy about this?

JG: Well, I'm just as excited as I can be because I think he's a fine young man and I think they're going to be very, very happy. They're very much in love. You can't ask for more than that.

LP: Judy Garland, nearly forty-five, married four times, is about to return to Hollywood to do another film. This is Leonard Probst, NBC News, New York.

TV INTERVIEW

BARBARA WALTERS | **March 6, 1967,** *Today* **(NBC News)**

Filmed in Judy's suite at the St. Regis Hotel, this interview was one of the earliest by up-and-coming broadcast journalist Barbara "*Today* Girl" Walters. Many years later, Walters recalled her appointment with Judy: "First of all, she kept me waiting more than four hours and I almost walked out. But, you know, it was Judy Garland! And then when she came out . . . she was *adorable* and I remember the laughter." Lorna and Joe joined their mother for the interview. Judy wore a light blue dress with navy trim belonging to Lorna. "She didn't have a dress of her own, and she was very tiny," recalled Walters. The edited piece aired on *Today* in two segments on the morning of March 16.

Segment One

Barbara Walters: You came here, of course, for your daughter Liza's wedding, which suddenly makes me feel very old, because I can remember, the way most of us can, when Liza was quite a little girl. Are you happy about this wedding?

Judy Garland: Oh, indeed, indeed, indeed! He's a marvelous boy, you know . . . Peter Allen. And she's a lovely lady. She's not a child. And they've been engaged for over two years. And I'm just terribly happy and terribly proud.

BW: Did you cry?

JG: No, I thought I was going to, and then I was so happy I didn't feel like crying at all.

BW: Did you give Liza any advice about marriage?

JG: No, I don't think so. I don't think I can *qualify* because I have not been too successful myself about marriage. Just in my children. But the thing is, she is a wise girl and she's very in love. And he's a very lovely guy who's mad about her, and you can't ask for more than that.

BW: I was reading a quote recently and you said, "I wish people would stop talking about my comebacks and my unhappiness. I have had so many happier days. I have so many happy days now." Do you recall saying this? It was just in the papers recently.

JG: Yes, well that's true, you know. Maybe it will distress a lot of people, but I've had an awfully nice life. [*Laughs.*] I really have had.

BW: I think it will surprise a lot of people who kind of like to think of you as a . . .

JG: Tragedy.

BW: Yeah, the poor little rich girl . . . the—

JG: [*Interrupting.*] No, never rich, just poor. And sad!

BW: Well, not that, but in the sense that . . . the one who had everything, but yet, you know, wasn't happy. What are the things that bring you the . . . I don't even have to ask you. I was going to say, "What are the things that bring you so much happiness today?" and you're hugging one of them right now.

JG: [*Hugging and gently stroking Joe's head.*] Well, first of all, my two friends here, myself, my oldest daughter, my son-in-law, my future, my past, my present, and my audiences. [*Pats Joe on the hip and smiles.*] And that ain't bad! [*Laughs.*]

BW: No, that's not bad. And I count myself among those of your audience who love you so much, so I'm doing this interview with great joy for me.

JG: Thank you, Barbara.

BW: Are you looking forward to being a grandmother? That's going to happen one of these days.

JG: Can't *wait!*

BW: Really?

JG: I can't *wait!* I want [Liza] to have a baby *immediately,* and then she can see the baby for only twenty-five minutes and then I'll be a babysitter.

BW: If you hadn't been an actress—if you can imagine being anything else but an actress—what do you think you might have wanted to be?

JG: Happily married. And just a nice lady.

BW: Do you think it's possible to be an actress and be happily married?

JG: Well, I don't think anybody who married me thought so, but *I* think it's possible. [*Laughs.*] I think . . . I don't see any reason . . . but I think it's probably a little difficult. It seems that every man that I've ever met, they sort of . . . well, they *know* that I'm Judy Garland when they start to go with me, and then the minute they sort of get entangled with me they say, "You know how difficult it is to be . . ." Well, why didn't they think of that before they, you know, took me out the first time? I don't know. I don't think I'm that difficult. [*To Lorna*] Do you? Or does it seem . . . It hasn't been too rough on . . . [*laughs*].

Lorna Luft: *No!*

JG: But at any rate, I would like that. I'm a good cook, by the way. And I think you can vouch . . . [*pointing microphone toward Lorna, who shies away*]. Say something good!

LL: *Yes!* [*All laugh.*]

BW: [*Laughs.*] No fair!

Joe Luft: She makes the best shepherd's pie!

JG: Shepherd's pie they like, yes.

BW: That's a pretty good recommendation. Do you want to get married again?

JG: You talking to Joe or . . .

BW: I'm talking to you. Joe hasn't been married *yet*!

LL: He caught the bridal bouquet at the wedding twice.

JG: Yes, he did! [*Kissing Joe's cheek.*]

BW: Ah. But do you think you do? Is it something that . . .

JG: I don't want to rush into it, no. I think I was married the first time when I was six months old, it seems to me. No, I'm not anxious to get married again. I don't see any necessity for that. Unless you've got somebody in mind . . . [*laughs*].

BW: Me? I don't know. You seem awfully nice. I'm going to look around. [*Judy laughs.*] Do you enjoy being recognized? I'm sure there's hardly a place you can go to where you're not.

JG: I don't like it too much. It's just that sometimes the lack of privacy . . . it's hard to just grow up in the public eye. And I'm a *terrible* eavesdropper. I *love* to eavesdrop and peek through keyholes, and I've never peeked through one keyhole without finding somebody looking back at me. [*Laughs.*] It's terrible!

BW: What are you the least tolerant of these days?

JG: The least tolerant? I'm the least tolerant of [*more deliberate*] any more lies or foolishness in print or spoken about me. That. And I think people should stop. I've never done anything. The only mistake I ever did . . . the only harm I ever did was sing "Over the Rainbow," [*Barbara laughs*] so I don't think that I should get any more than a *traffic ticket* for that! But to be called anything that is not true, I don't like it. I really have gotten to the age where I rebel, and I'm gonna *hit*, hit back!

BW: One of the very good things about television is that what you say is there. Nobody can put the adjectives to it. I can't. You know, I can't describe you. Everybody will see you as you are. So since we have this opportunity, are there any lies you like to clean up or correct? Are there things that have been said about you for years that you feel are untrue?

JG: Well, I think the fact that some kind of pattern of publicity started when I was very young and was becoming a famous person. This business of anybody implying that I'm either addicted to carpets or drinking or pills or . . . I wouldn't have had time to learn a *song* if I'd been as sick as they've printed me all the time. And temperamental. I haven't been able to *afford* to be temperamental. And I don't want to be temperamental. Now, nobody ever sues for slander because, obviously, all lawyers just say, "Well, forget it!" But the lawyer doesn't have to worry. But the newspapers—the scandal sheet—sells two million dollars. I mean two million copies. Or maybe makes two million dollars just with the front page JUDY GARLAND ADMITS SHE'S BROKE. And then it's all in quotes by a man that you've never—[to Lorna] pardon me, darling—I've never met. They must be stopped! That must be stopped! I want the money, I want a public apology, and I want them to be taken to court.

BW: Mm-hm.

JG: And I don't see any reason. I'm not a member of the Mafia. I'm not a cruel person. Why should I be run over? And why should my children be subjected to that kind of thing?

BW: Of course, we have heard for years about the concerts where there were times when you couldn't appear, and there was some conversation when you were doing a television show, and, of course, there *are* these rumors that "she's difficult, she's difficult, she's . . ." How do they—

JG: [*Interrupting.*] Well, I'm about as difficult as a daisy. I really am. Now, I do have times when I get the flu, and that's when they say, "Well, you know about *her* . . . it's not the flu." I catch cold now and then, but this business of being difficult is not true. It really isn't true. I may be pressed for time because I've been working so hard all my life, but I like to laugh, I like to have a bag of popcorn, go on a roller coaster now and then . . . but the fact of this thing about . . . People who haven't met me say, "Oh, I'm afraid to meet her!" Well, *why* are they afraid to meet me? I'm not going to hurt any[body], *bite* them, or have a conniption fit in the middle of the room. I like people. But they don't call me . . . [to Joe] but you call me, will ya? You know my number? [*Laughs and hugs Joe.*] No, I think my only anger is that it's just been such damn foolishness—[*to Joe and Lorna*] excuse me—about this difficult business. I've been working for forty-three years. Now, if I were as difficult or as ill [as they say], I wouldn't have been able to be working for forty-three years, so I think it's time to put a stop to all that.

BW: I heard recently that you no longer sing "Over the Rainbow." I hope that's not true.

JG: [*Shocked.*] Of course it's not true!

BW: Good.

JG: That's the best song ever written.

BW: Well, someone had said, "Judy Garland isn't singing 'Over the Rainbow' anymore."

JG: Now, who said that?

BW: A reporter. And I just heard it last week.

JG: Really? And what does his wife do? Sing?

BW: [*Laughs.*] I think she sings "Over the Rainbow."

JG: She probably . . . [*Laughs.*]

BW: Someday there will be a great deal of applause for a young lady named Lorna. And we asked Lorna earlier if she would sing something for us. This is *extremely* difficult to do, to sing without accompaniment, and in advance I want to tell you how grateful we are. Would you do something for us now?

LL: Well, I'll try. I do have a sore throat [*clears throat*] because of the weather in New York, but here goes nothing. [*Judy and Joe laugh and applaud as Lorna belts Petula Clark's "I Know a Place."*]

JG: Brilliant, Lorna! *Marvelous!* [*Leans in to kiss Lorna's neck.*]

BW: Lorna, you're wonderful and I thank you.

JG: Say, I must say, you're terribly good! Isn't she marvelous? There was no accompaniment.

BW: This is one time it wasn't motherly pride. You *are* marvelous.

LL: Thank you!

JG: [*Instructing the crew and others around the room.*] Everybody applaud now. Go ahead. Joe? [*Clapping.*]

BW: And we applaud you, too, Judy Garland. You've been a wonderful interview today.

JG: Why, thank you, Barbara.

BW: I'm so pleased to have had the opportunity to talk to you.

JG: [*Nudging Lorna.*] I'm so *impressed*!

BW: Thank you, Joe, as well.

JL: You're welcome! [*Judy smiles and laughs.*]

Segment Two

BW: How old were you when you got your first job?

JG: Thirty months.

BW: What was it?

JG: I was *singing*!

BW: Were you *really*? When you were that young? Did someone push you on a stage?

JG: My grandmother. I sang "Jingle Bells."

BW: And was that the beginning of the whole career?

JG: Yeah . . . been a long one!

BW: Yes. Did you have a stage mother, as we have heard about, the stage mothers?

JG: One that wouldn't quit! [*Shaking her head and smiling.*] My mother was truly a stage mother. [*To Lorna.*] A *mean* one, wasn't she? Well, you didn't know her, thank goodness, but she used to . . . . She was very jealous because she had absolutely no talent. [*To Lorna.*] Now she's gonna knock my earring off! [*Both giggle.*] My mother . . . You know, my mother died and whenever I talk about her—and I *should* because she was so wicked—but whenever I start to talk about her she inevitably [*gestures*] knocks one earring off. So she's still around. So, now Mother, [*pointing and looking upward*] you behave yourself! She would sort of stand in the wings when I was a little girl and if I didn't feel good, if I was sick to my tummy, she'd say, "You get out and sing or I'll wrap you around the bedpost and break you off short!" So I'd go out and sing.

BW: When you look back at your childhood . . .

JG: [*Groans.*] Ugh!

BW: Should I forget the whole period?

JG: [*Groans.*] Ugh! No, it's all right. [*Feigns panic, then smiles.*]

BW: Was there any part of it that was happy?

JG: Yeah, one day, about . . . [*laughs*]. No, let's see. I was . . . I didn't mind it too much when I was in vaudeville. You know, I wasn't always a movie star. I was on stage for ten years and that was kind of fun because Mickey Rooney was in vaudeville, too, and Donald O'Connor, and we didn't have the pressures that, later, we had when we got into movies. We used to play tag or backstage sometimes we'd run into the wings 'cause it was always dark. 'Cause we were in kind of *rotten* vaudeville where they ran movies and then threw five acts of vaudeville on in between a movie. And then they'd run the movie again and another show. We did nineteen shows a day, but I liked that better. I didn't want to get in the movies at *all*!

BW: When you were growing up in those Hollywood days, did you have dates? Did you go out at all?

JG: No, we worked all the time! We worked night and day. I've never been to a prom. We went to school on the lot and in those days you worked, oh, six days a week. and Mickey Rooney and I, for instance, would work sometimes seventy-two hours at a time.

BW: Do you still see Mickey Rooney at all?

JG: I see him whenever I can. He's the most *marvelous* gentleman and the most . . . well, I think he's the world's greatest talent and the loveliest person, too. But we never went out together. He liked other girls, which kind of miffed me for a while. No, I'd grown up with him in vaudeville anyway. . . . Neither one of us grew very tall. They worked us so hard we became Munchkins! [*Laughs.*]

BW: You know what I must ask you, before I forget? We used to read that you were dieting and I've said several times in this interview you are so tiny and you look to me, oh, I'd say about seventeen. Do you still have to diet?

JG: No, I don't have to. Finally I don't have to. About . . . [*to Lorna*]. When was it? About two years ago I went on a thirty-day fast. I fasted without vitamins or anything. I just had a cup of tea in the daytime and a cup of tea in the evening. And that seemed to sort of balance my metabolism, so I don't think I'll ever have a problem with gaining weight anymore, you know.

BW: I'd never realized that you were so tiny. Movies and television are very deceiving and when I saw you come out of the room . . . which is why I keep talking about what a little girl you look like. Could I ask you to stand up next to Lorna . . .

JG: My daughter . . .

BW: . . . so that the world can see that you're a very small young lady?

JG: Very small . . .

BW: And you're not . . . Well, you took your shoes off, I noticed.

JG: Well, I wear those four-and-a-half-inch heels so I can look like I have some status and . . . [*To Lorna.*] Come on, let's stand up and be counted, shall we? Will the real Lorna Luft stand up? Now, this is ridiculous, you know, when I try to say, [*looking up to Lorna*] "Liza [or] Lorna, you shouldn't stay out so late!"

BW: It's not like you can bawl them out when they're an inch or so taller than you are.

JG: Well, I'm only four feet eleven, you know. I'm glad that my daughters are taller.

BW: A lovely daughter. I just wanted everyone to see how tiny . . . [*Judy stands on tiptoes, looks down at Lorna and kisses her on the cheek.*] There we go!

JG: Can we sit down?

BW: Yes! You can sit down.

JG: [*To Joe.*] Do you want to stand up?

JL: No.

JG: OK! [*Laughs.*]

BW: Should we point out—I'm about to—that you're wearing your daughter Lorna's clothes today?

JG: Yes!

BW: A very pretty little dress and coat. [*To Lorna.*] How do you feel about that, Lorna?

LL: Well, we wear the same size clothes. I can't fit into Mama's clothes, but she can fit into mine. When I get a dress I usually get two! [*Judy laughs.*]

BW: We all remember *The Wizard of Oz* with so much joy and it's such a happy picture. Was it happy for you to make it?

JG: I enjoyed it very much. And I enjoy it today. [*To Lorna.*] I think you and I looked at it last time and it was all this *crying*! [*Laughs.*]

BW: I wondered. I was going to ask Lorna. What do you think of it?

LL: Oh, I just love it, you know. It's a classic, you know. It'll never die. You know?

BW: Do you feel as if you're looking at your mother?

LL: Oh, yes! But when you look at it you can really believe that's happening. It's not like something like a cartoon. You can *believe* there is a place called Oz.

BW: And your mother was just the age that you are now when she made it. [*Lorna nods her head.*] That must make you feel a little odd, doesn't it?

LL: No, not really.

JG: [*Laughs.*] Oh, darling . . .

BW: What about you, Joe, have you seen it?

JL: Yeah, and I could just watch it for a million times. [*All laugh.*] I never get tired of it.

BW: Aww.

OVER THE RAINBOW AND INTO THE VALLEY GOES OUR JUDY

JOHN GRUEN | April 2, 1967, *New York / World Journal Tribune Magazine*

"The sob queen of all time, Judy Garland had come to town," John Gruen recalled in his fascinating memoir, *Callas Kissed Me . . . Lenny Too!* "I instantly alerted the [*New York*] *Times* and asked to do the interview. I was overjoyed and hastened to prostrate myself at her feet, because, needless to say, I was one of her most ardent fans. . . . I desperately needed to come face to face with this forty-five-year-old monument to suffering, this paragon of survival and showbiz glitz and glitter."

Gruen's interview with Judy was conducted on March 9, 1967, but never appeared in the *Times*. Instead, the encounter was detailed in the *New York* magazine supplement to the short-lived *World Journal Tribune*, a hybrid newspaper with circulation limited to newsstand sales around the city. The publication survived a mere eight months, but *New York* was soon revamped as a glossy standalone magazine and has remained popular for many decades. This particular issue was one of the first known appearances of the now familiar *New York* typeface.

Garland was in town, staying at the St. Regis Hotel. She came for two reasons: to attend her daughter Liza Minnelli's wedding to actor Peter Allen and to hold a press conference, arranged by 20th Century Fox, about her forthcoming role in *Valley of the Dolls,* Jacqueline Susann's epic tribute to Hollywood and Broadway stardom at its most drug-drenched and sex-besotted. Miss Garland's role will be that of Helen Lawson, an aging queen of Broadway musicals who, as a recent ad informs us, "had the talent to get to the top—and had the claws to stay there."

This talony description does not really fit our Judy. Indeed, the character named Neely O'Hara comes much closer to the mark. Neely's blurb reads: "To her, stardom was too many minks, too many martinis and men." In effect, since the appearance of Susann's best-seller, the guessing games as to who was modeled after whom have been running rampant and Judy Garland's name has been high on the list as approximating the beautiful, desperate Neely.

Be that as it may, someone else will play that role because Judy has grown too old for the part. She is 45—not really old, not really young—about midstream in a life which, in terms of emotional investment, has left inner scars.

I appear at the St. Regis at 7 PM on the last day of Miss Garland's visit to New York. The plan is that we quietly dine together and talk about a million things. When I arrive, her suite is alive with children, grown-ups, ringing phones, and with Miss Garland herself, the center of all the commotion. Her daughter Liza, now Mrs. Peter Allen, greets me at the door. The Garland energy, enthusiasm and humor clings to this girl as to a magnet; she's an uncanny duplicate of her legendary mother.

Also on hand are Miss Garland's two children by Sid Luft, 14-year-old Lorna and 11-year-old Joe. They are both beautiful, Lorna in a pale-blonde, blue-eyed way, and Joe in a dark, intense, essentially mysterious way. Delores Cole [wife of Judy's conductor Bobby Cole] is present too, as is Liza's husband and a producer-friend of Miss Garland's.

Suitcases are open on the beds, clothes hang from hangers or lay on chairs and couches. Phonograph records, mainly of Judy and Liza, are strewn around the room. There are flowers, letters, bills, messages, photographs and empty glasses on the various tables of the three-room suite.

There, in the midst of this last-minute-in-New York chaos, stands Judy Garland. She's rail-thin, her sleeveless black dress emphasizing the thinness. Her face is gaunt; the eyes, enormous. There is electricity in her presence, but she seems disconnected just now. She reels around a bit, her speech comes in splutters, but she's cheerful, friendly, apologetic for the mess—and she's frantic. She had forgotten all about our dinner.

It takes one hour before children are sent off to their friends, before she finishes a private chat with her producer-friend, before she finally settles back on the couch, ready to talk to me.

"I can't keep track of time," she says, running her fingers through her hair. "I'm completely discombobulated. Let's please not go out to dinner. Let's have something sent up. I'm in the mood for some shrimp. And let's have a drink!"

"You know something? Someone came up to interview me this afternoon and said that people are saying I hit the bottle. Now, what does that mean—hit the bottle? Does it literally mean smacking the bottle? Or does it mean that I like to drink? I told the girl that I like to drink iced tea, like to drink soup, like to drink vodka and tonic. And, anyway, what kind of a question is *that?*"

Miss Garland is touchy on the subject of drinking. She has a natural anxiety about it. There is, alas, some truth to the gossip. But on this evening, while a glass or two of vodka and tonic does get put away, and while food arrives and does not get touched, Judy Garland seems very much her infectiously cheerful self. If I sense anxiety, it seems centered on one immediate problem, a problem that becomes more and more intense as phone calls from California keep interrupting our talk. Finally the subject of the California calls becomes clear, as Miss Garland in a somewhat shaky voice announces that the banks are foreclosing her Hollywood house.

"People are always keeping reality away from me. It's perfectly awful! It's awful finding out about things after the wolf is at the door. I don't understand it at all. This house thing is just like some of the other experiences I've had. Like the time this dear friend called to say that he was going to rent a car for me for life! The car was a lemon to begin with, but I was glad to have it and I thought it was marvelous of my friend to pay the bills on it.

"So I rode it around, never dreaming that after some months a huge bill would arrive charging me for the rental. I mean, that bill was astronomical but nobody ever bothered to tell me that I was now paying for it and not my dear friend.

"Or the time CBS rented a piano for my use while we were taping my television series. Again, after being reassured that CBS was paying for the rental, bills started pouring in charging the piano rental to *me!*

"I really don't know what happened with the house. Well, if worse comes to worse, I can always pitch a tent in front of the Beverly Hilton and Lorna can sing gospel hymns! That should see us through, somehow.

"In a way I'm glad they're taking the house. It's too big, too impractical. Besides, the man who lived there before didn't love his wife. That sort of put a pall on it from the beginning! There are acres of gardens, and a swimming pool, and the place needs at least four servants and four gardeners to keep it in shape. I never really liked it. It looks like a Gloria Swanson reject. I say good riddance!"

Everything is spoken with an anxious laugh. There is no bitterness, no anger. There is nervousness, however. A continuous lighting of cigarettes, an abrupt rush into an adjoining room to fetch a jacket, a tense choreography of gestures, all contrive to charge the atmosphere with a tension at once distracting and distressing.

Judy Garland has not appeared in a film since *I Could Go On Singing*, made in England in 1962. It was not a success, although Garland fans would have it otherwise. In the meantime she has concertized widely and her fame remains undisputed. Still, there have been arid periods, difficult periods during which creditors, an unkind press and personal traumas have somewhat tarnished the image of a glowing, courageous personality.

When Fox asked her to sign for *Valley of the Dolls*, she accepted immediately.

"So I'm cast in the part of an older woman. Well, I *am* an older woman. I'm not an ancient woman, but I can't go on being Dorothy for the rest of my life, now can I? Besides, there are bills to be paid, groceries to be bought and children to feed. I'm delighted to be in *Valley of the Dolls* although my slanderous press already has me walking off the set! Mind you, the set hasn't even been built, but already they have me walking off it!

"It's this kind of ugly slander that keeps me out of work. What am I supposed to do about it? I really need to work. I'm happiest when working, and when I work I give a lot.

"Sure there are mishaps, but what performer doesn't meet up with them? Sure it was awful when I arrived for a concert in Chicago and my voice gave out. I felt awful, but I swear to you I wanted to sing like anything. And I told all these people, all 5,000 of them, I told them I just couldn't sing anymore—that nothing would come out. I mean, I offered to do some acrobatics. After all, I did start out in show business as an acrobat. Besides, I couldn't bear losing all that money! Well, they understood. They let me off the hook!

"My job is entertaining. Fortunately I'm mad about an audience. I really, truly appreciate anyone taking time out and spending money to hear me sing and, believe me, I love singing for them. No matter how many people hurt me, when that orchestra starts playing . . . *I sing!*"

Judy's eyes light up and her words, spoken with that poignantly familiar break in the voice, ignite countless images of Garland singing all her songs, responding to the cheering crowds, transporting those who have cherished her ever since *The Wizard of Oz* and "Over the Rainbow" have made her name synonymous with heartbreak and bittersweet joys.

We touch on her legend. Garland gets up with a short laugh. She walks around the room, takes another sip of her drink, lights another cigarette. "If I'm such a legend, then why am I so lonely?"

"If I'm such a legend, then why do I sit at home for hours staring at the damned telephone, hoping it's out of order, even calling the operator asking her if she's *sure* it's not out of order? Let me tell you, legends are all very well if you've got somebody around who loves you, some man who's not afraid to be in love with Judy Garland!

"I mean, I'm not in the munitions business! Why should I always be rejected? All right, so I'm Judy Garland. But I've been Judy Garland forever. Luft always knew this, and Minnelli knew it, and Mark Herron knew it, although Herron married me strictly for business reasons, for purposes of his own. He was not kind to me.

"But I bear them no malice. Sid Luft turned out to be a nice man, after all, and Vincente is also very nice. They've given me beautiful, talented children. I haven't made out so badly, even though I often find it hard raising my kids without a father.

"I'm glad Liza is married, glad she's got a good career ahead of her, glad we're friends. As for Lorna and Joey, well, I guess I've uprooted them a lot, and I've not been very progressive about their education. I've even spanked them at times. But they're marvelous children and Lorna is already showing fantastic signs of becoming a fabulous singer. I think Lorna will make it very, very big one day."

Now Judy goes into another room. She quickly reappears with a record. "It just kills me about this record. Mercury pressed it in 1964 and never released it.* They say I sound lousy on it. They say I'm not up to snuff. Now just listen to this record and tell me if I sound lousy on it."

Judy puts the test pressing on the machine and a song [the title song] from Noël Coward's *Sail Away* starts it off. Judy comes on singing it in an up-beat tempo and the voice comes across fast, loud and clear. This is followed by "Something's Coming" from *West Side Story*, which Judy sings with that held-in, always charged intensity of hers.

As the song accumulates momentum, Judy in the room sings along with Judy on the record, throwing up that arm, hunching her body, now raising herself on the balls of her feet and belting out the song, now stopping and laughing and saying "Christ! That doesn't sound bad! That song works!"

The record spins along. Next comes "Just in Time" ("Listen to the key changes in there, will you. Doesn't that just kill you?"). Judy sings along again, her voice warm and supple, always a bit trembly.

The foreclosure of the house forgotten, the slander forgotten, the loneliness forgotten, Judy sings with Judy on the unreleased record and nothing really seems to matter. She's up there giving a show and she knows she's got everyone in the palm of her hands because she's Judy Garland and there's nobody— but nobody—like her.

---

*The intended album, *Judy Takes Broadway*, was recorded in a "live" recording session on April 26, 1962. Judy was suffering from laryngitis and unable to complete the recording. The project was shelved until 1989 when it was released with bonus material as *Judy Garland Live!*

TV INTERVIEW

JACK PAAR | May 7, 1967, *A Funny Thing Happened on the Way to Hollywood*

Videotaped at NBC's Studio 6B in New York's Rockefeller Center, this Jack Paar television special aired May 14, 1967.

Jack Paar: Somewhere over the rainbow is a land called Oz, which bears a striking resemblance to the Hollywood of the late '30s. In that enchanted land, good triumphs over evil and in breathtaking color, and people never lose their innocence, least of all little Dorothy from Kansas. But quite a bit of water has flown under the bridge since Dorothy first flew over that rainbow. In the intervening years, Oz and Hollywood have made a star of Dorothy, made her famous, made her grow up. The very talented stardom comes fast. Learning to live with it sometimes takes a little longer. No one knows that better today than the girl whose singing has a quality of heartbreak, ours or hers: the great Judy Garland.

[Judy enters to applause, carrying a broom, as she mimics sweeping the stage floor.]

Judy Garland: Oh, my goodness gracious!

JP: I see you found work back there. *[Audience laughs as Paar notes Judy's short skirt.]* And certainly your *knees* are over the rainbow, sweetie! *[Audience laughs.]*

JG: These are supposed to be the new knees.

JP: Well, honey, it's almost a thigh, I would say. *[Audience laughs.]*

JG: I don't know, it's not *mine*. [*Audience laughs.*]

JP: Well, whoever's it is. How are you, darling?

JG: Fine, darling, how are you?

JP: I'm glad you're here; glad you're happy and smiling.

[*Judy feigns tears.*]

JP: I was with her the other—

[*Judy interrupts with more false sob.*]

JP: . . . Last week . . . last week in Hollywood, and she could be in some of the most tragic situations sometimes.

JG: Oh, ho!

JP: But then she'll say, "You know, no matter how bad things are," and I waited for the rest, you know. "No matter how bad things are," she said, "they can always get worse." [*All laugh.*] "And somewhere behind every cloud . . ."

JG: There's a lot of rain! [*All laugh.*]

JP: Oh, but we're going to have fun tonight—we're going to talk—because no one can tell show business stories like Judy Garland. We've done shows in London, we've done them here and she has—

JG: Lost more friends! [*Audience laughs.*]

JP: Well, I suppose so. Did you ever hear from Dietrich after you told that story?*

JG: You know what? No, I never heard from her. That was my idea, you know.

JP: Do you ever hear from Deanna Durbin?

---

*Judy's hilarious telling of how Marlene Dietrich played a record of a [Dietrich] concert for Noël Coward, Judy and others was captured during a 1964 interview with Paar: "[Marlene] puts the record on and it was just applause . . . not one *note* of music! She didn't sing, there was no orchestra, just applause. And Noël turned to me in the middle and said, 'I hope there isn't another side.' And there *was!* . . . Marlene isn't one of our better singers, but she looks so marvelous."

JG: No, but her eyebrow is still around somewhere. [*Audience laughs.*] She had that one thick eyebrow that wouldn't quit.

JP: Just one eyebrow that went across?

JG: You know, just like a caterpillar. [*Audience laughs.*]

JP: What did you call her in those days when you . . .

JG: Hairy! [*All laugh.*]

JP: No, what'd you call her in those days when you . . .

JG: Edna Mae!

JP: All right, so now you've discovered that they've put you in pictures. Now there's Mickey Rooney. And is Lana Turner there yet?

JG: In school.

JP: Yeah, now they're on the M-G-M lot. Now these kids had to take regular lessons, do so many hours of work, run on the set and this one [*to Judy*] would run and do her little lessons and then run on *The Wizard of Oz* set and then have to read her lessons to Bert Lahr, who was a lion, and he would help her with her lessons. And can you imagine the kind of education you're gonna get doing history with a guy with whiskers? [*Judy laughs.*] It's absolutely *insane!* Tell 'em about Lana Turner and Mickey. Come on.

JG: What, you mean in school?

JP: *Anything!*

JG: Well, it was an odd class!

JP: They were an odd group.

JG: Yes. Freddie Bartholomew, myself, and Edna Mae Durbin. [*Gestures to brow; all laugh.*] And Mickey Rooney and Lana Turner. And we had a schoolteacher that wouldn't quit. She would be so mean. She scared me.

JP: Was she mean?

JG: Yes, a terrifying woman. And Mickey would always want to smoke, so he'd raise his hand and ask to go to the gentlemen's room as a little boy. Then Lana went out and smoked with him.

JP: Lana and Mickey were smoking.

JG: Yeah. And that's about all. I just burned inside of the schoolhouse.

JP: Was it strict? Did you actually graduate?

JG: Oh yes, I graduated from University . . . High School!

JP: High school.

JG: Yes, but with *strangers*!

JP: Was Mickey fun?

JG: Mickey was marvelous.

JP: And what was Lana like?

JG: She was wonderful, too. They were *smoking* all the time! [*All laugh.*]

JP: No wonder Mickey never grew up. Now we *know*! [*All laugh.*] Do you recall when the beautiful little thing came in, Elizabeth Taylor? Did you like her? Liz?

JG: With the chipmunks she had.

JP: Liz had a chipmunk?

JG: Yes.

JP: Is this true now, 'cause you've put me on?

JG: Called Nibbles.

JP: Nibbles?

JG: Yes.

JP: Let's hope it's Nibbles. [*All laugh.*]

JG: [*Nodding her head.*] Nibbles.

JP: Yes, and so what did Nibbles do?

JG: Not much.

JP: He didn't do much. And everywhere she went she had this little chipmunk. Everywhere she went, Mary had her little chipmunk, huh?

JG: *Elizabeth* had her little chipmunk.

JP: Did you like her then?

JG: Not very much. [*Audience laughs.*]

JP: You weren't so crazy on her, huh?

JG: No, she doesn't have very good manners.

JP: Really?

JG: No, and she has a *bad* voice.

JP: Her acting voice, you mean?

JG: Yeah. Somebody told her to *breathe* all the time she's talking. [*Produces an airy sound; audience laughs.*]

JP: Who did you like then?

JG: I liked Mickey Rooney. I liked Mr. Mayer.

JP: Did you like Mr. Mayer? [*Audience laughs.*]

JG: Yes, he was a very nice man.

JP: He was nice to you.

JG: Yes, he was a very great motion-picture maker.

JP: Did you like Jackie Cooper?

JG: I didn't know him.

JP: Didn't you know him?

JG: He was on another lot two blocks away.

JP: How about Freddie Bartholomew? You know he works in New York in an advertising agency?

JG: Yeah, he got smart.

JP: Would you ever see any of these people?

JG: Well, no. They wouldn't let us get together.

JP: They wouldn't?

JG: No. They wouldn't let us know we were a hit either.

JP: They never let you know?

JG: We found out though! [*Audience laughs.*]

JP: Hey, how about in *The Wizard of Oz*? That picture, they show it once a year and it must cost $300,000 or $400,000.

JG: Well, where's the money?

JP: I know. [*All laugh.*] Do you get a penny of that?

JG: *No!*

JP: Oh, I see. Well, what about the Moonchkins?

JG: Yeah, how about the . . . the *what?* [*Audience laughs.*]

JP: The Moo . . .

JG: The *MUNCHkins!*

JP: *MUNCHkins.* Yeah. Well, what did the Munchkins do? They were little dwarfs, weren't they?

JG: Well, they were very tiny. Yes.

JP: Were they little kids or little men?

JG: They were drunks. [*Audience laughs.*]

JP: They were little drunks? Wh-wh-wh-wh-what'd they . . . You've got me *stuttering!* [*All laugh.*] What'd they do? What'd they do?

JG: What'd they *do*?

JP: What'd the dwarfs do?

JG: Well, one of them who was about forty, a gentleman, asked me for dinner. And I couldn't say, "I don't wanna go out. I *can't* because you're a *midget*." I just said, "No, my mother wouldn't like it." And he said, "Ah, come on. Bring your ma, too!"

JP: How big was he?

JG: About two inches high. [*Audience laughs.*]

JP: Well, what could you do with him?

JG: I don't know . . .

JP: What could *he* do?

JG: Oh, they evidently did *a lot* because . . . [*Audience laughs.*]

JP: There was a lot of 'em!

JG: Oh, *hundreds and thousands*! And they put them all in one hotel room. Not one *room*, one hotel in Culver City. And they got smashed every night and they'd pick 'em up in butterfly nets! [*All laugh; audience applauds.*] They'd slam a tulip in their nose. Oh, the poor things. I imagine *they* get residuals. [*All laugh.*]

JP: What else are we gonna talk about?

JG: Well, whatever you want, darling.

JP: Well, let's see . . .

JG: We can always go back to Marlene . . . [*Audience laughs.*]

JP: Oh, Marlene.

JG: And her applause record.

JP: That's a funny thing. That didn't make her mad, huh? [. . .] But you are going home now, aren't you?

JG: No.

JP: Yes you are.

JG: You're going home.

JP: Well, we're going home together.

JG: Right.

JP: And . . .

JG: I don't wanna go home. You go home and I'll take over!

JP: No, no, no . . . [*All laugh; audience applauds; Judy kisses Jack.*] I gotta do a commercial. And God bless you and take good care of yourself.

JG: Good-bye!

[*Audience applauds; Judy picks up the broom and exits.*]

JUDY GEM
On Life

"I think [life] is to be enjoyed. And [it's important] to be economic in your life. Don't work too hard, don't live too hard. But laugh an awful lot. You must laugh a lot."

—To Barry Gray, July 1967

JUDY GEM
On Spirituality

"Of course I believe in God . . . because it's ridiculous to not believe in God . . . because I have proof [that He's there]. I've been protected and watched over, and my children have been. It's just a knowing and living knowledge that brings a great deal of comfort to me."

—To Barry Gray, July 1967

JUDY GEM
On "Over the Rainbow"

"[Am I] tired of 'Over the Rainbow'? Listen, it's like getting tired of breathing. The whole premise of the song is a question. A quest. At the end, it isn't, 'Well, I've found my world and I am a success and you and I will be together.' The lyric is having little bluebirds 'fly over the rainbow. Why, oh, why can't I?' It represents everyone's wondering why things can't be a little better."

—Cherry Hill (NJ) Press Conference, July 10, 1967

JUDY GEM
On Being Fired from *Valley of the Dolls*

"I got fired again. Oh, I know the studio says I 'withdrew for personal reasons,' but don't believe a word of it. Judy Garland was fired, canned. Why, I don't know. . . . It's just as well, though. I wanted the part, I needed the money, but I have to be honest: *Valley of the Dolls* isn't my kind of motion picture. I don't want to be a harridan on the screen, and I don't think people want me to be."

—To *McCall's*, August 1967

JUDY GEM
On the Legend

"I've heard how "difficult" it is to be with Judy Garland. Do you know how 'difficult' it is to be Judy Garland? And for me to live with me? I've had to do it—and what more unkind life can you think of than the one I've lived? I'm told I'm a legend. Fine. But I don't know what that means. I certainly didn't ask to be a legend. I was totally unprepared for it."

—To *McCall's*, August 1967

JUDY GEM

On the Palace Theatre

"It's a Mecca of artists, an artist's goal. Everybody who wanted to attain a dignity—without doing a play—by doing variety or vaudeville, their main goal was to play the Palace Theatre. This theater was the home and the place of all the European and all the world's stars, and you feel that when you walk on. You have a knowledge of it, even if you don't know about it. It comes to you through the theater itself."

—To Martin Block, *Guard Session*, August 1967

JUDY GEM

On Reliability

"I think that thing about 'Will she come out?' 'Will she appear?' 'Will she be all right?,' is gone. People feel, 'Well, of course she'll be all right, of course she'll be here.' Because they've seen me around too many years and they finally feel a little more secure. I never have *wanted* to miss *any* show . . . I usually *did* appear."

—To Leroy F. Aarons, *Providence (R.I.) Journal*, August 1967

JUDY GEM

On Happiness

"I'd like to explain myself a little. So much of the past that has been written about me, has been so completely, just 'authored.' Not even correct. . . . I think that the nicest thing to say is that I enjoy my work, that I'm a very happy woman, a very healthy woman, and that I look forward to my shows every night, and am having a marvelous life. I've had press agents that I've paid, to whom I've said, 'Why don't they put that in a magazine?' And they've said, 'No, they're not interested in that. That's not news. You have to do something terrible.' I don't believe you do. I think it might be awfully smashing news for people to find out that I'm a very contented, healthy, happy woman."

—To Stephen Rubin, United Press International, August 1967

JUDY GEM

On President John F. Kennedy

"I can honestly say that I was very honored to be friends with President Kennedy. . . . I was allowed to call him on the phone because I'd get a bit confused about my television shows and it seemed to me an awful lot of slipshod business was going on. And if I got into wondering about state income tax or government tax, well, I thought it was all right to call the president of the United States. And he always took time to talk to me. . . . He took the calls. I think he probably took *lots* of calls. Not just mine. But he was a very good friend, a very fine president, and a very fine man. . . . Mrs. Lincoln was President Kennedy's private secretary and it always used to be kind of funny. I'd say, 'This is Judy Garland calling President Kennedy at the White House in Washington,' and there'd be a bit of confusion. I'd say, 'If you can't get through, ask for Mrs. Lincoln,' and the operator would always say, 'Whoa. This is . . . really . . . She's really *gone* now! It's Judy Garland. She thinks Abraham Lincoln is still in the White House and [she's] asking to talk to Mrs. Lincoln!'"

—To Dale Remington, *Monitor* (NBC Radio), September 1967

JUDY GEM

On Her Homosexual Following

"For so many years I've been misquoted and treated rather brutally by the press, but I'll be damned if I'll have my audience mistreated."

—To Irv Kupcinet, *Kup's Show* (Chicago), September 1967

JUDY GEM

On Her Cult Following

"Maybe I'm some kind of female Billy Graham."

—To *Asbury Park Press*, June 26, 1968

TV INTERVIEW

DICK CAVETT | **December 13, 1968,** *The Dick Cavett Show*

Judy appeared with actor Lee Marvin and Ida Kaminska, a classical Yiddish the-
ater actress, on one of the last episodes of the morning edition of *The Dick
Cavett Show*, prior to his move to the late-night lineup. The taping took place on
December 13, 1968, and the show aired three days later.

Cavett detailed his Judy encounter in an "Opinionator" post for the *New
York Times* dated August 15, 2008: "Judy Garland did my old ABC morning show
shortly before she died. (That tape is gone. It was reused to tape *Let's Make a
Deal*. Trust me.) I think it was [one of] her last television appearance[s]—1968.
And what a comedian! She was garrulous, witty, and wickedly funny. What they
say was true. She made you feel you were an old friend, while keeping you in
stitches. But afterward we couldn't get her out of the dressing room. I left the
theater and later walked back well after tape time, and she was still there. She
couldn't make a false move onstage and so [she] did all she could to delay leaving it; and, equally, leaving the cozy womb of the dressing room. She was home
in those two places. Leave them, and you are back in so-called real life—where
it seemed poor Judy made only false moves."

Judy was accompanied by songwriter John Meyer, who later wrote of their
two-month relationship in *Heartbreaker*. "Cavett asked her to sing," he recalled
in the memoir. "Bobby Rosengarden's band played an introduction and Judy
sang 'The Prayer,' the song I'd composed [. . .] She did not sing it well. For open-
ers, the song was only a week old, and she barely knew it. Secondly, her voice
was in ragged shape. So, in addition to cracking vocally, halfway through her
rendition, Judy lost track of the melodic line and had to finish on an uncertain,
upward surge."

Judy and John watched the airing of *The Dick Cavett Show from* their room
at the Hilton. "My God, he's nervous," Judy said, watching the host cross and

uncross his legs, and fiddling with the arm of the chair. "Why do I make everyone so . . . nn, un*com*fortable?"

"Because, Judes," Meyer said, "no one knows whether you're going to sing 'Over the Rainbow' or open your veins."

"Sometimes I do both . . . at the same time," she giggled.

Dick Cavett: Occasionally on this kind of show you have this introduction problem of starting out by saying there's nothing to say about our next guest that's not already been said many times. And I'm in that situation now, so you may write your own introduction to this. Everything has been said about my next guest, over and over and over. She's the only person I know named Judy Garland. Here she is.

[*Audience applauds as Judy enters to "Over the Rainbow."*]

Judy Garland: Well, here we are.

DC: Two kisses. Are you sure you know who I am? [*Audience laughs.*]

JG: Of course! Why do you think I kissed you twice?

DC: Yeah, and thank you for the flowers.

JG: That's all right. You gave them to *me*. [*Audience laughs.*] You gave me a whole bunch of them, actually.

DC: That's right.

JG: I gave two of them back.

DC: Yes, I cut those this morning from my little window box.

JG: You did? Did you grow—

DC: It's so nice to meet you.

JG: It's nice to meet you. I'm a great fan of yours.

DC: I can't understand that. [*Audience laughs.*]

JG: Well, I'll tell you all about it. It's because . . . Now, come on. You can't understand it? Don't be *ridiculous*.

DC: There are certain people in the industry who are so "big," as we say, that you can't imagine them watching you. I mean, I can't imagine you or Bob Hope sitting in front of a TV screen and seeing me.

JG: I can't imagine Bob Hope watching you because he'd probably be jealous of your humor! [*Audience laughs.*]

DC: Oh, undoubtedly.

JG: But I can imagine everybody else would.

DC: Yes, he's very jealous of me. He keeps having to go to Vietnam to get away from the pressure.

JG: Well, he creates *wars* when there isn't a war, just to get away from the house, maybe. Bob goes and does a show and all of a sudden there's a war when there wasn't one there before.

DC: I hadn't noticed that it was in that order, but it's an interesting theory. You know, your fans sometimes are so enthusiastic that when one goes to see you . . .

JG: One fan? Or . . . [*Audience laughs.*] I'm glad I've got one left.

DC: No, when a person goes to see you, it's almost hard to hear you sometimes because your fans just won't let you finish a song.

JG: That's because they sing better than I do. [*Audience laughs.*] No, what do you mean, Dick?

DC: I don't know! [*Audience laughs.*]

JG: Well, what are we talking about now?

DC: I was thinking . . .

JG: Why don't we go back to Bob Hope or the flowers and I'll come on again.

DC: That was the best entrance anyone has made on this show.

JG: You should have seen me dressing upstairs. Do you remember a man named Owen McGiveney? No, you're too young. Everybody's much too young. [*To guest Ida Kaminska.*] Even *you're* much too young! [*Audience laughs.*] Owen McGiveney did nothing but change clothes. He wasn't witty or anything. He was in vaudeville. He'd just come on in one outfit and run off in the wings and come out in a whole new outfit in two seconds, and everybody thought it was pretty good. And I was like Owen McGiveney upstairs. I had odd and very strange . . . I don't mean strange . . . *nice* people, but strangers, working on my hair and makeup, and if I came out looking well, it's simply because of my good spirit! [*All laugh; audience applause.*]

DC: I don't think I could have said that better myself.

JG: No kidding! I don't think I could . . .

DC: Strange people *do* handle you when you're on a show like this. It's an odd feeling to go from studio to studio, especially for a lady, and suddenly all these people descend on you and they start doing things and . . .

JG: And you haven't met them and there isn't time to get acquainted, you know, and sort of say, "Well, it's nice to see you again," because, in the first place you haven't seen them before [*audience laughs*], and all they say is "Allright, come on! You're on in *four seconds!*" and you've just gotten into the studio and you don't know who you're working with or what songs are going to be up, but you bloody well do it. And I *don't know why!*

DC: Really? You're beginning to question the reason for all this foofaraw after all these . . .

JG: Do you mean showbiz?

DC: Showbiz, yeah.

JG: The biz?

DC: The biz.

JG: I think it's *hideous.* [*Audience laughs.*] Except for the audiences. I like them but I don't like all the ... well . . .

DC: Junk that goes with it.

JG: . . . the bloodstained runners that separate the artist from the audience. [*To audience.*] Well, you know about that. You all know about that. Maybe you're out there. I don't know. You know about it.

DC: I've been wondering myself. Listen, when I come back I have . . . you can stay a while can't you?

JG: Where are we going? [*All laugh and audience applauds.*]

DC: That's a damn good question because I always say "We're going away," but we don't. We stay right here.

JG: Oh?

DC: Well, let's see if we go away when I snap my fingers.

[*Commercial break.*]

DC: We're back. Have you noticed that we're back?

JG: Are we?

DC: We weren't anywhere at all. You're right about that.

JG: I've done so many comebacks, it's . . . [*All laugh.*] I'm the *Queen* of the Comebacks! And I'm getting tired of coming back, I really am. I can't even go into a restaurant and have to go to the powder room without making a comeback when I come out. [*All laugh.*]

DC: Well, you'll make another one about six minutes from now, too, because we'll have another break then and we'll have another comeback. Then we'll go away and not have been anywhere.

JG: I've not had a break for a long time. Do you have coffee breaks?

DC: Coffee breaks?

JG: Do you stretch them with Juicy Fruit? [*Audience laughs.*]

DC: We stretch them with anything we can get. [*All laugh.*]

JG: How does it feel to be a legend? [*All laugh and applaud.*]

DC: At this moment, rotten! [*All laugh.*]

JG: No, I mean . . . oh, level with me.

DC: I'm so seldom asked.

JG: Well, people are so afraid of you, you know. They don't dare. How does it feel to be a living Statue of Liberty?

DC: Very, very gratifying. [*Audience laughs.*] And I find it when a kid like yourself comes along and shows a little promise, [*audience laughs*] it's a pleasure to be able to give you a break.

JG: Oh, gee.

DC: I know that a lot of important people are watching this show. [*Audience laughs.*]

JG: Oh, gee. I hope so.

DC: I could throw up from this! [*All laugh.*]

JG: Oh no! I've got my black dress on. [*Audience laughs.*] And I brought my hat just in case anything like that might happen.

DC: Oh!

JG: What else have you got to say for yourself?

DC: You said something about a coffee break. See, I have some. I never offer my guests my coffee. And I have some extra New York tap water here.

JG: Your rose or your glove? [*Singing tune of "People Will Say We're in Love" from* Oklahoma!] Ba ba bum! Ba ba bum! Ba ba bum! Ba ba bum-bum!

DC: And they said we couldn't get her to sing on the show. [*Audience laughs.*]

JG: That's it! [*All laugh and audience applauds.*]

DC: That's not only it, it's all we can afford.

JG: I don't know what those curtains . . . after the television series I did . . . which unfortunately is buried somewhere in Newark . . . [*Audience laughs.] *Why*, I don't know! All twenty-six shows. We didn't have those kinds of classy curtains, and so you've got a little more money than we all think.

DC: Well, listen, those curtains are going to be available shortly. [*All laugh.*]

JG: What do you mean?

DC: Well, they're marked down because we're closing out in a month. [*Audience laughs.*]*

JG: Well, when are you coming back? Not to bring up the . . .

DC: Well, I've made so many comebacks that . . . [*All laugh.*] I don't really know!

JG: Oh, copycat.

DC: Yeah, I took your material. Do unknown songwriters—they must— come to you with manuscripts clutched under their arms and in their sweaty palms?

JG: Unknown songwriters?

DC: [Are] unknown songwriters [wanting] you to do their numbers all the time. This must have gone on for years and years! What do you do about that?

JG: Well, first of all, everyone who sings has people send them songs that they write . . . you know, amateur songwriters. The first thing you do is make sure you send them back after you read them over because they'll sue the Dickens out of you if they don't get them back. However I've got to tell you, there was one marvelous man called Peter A. Follo. F-O-L-L-O.

DC: Follo?

JG: Follo. And he was rather rich, evidently, because he sent me . . . This was years ago, just after we had lost the war completely, and Pearl Harbor was just bombed out and we were desperate.

DC: In '41, this was?

---

*Cavett was referring to the morning show's cancellation and his impending move to a late-night time slot.

JG: I don't remember, either that or the Civil War, when I was born. [*All laugh.*] But anyway, Peter A. Follo sent me a group of his amateur songs and it was leather bound and beautifully copied. And they were just terrible, terrible, *terrible* songs.

DC: [*Laughs.*] They were?

JG: They were the worst songs. So I had to keep them, even if he sued me. He wrote one song . . . Now, mind you . . . Pearl Harbor, they weren't kidding, you know. And then, I think, was it Mr. [Henry J.] Kaiser and Hildegard had to get a lot of ships built quickly so that we could defend ourselves. In the meantime, Peter A. Follo sent me these songs, and the first one was a kind of a peppy song called "You Lousy Jippy Jippy Japs." [*Audience laughs.*] And I'm sure he meant it well, but it was kind of a . . .

DC: A frisky little number.

JG: Yeah, frisky! I think he was Japanese.

DC: Poking fun at our yellow enemies. [*Audience laughs.*] That was the way they talked during the war. Did you remember the posters that showed the Japanese as rats?

JG: No, that was Peter A. Follo. He was the rat.

DC: Yeah?

JG: [*Singing and clapping.*] *You lousy jippy jippy Jap / I hate you so much / I'll make you go 'n' buy a crutch / Just wait and see / You lousy jippy jippy Jap / You lousy big rats. . .* And that's the most I can remember of it. [*Audience applauds.*]*

DC: You know, I remember when that was on the Hit Parade! [*Audience laughs.*] That's really a terrible song, isn't it?

JG: Well, it didn't inspire too much. Mr. Follo was an enemy, obviously, but he also wrote a song for everybody to join the army. A mobilization song. And he didn't like rhyming. He wrote words and lyrics and it went:

---

* As Meyer explained in a recent interview with this editor, "Judy and I were both blind to the offensive implications of singing 'You Lousy Jippy Jippy Jap' on a TV show that would be seen by an international audience. It's a tribute to Judy's immense and legendary star power that the team sent to interview us before the taping didn't call us on this and bring to our attention the racist aspect."

[singing] Uncle Sam is going to build an army / Uncle Sam is going to build a navy / And if you dare to come upon our shores / If you do we'll punch you on your jaws [pronounced "jors"] / *We are gonna certainly surprise you / And we'll knock out / For the U and S and A is going to knock you flat."* [*Audience applauds.*]

DC: We'll be back after these messages!

[*Commercial break*]

DC: Oh, we're caught talking. You were talking about how you were at M-G-M in what they always called the great days of M-G-M. The business has told stories about Louis B. Mayer, who was such a dominating figure in those days.

JG: Well, he was a dominating figure. He was a very good movie maker. He *did* make good movies. I don't know what happened. Well, first of all he *died!* [*Audience laughs.*] Then I suppose everything went into television and separate productions and all that. But Mr. Mayer was always really quite nice . . . very stern . . . very nice to me . . . except that he . . . [*Laughs.*] Can I tell a terrible story?

DC: Tell a terrible story? This is the place! [*Audience laughs.*]

JG: There was an anxious producer by the name of Harry Rapf. R-A-P-F.

DC: Rapf?

JG: Yes, which made you stop and think anyway, his name. [*Audience laughs.*] And I had only been at Metro for about six months and they didn't know what to do with me because I was at that rotten age. You had to be two or eighteen. There was no in-between. So I just went to school a lot. And didn't learn a *thing,* by the way. Except one day Mr. Mayer sort of ordered me into a private dining room at M-G-M, and there were just a lot of men eating and congratulating Mr. Mayer on the food from the commissary. They obviously wanted to stay in good with Mr. Mayer.

DC: As if he cooked it himself. [*Audience laughs.*]

JG: Yes! He did! [*All laugh.*]

DC: That's not the end of the story, is it?

JG: No, no. But if you want it be . . . [*Audience laughs.*]

DC: I'm sorry, I'll shut up.

JG: No, no, don't!

DC: So all these men are in the . . .

JG: No, there were about seven men in there and they were all trying to stay in good or stay with Mr. Mayer, and I was twelve or thirteen, and I was always just given chicken broth, but not a noodle in it because I had "baby fat." Everybody can have baby fat. That's not necessarily a criminal offense. But no matter what I ordered, I'd always get this rotten chicken soup. And even in Mr. Mayer's private dining room. Well, Harry Rapf was sitting here, and he had the most astounding nose, because it was very aquiline, but it went way over to the desk. [*Audience laughs.*]

DC: And came back again.

JG: And kept getting in my soup! [*All laugh.*] And they were all eating like mad, these gentlemen. You know, [saying] "Here, have some of this and some of that," and bypassing me as I sort of tried to get . . . well, anyway . . . Harry Rapf was perspiring—I suppose he was going to be fired or something—and the apple pie came on and my eyes bugged out. And they were all just eating, and I thought, "What am I doing here? I haven't been in a movie!" And nobody's paying any attention to me. And Harry Rapf finally broke the silence by saying with his mouth full of apple pie, "My goodness, Mr. Mayer! This is the best piece of apple pie I've ever had in my whole mouth!" [*All laugh.*] He was so *nervous*. He meant to say "my whole life." I laughed and I was never asked back.

DC: I think that's a great story! [*Laughs.*]

JG: Can you believe that? "The best piece of apple pie in my whole mouth!"

DC: You know Lee Marvin, don't you?

JG: Yes, I do.

DC: He'll be here in a minute, and maybe between us we'll coax you to sing. But I don't want to say that because I know we weren't supposed to. We'll be back after this message.

[*Commercial break.*]

[. . .]

DC: Can't you sing something for us? I know that it wasn't meant for tonight. [*Audience applauds.*]

JG: I think I probably would have *died* if you hadn't asked me. [*Audience laughs.*]

DC: How did you get that mic in your pocket? [*Audience laughs.*]

JG: Somebody handed it to me . . . and with my eyesight . . . Oh, dear heaven! No, this is . . . do you really want me . . . well, of course you want me.

DC: Yes. Obviously the audience doesn't want you to, but we do. That burst of applause was . . .

JG: [*To audience.*] Don't you? Oh, yes you do. [*Audience applauds.*] There's a new song which is an innovation for me because I've been singing caval-cade for years. But there's a marvelous songwriter by the name of Johnny Meyers, [*sic*] who wrote [what] I think [is] a lovely song and I might as well crack my way through it if it's all right with you.*

DC: Give it a crack.

JG: OK.

[*Sings "God Bless Johnny" and "Prayer".*]†

---

*"After two months of sleeping with me," Meyer wrote in *Heartbreaker*, "she still didn't know there was no S on the end of my name."

†Accompanying Judy to the Cavett taping was one of John Meyer's last contributions to her career. "A day later I was flat on my back with a debilitating case of the flu, so severe it took me weeks to recover," he recalls. "I had to watch from my sickbed as Judy sang my songs on *The Tonight Show* ['It's All for You' and 'After the Holidays'] and *The Merv Griffin Show* ['I'd Like to Hate Myself in the Morning']. This period is a bittersweet memory, as it marked Judy's leap from me to the man who became her final husband, Mickey Deans. But he didn't watch her closely enough."

JUDY GEM

On the Gumm Sisters

"[We were] *really* bad. I'm so tired of talking about the Gumm Sisters on every program. I think we've gone out of style again, and we never really were *in* style. . . . You notice you never picked up your *Ladies Home Hoo-Ha* or whatever it was [and read] 'Here's what the Gumm Sisters are doing today.' Nobody knew about the Gumm Sisters because we were a *bad act.* . . . I started in the act when I was about two. The others . . . the other two ugly sisters . . . They were really ugly. I'm gonna *talk*, finally! They were mean and ugly. And my mother was really a wreck. . . . There's just no reason to try to be Dorothy Adorable . . . They were *terrible!*"

— *The Merv Griffin Show*, December 19, 1968

THE PRIVATE AGONY AND THE JOY OF JUDY GARLAND

CLIVE HIRSCHHORN | January 16, 1969, *Sunday Express* (London)

Clive Hirschhorn was the film and theater critic for *Sunday Express* when he interviewed Judy Garland during her five-week run at London's Talk of the Town nightclub. "She was very late, and got a slow clap from the audience," Hirschhorn recalled to Michael Riedel of the *New York Post* in 2012. "She went up on her lines, and you really didn't know if she was going to make the top notes without cracking."

Hirschhorn went back to see the show again the following week and found Judy to be in better voice. "I met her backstage after the show, and she was in a good mood. She joked that my socks were too short. She talked about how M-G-M had hooked her and Mickey Rooney on drugs to keep them awake during filming . . . but she didn't moan about it. There was no malice or sense of exploitation."

Two months later, Hirschhorn attended the wedding reception for Judy and fifth husband Mickey Deans at Quaglino's, a popular West End restaurant. The star-studded guest list included Albert Finney, Margaret Leighton, Veronica Lake, Bette Davis, James Mason, and Eva Gabor, but none attended. Waiters with serviettes on their arms were standing by waiting to serve champagne, "But nobody came," he remembered. "There were more waiters than there were guests. Judy Garland getting married for the fifth time—who gives a shit? It was very, very sad."

The next day's headline read: JUDY WEDS BUT STARS STAY AWAY. Judy was in disbelief. "I can't understand it," she told the writer. "They all said they'd come."

It was a splendid performance Judy Garland delivered the night I saw her in London's Talk of the Town, and a capacity audience kept yelling for more.

And who can blame them? For when 46-year-old Miss Garland is on form, there is no star in the world today more exciting to watch or more thrilling to listen to.

Her singing is a rare combination of private agony and affirmation of pure physical joy. You cannot simply sit back and take her artistry for granted; you have to participate in it—share it with her. And if you're not quite sure why the atmosphere in the room is never the same after she has left the stage, you are probably being affected by the fallout of her stardust.

PLAYFUL

She was thrilled by her reception, and when we spoke together in her dressing-room after the show, I found her endearingly playful, warm, forthcoming, and relaxed . . . the very opposite, in fact, of so much of her publicity.

She had changed out of the gold trouser suit in which she appears on stage into a more feminine pair of black leotards and a red sweater. It suddenly struck me that not even in her youth, when she starred with Mickey Rooney in such films as *Babes in Arms* and *Strike Up the Band*, had she ever looked more appealing, and more vulnerable than she does now.

"You know," she said to me, "there are a lot of people around who think if you happen to know Judy Garland, or are friendly with her, you're someone to be pitied. They say—'You mean you actually *know* the woman? Ugh!' I really don't see why this should be. As far as I know, I'm a nice person, I do my best, and I don't try to hurt anybody.

"I guess that when you're well known or famous, people tend to be frightened of you. Or in awe of you. Either way, they don't understand you. They put you in a different category altogether. Either they think you're great, and they worship you—which is really rather silly—or they think you're a freak and treat you like one, which is just ridiculous.

"Sure, I've had problems, and temperaments and tantrums. But which one of us hasn't? If you want fame you have to pay for it—and brother, I have. Even from my earliest days at M-G-M, when I was a child star with the great Mickey Rooney—who, incidentally, I consider to be one of the finest talents ever to come out of Hollywood.

PRISONERS

"The growing pains of a young girl are bad enough in private; where they're exposed to the public . . . and when everything you say or don't say is reported in the press—well, it hardly makes for a smooth, easy life, does it?

"Mickey and I were prisoners at Metro. We were overworked and underfed. I remember they used to starve me whenever they thought I was putting on too much weight. Not that the food in the canteen at Metro was worth eating, mind you.

THE FUN

"Still, I mustn't complain. And I think it's wrong to be nostalgic about those 'good old days.' We all did well out of Metro, and Metro did well out of us. There were lots of good times, too, of course. Mickey and I had a lot of fun together.

"It's the fun," she said, "that gets you through life. That sees you through the heartache, and the tears, and the miserable periods. You just have to be able to laugh at everything—most of all at yourself. I'm always laughing at myself. I think I must be a very funny person to live with. Funny ha-ha . . ." she quickly added.

I asked her in what way.

"I don't know. If you spent 24 hours in my company, you'd know what I mean. Anyway, take my word for it. A sense of humor is everything. Without one you may just as well give up because you'll never be happy."

Is *she* happy?

"Sure I am. Don't I look happy? I'm just happy being in London. I love the place because I get this marvelous sense of well-being whenever I'm here. Though so far I haven't managed to move around very much. The only scenery I see is my hotel room, the hotel elevator, and my dressing room. That's because I sleep all day. But I'll get around to a bit of sight-seeing sooner or later. After New York, London's positively therapeutic! I don't know what it is about New York, but it seems to me to be going helter-skelter toward oblivion. Know what I mean? It's become so darned aggressive. D'you know something? I was once thrown out of a cab in New York—just because I asked the driver to go a little slower. And he had the nerve to make me pay the fare as far as he'd got! People in this country seem to have more manners. I guess it's because you're so much older than we are. And with age comes breeding.

HAPPINESS

"I'm also here because of the audiences. They still want me. Obviously there's something about me that appeals to them. I don't know exactly what it is, but it's nice to know that whatever it is, I've got it! Without my audience I'd be nothing. They honor me by paying to see me, and in return I try hard to do my best by them. If I feel I've succeeded in pleasing them, that's my justification and my happiness.

"But it is happiness of a certain sort only. A professional happiness. My private happiness is another matter completely. And I've found that in Mickey Deans (the man she plans to marry in the next couple of weeks when their license is granted). A good, responsive audience is all very well, but you can't take it home with you after the show.

"A woman needs more than applause to keep her going. It's too super-ficial, too frustrating, too soul-destroying just to live off applause, as I have often done that in the past, and to try and draw strength and secu-rity from it. It works for a while—but only a while. Because, late at night, when the paying customers have all gone home, the applause becomes a booming, empty echo, and that's not so pleasant. And then, even the echo dies away. And you're all alone. And frightened. And scared stiff.

"It's in moments such as these that you need another human being with you . . . somebody who really cares about *you*, and not just what you stand for. Someone who *loves* you. Fame is all very well, but it doesn't secure companionship and the feeling of possessing and being possessed.

"With Mickey I feel that at last I've found the love I've been searching for all my life. Searching and waiting for. (She has been married four times, and has three children.) I have made lots of mistakes in the past, but not this time. Mickey cares about me, and this is what I want now. I've been through the mill, as everyone knows. But I can take it. Especially now that Mickey's around. Life becomes so much easier to face if there's someone to face it with."

TV INTERVIEW

March 15, 1969, British Newsreel

Judy married Mickey Deans at noon at the Chelsea Registry Office on March 15, 1969. A short ceremony followed at St. Marylebone Parish Church, and this interview was conducted later that day.

It's a good day for you then?

Judy Garland: A lovely day. *Perfect* day.

How long have you known your husband?

JG: I've known my husband as long as he's known me! [*Laughs.*] For about three years.

And what are your plans now that you're married? To go on working?

JG: To be happy. [*Both laugh.*]

Are you going to go on working now?

JG: Do you want to ask my husband?

[To Mickey Deans.] Are you going to let her go on singing?

Mickey Deans: Well, we're looking at different contracts now completely. To go on singing . . . she can go on singing if she wants to. It's not work anymore, though. It doesn't have to be.

You're saying she doesn't have to. Is that because of the wedding present, five hundred cinemas?*

MD: She can buy hats with the money she gets from that. [*Judy laughs.*] My investments are entirely different. I'm very happy . . . She'll probably be in the kitchen, cooking, you know.

JG: [*Laughs.*] I'm a good cook.

MD: You can start being a housewife now.

JG: Well, I've wanted to be just married and happy for a long time.

JUDY GEM
On Her Marriage to Mickey Deans

"I mean it this time. I'm going to make it work for both of us—if it's the last thing I ever do in my whole life. There's too much at stake for it to fail. I see it as my very last bid for real peace of mind and contentment. I've suffered too much, and I've been unhappy too often. With Mickey I feel reborn. We're going to settle in London, you know. I don't know if London still needs me, but I certainly need it! It's good and kind to me. I feel at home here. The people understand me, and I'm not aware of the cruelty I've so often felt in the States. I've reached a point in my life where the most precious thing is compassion—and I get this here."

—To Clive Hirschhorn, (London) *Sunday Express*, March 15, 1969

---

*Mickey's wedding gift of a chain of movie houses across the United States to be known as Judy Garland Cinemas never materialized.

RADIO INTERVIEW

HANS VANGKILDE | March 26, 1969, Radio Denmark

Just days into her marriage with Mickey Deans, Judy and opening act Johnnie Ray set off on a four-city tour with stops in Stockholm, Gothenburg, and Malmö, Sweden, and concluding in Copenhagen, Denmark. Learning of the singer's arrival in Copenhagen, popular local radio personality Hans Vangkilde set out to secure an interview with Judy for his program on Radio Denmark, and became desperate when she didn't respond right away. During a two-year stay in New York City, Vangkilde had befriended Margaret Hamilton. It was a long shot, but he decided to lure Judy with a photo her fellow *Oz* actress had signed to his children, sending it to her hotel suite with a request for a visit. Judy responded and agreed to an interview.

"There was an immediate empathy between Judy and Vangkilde," explained author Anne Edwards, who interviewed Vankilde for her Garland biography, "and the interview became a very personal and honest discussion between the two. . . . She seemed happy as she asked Deans' opinion about everything, including him in all discussion. She held his hand, leaned against him, and kept referring to him as 'my man' or 'my husband' as he hovered close by, making flip side remarks."

Judy's voice was understandably brittle. She was terribly frail and not in any condition to be concertizing. Still, Mickey Deans saw his wife as an artist embarking on yet another comeback under his guidance. "I treasure the tape of that interview for the optimism and health in Judy's outlook," he recalled in *Weep No More, My Lady*, the biography he coauthored with Ann Pinchot. "This is a recording of a woman contemplating a new life. . . . It contains remarks that were familiar to me, since Judy had reiterated them, and they were memorable for their poignancy."

A day before their interview, Hans Vangkilde attended Judy's concert at Copenhagen's Falkoner Centret and witnessed what would be her final performance. "The air was thick with rumors that the star was no longer a star, that she had not only lost her voice, but that she could no longer even get through her program," wrote a critic for the *Politiken*. "Suddenly she stood on the enormous stage and disproved all the rumors in the world. . . . After a large number of curtain calls, she finally gave in to the deepest wish of the audience. She sat down on the stage floor and began to sing 'Over the Rainbow.' It was as though she sang it for the first time, with fervent innocence and sweetness. Tears came to one's eyes. All the spectators arose and cheered Judy Garland. She had a great triumph."

Hans Vangkilde: Haven't you had any fun in your life?

Judy Garland: Not until I met Mickey.

HV: But now you have?

JG: Oh, *yes.*

HV: Judy Garland, it's just about a year ago that we saw—

JG: [*Interrupting.*] Judy Garland-*Deans, please!*

HV: Oh, yes, *certainly!* I'm sorry. But then, Judy . . . That I'm allowed to say? Am I?

JG: Ask Mickey.

Mickey Deans: We're not going to call you *Sam,* that's for sure!

HV: Judy, we saw the first film in television last year. Your first film was shown in Danish television, *The Wizard from Oz* [*sic*].

JG: *The Wizard of Oz?*

HV: Yes.

JG: It was shown for the first time?

HV: Yes, in Danish television.

JG: Did people like it?

HV: They *loved* it.

JG: Did they?

HV: My little kid was just crying! [*Laughs.*]

JG: Oh, I *know*! I have three children and even I have had to reassure them when I'm sitting beside them that I haven't been stolen by the witch. It's a wonderful movie, though. They show it every year in America.

HV: They still do that in America?

JG: Yes.

HV: It's a long time ago now.

JG: Well, not that long. Let's not make it that long ago. [*Laughs.*] No. [*Sarcastically.*] About a *hundred and fifty years ago*!

HV: No, but what I'm aiming at is not to say anything wrong, but to state that—

JG: No, I didn't mean that. It *was* a long time ago!

HV: You have been in show business for—

JG: Too long!

HV: No, I don't think so.

JG: [*Laughs.*] Well, you don't have to *sing*! [*Laughs.*]

HV: Well, that's not the impression we got at the concert.

JG: Well, I like to sing now that I know I don't *have* to sing. Because I'm happily married to a man who's able to give me the protection and help that I need, and I can do a concert now and then if I *want* to. That's a much nicer feeling. That's why I had a good time at the concert you saw.

HV: We have a feeling that show business in America can be very tough to keep on top.

JG: Oh, it's *very* tough. You don't always keep on top, either. No one does. *I don't!* My life, my career's been like a roller coaster. [*Laughs.*] I'm either an enormous success or just a down-and-out *failure,* which is silly! Everyone always asks me, "How does it feel to make a *comeback*?" And I don't know where I've *been*! [*Laughs.*] I haven't been away, I've been working all the time.

HV: There's an old saying. I don't know whether it goes in the United States, too, but there's an old saying that it's cold on the top. It's very freezing on the top.

JG: It's *lonely* and cold. Lonely and cold. But when you . . . if you're lucky to find one person . . . I wanted to make sure . . . I was *nervous*!

HV: At the wedding?

JG: Of course. I'm a very . . . well, I was, literally, a blushing bride.

HV: You were?

JG: Yes. I know. But I was very happy.

HV: You still are?

JG: Oh, of course!

HV: We could see that on the stage, too.

JG: You could?

HV: Yes.

JG: I'm proud.

HV: I think that almost any Danish newspapers you could think of mentioned that your happiness showed and they could feel it in the way that you sang, too. Especially the song you sang to your husband.

JG: "At last I have someone who needs me." ["For Once in My Life."]

HV: We were just talking about the loneliness and the freezing top.

JG: Yes, well, you're either, as you put it, freezing at the top and lonely, or else you're surrounded by people who are not truthful.

HV: People who are using you.

JG: Yes, just use you, you know. And if you're as unaware as I am, and you're a woman, it can get pretty rough, sometimes. But it isn't that way anymore.

HV: It isn't?

JG: *No!* I can go *home* with my husband at night if I do a concert. I don't have to be alone in a hotel room.

HV: Where do you live?

JG: We live all over the place. [*Laughs.*]

HV: You do? But you have a home?

JG: We have a home in New York. We have a home in London.

HV: Where do you spend the most time?

JG: New York. And London. [*Both laugh.*] No, wherever my husband goes, I go. Except to Stockholm.

HV: Do you have a feeling that you have had a rich life?

JG: No. Not until now. I think it's been an *interesting* life. I've loved always giving performances to audiences because I think audiences are the most respectable people in the world because they pay money to come and sit for a long time. Whether you sing well or whether you sing badly, they've paid, and sometimes *saved* money, too, you know, so I have the highest respect. But I can't take the audience *home* with me. I couldn't before. I can't now, either, but I've got my love to keep me warm.

HV: Now you're talking about the audience. In other words, you mean that human beings are better when there are a lot of them than in singles?

JG: No, I mean in my line of business, in the entertaining business, if you're a woman and you have made a success of yourself by working . . . I've worked very hard, you know? And I was lucky enough, I guess, to plant a star. And then people wanted to either get in the act or else they wanted to rob. I mean emotionally or financially—whatever—and then walk away. It was always lonely.

HV: It's hard for us more anonymous people to understand the difference between being a well-known woman walking on the street . . . I'm anonymous when I walk on the street, but you're not. You always have somebody looking at you, somebody coming up greeting you, and . . .

JG: I don't mind that.

HV: You don't mind that?

JG: Not if they're nice, you know. I like to meet people.

HV: But what I mean is . . . isn't it sometimes hard for you not to be able to be yourself in the middle of a crowd?

JG: Talk to my husband about my shopping spree! [*Laughs.*] I ran through how many stores? [*Laughs.*]

HV: Yes, well, I'll talk to him a little later about *that*! [*All laugh.*] How is it to walk down the street in a foreign country—

JG: [*Interrupting.*] Fun. Fun. It's fun.

HV: Do people come up to you and say hello?

JG: Yes, they do . . .

HV: And it doesn't bother you?

JG: No, I'm too busy looking for a piece of porcelain if it's in Denmark, or wherever. I like to shop, I like to look in windows . . . Sometimes if I'm tired or after doing a performance or just before a performance I don't go out because when I do go shopping or anything, I wear myself out. [*Laughs.*]

HV: Judy, when you're not performing, when you're private . . .

JG: Yes?

HV: What do you do?

JG: I just look messy. [*All laugh.*]

HV: Is that a fact? I wouldn't believe that!

JG: I make *hats*!

HV: Oh, you do? Let's hear a little about that!

JG: Well, I *do*. I make hats. I made this hat.

HV: You have a very beautiful broad-rimmed, black hat with a silver lining on . . .

MD: That's mine! You have the wrong one on! [*Judy laughs.*]

HV: Do you *really* make hats?

JG: Yes, I really do make hats. I love to make hats, I like to design anything. I would love to have a chance sometime to learn to paint porcelain. You know, I don't know how to do that. I'd like to *learn*. And I'd like to do some interior decorating. In fact, I designed the dress I wore onstage at the concert you saw.

HV: Oh, yes. Do you do that always, yourself?

JG: No, I haven't had enough time. That was the first dress I have really had time to execute and design.

HV: Yes. Mickey, how is it to be married to a world-famous lady of the show business?

MD: I've never been married to a world-famous lady. I married a girl named Gladys.

JG: [*Laughs.*] He always calls me Gladys . . .

MD: That's her nickname from me. We say, "Gladys?" you know, and she calls me George. We sound very ridiculous to each other, calling each other this, and it's funny that way, you know. That is fun.

HV: But Mickey, don't you ever get a little jealous—I mean in the *real* sense jealous—when you see all the attention that your wife gets from other males?

MD: Well, I try to make sure that there are not too many around. Well, except the staff. [*Laughs.*] Of course, I'd get jealous. I love her very much, but . . . I want my wife to be admired as a woman, not just as a celebrity. The greatest fun we've had over here, I think, was going out one night and with my usual conservative dress that I wear . . . Judy's teasing me in back of me. That's why you can't see what's she's doing! [*Laughs.*] So a nice guy came over—a clean-cut looking boy—and asked my wife to dance. And since he was nice about it, I sort of gave him the look about it like, "take off." But they were so nice, the people sitting around us, that I thought they were sort of acting as a security guard, in a sense, without realizing it themselves. I said, "Would you like to come to the concert?" and arranged for the tickets. And he thanked me so much. And then he finally said to me, "What concert?" This was Saturday. [*Laughs.*] And he said "What concert?" And I said, "Well, my wife is a singer. " And he didn't know. Judy wasn't aware of this. And he was quite sincere! It wasn't a put-on. He didn't know! And then he was very embarrassed. He'd just picked up on a very, very, very pretty woman sitting there.

HV: [*To Judy.*] What do you think about it?

JG: I was very *proud!*

HV: Yes, I can understand that, because here, a young kid who apparently didn't know you, know your name or anything . . .

JG: I didn't know that he didn't know me until Mickey told me after we got home.

HV: In other words, you were appraised as a woman, and as an anonymous woman, when he asked you to dance?

JG: Yes! It was *lovely!* It's always nice for a woman to feel pretty or . . . yes, certainly!

JUDY GEM

"I've always taken *The Wizard of Oz* very seriously, you know. I believe in the idea of the rainbow. And I've spent my entire life trying to get over it."

—Source Unknown

EPILOGUE

On June 22, 1969, Judy Garland died in her London home of an accidental overdose of sleeping pills. She was forty-seven. Her passing made international front-page headlines and, in what *Variety* called her "last standing ovation," more than twenty-two thousand mourners and curiosity seekers filed past the glass-covered coffin at the Frank E. Campbell Funeral Home on Manhattan's Madison Avenue. "She was the most sympathetic, the funniest, the sharpest, and the most stimulating woman I ever knew," recalled James Mason, Judy's costar from *A Star is Born*, in his eulogy delivered June 27. "I traveled in her orbit only for a while, but it was an exciting while and one during which it seemed that the joys in her life outbalanced the miseries."

The joys in Judy's life certainly outbalanced the miseries, and in assessing her legacy, it's important to note that the successes outbalanced the failures. Today, the definition of Judy's greatness lies in her body of work, one that has essentially gone unsurpassed by any of her contemporaries and would rival that of any artist of her magnitude in the years since. Judy worked almost nonstop for forty-five of her forty-seven years in a career that traversed nearly every avenue in the entertainment industry. Aptly named "Miss Show Business," she made thirty-two feature films, hosted four television specials, taped a twenty-six-episode series, made countless TV guest appearances, recorded nearly one hundred singles and more than a dozen albums, appeared on hundreds of radio shows, and made upward of 1,500 live appearances.

The Judy Garland Show. Carnegie Hall. *A Star is Born*. The Palace. The Palladium. *Easter Parade*. *Meet Me in St. Louis*. Looking back over a career encompassing these highlights alone would qualify an entertainer for legend status. But then there is *The Wizard of Oz*. Declared by the Library of Congress to be "the most watched film ever," it is *Oz* that elevates Judy from "legend" to a realm of immortality, for when Dorothy entered that glorious Technicolor wonderland and set ruby-slippered foot down the Yellow Brick Road, she took with her legions of young people and gained an eternal audience of the young at heart.

In Judy's lifetime, she often repeated that it was the audience that nurtured and sustained her. Today is no different. Decades have passed, generations come and gone, but it remains the audience that nurtures and sustains the memory of Judy Garland. "During the bad days, I'm sure I would have perished without those wonderful audiences," she once pondered. "Without *that* and a sense of humor, I would have died. Even with my work and an active funny bone, I think there's something peculiar about me that I haven't died. It doesn't make much sense, but I just refused to die. When my number is up, I want a new one, and right now, my life is just beginning."*

---

*Judy Garland, "Judy Garland's Own Story: There'll Always Be an Encore," *McCall's*, February 1964.

SUGGESTED READING

The following books were instrumental during the research for this collection and are recommended to anyone wishing to further explore the details of the life and career of Judy Garland. Certain selections are out of print but still in circulation and available at local libraries or online.

Clarke, Gerald. *Get Happy: The Life of Judy Garland*. New York: Random House, 2000.

Coleman, Emily R. *The Complete Judy Garland: The Ultimate Guide to Her Career in Films, Records, Concerts, Radio, and Television, 1935–1969*. New York: HarperCollins, 1990.

Finch, Christopher. *Rainbow: The Stormy Life of Judy Garland*. New York: Grosset & Dunlap, 1975.

Frank, Gerold. *Judy*. New York: HarperCollins, 1975.

Fricke, John. *Judy: A Legendary Film Career*. Philadelphia: Running Press, 2011.

———*Judy Garland: World's Greatest Entertainer*. New York: Henry Holt, 1992.

Fricke, John and Lorna Luft. *Judy Garland: A Portrait in Art & Anecdote*. New York: Bulfinch Press, 2003.

Sanders, Coyne Steven. *Rainbow's End: The Judy Garland Show*. New York: William Morrow,1990.

Schechter, Scott. *Judy Garland: The Day-by-Day Chronicle of a Legend*. New York: Cooper Square Press, 2002.

CREDITS

Every effort has been made to contact copyright holders, and I gratefully acknowledge the help of all who gave permission for material to appear in this book. If an error or omission has been made, please bring it to the attention of the publisher. Nearly all of the pieces gathered from a variety of Hollywood fan magazines and other periodicals published prior to 1964 are now in the public domain. Except as noted, the images presented in this book—vintage photographs, magazine covers, and other memorabilia—are from the editor's personal collection.

"I've Been to the Land of Oz," by Judy Garland as told to Gladys Hall, reprinted by permission of John K. Ball and the Estate of Gladys Hall.

"Beginning Judy Garland's Gay Life Story," by Judy Garland as told to Gladys Hall, reprinted by permission of John K. Ball and the Estate of Gladys Hall.

"Judy Garland's Gay Life Story," by Judy Garland as told to Gladys Hall, reprinted by permission of John K. Ball and the Estate of Gladys Hall.

"My Story" by Judy Garland, as told to Michael Drury, reprinted by permission of Hearst Magazines.

"Judy Garland's Magic Word" by Liza Wilson, reprinted by permission of Hearst Magazines.

"JUDY," by James Goode, reprinted by permission of Damon Goode and the Estate of James Goode.

INDEX